AN ARCHAEOLOGY OF
SOUTH-EAST ENGLAND

AN ARCHAEOLOGY OF
SOUTH-EAST ENGLAND

A Study in Continuity by

Gordon J. Copley

*with 28 plates,
42 maps & diagrams*

PHOENIX HOUSE LTD
LONDON

To C.A.C.

© GORDON J. COPLEY 1958

Printed in Great Britain
in 11/13 point Monotype Plantin (110) by
Western Printing Services Ltd, Bristol for
Phoenix House Ltd, 38 William IV Street,
Charing Cross, W.C.2

FIRST PUBLISHED 1958

CONTENTS

List of Illustrations, 7
Note on the Maps, 9

PART I

I.	The Amateur in Archaeology	11
II.	The Natural Background	17
III.	The Palaeolithic Period (*from circa* 550,000 B.C.)	31
IV.	The Mesolithic Period (*from circa* 20,000 B.C.)	36
V.	The Neolithic Period (*from circa* 2,300 B.C.)	43
VI.	The Early and Middle Bronze Age (*from circa* 1,850 B.C.)	60
VII.	The Late Bronze Age (*from circa* 1,000 B.C.)	74
VIII.	The Early Iron Age, Phase A (*from circa* 450 B.C.)	85
IX.	The Early Iron Age, Phase B. (*from circa* 250 B.C.)	101
X.	The Early Iron Age (Belgic Settlement), Phase C (*from circa* 75 B.C.)	109
XI.	The Roman Occupation (*from* A.D. 43)	130
XII.	The Anglo-Saxon Settlement (*from circa* A.D. 450)	152
XIII.	The Middle Ages	178
XIV.	The Study of a Locality	201
XV.	Place-names and Fieldwork	217

General Bibliography, 228

PART II

Gazetteer	231

Index, 313

ACKNOWLEDGEMENTS TO THE PLATES

PLATES NOS. 3, 6, and 21 to Department of Antiquities, Ashmolean Museum

PLATES NOS. 5, 8, 10, and 15 to J. K. St. Joseph,
Crown Copyright Reserved

PLATE NO. 13 to J. Allan Cash

PLATE NO. 26 to Brian Hope-Taylor

PLATE NO. 28 to J. G. Hurst

Also PLATES NOS. 9 and 11—*Crown Copyright
Reserved*

All other photographs were taken by the author.

ILLUSTRATIONS

PLATES

between pages 176 *and* 177

1 Long Barrow, Rockbourne, Hants

2 Neolithic burial chamber, Aylesford, Kent

3 Cursus, Overy, Dorchester, Oxon, from the air

4 Round barrows, Dunstable, Beds, of the Early Bronze Age

5 Bell barrows, Bow Hill, Sussex, of the Middle Bronze Age, from the air

6 A Middle Bronze Age necropolis, Lambourn, Berks, from the air

7 A Late Bronze Age ranch boundary ditch, Martin, Hants

8 Celtic fields, Fore Down, Lullington, Sussex, from the air

9 Quarley hill-fort, Hants, from the air

10 Crop-marks, Standlake, Oxon, from the air

11 The Trundle hill-fort, Sussex, from the air

12 Uffington Castle and the Ridgeway, Berks

13 St. Catherine's hill-fort, Winchester

14 Hengistbury Head, Hants

15 Richborough Castle, Kent, from the air

16 Pevensey Castle, Sussex

17 The town wall, Verulamium (St. Alban's), Herts

18 The Roman theatre, Verulamium, Herts

19 Bokerly Dyke, Martin, Hants

20 A Roman barrow, one of the Bartlow Hills, Ashdon, Essex

21 A soil-mark site, Long Wittenham, Berks, from the air

22 A rampart of the Saxon *burh*, Wallingford, Berks

23 Strip fields, Uffington, Berks

24 A strip field still in cultivation, Dunstable, Beds

25 Grim's Ditch, Berkhampstead, Herts

26 A castle mound, Abinger, Surrey, as excavated

27 Manorial earthworks, Pirton, Herts

28 A deserted village, Romney Marsh, Kent

8 ILLUSTRATIONS

DISTRIBUTION MAPS

1 The Mesolithic Period 38
2 The Neolithic Period 45
3 The Middle Bronze Age 68
4 The Late Bronze Age 75
5 Iron Age Hill-Forts 89
6 The Late Iron Age 104
7 The Belgae 110
8 Roman Earthworks 141
9 The Saxon Period 160
10 The Middle Ages 182

REGIONAL MAPS

A Western Kent 50
B The Berkshire Downs 82
C Northern Hampshire 93
D The Chichester Region 114
E The Colchester Region 118
F Eastern Hertfordshire 121
G Eastern Surrey 138
H Western Hampshire 147
I The Goring Gap 156
J The Silchester Region 158
K Southern Buckinghamshire 181
L Eastern Sussex 187

DIAGRAMS

1 Chart of the Palaeolithic Period 21
2 Britain before separation from the Continent 24
3 Chart, South-Eastern Britain from Mesolithic times 28–9
4 Combe Hill Camp, Jevington, Sussex 44
5 The Dorchester Henge Sites 64
6 Bronze Age Barrows 69
7 Late Bronze Age Settlement: Plumpton Plain, Sussex 79
8 The Formation of Lynchets 80
9 Late Bronze Age ranch boundary ditch 81
10 Promontory Fort: Hengistbury Head 87
11 Hill-Fort Defences 95
12 Belgic Dykes 119
13 The Soldiers Ring, South Damerham, Hants. 136
14 Iron Age and Romano-British field-system, Farthingdown, Coulsdon, Surrey 137
15 The coast-line of the South-East in Roman times 145
16 A late Romano-British defensive earthwork, Bokerly Dyke, Martin, Hants. 155
17A Ancient woodland in Surrey as indicated by place-names 179
17B Ancient woodland in Surrey reconstructed on a geological basis 179
18 Castle mound at Pleshley, Essex 185
19 Deserted village and fields, Highclere and Burghclere, Berks. 193
20 Crop Marks over Buried Sites 208

NOTE ON THE MAPS

The Distribution Maps (1–10) are plotted on a base which shows the relative fertility of soils by means of stippling. The densest stippling indicates such soils as the brickearths; the blank areas are mainly of unmodified sands, acidic gravels, clays or tracts of the chalk uplands having a low fertility. County boundaries are shown with a broken line and the limits of the region on the north-west are marked with a thick unbroken line where they do not coincide with county boundaries.

The regional sketch-maps (A–L) are intended as a summary representation of the most interesting tracts of the South-East from the point of view of the field archaeologist. With a few exceptions (e.g. the sites of Roman houses on some of the maps) only visible earthworks have been plotted. The two Sussex maps (D and L) show elevation. On the remainder it was thought preferable to indicate water-courses in some detail since the amount and availability of surface water had a greater influence on the location of settlements of all periods than height above sea level. This is a generalization true, of course, only for lowland Britain.

The margins of both series of maps are marked with the national grid for convenience in identifying sites. Details relating to them may usually be found in the Gazetteer.

All of the maps are based upon the Ordnance Survey Map with the sanction of the Controller of H.M. Stationery Office.

PART I

CHAPTER I

The Amateur in Archaeology

THERE CAN BE few intelligent and educated people today who are not to some extent interested in the ancient past and in the processes of rediscovering it. Few of them can devote much time to the work, but of those who do, a few achieve great things in pushing forward the frontiers of knowledge and many more are able to make small but significant contributions to the subject. Among the most honoured names in modern British archaeology there is a handful of amateurs, men and women, who earn their living in one or other of the professions and devote their strenuous leisure to local research. Without them our knowledge of prehistory would be far scantier than it now is.

Let it be said emphatically that Britain excels in archaeological research mainly because of our good fortune in possessing a brilliant band of professional prehistorians: university teachers and museum curators who have constant access to great libraries and collections and who can spend some part of the year in field work. And the professional is usually the first to acknowledge that the distinction between himself and an outstanding amateur is one of degree rather than of kind; that it consists primarily in the amount of time which each can devote to the subject. Both have fully accepted the rigorous mental discipline of archaeology and are generous in their recognition of the lesser work of the amateur majority.

But at whatever level one works there can be no escape from the strict discipline that prehistory demands. In common with all other fields of serious study, whether in science or in the humanities, the handling of evidence must be unfaltering in its logic. It is, for instance, a waste of time and paper to elaborate a theory by selecting and stating those facts which accord with it and ignoring those that run counter to it. Publishers' lists for the last fifty years are littered with such works; and there are a few regularly reprinted that are an insult to the intelligence, yet which have remained available when valuable books have gone permanently out of print. Dr. Crawford has some amusing things to say about the cranks in an appendix to his *Archaeology in the Field*. Usually it is preferable for the amateur to do no more than set down all the relevant facts, though sometimes a theory will emerge from them and can be tested by reference to comparable work already in print. In general, however, most amateurs can make their best contributions by the discovery and publication of facts—the location of a barrow, group of Celtic fields or scatter of Roman brick in a ploughed field. The material is then available for the professional prehistorian who, with a wider and more detailed knowledge, can fit the new facts into the framework of established evidence and give them their due proportion and significance. This is a process that may prove disappointing to the original discoverer who lacks the breadth of experience to see his discoveries in true perspective.

But this does not reduce the value of his discoveries; their value is enhanced in that they fill in a blank in the vast and incomplete jigsaw puzzle of prehistory. The present state of our knowledge of the Iron Age, for instance, has become possible only as a result of many thousands of widely scattered finds and a few major excavations, the former mainly the work of amateurs and the latter undertaken most fruitfully by professionals seeking specific answers to questions posed before digging was begun. But the questions could not have been asked without the accumulation of data resulting from the scattered finds of amateurs; the sites excavated are sometimes amateur discoveries; and the excavation itself is almost invariably dependent on the brain and brawn of amateurs supervised, and sometimes inspired by, a professional, the master mind in a co-operative task. Finally, the evaluation of the evidence, the synthesis of scattered facts, and their orderly and intelligible presentation in a report, the end and crown of so much labour, is usually the work of the professional.

This is a broad simplification of what is in fact a complex relationship between two mutually dependent groups. The pity is that occasionally the amateur rashly exceeds his function and the professional belittles his own dependence on the amateur. A clear notion and recognition of the limitations and strengths of each side would obviate the wrangles that sometimes break forth into print. Happily, few engage in such fruitless debates and throughout the country in the rooms of both national and local societies and in the trenches of excavations, there is the closest co-operation. But tolerance will have to be shown by both groups from time to time.

Most amateurs will not want to dig except under skilled supervision, nor rush into print with new theories; yet many are enthusiastic enough to wish to undertake a role more active than that of paying a subscription and of listening to lectures by experts. And there is indeed useful work which they may accomplish if only they go about it in the right way.

For those living in the Home Counties I have tried to give an outline of present knowledge by compiling a prehistory of the region and a comprehensive list of sites and of the more significant finds arranged under counties and parishes. Large as the Gazetteer is, I make no pretence to have included everything in the region, though I believe that little of importance has been omitted. Therefore I hope that it may be possible to use the material there assembled as a starting-point for a limited local study which may be related to a broader body of knowledge. The inclusion of references in the Gazetteer would have more than doubled its length; but the chapter bibliographies and the suggestions in Chapter XIV should afford some compensations for this necessary defect. In the final chapter some attention is given to the use of place-names in field work.

The subject is one that may be studied at various levels. For some it is enough that they read round the subject and visit museums and field monuments—a relatively passive but nevertheless enjoyable pastime comparable with a mild interest in architecture, botany, meteorology or what you will. But among those whose interest is thus mildly aroused will be some who find themselves drawn further; they will visit a site in course of excavation, buy general works on the subject, and perhaps subscribe to an archaeological society. Interest increases as a consequence of meeting others pursuing the same aim; and a frequent outcome is a desire to take a more active part in the expectation of making a contribution to knowledge.

It is at this point that the Rubicon is crossed. Active participation can only be fruitful if it is based on accurate and detailed knowledge and experience. Some period must be spent on excavation under expert guidance—there are training courses available—and general works on prehistory must be absorbed. Then should follow the detailed study of selected excavation reports. The general works should come first so that the minute detail of the reports may be seen in due perspective. Then, in addition, field studies, preferably in the company of an experienced worker, should be sought whilst museum studies and independent field work (but not free-lance excavation) are being pursued.

For most people detailed study must then be followed in a restricted section of the subject. The restriction may be to one period, e.g. the Late Bronze Age, securely comprehended in relation to what went before and came after it; or there may be a limitation to a particular locality. It is amidst his own familiar landscape that the English amateur has given most to archaeology. Every hedgerow, every dip and fold of the land, every lane and copse within the parish are his affectionate acquaintances. As he comes to distinguish between the smoothing hand of nature and the deranging hand of man, whether historic or prehistoric, the details of the landscape take on new significances. Skylines long familiar are searched for those minor corrugations that tell of ancient disturbance of the soil not yet levelled by centuries of ploughing. Dark patches or scatters of alien flint or gravel in the arable are visited at each turning of the soil and especially when rain has rinsed surface objects clean so that the eye may detect them the more readily.

The townsman has fewer opportunities in his daily round. For him, too, any disturbance of the soil is of interest whether it be the laying of cables or trenching for foundations. Even in neighbourhoods built over for a century or more, man-made topographic features are sometimes still to be faintly discerned. The Holloway, which gave its name to a district of north London, has not altogether lost its hollowness; here and there side-streets still dip into it at points of intersection. The gradual lowering of the surface of this trunk-route by heavy use over more than a thousand years gave it a name which has still not lost its aptness. Another instance may be quoted from the south-western verge of London. The main road which skirts Marble Hill, Twickenham, can be seen to rise very gently until opposite the Palladian house and then fall in a very shallow slope. A side street, Sandycoombe road, drops similarly from the same faint eminence. Just within the Park fence is a broad mound (NG ref. 171739), cut through by the main road which is successor to a local road linking a ferry to Richmond on the north-east and the village of Twickenham on the south-west. The lane appears in eighteenth-century maps and very probably goes back to a time before the Middle Ages. But the mound may be older, for the varying levels of the main and side roads suggests that its material has slowly been scattered by passing traffic and that the process had gone far before the main road was metalled, probably in the earlier half of the nineteenth century. Greater certainty in the matter might be possible through a detailed study of the history of this one road in old maps and documents. Such an undertaking is, however, fraught with the disappointing possibility that the mound is a relic of eighteenth-century landscape-gardening, as may be some others nearer to Marble Hill House. These are almost completely denuded and carry trees planted 150 or more years ago. An alternative possibility is that the mound is a modern barrow heaped over the remains of a squire's favourite hunter. In any case, it is not a natural hillock.

Surface finds are not always elusive. Within a few weeks of moving into a new house my family had collected potsherds of cultures ranging from Iron Age 'A2' to Romano-British, and flints from a late Palaeolithic chopper to Bronze Age (?) fabricators. The most interesting find was made by a nine-year-old immediately after being allotted a portion of the garden. He picked up a rim-sherd of the Wealden culture although in colour it quite closely resembled that of the soil. Seldom do we take a walk without returning with some minor trophy.

My purpose in thus particularizing is to show that dwellers in towns and suburbs have their opportunities for field work if they will keep their eyes open. And, with so many possessing cars, the countryside is easily accessible, if only they will abandon them for cart-tracks and footpaths and the leisurely gait of the walker. A small tract of countryside may then become sufficiently familiar for its intensive study.

The Twickenham example mentioned above was chosen partly because its investigation might lead to disappointment. In probing the past it is only reasonable to expect that some lines of investigation can end only in the more recent past. Yet an eighteenth-century horse-burial, with superincumbent mound, is a part of archaeology just as much as the mint-fresh Victorian sixpence that I picked up recently in a Herefordshire churchyard. The former instance affords an apt illustration of the social life of its period; but, without the very full written records of the eighteenth century, fascinating speculations concerning contemporary 'hippolatry' (horrible coinage) would have been possible; nor need they have been very wide of the mark. In fact, though many a task of research may fail in its expected object, few of the failures are entirely not worth while. In any case, an archaeologist today sees the past as one continuous process, and he regards a seventeenth-century tradesman's token or an abandoned copper-mine of the last century, as equally significant with a Belgic coin or a Roman tile-kiln though, in fact, the earlier objects may yield information not otherwise obtainable.

Disappointment will certainly be met, though usually mitigated; but the pleasures of archaeology make full compensation for the setbacks. Indeed, an abortive line of inquiry can give intense pleasure while it is in progress. Field work will often take one to the less populous parts of the countryside where ancient monuments have suffered least and to which twentieth-century change has come most reluctantly. It is in such places, too, that the delicate balance between rural man and the natural environment has been least disturbed and where the past is most clearly seen through the present. There one perceives the present as a momentary culmination of the past and the present illustrating the past. The seamless garment of past and present becomes apparent in startling glimpses. A glance at Plate xxxvii of Sir Cyril Fox's *Archaeology of the Cambridge Region*, many a plate in the journal *Antiquity*, or the writings of Mr. T. C. Lethbridge will make clear my meaning more effectively than my words.

The mere collector of flints, sherds or coins is almost extinct, and public disapprobation should ultimately suppress the collecting habit, or at least make of it a secret vice. None of these things have value in themselves, but in a museum, available to all, and in collocation with other relics of the same culture, they can contribute their part to as full an understanding as possible of those early cultures of which knowledge is obtainable only from their material bric-a-brac and domestic rubbish. That is not to say that the field worker should leave non-structural finds *in situ*, but that he should first offer them to a local museum which will seldom want to retain them longer than to record the exact location of the find and its nature. Properly labelled they may make a welcome beginning to a local school collection and be the starting-point of an interest in archaeology for a few young people.

It should never be forgotten that all knowledge is always undergoing revision and that a young discipline such as archaeology is continuously being revised. New facts are constantly added to the data of any period and the whole subject is from time to time reshuffled. This enjoins caution in the study of any book, however eminent the author, which is much more than a decade old. Where there are later editions, these should be consulted in preference to the first. That is not to say that older books are worthless; used with circumspection, the best will always retain a high value for students and will command an exorbitant price in second-hand bookshops, especially in London. In this matter provincial shops are far more reasonable.

But the fluidity of archaeological knowledge enjoins caution in another respect. The amateur is likely to be ignorant of many current developments and his pronouncements are therefore likely to lack authority. If deeply interested in the subject, he will strive to become acquainted with the trends of research as soon as they are made generally available; and though there are national journals which go far towards supplying the deficiency, it must be said that a great deal of important information is tardily published, and that for months, even years, remains esoteric. This is partly due to the disparity between the large volume of research always in hand and the limited number of organs of publication, and partly, in some instances, to the dilatoriness of scholars. But few who have not undertaken the preparation of a report can realize the magnitude of the task.

For these reasons, then, I am sure that it is usually better for the amateur to stick to facts. However he may strive in his limited leisure to emulate the professional, he can seldom hope to rival him in overall knowledge and skill. For these in sufficient measure, abundant time is essential; and it is better to recognize one's limitations and to make due allowance for them than to entertain false hopes of emulating a Wheeler or a Hawkes through part-time studies.

CHAPTER II

The Natural Background

IT IS APPARENT that the further one peers back into the past, the more man was dominated by his environment. Dependence on nature's bounty and exposure to all her varied harshnesses is the normal lot of the most primitive communities. There has not been an unbroken progress in material things from earlier to later times and at intervals the struggle with environment has gone against 'that poor, bare forked animal . . . unaccommodated man'; for Lear on the heath, expelled from his palace, belongs to all times including the prehistoric. At one period there was a remarkable leap forward in material well-being through the introduction ready-made of an advanced Mediterranean culture; the Romano-British country gentleman in his 'villa' enjoyed a standard of comfort not to be surpassed among the wealthier classes until the nineteenth century; yet the sub-Roman era of the first half of the fifth century A.D. was one of almost unmitigated barbarism. But apart from the Roman episode in our history, progress in material standards has seldom suffered great setbacks, and on the whole it is true to say that the earlier the culture the more was it dominated by the natural background.

Clearly, a people who acquired very little by trade was dependent for its worldly goods on what nature provided. But the surviving objects of early cultures represent only a tiny proportion of the original whole. Much of the equipment of any culture is perishable. Without metals, and during the periods when metal was rare and expensive, implements had to be fashioned from hard natural substances such as rock and wood. Stone implements will normally survive, but those of wood do so only in very exceptional circumstances. But wood was certainly used for many other things besides tools, and it is only a fortunate chance that sometimes evidence of it is found as marks of discoloration in the soil, indicating the supporting posts of houses or religious sanctuaries. In damp peat it is possible for wooden objects to survive for a very long time in a recognizable form. Yet for every scrap of surviving evidence, enormous quantities must be irrecoverably lost, and we are left with only the merest glimpse of the full material accompaniment of ancient life.

Substances even more perishable than wood were certainly in daily use. Textiles, basketry, woven grasses or hair, objects made from bark and resins, besides possibly others of which we know nothing, must have been in common use; yet they rarely survive. Hence we depend largely on stone or metal implements and the almost ubiquitous and indestructible potsherds for much of our understanding of prehistoric life.

To peoples with few means of acquiring raw materials by trade, their local availability made much difference to the standard of living. After the palaeolithic period several kinds of wood were always abundant and to be had near at hand in southeastern Britain. Clay, too, for pot-making and for daubing on wattle walls of huts was never far to seek. The skins, sinews, horns, antlers and bones of animals were obtainable by hunting or from pit-fall traps; and, for pastoral or farming peoples, a good supply of animal products came from their own flocks and herds.

But ultimately the availability of these raw materials was dependent on two main factors: climate and soil; and for this reason it is necessary to give some thought to the geology of the region with its accompanying soil patterns, and to the climate as it varied from time to time: and, less important in so restricted a region, from place to place at any given time. This survey embraces Kent, Sussex, Surrey, Hampshire, Berkshire, Middlesex, Hertfordshire and Essex, the more southerly portions of Oxfordshire and Buckinghamshire and a small area of southern Bedfordshire (see map, p. 38). Broadly these counties comprise three natural regions of drainage: the London Basin, the Weald and the Hampshire Basin. The geological history of these regions is too complex and too little relevant to our present purpose to be given even in outline. The works of reference listed at the end of this chapter may be consulted by those who are interested.

The structure of the three regions has, however, a constant bearing on all periods of prehistory and of history, and cannot be lightly passed over. But we need go no further back in time than the Tertiary era when the vast bed of chalk, which characterises much of south-eastern Britain, was crumpled into immense troughs and upfolds. The Hampshire and London Basins are troughs subsequently overlain with sands, gravels and clays deposited by enormous volumes of water; the Weald, on the other hand, was originally a vast chalk dome, much cracked during its elevation, and since that time unceasingly worn down by wind, rain, river-action, and frost, agencies which have, of course, had their effect throughout Britain, but more drastically in the Weald than elsewhere in the South-east. The North and South Downs are vestigial stumps of the great chalk dome, and the Weald proper, between the two chalk ridges, represents the beds of rocks originally underlying the dome, and themselves much worn down by the weather of twenty-five million years or more.

The most prominent features of the region as a whole are the chalk downs: those surrounding the Weald, the uplands of northern Hampshire, the Berkshire Downs and their continuation north-eastward as the Chiltern Hills. The lofty sandstone ridges of the central Weald are, in comparison, of minor importance archaeologically; but a high Greensand massif such as Leith Hill in Surrey or Blackdown in Sussex, shared with other and lower Greensand tracts in affording a favourable habitat for mesolithic hunting-groups. The chalk plateaux, on the other hand, reveal abundant evidence of occupation from the neolithic to late Roman times, except where they are overlaid by gravel or clay deposits, especially on the Chilterns and North Downs, the western portion of the South Downs, patchily on the Hampshire uplands and sparsely on the Berkshire Downs.

Well drained, with light, easily-worked soils, and carrying only light woodland, the greater part of the chalk uplands were highly attractive to prehistoric peoples. All of the main ridges converge towards Salisbury Plain, the 'metropolitan' region of southern Britain for much of prehistoric times. Communication was relatively easy along the downs as they are broken only by occasional river-gaps, none of which presented a serious obstacle to movement. Indeed, so thickly do relics of ancient peoples cluster on the downs that attention was for long diverted from the lower ground, and the distributions of prehistoric cultures were much distorted as a consequence. We now know that suitable riverside areas were equally favoured, but intensive occupation during historic times has much obscured or even destroyed the vestiges of earlier peoples.

Along most of the rivers, and especially beside the Thames and its tributaries, there are tracts of gravel deposited by the rivers at different stages of their evolution, and tracts of fertile loam, called brickearth, which was also laid down by the rivers in flood and possibly added to by wind-blown deposits, called *loess*, during long epochs of drought and high winds. *Loess* has been detected at Swanscombe (Kent) and at Iver (Bucks). Both the gravels and the brickearth have some characteristics like those of chalk, especially in their porosity. They were therefore well suited for habitation and for the production of food. Moreover, lightly wooded as they were, the task of clearance was less onerous and they could the sooner be brought to productivity. What is more, they could be traversed as easily as the chalk ridges, and the rivers themselves afforded means of communication in dug-out canoes. Besides the riverside tracts of brickearth there are extensive spreads of it along the South Coast extending westward from Brighton and irregularly as far as Southampton Water. The other main tracts occur in south-west Middlesex, and in south-east and north-east Essex. Smaller patches of similar soil are found in the Lea valley and in those of the Kentish Stour and Medway just south of where they break through the North Downs.

Elsewhere soils vary from the lightest of sands to the stickiest of clays. As noticed earlier, the Greensand exposures of the Weald were favoured hunting-grounds of mesolithic tribes. Vestiges of them have been found also on the Tertiary sands and gravels of the London and Hampshire Basins and in the valley of the Essex Colne, in tracts generally similar to the Wealden Greensand. But the vast clay belts of the south-east, on the other hand, reveal few traces of human occupation until the end of the Iron Age. The implements of Palaeolithic man, however, have been recovered from the margins of the gluey clay-with-flints on the north Hampshire downs, and mesolithic tools from similar terrain on the southern Chilterns at Turville in Buckinghamshire. For the rest, the clay-lands remained almost barren of occupation until the Middle Ages.

The expanse of south-eastern England is much broken up by these broad clay belts, and they remained a serious obstacle to movement until quite recent centuries. Apart from their stickiness except in times of drought, they bore dense oak forest with an even denser undergrowth of brambles, thorn and hazel. Southern Essex, southern Hertfordshire and northern Middlesex are covered by a broad area of intractable London clay which is cut through only by the continuous alluvial spreads that border the river Lea. These afford a corridor leading northwards from the Thames valley with its gravel terraces to the light though very variable boulder-clays and gravels of northern Essex and Hertfordshire. West and north of the Chiltern escarpment are yet vaster expanses of stiff soils composed of bands of the Gault and Kimmeridge clays, separated in some areas by a narrow zone of Greensand. These beds trend, like all the local rock exposures, from the middle Thames north-eastward following the scarp of the Chiltern Hills. The latter, linking up with the chalk of Berkshire and Wiltshire to the south-west and with the Breckland of Norfolk to the north-east, afforded an easily traversed route of access into the very heart of southern England. From the tenth century A.D. at least, this route has been known as the Icknield Way and along it there passed several waves of immigrants in prehistoric and early historic times.

In Kent, Surrey and Sussex, almost completely surrounding the central Weald, is a broad belt of Weald clay even now sparsely settled except along the main lines of communication from north to south. Apart from some pottery-making at the end of the Iron Age this cold and heavily wooded wet soil was scarcely trodden by early man. The same is true of the London clay belt of southern Hampshire. The Forest of Bere survives as a shrunken remnant of the dense oak woodland of that region.

The broad areas of acid sands and gravels such as the New Forest and the Bagshot heath country are not without their interest for prehistorians. During the Bronze Age, at any rate, they carried a moderate-sized population of pastoralists who buried their dead in several kinds of round barrows; and there are, in both regions, unexcavated earthworks which may indicate the presence of Iron Age people, though their distinctive hill-forts are generally to be seen only on the fringes of these regions.

Finally, the ancient marshlands merit some attention. The lower land beside watercourses, large and small, was in many areas impassable before it was drained. On both sides of the lower Thames, and on the coastal margins of Essex and northern Kent are marshy tracts that reveal only a very limited occupation, mainly from the Late Bronze Age onwards, wherever gravel patches made habitation possible. The marshes of the Wantsum that divide the Isle of Thanet from the Kentish mainland afforded a sea-route for shipping until the beginning of the eighteenth century. Much earlier, the arm of the sea now represented by the Pevensey Levels, had similarly begun to silt up, but the town of Pevensey remained an active member of the Cinque Ports during the Middle Ages. The headland of Dungeness is also of recent geological origin. By late Roman times its northerly portion, Romney Marsh, had grown enough for some settlement to be possible; and there has been a steady accretion since, with

CHART OF THE PALAEOLITHIC PERIOD

TIME SCALE	CLIMATE	CORE CULTURES	FLAKE CULTURES	BLADE CULTURES
A.D.				
	ICE RECESSION			MESOLITHIC
22,000 B.C.	FOURTH GLACIATION–phase C (Würm 3)			Early Tardenoisian
	ICE RECESSION			MAGDALENIAN
72,000 B.C.	FOURTH GLACIATION–phase B (Würm 2)		↑	Solutrian Upper Aurignacian
	ICE RECESSION		↑	Mid. Aurignacian
100,000 B.C.			↑ Late Levallois	AURIGNACIAN 100,000
115,000 B.C.	FOURTH GLACIATION–phase A (Würm 1)	Micoquian Upper Acheulian ?	Mousterian	
	THIRD INTER-GLACIAL (c. 60,000 years)		↑	
187,000 B.C.	THIRD GLACIATION–phase B (Riss 2)	↑	Middle Levallois	
200,000 B.C.				200,000
230,000 B.C.	THIRD GLACIATION–phase A (Riss 1)	Middle Acheulian	Early Levallois	
	ICE RECESSION		? Levallois technique appearing ?	
300,000 B.C.		↓		300,000
	SECOND INTER-GLACIAL (c. 190,000 years)	↑		
400,000 B.C.		Lower Acheulian	Clactonian II	400,000
435,000 B.C.	SECOND GLACIATION–phase B (Mindel 2)			
	ICE RECESSION			
476,000 B.C.	SECOND GLACIATION–phase A (Mindel 1)	↓ ?		
500,000 B.C.	FIRST INTER-GLACIAL (c. 60,000 years)	Abbevillean	? Clactonian I	500,000
550,000 B.C.	FIRST GLACIATION–phase B (Günz 2)	(CROMERIAN)		
	ICE RECESSION	(NORVICIAN)		
600,000 B.C.	FIRST GLACIATION–phase A (Günz 1)	(IPSVICIAN)		600,000

After Zeuner. N.B.—Not all of this is relevant to South-eastern England.

FIG I Chart of the Palaeolithic Period

now a bold headland where once was a large inlet (Figure 15). (Note: The recent discovery of a Romano-British earthwork and a trackway with second century pottery at Lydd suggest that Dungeness had reached almost its present extent by that time.)

Altogether the modern map is a poor guide to prehistoric geography and it must be used with caution. Even apart from the deposition of silt, which has placed the Roman naval bases of Richborough and Pevensey a mile from the sea, and apart from the unceasing erosion which has almost engulfed the Roman fort at Reculver and destroyed without trace the one at Walton, Suffolk, other natural processes have been at work and are still continuing, so that the dividing line between land and sea has never for long been stable.

A main factor in the changes in our coastline has been the variation in level between land and sea. Four main glaciations, with three warmer intervals, alternately locked up enormous quantities of water in vast ice-sheets, and then released it slowly as melt-water. At their maximum in the penultimate ice-age (see Figures 1 and 2), glaciers reached southward to near Finchley (Middlesex) and like a plane they smoothed down the regions to the north of the London Basin and spread a variable layer of chalk, gravel and clay debris across northern Hertfordshire and Essex, greatly modifying the surface geology of those regions. In northern Essex the London Clay is overlaid by this boulder-clay which gives rise to good arable soils over wide areas; and the distributions of prehistoric occupation in the county as a whole reveals how much more the modified soils of the north were preferred.

As the ice-sheet melted, much sand, gravel and clay was redeposited by melt-water in the wake of the retreating glacier, causing further modifications in the surface geology over wide areas. Land to the south of the ice-sheet, though not covered by it, was deeply frozen and, as it thawed out, tended to slip down the steeper slopes, especially in chalk country, to form masses of so-called Combe Rock in the valleys.

The sea, too, alternately increased and decreased in depth as arctic gave way to temperate conditions; but the enormous weight of ice on the land surfaces tended to depress certain regions relatively to sea-level, so that the contraction in the volume of sea-water was partly offset by the depression of the land. Conversely, with the retreat of the ice-sheet and the removal of the superincumbent load of ice, the land level rose; but the melt-waters added so much to the volume of the sea that the water-level rose at a greater rate than did the land as it was released from the weight of glaciers. Consequently there are remnants of ancient shore-lines, distant from the present coastline, and at varying levels above it. The only ones of archaeological significance in our region are those situated at varying heights from 70 to 135 feet above present sea level between Arundel and Goodwood in Sussex. The different heights correspond to phases in the emergence or submergence in the local land surface. A totally different phase is represented by the beach at 15 feet to be seen in the cliff at Black Rock, Brighton, which extends westwards as far as Selsey.

The higher of the old shore-lines of west Sussex was probably formed during the warm interval that occurred between the second and third of the four main glaciations of Europe, roughly between 400,000 and 300,000 B.C. Hand-axes recovered from these beaches are assigned to the Clactonian and Acheulian phases of palaeolithic culture, and are broadly contemporary with similar objects from the so-called 100-foot terrace of the Thames valley. At Swanscombe in Kent part of a skull of Acheulian man was recovered from that terrace. The river terraces and the old shore-lines were in fact formed contemporaneously by the same agency. With a higher sea level, that of the rivers necessarily rose in conformity. But the rivers were certainly far greater in volume than today and their currents were faster as large quantities of water were unlocked from the glaciers during the earlier stages of a warm phase of climate; and the sheer volume and speed of the water shifted vast quantities of sand and gravel to form terraces along the river-beds and banks.

The 15-foot raised beach at Black Rock corresponds to the 50-foot terrace of the Thames, the difference in height representing the gradient of the river between the terrace and the sea. This terrace and raised beach were laid down during the warm phase between the third and fourth periods of glaciation (roughly from 180,000 to 120,000 B.C.), and in them have been found the flint implements of Mousterian (or Levalloisian) man.

Another event connected with the final retreat of the ice-sheet was the separation of Britain from the Continent. There had been earlier separations but for some time before and after the final retreat began (c. 20,000 B.C.) the level of the sea was probably rather more than 300 feet below the present mean level of tides, and the English Channel did not therefore exist. (During the final glaciation the ice-sheet did not actually cover our region; its nearest approach was to the northern coast of Norfolk.) With the melting of the ice, sea-level slowly rose until it flooded through the low marshy gap between Kent and Artois, somewhere in the millennium 7,000 to 6,000 B.C., or perhaps even later. Until the separation, an ever-narrowing land-bridge across dunes and marshes afforded access from what are now north-east France, Holland and Belgium direct into south-eastern England. At its maximum extent the land-bridge gave relatively dry access from the Danish coast to eastern England, with the southern limit of the North Sea extending from the Lincolnshire coast east-north-eastwards to just north of Jutland. The mesolithic (Maglemose) fish-spears dredged from the Leman-Ower Banks were almost certainly used against freshwater pike in the meres scattered across this land surface, and, taken together with the identity of culture at this time in Britain, Germany and Denmark, they suggest a common way of life extending across a greatly enlarged north European Plain (Figure 2).

There is evidence for a long-continuing process of submergence of land surfaces. Round about 8,000 B.C. what is now the East Anglian Fenland was some 180 feet above modern sea level. At the beginning of the neolithic period, about 2,300 B.C., it it had sunk to 20 feet with a fairly rapid continuance during the next three centuries until the land surface was below sea level and a six-foot layer of 'buttery clay' was

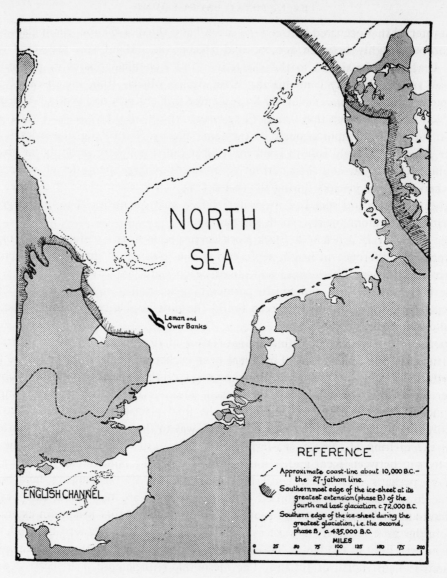

FIG 2 Britain before separation from the Continent

deposited upon it. In the ensuing Bronze Age occurred a brief reversal of the process so that an emergence to 15 feet above sea level took place. There followed further slight fluctuations, with a total depression of 20 feet below the Bronze Age level during the Iron Age; but during the Roman period re-emergence made possible an intensive occupation of the silt Fens, traces of which can be seen from the air and even, in suitable conditions, from the ground. In the third century A.D. a slight inundation occurred and protective banks were constructed in a vain attempt to stem the rising waters. Final submergence came in the fifth century, and evidence for early Anglo-Saxon occupation is limited to the Fen islands; the silt lands and the equally low-lying peat were waterlogged and shunned (Figure 3).

This process of submergence probably affected much of south-east England and there is, in fact, evidence for it in the late Roman period from the Thames estuary, from the valley of the Kentish Stour at Canterbury and on the Kentish and Hampshire coasts. And the process continues to the present day at a rate of six to twelve inches in a century. As an indirect result of it, the shallow inlets that once bore Roman galleys in the fourth century are now dry land; for as the land level sank, the gradients of the rivers declined, with a consequent slackening in current and an increased deposition of silt in their estuaries. Hence the dry land that now separates the Roman naval bases of Pevensey and Richborough from the sea.

Elsewhere the coastal erosion that began with the resubmergence of the southern North Sea and the re-opening of the Strait of Dover has continued its course with only minor regressions. The sites of the Roman forts at Bradwell (Essex) and Reculver (Kent) are half destroyed by the waves; one of the Roman buildings on the cliffs at Folkestone has similarly suffered; and villages founded in the Saxon period, 'Consumpta per Mare' in Essex, and such Sussex villages as Cudlow and Wittering and the Saxon city of Selsey, have been swallowed by the sea without a trace being left.

Yet another factor that has influenced settlement is the availability of fresh water. A glance at any relevant sheet of the Ordnance Survey One-Inch maps will show that nowhere in the south-east is one more than a few hundred yards from fresh water; and before the days of piped supplies, dwellings were necessarily placed near to it. There can be little doubt that in the prehistoric period natural supplies were even more abundant than today, even during the drier climatic phases which will shortly be discussed. Much low-lying ground that is today passable on foot even in winter was then waterlogged and impassable; medieval and modern drainage works have indeed changed the face of the land. But apart from that, on the downland plateaux there has been a steady decline in the level of water in the chalk; and evidence from Woodyates in Cranborne Chase for example, just to the west of our region, shows that in late Roman times the bottom of a well could be fully sixty feet above those of modern wells in the same neighbourhood.

Saxon settlements are almost invariably by a stream or at its source, yet in the district immediately north and west of Andover a number of hamlets are at the heads of chalk valleys now dry. Several of these places are mentioned in the eleventh-century Domesday Book. At the time of their foundation in the Saxon period they were almost certainly made beside springs flowing from the heads of the valleys. As the water-table declined the settlements were left high and dry except at long intervals when a season of heavy rainfall causes the table to be temporarily restored and the winter-bournes to flow from a point nearer to the old source-level.

During the half a million years since man's first appearance in Britain there have also been fluctuations in climate. It has been convenient to speak of four main glaciations and of three intervening milder phases; yet within the period of each ice age there were minor recessions, one in each of the first three, and two during the last glaciation (see Figure 1, p. 21). The effects of extremes of temperature and of the presence or absence of a continuous ice-sheet are profound even for civilized communities; for men in a state of savagery these changes, though doubtless imperceptible to any single generation because of their gradualness, were catastrophic. Unconscious of the advancing ice, they continued their hunting and food-gathering, moving always, generation by generation, before it, keeping in step with the southward migration of the animal and plant communities upon which they were entirely dependent for their sustenance. As cold phase gave place to warm, a slow reverse migration ensued.

Although the ice-sheet at its maximum did not cover England south of the Thames, yet the land-surface there and for some distance further to the south could support little life. The soil was frozen to some depth and glacial melt-water must have flowed over wide areas. Even during the final glaciation when much even of midland and north-eastern England were free of ice, the south-east could barely support human life. Britain, continuous with the Eurasian land-mass, was on the outer fringes of human settlement, with a probable population of less than 300 at any one time. The region was a tundra in this sub-Arctic period with a characteristic vegetation of moss, lichens, dwarf birch and dwarf willow, tiny shrubs a few inches high and largely confined to the sides of valleys. The rest of the region was barren.

From 20,000 B.C. (a date that is only a vague approximation) the climate softened as the ice-sheet waned and shrank northward. In its wake followed plants, trees, elk, wild oxen and herds of reindeer and horses, all of them tolerant of cold but not of perennially frozen soil. Birch and pine were among the first immigrants, with the birch for long dominant. The landscape was relatively open, with birch woods inter-mixed with pine and eventually a strong undergrowth of herbaceous plants. Willows occurred sparsely in the damper hollows.

With the onset of still greater warmth from about 7,000 B.C. the pine replaced the birch as the dominant tree and, because of the shade cast by its foliage when growing in close canopy, and of the dense carpet of its fallen needles, other plants were largely suppressed. But the birch lingered on and afforded suitable conditions for hazel to gain a first foothold. Broad-leaved trees of the temperate high forest begin to appear at about the same time as the hazel shows an enormous increase and as the pine was reduced in numbers. This change has been dated to about 6,000 B.C. Oak and elm were among the earliest invaders at this period and the alder followed soon afterwards. With their increase, a sign of yet greater warmth, the hazel declined moderately, crowded out in the struggle for light and sustenance with loftier competitors.

Round about 5,500 B.C. climatic conditions were so favourable that deciduous high forest flourished exceedingly. Much of the land was clothed in mixed oak forest with alder, elm and lime present in varying numbers. On poor soils birch and pine probably remained, scattered in open canopy. This favourable climatic phase is commonly referred to as the Atlantic period, and was characterized by prevailing westerly winds with much rain; annual mean temperatures were rather above those of recent centuries. The preceding 'Boreal' phase was drier and warmer than the Atlantic period. The two together cover the era during which the mesolithic tribes were in occupation of the land (c. 7,000–2,000 B.C.).

At the time when the first neolithic farmers were settling in the south-east there was a gradual though slight fall in temperatures and a decrease in rainfall. The birch extended its dominion again whilst the warmth-loving mixed oak forest declined somewhat. The beech, which arrived in small numbers late in the Atlantic phase of climate and had maintained itself sparsely in suitable localities, showed a modest increase at the same time as the birch was spreading. This sub-Boreal phase, drier and rather cooler than the Atlantic, lasted from c. 2,000 B.C. until 700 B.C., that is, for the greater part of the Neolithic and Bronze Ages. The ensuing onset of wetter and still cooler summers (the sub-Atlantic phase) roughly coincided with the arrival of Late Bronze Age farmers practising a more intensive agriculture. In the growing and harvesting of cereal crops they were faced with the same difficulties of weather as are normally experienced today in the westerly parts of the British Isles. This phase continued with little amelioration until the middle of the Roman period (c. 200 A.D.) when there was a slow change to the phase still current, with drier and slighter warmer weather, at any rate in the south-east of Britain.

These climatic phases have been described at some length because they are of fundamental importance to a proper understanding of the changes that took place in the economy of prehistoric peoples. Many of these economic changes were, of course, due to the introduction of new techniques by successive waves of immigrants; but there must also have been some unconscious adjustment to slow climatic change with its attendant modifications of the natural plant communities and of animal life, on both of which early man depended so greatly for his livelihood.

The highly complex evidence on which much of this chapter is based will be found in Zeuner's book cited in the following bibliography, and a summary of the main points will be found in Figure 3 on p. 28–29.

Date	6,000 B.C.	5,000 B.C.	4,000 B.C.	3,000 B.C.
Climatic Phases	BOREAL PHASE of dry and warm summers and cold winters	? ?	ATLANTIC PHASE Moist and warm (temperatures rather above those of present day)	
Forest Succession	Birch, then pine dominant	Expansion of mixed oak forest Elm, lime and beech Alder becomes abundant Hazel at maximum Birch declining Pine declining		MIXED OAK FOR Hazel abunda De
Development of Grassland	Grass and herbs abundant			
Domestic Animals		Dog ? Horse (wild ?)		
Introduction of Plants and Weeds of Cultivation				
Relative Levels of Land and Sea	+180 feet (height above present sea-level) Separation of Britain from Continent SUBSIDENCE			
Cultures	MESOLITHIC Maglemosean (Forest Folk) Tardenoisean			

FIG 3 SOUTH-EASTERN BRITAIN

					Date
2,000 B.C.	1,000 B.C.	A.D.	A.D. 1,000		

				Climatic Phases
SUB-BOREAL PHASE Drier with warm summers	SUB-ATLANTIC PHASE Wet, cool summers	PRESENT CLIMATIC PHASE		

Forest Succession

Increase of pine and yew

DOMINANT———————————————————————→

ne in elm   Increase of birch

			Development of Grassland
'Extensive' system of cultivation begins—burning and grazing create arable and pasture	Increase of population and of grazing, together with the introduction of 'intensive' agriculture hasten deforestation	Heavy inroads into forests. Exploitation of clay soils	

				Domestic Animals
Swine and cattle numerous—fewer sheep and goats Dog	Shorthorn cattle	Sheep dominant Cattle numerous Fewer swine	Great increase in swine pastured in forests	
	Small domesticated horse			

			Introduction of Plants and Weeds of Cultivation
Wheat Flax Barley	Spelt Celtic bean Oats Making of hay		
Great increase in plantain	Rye ? Rye		

Relative Levels of Land and Sea

₂o feet   − 6 feet   + 15 feet   − 5 feet   + 5 feet ?   o

————————————————→EMERGENCE   SUBSIDENCE→EMERGENCE SUBSIDENCE--------------→

					Cultures
---SECONDARY NEOLITHIC	Wessex Culture Food	Urnfield people	Iron Age 'C'	SAXON	NORMAN
WINDMILL	Vessel	Deverel-	Iron Age	SETTLE-	CONQUEST
HILL	People	Rimbury	'B'	MENT	
CULTURE 'B' Beakers		Culture			
	'A' Beakers			ROMAN→	DANISH
				PERIOD→	RAIDS
		Iron Age 'A'			

n Mesolithic Times

BIBLIOGRAPHY TO CHAPTER II

For the correlation of the climatic, vegetational and prehistoric cultural phases see F. E. Zeuner, *Dating the Past* (1952), chapter IV, pp. 92 f., and *Sir Cyril Fox, *The Personality of Britain* (1953), pp. 51 f. A useful summary of the evidence relating to animal and plant life may be found in the final pages of **The Succession of Life through Geological Time* (1949), published by H.M.S.O. For the geological evidence see British Regional Geology (a) **London and the Thames Valley* (1947) by R. L. Sherlock, (b) **The Wealden District* (1948) by F. H. Edmonds, and (v) **The Hampshire Basin* (1948) by C. P. Chatwin. The standard work on vegetational history is *The British Islands and their Vegetation* (1949) by Sir A. G. Tansley, of which see especially chapter VIII. Mention should here be made of Professor S. W. Wooldridge's *The Weald* (1953), a detailed study of the historical geography of that region; and his contribution to *Geographical Journal* 78, pp. 243 f., contains much that is valuable and relevant on the soils of Herts and Essex. See also *Antiquity VII* and *Geography* 20, pp. 161 f., for his discussion of soils over much of our region.

The variations of land and sea level in East Anglia are discussed by C. W. Phillips in *Aspects of Archaeology*, essays presented to O. G. S. Crawford, pp. 258 f.

* Inexpensive works.

CHAPTER III

The Palaeolithic Period

(*c*. 550,000 - *c*. 10,000 B.C.)

OF ALL PREHISTORIC peoples in Britain those of the Old Stone Age have left relatively fewest relics of their existence although they were the longest here. Indeed, their half-million years can show less, far less, than the 300 years or so during which the New Stone Age farmers retained their distinctive way of life. There is only one piece of scratched bone bearing the outline of a man to compare with the contemporary cave-art of France and Spain, and a few barely recognizable hearth-sites to set against the palaeolithic long-house sites of Russia. Otherwise, finds in Britain have been limited to a few bone and fewer wooden implements and large numbers of flint 'hand-axes' so called, though their actual use is unknown.

It is not my purpose to describe the differences in the forms of hand-axes, their techniques of manufacture or to do more than outline the successive cultures deduced from these facts. That information may be had from books listed in the bibliography at the end of this chapter. But, in that relics of the period are discoverable in the Home Counties, I offer a minimum of information here. The chart, Figure 1, on p. 21 may be found useful in providing a relative chronology for the period.

The fewness of finds, except of the almost indestructible hand-axes, is due to the immense changes made in the landscape by the four great glaciations. Their direct affect north of the Thames was to scrape the surface like a colossal bulldozer so that vestiges of dwelling-places were either erased completely or were overlaid by glacial gravels which are themselves sometimes covered by the deposits of a later glaciation. Even south of the Thames much the same sort of thing could occur. A working-floor with Acheulian axes and the flint waste from their manufacture was found on the ancient shore-line at Slindon in west Sussex, where it had been overlaid by a deposit of chalk sludge (Combe Rock) that had slipped from the steep slope of Nore Hill during the third glaciation.

The days are long past when one could go 'flinting' in gravel-heaps dumped along the highways for use as road-metal. Many finds of hand-axes are, however, made far from the spot at which their owners abandoned them. They have been swept along with other hard debris in one of the inundations which carved the landscape immediately to the south of the ice-sheet. Often they have been blunted, smoothed and scratched as a result of being hurtled along in contact with the gravel in which they

31

are found. Even where they are recovered with sharp edges it would be unwise to assume that they have not moved from the spot where the hand of man last touched them. It is true that a few flake-implements have been recovered from the edges of the clay-with-flints of the north Hampshire downs and rarely at other places in the same deposit (e.g. Wrotham, Kent); but these are exceptional. Certainly most of the palaeoliths are found during commercial excavations for gravel in the river-terraces of south-east England. The Thames 100-foot terrace from near Oxford to North-fleet in Kent has yielded them in abundance, and those who are interested seem to make a practice of watching these excavations and of ingratiating themselves with the foreman to make access easier and to swell their collections from finds made during their absence. Apart from the water that almost invariably fills them, abandoned gravel-pits offer fewer obstacles to the earnest seeker.

At Great Clacton and at Lion Point, Jaywick, both in Essex, evidence of occupation by one of the early flake-using peoples has come to light. They are called Clactonian after the site where they were first recognized. About one in ten of their implements were fashioned by trimming flint nodules to the required shape, producing what are known as core-tools; but the remainder of their implements were made by striking a flake from a flint-core and then trimming the flake to the desired shape. Among the finds was a spear-point of yew-wood, highly mineralized, and originally sharpened with a flint tool. Besides this almost unique object, several animal bones, including the radius of a rhinoceros, were recovered bearing signs of shaping for use as tools. Unworked bones of extinct species of elephant and fallow deer were also found.

The Clacton site was on the shore of a channel of the ancient Thames; that at Jaywick is on the foreshore below the present level of high tide. Recently I was shown worked bone and flint implements discovered over half a century after the first finds at the latter site. No evidence for the use of fire was found at either spot, but a working-floor, with implements and the waste from their manufacture, discovered at Stoke Newington, London, did afford evidence of its use by later people of the Clactonian culture. Levalloisian working-floors occurred at Crayford and Northfleet in Kent and at Acton, Middlesex; and a similar site, but of Acheulian man, at Caddington, as well as at Luton (Beds). The Chilterns further to the south were equally attractive because of the abundantly available flint, but knapping-floors have not yet been located there. Most of the evidence for palaeolithic man comes from the gravel terraces of the Thames and its tributaries, the Colne and Lea, including the abandoned channel of the Thames between Caversham and Henley (Oxon); but living sites are rarely discovered. Mention should therefore be made of those at Frindsbury and Bapchild in Kent where Mousterian man left the remains of his flint-working. Though some of the more important gravel pits are now worked out, increasing commercial demands for gravel constantly necessitate the opening of new ones, some of which may be expected to yield further information concerning this little-known period.

Rarely, human remains are found, as at the Barnfield Pit at Swanscombe, Kent, where, in 1935 and in 1955, parts of a skull have been recovered in close association with hand-axes. The latter permit the inference that these bones, the most ancient that closely resemble those of modern man, belong to the Middle Acheulian period (*c.* 200,000 B.C.) during the second glaciation. These finds also indicate that the *homo sapiens* stock, of which all modern races are members, must go back to a time much earlier than two thousand centuries B.C.; for these Swanscombe remains show 'a high degree of evolution'. A further assumption is that the core hand-axe was normally associated with *homo sapiens* and that flake implements were the handiwork of a distinct human stock, Neanderthal man. His remains have not been found in Britain and he seems to have become extinct about 72,000 B.C. It is possible, however, that his distinctly simian characteristics were smoothed away by cross-breeding with *sapiens*; but there is little evidence in support of this belief. At any rate, the flake industries, Clactonian, Levalloisian and Mousterian, begin to fade out at the beginning of the last glaciation (*c.* 100,000 B.C.), but not before they had influenced the hand-axe peoples and had been influenced by them in their techniques of flint-knapping.

At least two phases of the Levalloisian seem to begin contemporaneously with the onset of a glaciation (namely, the third), which suggests that the Neanderthalers adapted their way of life to the onset of arctic conditions and stayed on in the tundra zone beyond the edge of the ice. The Acheulians, on the other hand, seem to have retreated from it, continuing no doubt their pursuit of the warmth-loving animals on whom they depended for existence.

Altogether the evidence is far too slight to enable us to reconstruct the life and habits of Old Stone Age peoples. Some of the French and Spanish cave paintings graphically record the hunting methods and the varied prey of the late palaeolithic; and it is not unreasonable to assume that during similar phases of the early and middle palaeolithic periods a similar way of life had existed, but with less highly specialized implements of the chase.

In the cold phases small family groups preyed on the mammoth, bison and reindeer; in the warm phases the elephant, the hippopotamus and other animals of modern tropical distribution were hunted. In both cold and warm phases, roots, nuts, berries and the larvae of insects, as well as the leaves and shoots of many herbaceous plants, probably constituted an important part of the diet.

With the onset of the Upper (Late) Palaeolithic we can get a little nearer to the humanity that lies behind the poor relics that survive. The flake industries that are sometimes thought to characterize Neanderthal man became dominant for a time around 100,000 B.C.; the core cultures disappear from Britain. Then a series of folk migrations from the Near East set in, ultimately reaching the ice-free areas of southern Britain by various routes, but eventually crossing the broad land-link which was later to become the English Channel.

C

Hunters of mammoth, of reindeer and of horses probably came in separate groups by different routes and at wide intervals of time, for the Upper Palaeolithic lasted for 75,000 years. Like Neanderthal man the immigrants were compelled to shelter in caves from the rigorous severities of the second and third phases of the last glaciation. Their manner of life, too, was not dissimilar in that they were hunters and collectors of plant food. The cave-dwellings of the Mendips, Wales, Derbyshire and Devonshire, and especially those of France, have furnished sequences of occupation-floors which make it possible to study the cultural development of these peoples; and the great quantities of animal bones from some caves indicate the abundance of the kinds of prey hunted, though it has to be remembered that these deposits of bones may represent the accumulation of refuse over many centuries. In the Home Counties such evidence is lacking. At Oldbury Hill at Ightham in Kent a rock-shelter of this period may be seen, though it was much damaged by quarrying for road-metal in the early nineteenth century. The occupants of the shelter were probably living just before the beginning of the fourth glaciation (c. 115,000 B.C.). Judging from the implements found on the site of the Admiralty in London there once existed an occupation-site there too, but not in a cave. Caves near Dorking, Farnham and Guildford are probably not ancient but, like the Chislehurst caves, were excavated as quarries. However there may well be others like the Oldbury shelter now masked by a covering of sand and earth at the entrance.

Men and women of this period certainly belonged to the species of man of which we are members. The skeletal remains of North American Indians are most nearly comparable with those of Upper Palaeolithic man, though the latter may have interbred with the Neanderthal stock and inherited some of its physical characteristics.

Figure 1 indicates the sequence of cultures during this period, from the Aurignacian onwards to the pre-Tardenoisian which merges with one of the main mesolithic cultures. Few significant finds relating to these tribes have come from the Home Counties, perhaps because their open habitation-sites are more easily destroyed than the occupation-levels in caves. It may be inferred, however, that the Mousterian and Levalloisian flake-implement peoples were displaced here as elsewhere by immigrant Aurignacians. The latter possessed a more highly specialized and more finely-made range of tools than any of their predecessors. These tools are smaller and the so-called 'blade' is a characteristic of their equipment. It is fashioned for special tasks like the carving of bone for such things as fish-hooks and for the dressing of leather for clothes.

Forced to retreat by the southward extension of the ice-sheet round about 115,000 B.C., they seem to have been replaced by new migrants, the Gravettians (or Upper Aurignacians), ultimately from southern Russia. With them arrived a few Solutrians, a people better known from their remains in France and Spain. The ice-free phase that occurred between the two earlier glaciations of the final ice-age is almost a blank in Britain, but a skeleton with implements that may be Aurignacian and probably of this ice-free phase, was found at Halling on the Medway, and may indicate that southern Britain was not entirely deserted at this time.

The warm epoch between the two later arctic phases of the last glaciation saw a local development of the Gravettian, namely the Creswellian culture, so called from the type-site found in a cave in Creswell Crags in Derbyshire. In the same period Britain was visited by hunting parties of the Magdalenian folk of whom slight remains have been found. But the Creswellian people are the more important, for it is likely that their descendants formed one folk-element among the mesolithic tribes whose remains are so abundant in the Home Counties.

The transition from the end of the Palaeolithic Age to the Mesolithic is more than usually obscure and only further finds of late palaeolithic and of early mesolithic sites can bridge the gap. With cave-sites lacking in south-east England it is more likely that the Gravettians dwelt in huts not unlike those shortly to be described. But their detection can hardly be made except through great vigilance coupled with luck, and the vigilance must be backed by a detailed acquaintance with the material equipment of both periods.

BIBLIOGRAPHY TO CHAPTER III

*K. P. Oakley, *Man the Toolmaker* (1950) is valuable for its clear explanations of the techniques of flint-knapping and of the various types of flint tools. Complementary to this, and equally authoritative, is another British Museum publication, *W. Watson, *Flint Implements, An Account of Stone Age Techniques and Cultures* (1950). Of interest also is *W. Le Gros Clark's *History of the Primates: An Introduction to the Study of Fossil Man* (1949), from the same source. More general works are M. C. Burkitt's *The Old Stone Age* (1956), D. A. E. Garrod's *The Upper Palaeolithic Age* (1926), which should be supplemented by her paper in *The Proceedings of the Prehistoric Society* 4 (1938) and F. S. Zeuner's *Dating the Past* (1952), especially chapter VI, D, pp. 182 f. This last work contains a very full bibliography. For the non-specialist reader there is *V. G. Childe's *Man Makes Himself* (1941) and *J. D. G. Clark's *From Savagery to Civilization* (1946).

* Inexpensive books.

CHAPTER IV

The Mesolithic Period

THE CONTINUITY OF CULTURE so easily discernible in recent centuries is less apparent in the earlier millennia of prehistory on account of the paucity of evidence; and that evidence is highly selective, for its survival is dependent on the whims of time, or rather on its accessibility to the bacteria of decay. Always there must be borne in mind the fragmentary nature of the evidence for any prehistoric age. What survives may provide only a very distorted picture of life as it was actually lived.

If we had nothing but the material collected in south-east England on which to base an account of the life of mesolithic people, the amount of surmise in that account would be greater than the ascertained facts. Fortunately there is evidence from the Continental territories of these tribes, as well as from a careful excavation in north-east England, to fill out the picture. The Maglemosian site at Star Carr, Seamer, near Scarborough (N.G. 027809) yielded a great quantity of organic material preserved in the peat-bed of a swamp on the edge of a former lake. Brushwood from the birch, reinforced with stones and clay, had been used to afford a firm footing. Flint cores, cast aside after the detachment of flakes suitable for tools, were found in some numbers, besides the flake-tools themselves. One of these retained traces of the birch-resin by means of which it had been secured to an arrow-shaft. Mattocks of elk-antler have the cutting-edge ground to a shape similar to that of a neolithic polished axe; and one of the mattocks retained traces of its wooden handle. There were also scrapers for the preparation of skins, made from the bones of wild oxen, and barbed points made from red-deer antlers were designed for use as fish-spears. Equally significant for the understanding of these people was a wooden paddle.

Clearly fishing and the hunting of wild cattle, elk and red deer were the main occupations, presumably of the men; skin-dressing for the making of clothes, for containers and hunting-accoutrements, was a task for the women. Rolls of birch-bark from the site were the raw material from which box-like objects could be sewn, to serve as containers for small objects such as nuts and wild fruits. It is noteworthy that the dominant tree of the period, the birch, played a very large part in the economy of these people of Star Carr.

These Forest Folk (Maglemosians) were dwelling beside this northern lake during the eighth millennium before Christ, that is during the Boreal phase of dry, warm summers and cold winters. They were among the earlier mesolithic immigrants into Britain, crossing the territory not then inundated by the North Sea and no doubt dwelling among the dunes and meres that ran without interruption from the higher land that was yet to be eastern England, across to southern Scandinavia. One such group lost a fish-spear which in recent times was dredged up, with fresh-water peat adhering, from between the Leman and Ower banks, well out to sea from the Norfolk coast (see map, Figure 2). Groups of them settled in eastern and south-eastern England and their fish-spears have been found near Royston (Herts), in the Thames at Battersea and Wandsworth (London), and in the river Test in Hampshire. Their settlements were placed on low ground near to ancient marshland; and, in our region, one of them came to light by the river Lea at Broxbourne (Herts) and others are known from the valley of the Essex Colne and from beside the Kennet at Thatcham (Berks). At Broxbourne their equipment of flint tools was well represented, especially the tiny flint points and knife-edges, called microliths. These could be used singly as arrowheads or for the shaping of bone, antler, or wood, or they could be used in composite tools which had a series of flint flakes mounted in wood like the teeth of a coarse saw. The most significant wood-working implement, however, was the axe, now increasingly employed for the felling of trees and for the shaping of wood.

As the climate softened towards the end of the Boreal phase, the dominance of the birch gradually gave way to high forest in which oaks formed a majority of the larger trees; and for the three to four thousand years of the Atlantic phase of climate there was a proliferation of warmth-loving plants unequalled since in Europe. With a mean annual temperature about two degrees Centigrade above that of today, and with greater precipitation, the tree-line extended higher than it does today in mountainous regions, and on porous soils such as the sandstones and chalk of the south-east the greater humidity favoured the growth of deciduous trees in localities where today there is open country, though felling in recent centuries has also contributed to this change in the landscape.

The axe gained in importance in such an environment and probably remained the most essential tool even as late as the Middle Ages. In its mesolithic form it was a roughly flaked, elongated core-tool with an efficient edge (the tranchet axe). The edge was produced by the detachment of a tranverse flake from one of the ends, and the axe could be re-sharpened again and again by the removal of further similar flakes. Though much smaller, arrowheads were produced by the same method, with a chisel-like edge which continued to be employed in neolithic times. It appears to have been derived from an older palaeolithic culture and was first introduced into Britain by the Maglemosians. (*Petit tranchet* arrow-head.)

They influenced or intermarried with a second group of mesolithic tribes, this time from the Continental regions forming parts of Belgium and northern France. They are known as the Tardenoisian from the type-site in the Département de l'Aisne. By the time they migrated Britain had become an island, but the Channel was far narrower than it is today. They settled for preference, it seems, in sandy tracts, especially on the Lower Greensand of the Weald where clear evidence of their brief

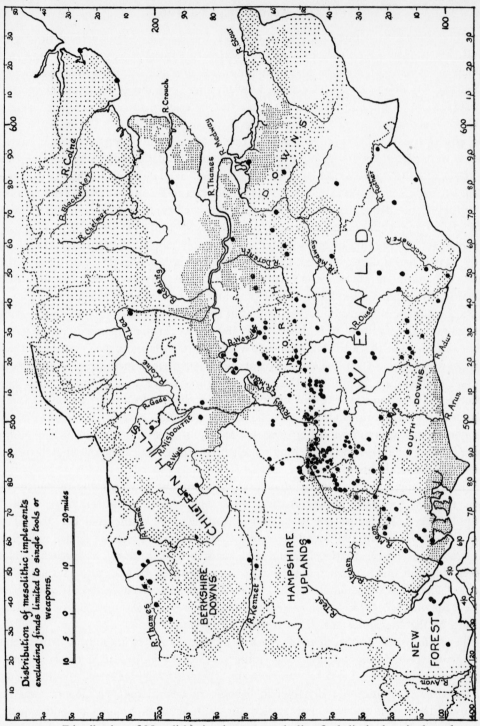

MAP I Distribution of Mesolithic implements excluding finds limited to single tools or weapons

occupation has come to light in scores of places (see map 1). Two distinct flint-knapping traditions, possibly representing distinct waves of immigrants, appear to be present. The one is broad-bladed, mainly found intermingled with Maglemosian traditions and closest to its Continental prototypes; the other has narrower blades often of sharply angular form (geometric microliths), and these commonly occur on south-eastern sites as one element in the culture.

Hut-sites have been found near Farnham and near Abinger in Surrey and at Selmeston and Hassocks in Sussex, and tranchet axes, suggesting Maglemosian influence, have come from all of them. Moreover, microliths of Tardenoisian ancestry have been found in large numbers on all these sites, thus indicating the cultural fusion between the two peoples. The most recently excavated dwelling was that at Abinger. It was about ten and a half by fourteen feet and roughly V-shaped in section with a sloping ledge on one side, possibly a sleeping place. Two post-holes were distinguished at one end of the dwelling-pit. 'It would seem possible that these two post-holes carried short forked poles with a horizontal cross piece between the forks, and that the structure forming the roof of the pit consisted of a framework of branches and saplings leaning against the cross piece and with their ends resting on the land surface surrounding the edge of the pit. Some such structure, covered over with grass and bracken, and then perhaps the skins of deer, would provide a reasonably waterproof roofing to the pit and convert it into comfortable and warm sleeping quarters.' A rough wall made of stones, clay and earth may have been built between the posts. Traces of two cooking hearths were found just outside the limits of this lean-to structure. By contrast, a rock-shelter is known to have been used by this people at Balcombe in Sussex.

There, especially in the Horsham district, and to some extent in Surrey, Hampshire and Kent, the microlith assumes a characteristic form with a concave base, produced by trimming away minute secondary flakes. This should be a distinctively Tardenoisian contribution to the culture, for in a less evolved form it has also occurred on Belgian sites of the Middle Tardenoisian period. Another specialized and very local form is the 'Frensham point', known so far at only three find-sites in West Surrey. But the Wealden culture is not limited to the south-eastern counties where it was first recognized. In Oxfordshire and Berkshire, in northern Hampshire and from places on both sides of Southampton Water, as well as in the Isle of Wight, ample evidence of the handiwork of the same people has been picked up from the ground surface. Their occupation sites are known even further afield in Dorset, Somerset, west Cornwall and Wales; and the presence of flint artifacts in these regions, so far from the chalk country where the material naturally occurs, has led to the suggestion that there was a migration westward from the Weald. But the movement was not all westward, for Portland chert from Dorset was the material of microliths found in both Surrey and Cornwall; and siltstone pebble implements of Cornish origin have turned up in the western Weald. In this same area, too, 'mace-heads' made from quartzite pebbles from outside the Weald, have been found on more than two dozen sites, and implements of coloured flint, from East Anglia or further north along the East Coast, have been recovered from a dozen sites in Surrey. If these wide dispersals of raw materials were not a result of tribal migration, they may represent evidence of trading activity, a pursuit in which their secondary neolithic descendants were much concerned.

Although vestiges of mesolithic hunting-camps or of more permanent settlements are frequently discovered in the Lower Greensand areas, this is mainly because they have been less disturbed by cultivation; whereas on other formations they have been obliterated by the plough. Yet sites are, in fact, known from the Weald Clay near Chiddingfold in Surrey and from the Clay-with-Flints round Dummer in Hampshire. In north-west Surrey, in the the New Forest at Beaulieu, Denny Lodge, and Wootton and at Cams on Portsmouth Harbour, the Tertiary gravels were occupied. Numerous sites are known from the Hastings Sands of the High Weald of Sussex which, for much of its extent, is similar to the Greensand; and two sites on the South Downs, at Seaford and Peacehaven are situated on sandy patches overlying the chalk.

The evidence for south-east England is limited to flint and stone implements mainly because of the preference of this people for well-drained soils. The acidity of the sands soon destroys all organic materials whether vegetable substances or skeletal remains. Consequently we know nothing of the burial customs of mesolithic people and it was necessary to look to the Seamer settlement in Yorkshire to gain a fuller notion of their equipment.

The relatively open forests of the sandstone country favoured hunting more than the dense growths on heavier soils, though the Chiddingfold sites show that game was pursued and temporary lodgement made even in the thickest forest. Yet more permanent habitation was conditioned not merely by proximity to game, for it was then abundant in all kinds of country; but well-drained soils for dwelling upon, a good spring for fresh water and a not-too-distant supply of flint were obviously considerations of prime importance for these people. Such clues as these should make it possible to locate more of their dwellings; and the presence of a strong spring, in conjunction with the other factors, should narrow the search.

The flint implements of the mesolithic peoples are not usually difficult to distinguish from those of later ages. Size is an important criterion for all but the tranchet axes, which are themselves easily distinguishable from the stone and flint axes of later cultures. Microliths are seldom more than two inches long and, though they assume various forms, they are usually pointed at one end and functionless edges are blunted by minute secondary flaking. The cores from which flakes were struck are roughly conical in outline, though sometimes they are found to have been truncated preparatory to re-use. The upper surface produced by the truncation afforded a new platform for the detachment of further flakes. Sometimes the base of a used core was

removed for the same purpose. This technique is similar to that used in the resharpen-
ing of tranchet axes. Another flint type characteristic of these people is a tiny saw
from one to two inches long, produced by minute notches made at regular intervals
along the cutting-edge of a blade. Of the micro-burin and its origin as a waste product
from microliths produced by the notch technique I must pass over. It is well described
and illustrated by Mr. W. F. Rankine in his excellent book *A Mesolithic Survey of
the West Surrey Greensand*. No one interested in this period can afford to be without it.

A late mesolithic site of some importance came to light at Lower Halstow on the
estuary of the Medway. Several hearths were distinguished, a few microlithic points
similar to some from the Essex coast, and, very significant, the Thames 'pick'. This
has been so named from its frequent occurrence in that river and its tributaries; but
it is to be found widely in south-east England including one recovered from very
near the mesolithic dwellings at Farnham, Surrey. It is considered to be a form
evolved late in the period, and has the characteristic cutting edge of the tranchet axe
and *petit tranchet* arrow-head.

One interesting point about this Kentish site is botanical. The marsh clay on which
the hearths were found afforded evidence that the lime-tree had supplanted the pine
as the dominant tree—an indication that the dry, cold Boreal had given way to the
moister and warmer Atlantic phase of climate. Immediately overlying the site were
peaty layers which could not have formed until the rainier conditions of the later
phase were well established.

The Lower Halstow culture is known also from Clacton and Walton on the Naze
on the Essex coast, where it occurs on a submerged land surface now accessible only
at low tide. Obviously there has been a rise in the level of the sea since late mesolithic
times, the later part of the process of land-submergence discussed on p. 22f. The
same process had inundated the southern North Sea which had been crossed on foot
by the Maglemosians, and had flooded south-westwards to form the English Channel
which had not long existed at the time of the Tardenoisian immigration. Microliths are
found below high-tide mark near Titchfield Haven (Hants), though they may have
been moved there by the sea-tide or a river-current; in a similar position off Cams in
Fareham parish, Hampshire, they are almost certainly on a submerged land surface.

With the advent of Western Neolithic (Windwill Hill) farming communities, the
earlier inhabitants of south-eastern Britain did not become extinct; indeed, they
ultimately became the dominant people, strengthened by contacts with the newcomers. But some section of them appears to have persisted in their aboriginal way
of life. In the Mendips and in Staffordshire, hunters with microlithic arrow-points
survived into the Early Bronze Age; and at Pulborough, Sussex, on the Lower Greensand, mesolithic cores and flint waste, a Thames pick and the sharpening flake from
a tranchet axe were found apparently in association with some 2,300 flint daggers or
fragments of them; but there were no microliths. Though the daggers are not of
typical Early Bronze Age form, it is likely that they were being manufactured in that

period by a mesolithic tribal group. Such an occupation would be natural among the Peterborough Folk, themselves descended in part from the native mesolithic peoples. It should be noted, however, that the site was not examined scientifically, and it is possible that the dagger factory was later than the mesolithic occupation and not in fact associated with it.

The preference of the Windmill Hill neolithic groups for the chalk uplands resulted in little competition for living-places with the mesolithic people of the Weald; and it is quite likely that the two could exist side by side with little contact between them for some considerable time. But their was some borrowing of ideas. A chert adze of mesolithic form from Thakeham, Sussex, is partly polished in the neolithic manner, thus adding much to its efficiency as a cutting tool. And, as an element in the secondary neolithic peoples, the old mesolithic Tardenoisians reveal a vigour and enterprise that ensured the survival of their traditions, much changed of course, for long after the disappearance of the Windmill Hill people.

BIBLIOGRAPHY TO CHAPTER IV

The Mesolithic Age in Britain (1932) by J. G. D. Clark, with a map of Wealden sites, is the most complete and fundamental study of the British evidence, which he put into its wider setting in *The Mesolithic Settlement of Northern Europe* (1936). W. F. Rankine's *A Mesolithic Survey of the West Surrey Greensand* (1951), published by the Surrey Archaeological Society, is valuable both for its local and wider implications. His contribution to *A Survey of the Prehistory of the Farnham District* (1939), pp. 61 f. (Surrey Arch. Collections) affords a useful and detailed summary also. See also his papers in *Archaeological News Letter*, vols. 4, no. 4; 4, no. 10; 5, no. 3; and 5, no. 5; in the *Proceedings of the Hampshire Field Club*, vol. 18, part 2; in the *Proceedings of the Prehistoric Society* for 1939 (with J. G. D. Clark on the Farnham dwellings), and for 1949 (on mace-heads, which are not discussed in my chapter); and in *Surrey Archaeological Collections*, 46, 49 and 50.

See also *Oxoniensia*, 17–18, for finds in the Oxford area.

The Excavations at Star Carr: An Early Mesolithic Site (1954), also by Clark, is necessary for a complete understanding of what is known about the period. See also his papers on the Horsham culture and the classification of microliths in *Archaeological Journal*, XC (1934). L. S. B. Leakey's *Mesolithic Site at Abinger Common* (1951), published by the Surrey Archaeological Society, is the source of my quotation on p. 39, and is well worthy of complete perusal.

The relevant chapters of the general works listed in the General Bibliography on p. 228f. contain summary accounts of the period.

* Inexpensive works.

CHAPTER V

The Neolithic Period

WE SAW IN the last chapter how it was possible for peoples originating from Scandinavia, from Belgium and northern France to reach a common destination in Britain and there to mingle and evolve new cultures. British prehistory saw this occur again and again. Our south and east coasts with their sheltered natural harbours, easy natural routes by river or ridgeway into a rich and varied hinterland, and the comparatively narrow stretches of sea separating these shores from the continental mainland, made of Britain a land attractive to those dispossessed by over-population or by the pressure of more warlike peoples from the east.

The Windmill Hill tribes, who began crossing the Channel from northern France in about 2,300 B.C. were descended, in part at least, from peoples who had been living in small communities in the countries immediately to the east of the Mediterranean in the sixth millennium B.C. In these territories, which naturally supported plants ancestral to modern cereals and some of the animals suitable for domestication, a system of simple 'extensive' farming was practised. This method involved an almost annual breaking of new ground for crops, since manuring or fallowing to restore fertility were apparently unknown. Land could be re-used only after the lapse of some years, but suitable light soils of sufficient natural fertility to be worth cultivation occur only patchily, and, with an increase in population, migratory movements began in order to satisfy the frequent and increasing need for new land. Spreading along the southern edge of the north European plain from the Black Sea to northern France is a discontinuous belt of light but rich *loess* soils which seem to have afforded an avenue for a people accustomed to light-soil agriculture. Similar deposits occur in southern England and have been recognized at Iver (Bucks) and at Swanscombe (Kent). But the soils overlying the chalk downs were a good substitute, and in Sussex and Hampshire especially, these earliest of our farming communities have left many traces of their former presence.

Valley brick-earths and gravel-spreads were perhaps equally attractive to them, but unlike the downlands, these riverside tracts have been densely settled, continuously farmed and latterly largely buried by the ever-spreading Wen, so that lowland traces of the Neolithic period are fewer. Moreover, in such situations there was competition from the secondary neolithic peoples; and judging from the quantity of Peterborough ware and related objects dredged from the lower reaches of the Thames, the Windmill Hill peoples were restricted to the middle reaches from Marlow to Abingdon.

Even there, signs of secondary neolithic occupation came to light, though whether contemporaneous with that of their rivals it is not possible to say. The most important lowland site of a developed Windmill Hill community, that at Abingdon, belongs to the middle neolithic, yet even there a few tiny sherds of secondary neolithic ware were found.

Four pastoral enclosures ('camps') of this period are known in Sussex, one of them on Barkhale Down, Bignor, shamelessly half ploughed down in quite recent

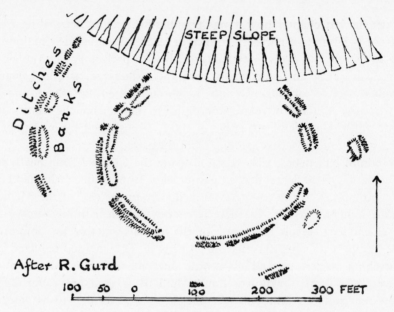

Based on Figure I p. 106 of 'Sussex Archaeological Collections' 89

FIG 4 Combe Hill Camp, Jevington, Sussex

years. Kent, Surrey and Hampshire and the south midland counties have none apart from that at Abingdon, now destroyed, and the 'Maiden Bower' at Houghton Regis (Beds), which lies beneath an Iron Age promontory fort. Others exist in Devon, Dorset and Wiltshire. There may be some yet to be discovered, especially on the Hampshire chalk where long barrows of the Windmill Hill people are particularly numerous (see Distribution Map 2 and Plate 11).

To a predominantly pastoral people the chalk downs were attractive because they were only lightly wooded over large areas. The denser forest on areas of clay-with-flints in west Sussex, along the North Downs, on the Hampshire Downs and on the southern Chilterns were largely avoided. Elsewhere on the chalk it was a matter of no great difficulty with the surprisingly efficient polished axe to fell and then to burn in order to create fields which could be broken with the hoe. The grazing of cattle and pigs in the woodlands destroyed seedlings that might have maintained the forested

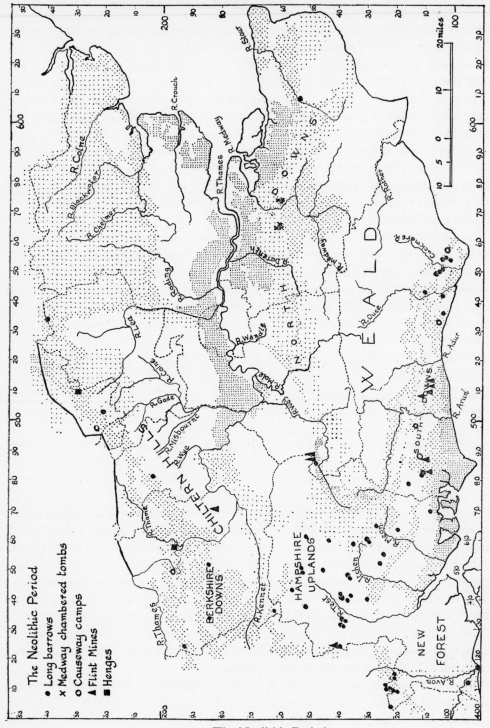

The Neolithic Period

• Long barrows
× Medway chambered tombs
○ Causeway camps
▲ Flint Mines
■ Henges

MAP 2 The Neolithic Period

character of the Downs; and the process of deforestation was greatly hastened by the constant need to move the cultivation plots and break new ground. The abandoned fields would soon afford grass for the cattle whose grazing in these open patches would prevent a reversion to woodland.

The cattle enclosures, called 'causeway-camps', are usually ovoid in shape, sometimes with only one surrounding bank, but usually with two or more arranged concentrically. The ditches are not continuous, but gaps of undisturbed chalk were left at irregular intervals, hence the term 'causeway'. The segments of ditch were probably each dug by a different gang, who piled the excavated soil and chalk on the inner, upper, side of the ditch (Figure 4). That at Abingdon was constructed so as to isolate a spur of land between two brooks and it forms a 'promontory' camp analogous in form with the promontory forts of the Iron Age.

The ditch itself was not functional; it merely provided material for the bank within which a fence or palisade was constructed. A timber gateway controlled access to the enclosure across one of the causeways. There is no evidence from our region of permanent occupation within the camps; nothing to suggest hut-sites has so far been revealed by excavation. But the ditches themselves have afforded material suggesting seasonal occupation—pottery, bones and ashes—and the bones, which were of domestic animals, together with the shells of hazel-nuts and remains of crab apples, go further in implying that the ditches were occupied in late summer or autumn. At Whitehawk the presence of human bones among the food-waste points to cannibalism, with a special preference for the brains of young people. The animal bones, too, were of immature cattle, and this fact more than any other affords a clue to the purpose of the camps.

They were for coralling the herds after their rounding-up from the open expanses of downland. Only thus could a proper selection be made of the few beasts that were to be kept over the winter as breeding stock for the following year. The remainder were pole-axed. The hides would be prepared as leather which served so many essential purposes. The bones, such as were suitable, provided awls and needles, and the sinews were used as thread. The flint scrapers and points that are found in the camps were used in the dressing of the hides. The few animals that were spared could not be maintained with fodder as we understand it. If analogy be any guide, they were fed with tree-bark and with dried foliage, possibly eked out with a little hay. Such a diet meant stunted, undergrown beasts and, as late as the Middle Ages, Danish cattle had to be carried from the stalls to spring pasture, so weak were they and so light after their winter fast. What with the autumn slaughter and the deprivations of winter, only about one beast in five survived to maturity. Much the same could be said of man himself in this and in succeeding periods.

The causewayed camps in the lowest and so earliest levels of their ditches have yielded mostly pottery of the Windmill Hill culture or of closely related types. Usually the vessels are round-bottomed and would not stand upright without support; and in some forms there is a shoulder (carination) in the upper half of the side. Few bear decoration and those show only rudimentary patterns of lines and dots. Pots from westerly sites such as the Holdenhurst long barrow in Hampshire sometimes have two unpierced handles (lugs), a trait derived perhaps from Brittany. But the Holdenhurst sherds belong to a western type of ware of which the type-site is Hembury in Devon.

The camp at Abingdon produced a more evolved style with more decoration, and the lugs have become strap-handles. Similar sherds occurred at Selsey in Sussex and at the Maiden Bower in Bedfordshire. A further development is seen on pottery from some East Anglian sites and from an anomalous kidney-shaped barrow at Monks Risborough (Bucks). There was also a link in style between this and the Bedfordshire site. Finally, distinctive pottery from Whitehawk, imitating the forms of leathern vessels, are believed to owe something to the mesolithic folk of the region.

The pottery of the secondary peoples and others has been found in some of the camps, but usually in the later levels. A sequence, not equally apparent at all sites, of Windmill Hill, Ebbsfleet and Peterborough wares and then beakers throws some light on the relative age of these cultures. The camp at Combe Hill, Jevington (Sussex) (Figure 4) is exceptional in yielding only Ebbsfleet ware, a secondary type of which more will shortly be said. Sherds of this ware were found at Whitehawk but they were intermixed with Windmill Hill pottery.

Although hut-sites have not been found in or near the camps, a few have been located elsewhere. They occurred at Michelmersh and Southbourne in Hampshire and at Marlow, (Bucks); another at Clapham in Sussex, with a roughly oval base, contained scraps of Windmill Hill pottery as did the Michelmersh hut. At Selsey both Windmill Hill and Abingdon wares were recovered from a habitation site and the same is true of the circular huts on the Essex coast at Clacton and Jaywick. There, in addition, Rinyo-Clacton grooved ware, another secondary type and still later in date, 'B' beaker with rusticated ware, were all found; but their relative positions could not be determined. Two deductions are permissible from these instances and from a similar tribal inter-mixture in the types of flint implements from a few other sites. One is that the two peoples eventually intermingled; the other, that the secondary tribes took over some of the dwelling places of the Windmill Hill people. The latter explanation is true in some instances where the Windmill Hill occupation layers are overlaid by a sterile stratum of silt and this in turn by a layer containing secondary neolithic sherds. Maiden Castle (Dorset) and Windmill Hill, the type-site itself at Avebury (Wilts) are such instances. But at Abingdon and Whitehawk the camps were apparently in use by both peoples for a time, but not necessarily simultaneously. It is important to note that the further west one goes the later seems the secondary neolithic occupation. This suggests a slow westward infiltration of secondary tribal groups into Windmill Hill territory which, in its more westerly regions, had ceased apparently to be occupied by the makers of causewayed camps at the time it was reached by the secondary people. The further suggestion that the camp-makers had withdrawn westward in face of this advance is perhaps straining the scanty evidence too far. Yet it accords with the fact that, at any rate in the south and south-east of Britain the Windmill Hill culture shows a comparatively short period of development and then flickers out leaving scarcely a trace. In its place appears the culture of the warlike Beaker tribes, briefly dominant and soon eclipsed by people clearly descended from the secondary neolithic strain, and who, themselves, had almost certainly remained in the region during the hegemony of the Beaker folk. Furthermore, there are indications that secondary neolithic and Beaker tribes gradually merged and that they came to possess a material culture that reveals its debt to both stocks by the Middle Bronze Age.

As we have seen, the Windmill Hill people were equipped with flint scrapers and points for the preparation of hides; for tree-felling and woodworking they had axes of flint or stone, some of which were rubbed to a smooth surface to improve their cutting power. For hunting they tipped their arrows with small, finely-flaked, leaf-shaped heads. Their barley and wheat were ground to flour on a grain-rubber, which is a sandstone block with a saucer-shaped hollow on which a bun-shaped stone could be wielded with a grinding motion.

A belief in the supernatural is revealed by chalk figurines of pregnant women and by the phallic carvings found in some of the causewayed camps. They suggest a fertility cult comparable to those known from the eastern Mediterranean. But it is from their burial practices that most may be learned of the beliefs of the Windmill Hill people.

Occasionally the burial of a solitary individual comes to light, as at Pangbourne in Berkshire, or in a ditch of the Whitehawk camp where two separate female burials were each accompanied by fossil sea-urchins. A male skeleton was found at the same place with a funerary offering of mussel-shells. Above the filled-in mineshafts at Blackpatch two round barrows each contained a male skeleton, one of which had been provided with neolithic flint-implements. With the latter was a female skeleton and over these two associated interments a cremation had been scattered. In all these instances from Sussex the body had been buried in a crouched position like Beaker burials. The discovery of human bones that had been cast aside after a cannibalistic meal has been alluded to earlier. These human remains were not interred but were simply treated as rubbish. Evidence of this kind has come from two Wiltshire sites and from Whitehawk and Maiden Bower. In the flintmines at Cissbury and Blackpatch, as well as in Grime's Graves in Norfolk, bodies were cast unceremoniously into worked-out shafts with the chalk rubble of their filling; but no suggestion of cannibalism is involved in these instances.

Solitary burial is not the typical rite of the Windmill Hill people; most commonly they interred their dead in the earthen long barrows which are the most conspicuous monuments surviving from the period (Map 2). At least a dozen of them still remain on the Sussex Downs, three in the extreme west of the county and the remainder between Brighton and Eastbourne. Along the chalk to the westward in Hampshire there is a concentration of nine near the valley of the upper Test and others scattered elsewhere in the county. In Dorset and especially in Wiltshire they are very numerous. Berkshire has three of these earthen long barrows, at Churn Knob, Blewbury, at Lambourn and at Combe Gibbet in the extreme south-west corner of the country. The famous Wayland's Smithy, Ashbury, is a chambered tomb built by the related Severn-Cotswold people who formed a branch of the Western Neolithic community. Sherds of Windmill Hill ware have come from a dozen of these chambered long barrows in Gloucestershire and Wiltshire. The two kinds of burial places have a similar external appearance and both are often placed on conspicuous ridges. The Windmill Hill people and the Severn-Cotswold people had also in common the use of similar undecorated pottery, leaf-shaped arrowheads and flint or stone axes indistinguishable in form.

There are three widely spaced neolithic barrows on the Chilterns, one at Monks Risborough, with a wooden burial chamber and a kidney-shaped mound, and the others at Dunstable (Beds), now destroyed, and at Royston (Herts). There are also two near together on the continuation of the same chalk ridge in Norfolk. A third in the same county, at Ditchingham, near the river Waveney, far from the chalk, is comparable with the barrow which formerly existed at Holdenhurst (Hants) sited on Tertiary deposits. The location of these two barrows together with that of the Abingdon camp and of the numerous finds along the Thames should make us cautious not to overstress the upland distribution of the Windmill Hill culture, at any rate in its later phases. On the North Downs only two long barrows are known, one that was destroyed at Badshot Lea near Farnham (Surrey) and Julliberries' Grave at Chilham (Kent).

The Holdenhurst barrow is of further interest because of the pottery recovered from its ditch. As in some of the camps, sherds of Windmill Hill type occurred in the earliest silting of the ditch, followed at intervals by secondary neolithic (Peterborough) and soon afterwards by beaker sherds. This fact, together with the knowledge won from other unchambered long barrows and with the close identity of distribution between the barrows and the camps, goes far to prove that both kinds of earthwork were made by the same people.

The external appearance of long barrows varies little except in size, but internally excavation has revealed a bewildering variety of construction. For these the reader is referred to pp. 50 f. of Professor Piggott's monumental work cited at the end of this chapter. One group must, however, receive brief attention. In the Medway valley, in the parishes of Addington, Aylesford and Trottiscliffe are the remains of some half a dozen megalithic structures in many respects comparable with the chambered tombs of the Severn-Cotswold culture (Map 2 and Map A). They may be ultimately related; but the more immediate ancestry of these barrows may be traced in similar structures across the North Sea in Holland, north Germany and Scandinavia.

D

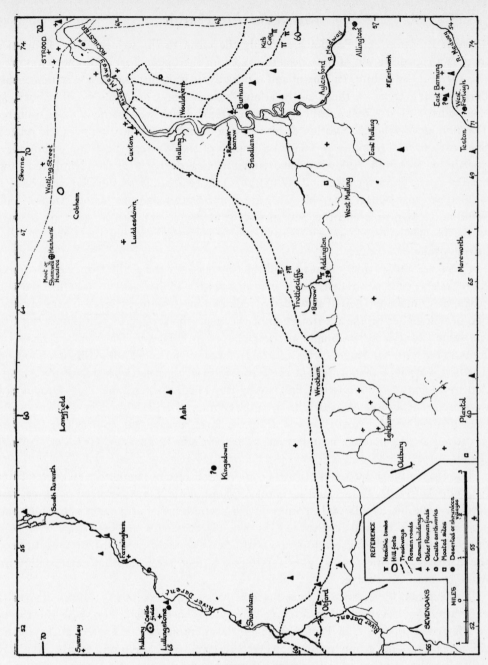

MAP A Western Kent

Some sort of movement from these regions into Britain, whether of migration or of trade it is impossible to say, is indicated by finds of thin-butted axes at such places as Enfield (Middlesex) and Canterbury, in the earthen long barrow at Chilham and at other places near the Thames and Medway estuaries. Across the North Sea these axes are associated with megalithic tombs comparable with those in the Medway valley; and some pottery from Orpington (Kent), having the same Continental origin, may be further evidence to the same effect.

In some instances it is clear that bodies were not interred in long barrows immediately after death, for the skeletons of a number of individuals have been found disarticulated and the bones intermingled. As there was no indication that the burial chamber had been disturbed since being sealed after the last burial, it follows that the flesh had gone from the bones and that they had fallen apart before interment. Evidence from Dorset suggests that bodies were reserved for some time in a mortuary enclosure or house before burial took place in the communal tomb (Figure 5, site VIII). The turf structure in the Holdenhurst barrow and the elaborate timberwork in the Whiteleaf barrow may have been mortuary houses that were later covered by the mound of earth as the final ritual act of burial. There is evidence, too, that this last ceremony sometimes included a ritual feast. At Badshot and elsewhere there were many bones split for the extraction of the marrow and then cast into the newly dug ditch; but nowhere in our region have vestiges of funeral dances been noted such as were detected in the forecourt of a Cotswold chambered tomb.

Late in the period communal burial in round barrows was not infrequent. This practice was most common in Yorkshire, but instances are known from Royston (Herts), and it is conceivable that the Whiteleaf barrow may be simply a damaged round barrow. Sherds of Abingdon ware and tranchet arrowheads were found in a round mound covering a secondary neolithic burial on Dunstable Downs (Beds); but such small objects may well have been scraped from the surrounding ground surface when the barrow was being made.

The secondary neolithic cultures are still but vaguely known and their interrelations can barely be guessed. They overlap in time and in spatial distribution with each other and with the Windmill Hill peoples whom they eventually replaced. The latter had introduced into Britain the cultivation of cereals, with the hoe as their main agricultural implement, and they were the first to herd cattle. But these skills were almost certainly acquired from them by the secondary tribes. Indeed, the causeway camp on Combe Hill at Jevington in Sussex (Figure 4) yielded only Ebbsfleet ware which is probably an early variety of the Peterborough ware; and in the same camp was found a grain rubber. These two facts serve to associate the secondary people at Jevington with both herding and corn-growing. At Whitehawk pottery of both the Windmill Hill type and of Ebbsfleet type were found intermixed. Much further west, at Windmill Hill itself, Peterborough ware was in use only after an interval had elapsed after the original occupants of the camp had gone from it. But in the south-east, at any rate, there must have been frequent contact between the two peoples; and, having learned to grow cereals, the secondary tribes no doubt continued the practice, though stock-raising, with hunting, fishing and some food-collecting was probably far more important in their economy than corn-growing.

It is likely that the secondary neolithic people of the south-east resulted from a fusion between the mesolithic aborigines and newcomers from across the North Sea. The two elements were, in fact, ultimately of the same stock, for some of the mesolithic people of our region were themselves earlier emigrants from among the Forest Folk, some of whom now followed them to Britain. The relative chronology of Windmill Hill and secondary neolithic pottery noted earlier suggests a slow movement westward of the latter people from their landing-places in the east and south-east of England; but the evidence is insufficient to justify such a conclusion.

Peterborough ware is heavier and cruder than pottery of the Windmill Hill type; it is often much ornamented with maggot-like impressions produced by pressing twisted cord into the unfired clay. The bones of small animals or birds were used to make deep pittings, especially in the zone immediately beneath the rim. The total effect is that of an imitation in clay of the texture of basketry, and it is widely held that plaited containers were ancestral to the Peterborough wares and to related pots of north-west Europe.

The culture takes its name from the type-site in Northamptonshire but, although its pottery is found scattered thinly in the Midlands and north of England, it is common-est in Wessex, the Thames valley and along the Sussex coast, more often in low-lying situations than on high ground. At Peterborough itself, and at Grovehurst in Milton Regis (Kent) traces of habitations were found. Shallow circular depressions about three feet deep and eleven feet across revealed the confined area of the living-space; and clay daub that had once adhered to wattlework walls at Grovehurst gave some hint of how wind and rain were kept out.

The tools of this people are not distinctive. Leaf-shaped arrowheads, and axes indistinguishable from those of the Windmill Hill folk, have been found at several places with Peterborough pottery; but there are no implement-types so frequently found in association with it as to be termed characteristic of this culture. In common with other secondary neolithic cultures, arrowheads with a chisel edge, mesolithic in origin, were used by the Peterborough people.

Even more shadowy are the two secondary cultures known as the Rinyo-Clacton and the Dorchester; but, as type-sites of both occur in our region, they require some attention. The Great Clacton site yielded pottery similar to that from the Abingdon camp and secondary wares of the Peterborough and Rinyo-Clacton cultures. Palae-oliths and sherds of the earliest ('B') beakers have also been found there. A generally similar collocation of these cultures occurs at Jaywick to the south and at Walton-on-the-Naze to the north. At all three sites the Lower Halstow culture, already alluded to, was represented. It has been suggested that this late mesolithic people survived at

Halstow into the neolithic period and that the two people, mesolithic and neolithic, were in contemporary occupation of that Kentish site. Yet the surviving evidence suggests succession rather than contemporaneity of occupation, though it is all too seldom that the stratigraphy of sites allows more than a guess in this matter. At any rate, occupation in both the mesolithic and neolithic periods is attested at Farnham, Abinger and Ewell in Surrey, at Selmeston and Peacehaven in Sussex besides Lower Halstow, Kent, and a number of other places in the south-east; and in most instances the abundant spring that attracted the earliest inhabitants has continued as a focus of settlement through succeeding prehistoric and historic phases.

The distribution of Rinyo-Clacton pottery (or Grooved Ware, as it was formerly called) is curiously scattered. It has been found in fullest context in the neolithic villages of Skara Brae and Rinyo in the Orkney Islands, and finds have come from mid-Scotland and the north-east of England. The heaviest concentration of it is on the Wessex chalk and upper Thames, with outliers at Holdenhurst and Hurn near the Hampshire coast, at Saunderton (Bucks), and one so far isolated occurrence at East Malling in Kent. It has also been found at places in East Anglia. It is generally of thinner fabric than other neolithic wares, and the ornament commonly consists of grooved chevrons sometimes alternating in zones with horizontal lines. In the southern province of the culture ornament is added within and just beneath the rim. A flower pot shape is common, though the walls of many pots form nearly a right-angle with the invariably flat base.

The other equipment of this people (if the pottery does, in fact, represent a distinct people) is hardly distinguishable from that of the Windmill Hill or Peterborough folk. Both leaf-shaped and chisel-edged tranchet arrowheads were used; scrapers and small saw-edged flakes occur in association with this pottery. At the henge-sites, shortly to be described, it is found with the other three main neolithic wares and with beaker-sherds. At Durrington Walls, in Wiltshire, the largest known henge-monument, a habitation site of this people has come to light. Among them were a few users of Peterborough ware. However, the significant point about this site was the light it shed on the economy of the Rinyo-Clacton people. Of the large number of animal bones recovered, roughly two-thirds were of swine, one-third of cattle with a few sheep or goats and an even smaller number of horses. This predominance of swine makes possible an instructive comparison with sites such as The Trundle in Singleton, Sussex, with Whitehawk, Brighton or with Windmill Hill. The makers of the camps were mainly occupied with the herding of cattle, the bones of which predominate at these places, whereas pigs come a poor second and sheep-bones are few or absent. This suggests that by the late neolithic period the process of forest-clearance had not gone far, for both cattle and swine are native to forests but sheep can thrive only in open country. By the Iron Age, on the other hand, at hill-forts such as Quarley or Meon Hill (Stockbridge), both in Hampshire, sheep are next in order of importance only to cattle; and on some Romano-British sites they actually exceed them in number. Thus, by indirect evidence, it is possible to gain some idea of the changing landscape; and it will be necessary to revert to this topic later.

The Dorchester culture is the only other one of the secondary neolithic cultures that occurs in our region. It is to my mind doubtful whether it represents a distinct group of people, but rather a merging of cultures at nodal points of prehistoric communication, such as Dorchester, where the main highway of the Thames is crossed by a trunk route, the Icknield Way, and Berkshire ridgeway, the importance of which at this period is manifest by the distribution of long barrows, camps and settlements along the course of the route. Similarly, the earliest Stonehenge, which is also regarded as a monument of the Dorchester culture, is nodal to prehistoric communications. Of the two other known sites of this culture, the Dunstable long barrow is on the line of the Icknield Way; and the round barrow at Stanton Harcourt is within easy reach of Dorchester either by water or along the gravel which here overlies the Oxford Clay.

But the sites at Dorchester are of great interest, and their excavation and interpretation is a masterpiece of modern archaeological method. Briefly, they consisted of enclosures of so-called henge type, though there were no standing stones or timber posts with lintels as the word 'henge' implies (Figure 5). Within a circular ditch pits had been dug for some unknown ritual purpose. Some of the pits had been used for the interment of cremations that had once been contained in skin bags, usually secured with a bone skewer-pin characteristic of the Rinyo-Clacton folk. Associated with one or other of these monuments occurred sherds of pottery: Windmill Hill, Abingdon, Peterborough and Rinyo-Clacton wares, and implements of tranchet type. The only distinguishing feature that would justify the term 'Dorchester culture' was the use of some of these henges as cremation cemeteries. But even this trait was present, either in the form of partial burning among the Wessex long barrow people, or of more complete incineration of the bodies in a flue constructed within some Yorkshire barrows of the neolithic period. What is new at Dorchester is not the burial-rite so much as the number of cremations together within a ritual monument. More recently, a similar henge has been discovered at Streatley in Bedfordshire.

Associated with the henge-sites at Dorchester was a cursus which consists of parallel ditches some 4,000 feet long with 210 feet between them (Figure 5). In the earliest silting were found a polished flint axe, a leaf-shaped arrowhead and the early variety of Peterborough pottery (Ebbsfleet ware) such as was recovered from the ditch of the causeway camp at Combe Hill, Jevington. It will be apparent, then, that the Dorchester cursus, like the henge monuments, exhibits a mixed primary and secondary culture. The purpose of these extensive earthworks is also unknown, but the famous example near Stonehenge and the even larger one in Cranborne Chase are both aligned on long barrows, and they may well have served some ritual purpose in connection with the burial of the dead. (See Plate 3 for another cursus at Dorchester.)

Like most of the Dorchester sites, the cursus was discovered from the air and excavation was necessary before its destruction by gravel-digging. Similar cursus monuments are known at North Stoke and Benson (Oxon), and at Sutton Courtenay, just across the Thames in Berkshire. At the Oxfordshire sites, and upstream at Eynsham and Stanton Harcourt, other henges have been discovered as the result of aerial survey, and it is evident that taking burials, habitations and ritual structures together, occupation of the gravel-spreads beside the middle and upper Thames was dense in the late neolithic period; and it continued to be so throughout subsequent prehistoric and historic phases. Such a continuity of dense occupation must mean that many sites of the earlier periods have been obliterated; the number still remaining is therefore all the more remarkable.

Another interesting feature of the neolithic period, and well represented in our region, are the flint-mines. Seven of them, including five explored by excavation, are known from the South Downs alone. Only one so far has been located in Hampshire, at Martin's Clump, Over Wallop, and one in the southern Chilterns at Rotherfield Peppard (Oxon). On the continuation of the Chilterns at Weeting (Norfolk) are situated the most famous of all, Grime's Graves. The mine at East Horsley (Surrey), which was thought by its discoverer to be neolithic, is now considered to be medieval, though neolithic occupation was evident at this place and there are two groups of filled-in mineshafts a little north-east of Farnham in the same county (Map 2). Just over the Hampshire-Wiltshire border from Over Wallop two further mines are known, that on Easton Down being particularly interesting. In my own journeyings through Wiltshire I have twice observed a site which strongly suggests the presence of filled-in mine shafts. It is on the western extremity of Long Knoll, Kilmington (actually on the parish boundary; N.G. ref. 785377), and about two miles from the neolithic causeway camp recently discovered by Professor Piggot. It would not surprise me to learn, however, that these bumps and hollows (which I have seen only from a distance) were the result of military activity—the craters of small practice bombs, or mortar shells or something of the kind. Given the leisure to make local inquiry, the possibility of modern disturbance might have been verified.

Occasionally supplies of useful flint, which is only to be had from the stratum called the Upper Chalk, were accessible at ground-surface, as at East Horsley; but usually shafts had to be dug with antler-picks in the same way as the ditches of a causeway camp or cursus. Shovelling was done with the shoulder-blades of oxen. When the shaft had reached down to a seam of flint, horizontal tunnels were cut following its bedding; and the chalk débris from the workings was moved in wicker baskets to parts already exhausted of flint. Light was obtained from wicks floating in tallow contained in a chalk cup. The marks of soot from these lamps are still to be seen in the mine galleries as well as the marks of picks. ('Levers' would be an apter word, but 'picks' is the term commonly used.) These sometimes bear the chalky fingerprints of the last neolithic miners to use them.

The flint nodules were roughed out into axes on the ground surface and then traded away for the food and drink which the miners themselves could not produce. A hoard of these rough-outs found at Peaslake in Shere (Surrey) was almost certainly on its way from a mine to a customer when abandoned. The hoard of seven found upright in the soil at Great Baddow, in Essex, seems to have had a votary significance.

The flint mines were almost certainly the work of Windmill Hill people in the first place, and typical pottery of theirs was found in shafts at Cissbury. But the mines continued in use for a longer period than that of the Windmill Hill culture, and besides Peterborough sherds, actual burials of the Early Bronze Age Beaker people were discovered in shafts at two Sussex mines, namely Blackpatch (Patching) and Church Hill (Findon). At the latter place it was proved that Middle Bronze Age barrows were built whilst the mines were still working.

But axes of fine-grained rock were being imported into the south-east from distant mountain-sides in the Highland Zone. Manufacturing-sites of roughed-out axes of igneous rock have been identified at two places near Penmaenmawr in Caernarvon-shire whence they were traded widely into the Lowland Zone of Britain. The densest concentration of these axes was in the Avebury district and the south-west midlands, but a few did reach the south-east. At least three have been found near the Hampshire coast, and a pair at Kingsclere in the north of the county probably came origin-ally from the Arenigs in Merionethshire. The contemporary use of these distant products is proved by the discovery of a Graig Lwyd (Penmaenmawr) axe in associa-tion with Rinyo-Clacton pottery at Avebury.

The axe factory at Pike o' Stickle in Great Langdale, Westmorland, had similarly wide trading connections. A Langdale axe was found in the causeway camp at Abing-don; others, to the west at Sutton Courtenay and near Faringdon in Berkshire, and across the Thames at Chalgrove (Oxon). In Surrey one occurred near the headwaters of the Wey. Exports from a factory at Tievebulliagh in Northern Ireland, have been little studied yet, but one has been found in our region at Sittingbourne, Kent.

So far only one Cornish factory site, near Callington, has been identified, but products that certainly came from the far south-west occur from time to time on south-eastern sites. Such are the greenstone axes from Cold Ash (Berks) and Bled-low (Bucks.). Even further afield, from Brittany, came the jadeite axes such as those from Canterbury and from the Southend district. West Wales contributed a quota to the complex trading pattern of neolithic Britain, and the Presely Hills of Pembroke-shire, whence came the bluestone circle of Stonehenge, were sending axes into Hamp-shire (e.g. Bankes Heath, Bournemouth) as well as into more westerly counties. Numerous axes of dolerite from Wales and the borderland have been found in Hamp-shire particularly, but Berkshire, Hertfordshire and even London (Pimlico) have yielded specimens.

The importation from across the North Sea of Scandinavian axes was noted in connection with the Medway megalithic monuments, but according to present know-ledge, overseas trading was mainly concerned in the export of stone axes from the workshops in the Highland Zone across the Channel to France. The concentration of finds from near the fine natural harbours of Christchurch and Southampton Water is some indication of the route taken. But although the neolithic material of northern France has been little studied, it is already clear that Graig Lwyd axes reached Brittany and the Channel Isles; yet blades of the fine honey-coloured flint of Grand Pressigny (Touraine) probably never came to Britain, though they were sent far and wide to Switzerland, the Low Countries and to the Channel Isles. It is likely that there was little point in exchanging the products of British flint-mines with those of Pressigny; the local and familiar article was preferred in both regions.

The trade in stone implements was mainly in the hands of the secondary peoples. At Graig Lwyd they produced the rough-outs, and when these had reached their destinations they were, where stratigraphy permits any pronouncement, generally used by secondary folk after the disappearance of the Windmill Hill people.

The survival of the secondary culture into the Beaker period is well documented on numerous sepulchral and habitation sites. Scraps of beaker pottery (the earlier 'B' type) begin to occur in stratigraphical positions that suggest that the neolithic had run only half its course; and it is not unusual now to lump the Beaker period with the Neolithic Age. The later 'A' beaker was represented by sherds intermixed with Peterborough pottery and a scrap of Rinyo-Clacton ware in association with the burials found in the West Kennet long barrow (Wilts) and in a long barrow at West Runton (Norfolk); in the causewayed camp at Maiden Castle (Dorset) the same mixture was found but without the Rinyo-Clacton ware. At the henge monument called the 'Sanctuary' near Overton (Wilts), which is part of the Avebury complex, 'B' beaker sherds were associated with Peterborough pottery. On the submerged land surface of Essex the East Anglian variety of Abingdon ware (primary neolithic), Ebbsfleet, Rinyo-Clacton (both secondary) and 'B' beaker appear to be roughly contemporary, though appearances here may be very deceptive. To go further afield, in the Giants' Hills long barrow at Skendleby (Lincs.), sherds of 'B' beaker occurred in the mound itself and had obviously been scraped up from the ground surface when the barrow was being made, so that obviously here beaker pottery was in use before the building of the barrow. The complete absence of vestiges of the Beaker people from within the Class I henge monuments at Dorchester on Thames is noteworthy in view of their abundant relics along the middle and upper Thames and in view of their association with the more developed henge monuments (of Class II) at Dorchester and elsewhere.

That the long-headed Windmill Hill stock did not die out, as did the culture of that name, is suggested by the association of long skulls with the broad type that is normally found in burials of the Beaker Folk. Evidence of this survival has come to light in Bedfordshire where, at Clifton, a cemetery of five skeletons with a late type of beaker-pot included two men and a woman of long-headed, neolithic type. At Sutton Courtenay (Berks) there occurred a less certain association of long and broad skulls with Rinyo-Clacton ware; beaker burials were nearby. And in a flint-mine shaft at

Cissbury (Sussex), and in a grave near the Blackpatch mines, skulls occurred which seem to indicate a cross between the Neolithic and Beaker strains.

Before leaving the neolithic period something should be said concerning the vegetational history of the time in relation to the neolithic economy. The warm and moist Atlantic phase was giving way to the drier sub-Boreal, but almost throughout the region conditions of soil and climate had favoured the growth of broad-leaved forest. Only on the windswept summits of the downlands was growth checked, and there scrub and coarse herbage afforded a more open landscape. Elsewhere on the chalk, with a normally deeper soil than to-day, woodland flourished only less luxuriantly than on the deep soils of the valleys. Mixed oak-forest, with some lime and beech, spread above a lush undergrowth of hazel which gave place to alder in the damper areas of lowland.

It has often been asserted that the beech was absent from Britain at this time and that it entered later in prehistory. But its seed cannot be bird-borne or wind-borne, so that, once the Channel had been formed about 5,000 years before the first neolithic immigrations, it is unlikely that sufficient seed could reach these shores by natural agencies for it to establish the colonies that must have preceded its later dominance in favourable situations of soil and drainage. Yet its charcoal and pollen-grains have been recovered from a number of neolithic contexts, too many, indeed, for it to have been a tree of only sporadic occurrence. Its pollen grains appear in small numbers in East Anglian peat formed towards the end of the Atlantic phase of climate; but the nearest favourable habitat for it was probably the East Anglian heights and perhaps the Brecklands. In those places it could have been dominant without leaving a trace in the Fenland peat. Moreover, it could have existed for many centuries in the southeast before it reached East Anglia by natural slow expansion of its territory. At any rate, by late neolithic times, beechwood was being shaped for the hafts of axes at Ehenside Tarn in Westmorland, and an even longer lapse of time must be allowed for such an extension to the north-west of England.

The neolithic agriculturists initiated a process of deforestation which has still not ended. Predominant among their livestock were cattle and swine, both by nature woodland animals, and it was they who pushed back the forest edges more quickly than would have happened if hoe-agriculture had been the only agent of destruction. In this period, sheep and goats were few and they could only attain to dominance in the Iron Age in consequence of earlier clearance by cattle and swine. Clearance resulted in a drying-out of the soil with a consequent deterioration in the habitat of the liver-fluke, the worst parasitical scourge of sheep. Moreover, clearance permitted the luxuriant growth of those grasses and herbs on which sheep thrive best; and the open chalk downs of southern England afforded optimum conditions for flocks from Iron Age times until recent decades.

The change from woodland and scrub to open grassland is traceable in the type of snail shells found in levels attributable to the neolithic and subsequent periods, and this kind of evidence shows that already by the Late Bronze Age the chalk downs had undergone much clearance; and the lynchets of Celtic fields, some of which can be shown to belong to that period, prove that a more efficient agriculture had hastened the process. In short, neolithic tillage and herding radically affected the natural plant communities which, in turn, made possible an expansion of sheep population and a greater extension of the arable.

BIBLIOGRAPHY TO CHAPTER V

S. Piggott's *Neolithic Cultures of the British Isles* (1954) is the standard work, with full references to periodical literature. On the economic aspects of the period, in a European setting, see J. G. D. Clark, *Prehistoric Europe* (1952). The important series of Sussex sites are discussed by E. C. Curwen in *The Archaeology of Sussex* (1954) chapters V and VI. Of great importance, and too recent for discussion in most general works, is *Excavations at Dorchester, Oxon.* (1951) by J. R. C. Atkinson, C. M. Piggott and N. K. Sandars—First Report, with a chapter on henge monuments. Some of the more important articles and general works are: E. T. Leeds, *Antiquaries Journal*, VII and VIII, on the Abingdon camp; S. Piggott, *Archaeological Journal*, 88, on neolithic pottery; V. G. Childe in the same volume on the continental affinities of this pottery; E. C. Curwen in *Antiquity*, IV, on causewayed camps; G. E. Daniel, *The Chambered Tombs of England and Wales* (1950); S. Piggott and A. Keiller, 'The Badshot Long Barrow' in *A Survey of the Prehistory of the Farnham District*, pp. 133 f. (1939); R. F. Jessup, 'Excavations at Julliberrie's Grave, Chilham,' in *Antiquaries Journal*, XIX; S. Piggott, 'The Holdenhurst Long Barrow,' in *Proceedings of the Prehistoric Society*, III; B. Bunch and C. I. Fell, 'Stone-axe Factory at Pike o' Stickle, Westmorland,' in the same journal, vol. XV; S. H. Warren, 'The Graig Lwyd Axe Factory,' in the *Journal of the Royal Anthropological Institute*, 49 and 51. For the extensive literature on the Grime's Graves flint-mines see Curwen, above. *The Later Prehistoric Antiquities of the British Isles* (1953) is valuable for its text and especially for its illustrations for this and later periods down to the Iron Age. It is published by the British Museum.

* An inexpensive work.

CHAPTER VI

The Early and Middle Bronze Age

THERE IS GOOD reason for treating the Beaker Folk as a part of the neolithic complex, for few of these immigrants had the use of copper or bronze, and it is doubtful whether any of them were acquainted with the techniques of producing and shaping metal. The few bronze daggers found in their graves were probably acquired by trade from Ireland or perhaps as loot before they crossed to Britain. I have kept to the traditional division between the Neolithic and Bronze Ages simply as a matter of convenience. Already in the last chapter some attention was given incidentally to this people because of the considerable chronological and cultural overlap between them and those whom they conquered.

Within the limits of the Home Counties as here understood over seventy Beaker burials have come to light, apart from numerous potsherds from the Thames and a widespread occurrence of their flint arrowheads and daggers. But the main concentrations of these peoples (for at least two main groups are distinguishable) are to be found stretching from west Dorset to north Wiltshire, from the Suffolk coast to the Wash, on the Yorkshire Wolds, in the Peak district and in Northumberland. In south-eastern England smaller groups of finds have come from the South Downs, from east Kent, north-east Essex, and a relatively dense concentration from the Thames valley near Oxford. Scattered burials have been discovered elsewhere in our region.

These people have been named from the drinking-cup which they commonly placed with their dead. It probably contained milk, for they were mainly a pastoral people, constantly on the move seeking new grazing grounds for their herds. It is believed that they remained for a comparatively short time in any area. Their weapons were daggers and bows, and, in contrast with earlier peoples, they buried their dead singly in a crouched position, often under a bowl barrow if they were of the 'B1' group, or rarely under a bell barrow.

Two main groups of these immigrants are distinguished as 'A' and 'B', though the 'B' tribes actually came here first. The sub-group, 'B1', after moving across Spain and southern France to Brittany, crossed to the Hampshire coast near or at Christchurch and thence spread northwards after leaving vestiges of their passing. They extended inland along the Avon and between the Test and Itchen, spreading at least as far as Cholsey and Radley beside the Thames in Berkshire. The 'B2' sub-group migrated from the eastern Pyrenees to Holland and the middle Rhine and eventually

60

to Kent, Sussex, Essex and the middle Thames where they overlapped the area of 'B1' occupation, assuming that both sub-groups were in that area contemporaneously.

The 'A' Beaker Folk were also immigrants from the Rhineland and beyond, and their typical flint dagger, made thus perhaps because of their remoteness from copper ores, has been found in some numbers in and along the Thames from its confluence with the Lea westward to the Wey. The eastern parts of Essex and Sussex show minor concentrations and there is a scatter elsewhere in our region. Beside the main immigration up the Thames, the 'A' Beaker Folk came in via the Wash and are strongly represented by finds to the east of the Cam and Ouse. Some of the latter may have moved south-westward along the Icknield route to the middle Thames, but finds along that river in southern Essex suggest that the concentration of 'A' Beaker people upstream from London arrived via the Thames rather than the Icknield Way.

The 'B' groups were equipped with tanged copper daggers, and their arrows were headed with barbed and tanged points of flint. Whereas the 'B1' group practised burial beneath barrows, the 'B2' group were commonly buried in flat graves and unaccompanied by funerary deposits apart from the beaker. As for the pots themselves, they are of well-made thin ware, and the B varieties, in common with the ancestral bell-beakers of the Continent, have a profile with a double curve of shallow S-shape. The decoration of the 'B1' pots is usually limited to horizontal bands of tiny jabs with a pointed implement or with a finely toothed comb; 'B2' beakers are decorated more perfunctorily, often by the impress of a cord twined round the pot before firing.

'A' beakers are more angular because of their constricted waist, and their decoration is more elaborate, taking the form of zones of triangles and lozenges which give a feeling of vertical pattern rather than the horizontal banding of the 'B' types. Before their migration to Britain the 'A' folk had interbred with the battle-axe tribes of Central Europe, and had retained some of their traditions. These found expression somewhat later in our region in the fine battle-axes found in the Hove barrow, in that from one of the Lambourn (Berks) barrows, or the one from Botley (Hants.). But besides the flint daggers, battle-axes and archers' equipment, a member of the 'A' group might be buried with a copper or bronze flat dagger with rounded base and rivets to secure the haft. Finds of these are most numerous in Wessex, the Peak District, and East Yorkshire. In our region they occur as the easternmost sector of the Wessex concentration, with half a dozen in Berkshire, about the same number in Hampshire and three outliers in Kent. They are almost certainly imports from Ireland, the first of a trade in bronze implements which was later to grow considerably.

More complicated are the relationships of the 'C' beakers. Some are degenerate and probably late forms of the 'A' or 'B' types; but not a few suggest that the main 'A' and 'B' peoples had intermarried, and that the purer traditions of both had become mixed by contact with each other. This is most evident in Oxfordshire and in the Highland Zone. In equipment the 'C' group has more in common with 'A' and is often termed 'A-C' in consequence. Their relics are found most commonly in the west and north, but they do occur on the fringes of our region, not only round Oxford as a group, but as scattered single examples at such places as Inkpen (Berks), Hitchin (Herts), Clifton and Shefford (Beds), and at Great Chesterford (Essex). Within the 'A' group should be included handled beakers of which two come from just outside our region at Eynsham and Cassington (Oxon), the sites of beaker cemeteries. Within the region, Abingdon (Berks) has produced one and Sible Hedingham (Essex) two. Some of these were conscious imitations in pottery of wooden prototypes, which may quite well have been commonly used in this period but have been lost without trace. At any rate a sherd of such a pottery beaker, with a representation of wooden growth-rings on the bottom, was recovered from the Thames, and a complete handled beaker, similarly decorated, was found at Bottisham (Cambs). And such imitations in pottery of vessels made in other materials recall the pots of Abingdon ware from the White-hawk causewayed camp which have diagonal slashes on the rims and shoulders imita-ting the stitching which secured the hoops to the leather of their prototypes.

Associated with the 'A' beaker people, and with secondary neolithic cultures, is the so-called rusticated ware, of which the whole surface is pinched up to produce a much-roughened appearance. The closest analogies for this pottery are to be found in Holland where, too, it is associated with beakers. It has been thought to represent an intrusion into the Beaker traditions of a custom of the mesolithic Forest Folk; but so little of it has so far been found that its full significance is far from clear. Several sherds were found scattered through the filling of a flint-mine shaft at Church Hill (Findon). Below them, in earlier tips of chalk débris, was an unusual kind of beaker, probably of the Middle Bronze Age. Most extraordinary, however, was the fact that it contained a cremation, which is in contrast with the normal Beaker practice of inhumation. Rusticated ware was also found in the flint-mines called Grime's Graves in Norfolk, and in our region it occurred, again with beaker fragments, in an Early Bronze Age dwelling-site in the upper levels of Whitehawk camp. These beaker sherds were similar to the very late Findon pot just mentioned. Rusticated ware occurred also at Colchester and on the Essex coast and, at the other end of our region, at Holden-hurst (Bournemouth) (where it was associated with 'A' beaker), and at Moordown, in the same district. Here sufficient of it survived for a tentative reconstruction of the vessel to be made, revealing that it has something of the flower-pot shape of Rinyo-Clacton ware. It would seem that the rusticated pottery belongs to the period of overlap between the secondary neolithic and beakers, and its occurrence in henge monuments at Arminghall (Norfolk), Gorsey Bigbury (Som) and at Stonehenge and Woodhenge (Wilts) goes some way to confirm that belief.

Dwelling-places of the Beaker folk are seldom found. One at Whitehawk is of interest in that a foot of silt separated the latest level of neolithic occupation from that of the Beaker inhabitants, which indicates some considerable lapse of time between the two peoples' use of the site. Apart from a pit which had soon been filled, there was no sign of any structure. An 'A'-type beaker was found in a dwelling-pit at Lymore in Lymington (Hants); a 'B' beaker at Kingston Buci (Sussex) in what may have been a dwelling; and at Hitcham (Bucks), pits three to seven feet deep and from fourteen to twenty feet in diameter, with evidence for stakes leaning from the edge to a central support, contained domestic refuse, beaker sherds and those of later vessels, so that an Early Bronze Age date for this dwelling is not certain. But the best account of Beaker habitations is to be found in the *Wiltshire Archaeological Magazine*, volumes 45 and 46. Flint-mines at Easton Down, Winterslow, produced material of both the Windmill Hill and Peterborough peoples, but were most intensively worked by the Beaker folk who set up a number of their huts nearby. They were of varying plan, some round, some oval, and all irregular in shape. They were sunk into the surface from six to eighteen inches and, even in the elongated form, were not over ten feet across in the longest dimension. Stake-holes about six inches deep and from four to six in diameter surrounded these shacks and probably supported a thatched roof. Among the occupation refuse were the bones of cattle, pigs and sheep; and in an ashpit there was charcoal of both dediduous and coniferous wood, the latter a surprising find in the south at this period.

The information from Easton Down, just beyond the Hampshire border, and from the Findon flint-mines in Sussex, shows that the exploitation of the mines continued at least until the later part of the Beaker period; and the discovery of beaker sherds with a cremated burial beneath a flint-knapping floor at Blackpatch affords some confirmation of the continuance. Indeed, there was clear indication here that a barrow containing a Middle Bronze Age overhanging-rim urn, had been constructed while one at least of the mine-shafts was still open; yet the flint implements from the knapping-floor are to all appearances purely neolithic in form.

In contrast with earlier inhabitants of Britain, the Beaker folk were warlike and well armed for conquest. It is assumed that they established themselves as a warrior caste dominating the neolithic peoples whom they had subdued; and no doubt they exacted tribute from them. With surplus wealth thus acquired they could purchase imported luxuries such as the greenstone axes from Brittany, weapons of copper from Ireland and ornaments of jet from Yorkshire. A woman of the 'B1' group, buried under a barrow at Radley (Berks) possessed golden ear-ornaments whose closest parallels are found in Spain.

Burial in barrows suggests some belief in an after-life as do the ritual henge monuments which are, in their double-entrance form (Class II), associated with Beaker remains. At Dorchester such a structure was discovered (site XIII) with two entrance-causeways through double concentric ditches which were over thirty feet wide and five feet deep (Figure 5). A low bank had been piled between the ditches, which had an extreme diameter of 620 feet. No sockets for posts or standing stones were found. The only evidence of the period of construction came from the earliest silting of the inner ditch. There, fragments of 'B1' beaker occurred, and just outside one of

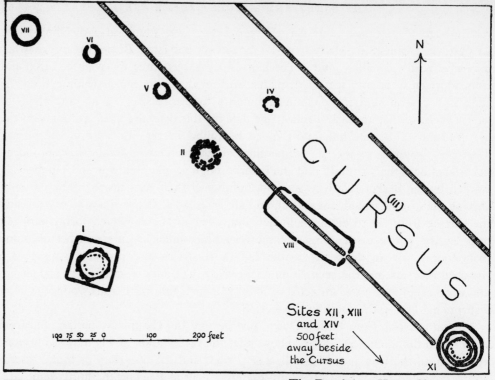

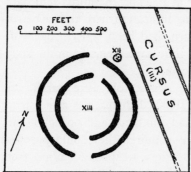

FIG 5A The Dorchester Henge Sites
FIG 5B Beaker Monuments, Dorchester, Oxon
(Only the ditches are shown)

Site I: A Class I henge monument containing a crouched inhumation and four cremation burials. The pottery in use was of the Abingdon type. Part of the site was later used for temporary shelter, the occupants of which used Peterborough ware (v.p. 54).

Sit II: Of three phases: (*a*) an innermost uncompleted ring-ditch; (*b*) a second ditch probably an internal bank; and (*c*) an outermost ditch with inner bank containing cremations. Finds relate the site to the Peterborough and Rinyo-Clacton Cultures.

Site III: The cursus, possibly made by users of Abingdon ware. Spoil from the ditches was piled to form an internal bank. Total length over 4,000 feet. (v. p. 54 and cf. Plate 3).

Site IV: A Class I henge with outer bank enclosing 25 cremations. Its entrance-gap was on the south-east.

Site V: Similar to IV but with entrance-causeway in the north-west sector.

Site VI: Similar to V.

Site VII: Ditch of a bell(?) barrow. Secondary Saxon inhumations round the edges.

Site VIII: Probably a mortuary enclosure (v.p. 51). In its shape and its position relative to the cursus (which it preceded), it is analogous to a long barrow.

Site IX (omitted from plan): Linear ditches. *Site C* (omitted): Pits of uncertain purpose.

Site XI: A Class I henge of three roughly concentric ditches with an inner ring of pits, probably not all contemporary. Three pits contained cremations and a fourth a sherd of Ebbsfleet-type pottery.

Site XII: A 'BI' Beaker burial in a wicker coffin. A low mound had covered it, and the remains of what had probably been a mortuary sledge were found in the enlarged ditch.

Site XIII: 'The Big Rings', a Class II henge with two opposite entrances and a bank between the ditches. Sherds of 'BI' beaker came from the primary silting.

Site XIV: A small ring ditch near the southern entrance to XIII and within its outer ditch (omitted from plan). (See p. 54 and pp. 63–5.)

Based on 'Excavations at Dorchester' (1951), parts of Figure 2 (pub. Ashmolean Museum, Oxford).

the entrances was a barrow-burial of the same Beaker group (site XII). The man had been enclosed in a wicker coffin and interred in an oval grave with his tanged copper dagger, a riveted knife and an archer's wrist-guard of greenstone. The barrow was composed of earth taken from the ditch surrounding the burial. In a pit associated with the interment were the remains of what seems to have been a wooden sledge, probably the one on which the corpse had been brought to the place of burial. This is the one clue we have as yet to methods of transport in the Beaker period. The closest analogies for this beaker were to the south in Wiltshire; the only henge monuments comparable with that described above are to be seen on Thornborough, Hutton and Cana Moors near Ripon (Yorks).

The Food Vessel Culture

It is in Yorkshire particularly, and in the north and west generally, that the Food Vessel culture flourished. Its appearance in the south-east was fitful and probably brief as it was overlaid early in its development by the astonishing florescence of the Wessex Culture. In our region the Food Vessel people left few traces: a pot or two each at Seale and Farnham (Surrey), at Burpham? (Sussex), at Beaulieu (Hampshire), half a dozen on the middle Thames at, for example, Drayton and Radley (Berks), and at Oxford, besides a few in the north-eastern part of the region (e.g. a handled vessel at Great Chesterford and a more normal example at Great Oakley, both in Essex). There can be little doubt that the Beaker and Food Vessel peoples overlapped in time and that the latter owed something to the former in their traditions of pot-making. Yet there was a larger contribution from the secondary neolithic cultures than from the Beaker culture to the style and fabric of food vessels. This is best illustrated by a pot from Dippenhall, near Farnham (Surrey), which is of the same fabric as Peterborough ware from the ditch of the Badshot long barrow situated barely four miles to the east. What may be even more significant is the cord ornamentation common to both.

Little is known of the economy of this people. The impression of barley-grains on a food vessel from the Oxford region suggests that they grew corn; though it might equally well have been acquired, for like the Beaker folk they were predominantly herdsmen. Beneath the Roman villa at Park Street (St. Stephens, Herts), a shallow pit, eight feet by four and a half deep, with post-holes at each end, contained a sherd of this ware with cord ornamentation. This is the only instance of a possible dwelling-place so far to be found in the Home Counties. The sherd emphasizes the secondary neolithic ancestry of this people.

More widely known in the south-east are the plano-convex flint knives (or 'slug-knives' from their typical silhouette) which have been recovered in association with food vessels in the north. It is likely, too, that this period witnessed the importation and use of the flat axes of copper or bronze, though only once has one of these been

E

recovered in association with objects assignable to a particular culture, and that was a food vessel. However, there are indications that these people were skilful carpenters requiring such tools; and even their pots are thought to be cheap substitutes for wooden bowls, for, like the handled beakers, some have imitation growth-rings on their bases.

Information concerning their burial customs is seldom to be had from the south-east, but in the north four out of five burials with food vessels were of the crouched body, like those of the Beaker folk; the remainder were cremations. A few of the latter occur under barrows; but more usually both kinds of interment were made in cists (boxes of stone slabs) or pits, without a barrow above. An inhumation beneath a barrow on Beaulieu Heath (Hants) was exceptional. The mound was of turves and there had been a surrounding ditch.

The submergence in our region of the Food Vessel people by warriors of the Wessex Culture has already been referred to; but much of the south-east appears to have remained little affected by either and it is likely that the secondary neolithic Peterborough culture persisted and underwent gradual modification, first through contact with the Beaker folk and subsequently with the hybrid cultures, that resulted from their transitory sway over the region.

The Wessex Culture

There are some who believe that the Wessex warriors irrupted into southern Britain from Brittany or north-west Germany, where some contemporary analogies to its material culture are known. Others have seen in their emergence a response to broader commercial opportunities by a native people. Cultural modifications brought about by wide trading contacts are a familiar element in twentieth-century sociology; few peoples, civilized or barbarous, have escaped such influences in the modern world even though some have consciously resisted them; in the sixteenth century B.C. conscious resistance was unlikely, and the acceptance or purchase of the exotic objects that make this culture so remarkable may be no more than a widening of trading contacts that already in the neolithic period had become transmarine. At any rate, the persistence of the secondary neolithic stock, well versed in the pursuit of trade, makes such a development a reasonable assumption.

And there is indeed evidence that the secondary neolithic peoples made some contribution to the Wessex Culture. The perforated antler mace-heads characteristic of the Dorchester Culture, and ultimately derived from the Maglemosean, recur in burials of Wessex warriors, as for instance at Lambourn (Berks). This symbol of authority was deposited with a ceremonial battle-axe, and the two kinds of objects have been found together in several burials of this culture.

Cattle breeders like the Beaker folk, the Wessex people were also like them constantly on the move and their dwellings were no doubt of the flimsiest. None is yet known and knowledge of this people is derived solely from their funerary deposits and their burial-mounds. The increasing dryness of climate may in part explain their absence from the territories inhabited by the Neolithic and Beaker tribes; with a smaller rainfall and a decline in the water-table in the soil, lower ground probably became habitable, and the activities of medieval and modern man may have destroyed the few dwelling-sites necessary to a scanty aristocracy.

They had surplus wealth with which to obtain the metals which their smiths wrought into hammer-flanged axes and riveted daggers, often ogival in outline. Irish gold, Baltic amber, such as composes the magnificent cup from the Hove (Sussex) barrow, and beads of bluish faïence from the eastern Mediterranean were thus acquired. Contacts with northern Europe are emphasized by the occurrence in the Hove, and other burials, of battle-axes of Scandinavian type; and the axe and dagger carvings recently discovered on the uprights of the Stonehenge trilithons point to intercourse with Mycenean Greece as well as with Ireland.

Once again the south-east is on the fringe of a dominant culture. The Wessex chalklands, centre of natural communications and containing the great sanctuaries of Avebury and Stonehenge, remained the metropolitan region of England. But the Wessex Culture reached out from Hampshire eastwards into downland Sussex and northward to the middle Thames. Even distant Kent had stray burials of Wessex warriors at Aylesford and Ringwould, the latter accompanied by faïence beads, and both with typical metal goods. In Sussex, besides the rich interment at Hove, the Culture is represented by faïence pendants from barrows at Clayton and Lewes; and from the latter interment came one of the more familiar segmented faïence beads (Map 3).

In southern Hampshire, on Portsdown (Portsmouth), a cremation with amber and shale beads and an 'incense' pot were found together with a shale button covered with beaten gold. Further north, at Stockbridge, a similar interment from a small barrow was contained in a collared urn with various beads of jet, shale, calcite, lignite and faïence. In most respects a cremation within a ring-ditch at Radley (Berks) was similar. Other ring-ditches in the middle Thames district, known mainly from aerial observation, may belong to this Culture. (See Plates 3 and 21.)

But for the field-worker the greatest interest attaches to the barrows beneath which the Wessex people were buried. They are typically of the bell, disc or possibly pond categories (Figure 6, c–f.) and are better represented in our region (though few have been excavated) than the material just cited would suggest. Bell barrows occur in the New Forest, in Berkshire, Buckinghamshire, Sussex and Surrey; good examples of disc barrows may be seen at Petersfield Heath (Hants) and in the New Forest, as well as at the remarkable prehistoric necropolis near Lambourn (Berks). Instances are too numerous to give in detail but many more are noted in the Gazetteer. Barrows with a berm broader than that of a typical bell barrow and a central tump larger than that of a disc barrow (in fact, intermediate in form between the two), may be seen at Elstead, Worplesden and Wotton (Surrey) and at Bealieu (Hants). Pond

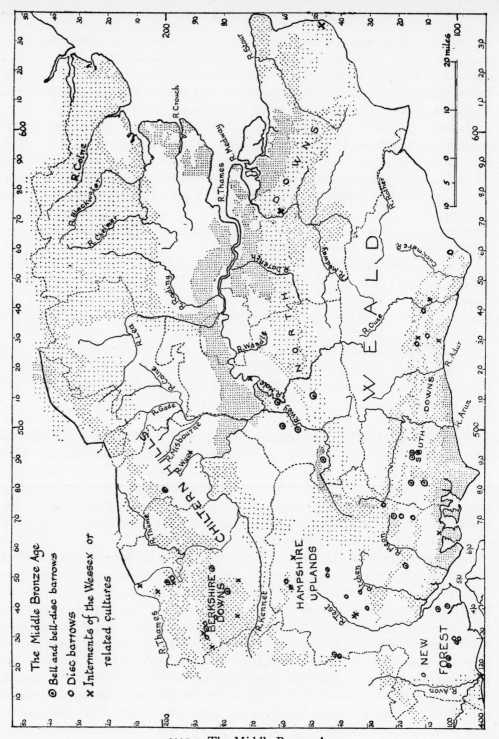

The Middle Bronze Age

⊚ Bell and bell-disc barrows

○ Disc barrows

✕ Interments of the Wessex or
related cultures

MAP 3 The Middle Bronze Age

barrows, which in Dorset at any rate, came first into use among the Food Vessel people, are said to occur in West Sussex (Bow Hill, Stoughton?), in Hampshire on Beaulieu Heath and at Warnford (?) and elsewhere. As superficially they are mere shallow depressions in the ground, usually obscured by bracken or long grass, they are extremely difficult to locate (Figure 6 h). A very few saucer barrows, such as those at Petersfield and on Ibsley Common (Hants) may also be of this period (Figure 6 g).

About one-third of all known interments of the Wessex chieftains were of the

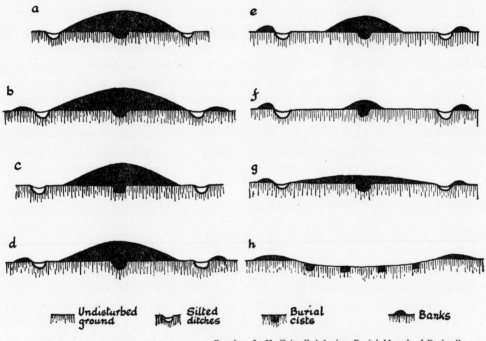

Based on L. V. Grinsell, 'Ancient Burial Mounds of England' (1953), Figure 2 (pub. Methuen).

FIG 6 Bronze Age Barrows: (a) bowl barrow with ditch; (b) bowl barrow with ditch and outer bank; (c) bell barrow; (d) bell barrow with outer bank; (e) intermediate bell-disc barrow; (f) disc barrow; (g) saucer barrow; (h) pond barrow. N.B. The cists in this type may be numerous and asymmetrical in their placing

unburned body in a crouched position; the remainder were cremations, usually in an urn, and sometimes with a tiny accessory vessel such as an 'incense' cup. A few, especially among the related Urn Folk of the north, might be made in coffins hollowed out of tree trunks; such were found under the Hove barrow and, more recently, under a bell barrow, now destroyed, at Bishops Waltham (Hants), Perhaps roughly contemporary and certainly of outstanding interest were the mortuary houses found in two barrows at Beaulieu. Skilful excavation brought to light the traces of bounding post-holes of a structure about five and a half feet square with two post-holes in the central axis for the support of a roof-ridge. This is the closest that we can get to a visualization of houses of the Middle Bronze Age. A somewhat different structure was long ago found with a cremation and a small 'incense' cup in the centre of a bell barrow at Beedon (Berks). It consisted of a ring of seven post-holes in the old ground surface, containing traces of wood. The holes lay beneath a layer of decayed wood which might conceivably have roofed the building. This also may represent a mortuary house or a sepulchral 'henge' structure, similar to the palisade barrows of eastern Holland and of south and west Wales.

Pottery finds in our region that belong distinctively to the Wessex Culture and not to a contemporary variation of it are so few that they are not discussed here. Reference may be made to such works as Professor V. G. Childe's *Prehistoric Communities of the British Isles*, chapter VIII, where detailed references will be found. More interest attaches to the faïence beads that have been found with over two dozen interments of this people. These beads were imported ready-made from somewhere in the eastern Mediterranean lands; a close parallel for them was found in an Egyptian burial confidently dated to *c.* 1400 B.C. This fact, and the chronological implications derived from contemporary imports into southern Britain, have led to the conclusion, not altogether undisputed in its premises, that the Wessex Culture flourished from about 1550 until about 1350 B.C. and thereafter began to lose its character as it became merged with the more broadly based culture of the Urn Folk.

The Urn Folk

It is likely that the Wessex and Food Vessel Cultures were largely contemporary, the Wessex people being mainly of southern distribution, the Food Vessel folk northern. The Urn Folk, who were widespread throughout the British Isles, were in direct line of descent from the secondary neolithic, especially Peterborough, peoples, with some cultural contribution from the Food Vessel tribes. They overlapped temporally with the Wessex people, but seem to have endured for long after them. A form of society appears to have developed which, judging from the wide homogeneity of burial-custom, was more egalitarian than that which it replaced; for, among the Urn Folk, few burials are known that could represent members of a ruling class such as the Wessex people seem to have been. But such a conclusion can be only tentative.

Single-grave burials are the rule in our religion, either with or without a barrow above. Cremation was the almost invariable burial-rite and the ashes of the dead were placed in large urns just below the old turf-line. From about 1200 B.C. inhumation of the unburned body ceased to be practised throughout Britain and a uniformity of culture prevailed which had never before existed and which was not to be interrupted until an invasion that conventionally ushers in the Late Bronze Age in about 800 B.C.

Much timber is necessary for the thorough cremation of the human body, and the widespread adoption of this custom must necessarily have made increasing inroads on the forests bounding the regions of settlement. This increased the area of pasture and made possible an expansion of the herds which continued to be the mainstay of human existence. But larger herds enabled more mouths to be fed; or rather, it allowed more infants to reach maturity and thus increase the rate of breeding and the population. This, besides a drier phase of climate, probably accounts for an expansion of the habitable areas which is especially noteworthy in the Highland Zone, on Dartmoor in particular. In the South-East barrows contemporary with the Wessex Culture, if not of it, are found on the lower ground and especially on heathy sands and gravels as at Worplesdon, Wimbledon, and Reigate in Surrey, and at Petersfield (Hants), in the New Forest and on the Wealden greensands—all of them areas comparatively unfrequented since mesolithic times. What for a millennium had been occasional hunting grounds now became more frequently traversed by these nomadic herdsmen; and in their wanderings they sometimes halted to burn and bury their dead. In so doing they were adding to the acreage of their pastures and occasionally leaving monuments which are, with their funerary contents, almost the sole evidence for their ever having lived.

It may well be that so few habitations of the period are known because the majority of them were located on soils which rapidly destroy all organic remains. Moreover, these dwellings were probably flimsy tent-like structures such as nomads commonly use and which leave little trace. Similar mesolithic dwellings are now being recognized because attention is drawn to the sites by easily-identified microlithic implements and waste chips from their manufacture. If more were known of distinctively Middle Bronze Age flint types, the dwelling-sites would perhaps sometimes be traceable by this means; and there is little doubt that flint was much used at this time, especially as it continued in use in the Iron Age when metal became cheap and relatively abundant. Indeed, Middle Bronze Age sherds are said to have come from the filling of a flint-mine shaft at Findon; and, as already noticed, at Blackpatch there was good reason to believe that a Middle Bronze Age barrow had been constructed of chalk-blocks from a shaft then being dug. The associated flint-types, however, were almost indistinguishable from those found in neolithic shafts. This close similarity may account for the rare identification of these dwellings. But what is true of Blackpatch need not be true elsewhere, for the Middle Bronze Age reveals some local diversity of culture within its overall uniformity; and diversity could occur in flint types as well as in pottery.

At Stockbridge (Hants) a dwelling site yielded sherds of urns, and flint implements that are considered distinctive of this period; and its location shows, as do many barrows, that the old primary areas of occupation were by no means abandoned. The traces of habitation at Sutton Courtenay (Berks), on the same site as the pagan Saxon village, indicated that this area, too, had continued in unbroken occupation from at least the late neolithic; and in the middle Thames valley generally, above the Goring Gap, air photography has shown numerous sites of ring-ditches, which may have been sepulchral as at Radley, or places of habitation as at Sutton Courtenay. It should be added, however, that a ring-ditch at Radley was associated with a food vessel of the earlier, and with a lugged biconical urn of the later Bronze Age. The ditches, in most instances, are probably all that remain from the ploughed-down structures of bell or disc barrows (Figure 5a and Plates 3 and 21).

The agricultural economy of this period is barely known at all from evidence discovered in the Home Counties; and little enough that is not guesswork is known from other parts of Britain. On Ram's Hill, Uffington (Berks) a ditched earthwork enclosure was seen from the air, and on excavation proved to be the work of the Urn Folk. It was probably made for the safe keeping of cattle; but besides herding, some hoe cultivation of cereals was practised, for the impression of a grain of spelt, a primitive form of wheat, has been found on a collared urn such as came from the Ram's Hill cattle pound; and barley continued to be cultivated as it had been by the Food Vessel people. Even flax impressions are known from this period; and flax normally implied weaving. But no contemporary fields have certainly been identified anywhere, for they were probably obliterated by the more intensive plough cultivation of the Late Bronze and subsequent Ages.

Perhaps this rudimentary hoe agriculture, or, more likely, the rearing of cattle, yielded produce surplus to the basic requirements of these peoples; for only by means of such a surplus could their few bronze weapons be acquired. These were obviously not local products in a region devoid of copper or tin ores, and flint was of necessity still mined and used for most ordinary purposes. It is likely that bronze-smiths, like the tinkers of a later age, had no local roots or tribal ties but wandered from place to place bartering their wares for food, drink and shelter. Already in the Beaker phase Irish copper and bronze tools were being imported into the South-East along the trade-routes pioneered by secondary neolithic traders in stone axes from Cornwall, from west and north Wales, and from the Lake District. Through their wealth the Wessex chiefs had been enabled to widen the scope of trade, and the partly contemporary Urn Folk had no doubt made the southern British market the more profitable by their purchases. At least we know that itinerant merchants of bronze implements were active in this period: and their stock-in-trade, which they hid in times of danger, but failed to recover afterwards, has come to light again in a number of places.

The characteristic tools and weapons include axes with strengthening flanges, cast not hammered as heretofore; spearheads attached to the shafts by tangs; and daggers sometimes ogival in outline, strengthened with central ribs or with grooves. Later, development from the flanged axe to the palstave occurred, but the earlier forms probably continued in use alongside the newer type for some time. The same is no doubt true of spearheads which were now given basal loops by means of which they could be attached to the shaft by leathern thongs; and the daggers were lengthened into dirks or rapiers. These arms may betoken a warrior aristocracy concerning whom archaeology is otherwise silent, for the later weapons are never found in graves, but are discovered singly without association. The dredging of the Thames has produced very many such isolated finds of all periods, prehistoric and historic. But the merchants' hoards, above all, afford information concerning the contemporaneity of types of weapons; and roughly chronological series of each type have been worked out by specialists. The only supposedly dateable objects found in association with weapons are the faïence beads; and these have occurred only with the earlier types of the Middle Bronze Age. It may well be that new dating techniques will be elaborated before long to provide a firmer basis for the chronology of this period.

The end of the period is ushered in by the arrival of refugees in Sussex and Kent who had crossed from northern France. At Playden (Sussex) a Wealden habitation site has been excavated which suggests that some of the natives fled from the Downs to their pastures and hunting grounds further north. There they built a ring-ditch dwelling in the forest and near it an enclosure, probably for swine, which were made safe from wolves by a wattle fence and a ditch. The pottery found on the site suggested a fusion between the styles of the natives and those of the invaders. A similar intermixture of Middle and Late Bronze pottery styles is to be seen in sherds from Castle Hill, Newhaven. Here, it may be conjectured, the invaders had paired with native wives whose pots were made to please the taste of their new lords but who could not altogether forget their traditional style of potting.

BIBLIOGRAPHY TO CHAPTER VI

No book has yet been devoted solely to this period, but the following papers, with the references contained in them, afford the necessary detail for a closer study of the Early and Middle Bronze Age. J. G. D. Clark, 'The Dual Character of the Beaker Invasion,' in *Antiquity*, V.; E. T. Leeds, 'Beakers of the Upper Thames District,' in *Oxoniensia*, III; J. B. Calkin, 'A Local Survey of the Early Bronze Age,' in *Proceedings of the Bournemouth Natural History Society*, 28; J. G. D. Clark, 'Plano-Convex Knives,' in *Antiquaries Journal*, XII; W. F. Grimes, 'The Bronze Age Flint Dagger,' in *Proceedings of the Prehistoric Society of East Anglia*, 6; and see his *Prehistory of Wales* (1951), pp. 64 f., on the development of metal goods, and techniques of producing and hafting them; S. Piggott, 'The Early Bronze Age in Wessex,' in *Proceedings of the Prehistoric Society*, IV; L. V. Grinsell, 'Bronze Age round barrows of Wessex,' in the same journal as the last, vol. VII; and for regional surveys and local bibliographies of barrows see his *Ancient Burial Mounds of England* (2nd ed., 1953). For the Radley interments, see *Oxoniensia*, vols. I to XIII passim; for the Stockbridge interments, see *Antiquaries Journal*, 20 and 28, and for the dwellings, *Proceedings of the Prehistoric Society*, IV; for the Playden site, see Curwen, *Archaeology of Sussex*, pp. 184–6; for Sutton Courtenay, see *Archaeologia*, 76.

CHAPTER VII

The Late Bronze Age

THE FIRST OF the three phases of the Late Bronze Age began about 1000 B.C. and is mainly significant for the greater abundance of metal and for the introduction of foreign tools and weapons produced by techniques novel to this country. The vastly expanded trade in metal goods was handled by wandering merchants who themselves produced the new types as fast as they could accumulate sufficient scrap bronze or acquire the unworked metals from Ireland. The number of hoards of scrap discovered in south-east England is very great (Map 4), though not all belong to this earliest phase of the Late Bronze Age and already in the previous period a few hoards containing broken and worn-out tools were being hidden.

The abundance of bronze made possible its use in a wider variety of articles and for humbler uses. Tools of the carpenter and the bronze-founder become relatively common, and the needs of the farmer were not overlooked. Buckets and great cauldrons, probably the possessions of chieftains, were acquired for some ceremonial purpose; and improved forms of swords, shields and spearheads provided for the warrior. Most significant are the newly-introduced 'leaf-shaped' swords constructed so as to be equally effective either for slashing or for stabbing, thereby indicating a change in fighting tactics. With this innovation came the leaf-shaped spearhead, secured to the shaft by means of a rivet; and, most common of Late Bronze Age finds, the socketed axe. But the older palstave was not altogether superseded, and spearheads with basal loops continued to be collected for scrap for some long time.

But the population remained very largely the same, following their herds from pasture to fresh pasture, cremating their dead and interring them in urns of devolved Middle Bronze Age form. Very probably the bronze merchants were but a score or so at any one time, detribalized and separate from the life of ordinary people. The not infrequent recovery of their hoards from what must then have been forested areas (e.g. Harty in Kent and Dagenham in Essex) suggests that they secreted themselves to perform the mysteries of their trade where wood fuel was abundant and where prying eyes could not discover their techniques and deprive them of livelihood.

The second phase possibly covered the two centuries from about 800 to 600 B.C. It is characterized by the introduction of yet further new types of metal-goods and by new burial rites, new forms of pottery and by a revolution in farming methods. It is reasonably certain that the changes were introduced by refugees crowded out from northern France by the expansion of the Urnfield Folk who had spread to the Channel

74

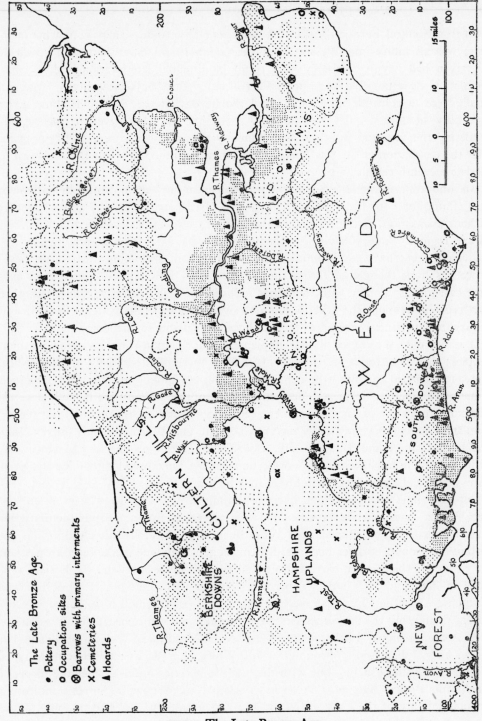

MAP 4 The Late Bronze Age

coast from Central Europe. Within the same general period, perhaps somewhat later, there was an influx into Wessex from the region round Cherbourg. An epoch of migration had begun, probably as a result of climatic deterioration and of over-population made possible by improved cereal cultivation. Folk-movements, large and small, were to continue in Europe until the heyday of the Roman Empire. Even then only an uneasy quiet was achieved; and that was short-lived in the regions bordering the Imperial frontiers. Subsequently the migrations were to begin again, after the dissolution of the *pax Romana*; and they continued to affect Britain down to the late eleventh century A.D.

An innovation in metal-types that is widespread in our region, found in settlement sites (Plumpton, site B, in Sussex), in hoards (Eastbourne, Sussex) and frequently without association, is the winged axe which was originally developed in the West Alpine regions. Pottery having associations with the same Continental region was recovered from the same Plumpton site. At Farnham and Kingston (Surrey) evidence has come to light of similar immigrants. Poor imitations of the winged axes were cast in this country with the wings reduced to mere decorative ridges. Another new type of weapon, the 'carp's tongue' sword, came from western France; and bronze sickles, either socketed or tanged, became available to farmers.

It is not only the influx of new implements that demonstrates invasion by alien peoples; their cemeteries are quite distinct from those of the natives. In Hampshire low saucer-shaped barrows with a shallow ditch, as at Colbury and Plaitford contained numerous cremations in urns. These and the culture they typify are named Deverel-Rimbury from the two Late Bronze Age cemeteries found at those two Dorset places. Similar barrows are known at Wonersh, Chobham and Worplesdon in Surrey, Inkpen in Berkshire, and Hadden Hill, Bournemouth, though the last instance was without a ditch and the one at Worplesdon had an interrupted ditch. Rarely, as at Ramsgate (Kent), an inhumation burial may be found.

But sometimes barrows of the Early or Middle Bronze Age were re-used and the Late Bronze Age secondary interments were placed in any of its four sectors other than the northern one. Occasionally, also, the interments were made close to, but not within, the mound of older barrows. All this is generally true of the western parts of our region; in the eastern, barrows were seldom built or re-used and the burials were made in flat ground without a superincumbent mound. This practice has been encountered, exceptionally, as far west as Pokesdown (Bournemouth) and Brown Candover (Hants); but the flat cemeteries are predominantly south-eastern in distribution, as at Acton, Ashford, Littleton and Yiewsley in Middlesex, Walton-on-Thames in Surrey and Alphamstone, Manningtree and White Colne in Essex. Three main types of urns are distinguishable, but with them are sometimes found degenerate forms of the Middle Bronze Age, as at Pokesdown (Hants) and Wonersh (Surrey), indicating an inter-mixture of the newcomers and the natives and the survival of some of the latter, at least among the women, who were normally the potters. Of the introduced types the globular urns are least common, but this type is mainly found just outside the western limits of our region, in Wiltshire and Dorset. Their immediate prototypes occur in Dutch Limburg and they represent a cultural fusion of the Continental Urnfield Folk and the Lusatian (Lausitz) culture of the north European plain between the Elbe and the Vistula.

The far more common barrel and bucket urns also have an immediate origin on the lower Rhine, whence their makers, in company with those who made the globular urns, crossed to the east and south coasts of Britain and made their way inland from the natural harbours of our region. The Essex Blackwater and Colne, and the Thames, Southampton Water, and Christchurch Harbour afforded sheltered landfalls and relatively easy routes to the hinterland.

It is seldom that metal goods of this period are found with pottery, as at Plumpton Plain 'B', which yielded a fragment of a winged axe as well as pottery of West Alpine provenance. But the general distribution of these axes and of the carp's tongue swords on the one hand, and of urns of the Deverel-Rimbury type on the other, suggest that they are different facets of the same culture. The absence of these axes and swords from Wessex is not easy to explain in view of the considerable numbers of them found on the other side of the Channel in Normandy and Brittany. Elsewhere in France they have been found mainly along the river valleys that trend northward and northwestward from the Vosges massif, and their distribution indicates the routes taken by migrants from the lake-dwellings of western Switzerland and Savoy. It was along the valleys of Seine, Marne and Loire that these first Celtic speakers to reach Britain made their way, halting awhile on the French coast before pressure of population urged them to cross the Channel. With them, too, they imported the common socketed axe and the barrel and bucket-shaped urns, cultural loans from the Lusatian culture. In Britain, then, there finally settled down, though not quite contemporaneously, immigrant groups from the Continental coastline between the Rhine to the north and the Loire to the south. But their more enduring innovations were a settled habit of life, in place of the nomadic customs of earlier immigrants, and a system of agriculture that was to be normal over large areas of England for more than a thousand years. Most persistent of all is their speech, which, strengthened by mass immigrations in the Iron Age, remains vigorous in Wales today and survived in Cornwall until the eithteenth century.

The closest analogy to the lake-side dwellings of Switzerland is the 'Old England' site at Brentford (Middx). Pottery indented with finger-tip ornament, winged and socketed axes, carp's-tongue swords and other typical metal goods were found in association, though not all were precisely contemporary. Downstream at Southchurch (Essex) enough was recovered to suggest a settlement of similar people in a similar Thames-side setting; and upstream at Taplow (Bucks) a riverside hamlet may well have first been built at about the same time. Lakeside dwellings of indeterminate date, but possibly of this period, came to light at Braintree (Essex).

But more instructive are the downland settlements of Sussex from which a considerable body of information concerning the economy of these immigrants has been obtained. About a dozen of these hamlets or farmsteads have been located and several have been excavated. One of them, on Itford Hill, in Beddingham parish, was recently investigated very fully over a period of five seasons. Thirteen round huts and eight enclosures with an accompanying 'hollow-way' and slight traces of fields were identified. The huts had diameters ranging from fifteen to twenty-two feet; their roofs were supported on a circle of poles sunk into the chalk. The floors were levelled by cutting into the slope on which the settlement is situated. Porches projecting on the south side were built on four of the huts which are considered to have been dwellings; the other nine served for storage or as workshops. The dwelling huts had central posts suggesting conical roofs and the largest of them, perhaps the chief's, had a large chalk phallus set up beside the inner doorway as a talisman of fertility to bring bounteous increase to crops and herds. Some of the ancillary huts covered small storage pits three feet across and two feet deep, one of which yielded many potsherds and another about twelve pounds of carbonized barley. Saddle-querns for grinding the grain and post-holes for the two upright beams of a weaving loom, with cylindrical loom-weights, afford clues to the occupations of the women. A possible corn-drying kiln was also found on the site.

Slingstones for hunting indicate that the herds did not supply all the meat required, especially in winter; and winkle and mussel shells betoken a varied diet. The skeleton of an ox represents one of the main farming activities of these settlers; the looms, however, render it likely that sheep were kept too.

This settlement had a relatively short life, for there were few indications of rebuilding in the huts. It was occupied in the earlier part of the second phase of the Late Bronze Age, probably soon after 800 B.C., and some of the pottery showed that this farming community had migrated from northern France. Somewhat later in the second phase (c. 700 to 500 B.C.) was the settlement on New Barn Down (Patching). It resembled one of the Itford enclosures in being surrounded by a fence of posts and in having a ditchless bank on the north side to give shelter to a group of five similar round huts. A farmyard enclosure, field lynchets and an associated 'hollow way' make possible a fairly complete plan of one of our earliest known farmsteads.

The settlers at Itford and New Barn Down sprang from people long resident in northern France. From there also came settlers to Birchington (Kent), to the earlier farmstead at Plumpton Plain (site 'A') in Sussex (Figure 7), and to other localities on the South Downs such as Park Brow in Sompting and High Down, Ferring. Further to the west, in Hampshire, evidence of the Deverel-Rimbury peoples is mainly confined to their earthworks and cemeteries; but the pottery from the latter suggests an immediate origin in the Cherbourg peninsula.

The West Alpine contribution to our Late Bronze Age population is most clearly shown in the south by Site 'B' at Plumpton Plain of about the seventh century B.C.,

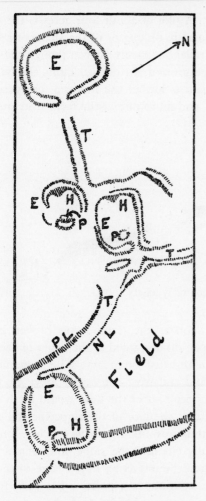

FIG 7 Late Bronze Age Settlement: Plumpton Plain, Sussex, Site A; E enclosures, H huts revealed by post holes, P ponds, T tracks, PL positive lynchet, NL negative lynchet (from *The Archaeology of Sussex*, 1954, by E. Cecil Curwen).

and it was there too that fragments of a store-jar were found that seemed to indicate that Middle Bronze Age groups had survived locally until far into the Late Bronze Age and had mingled with the new settlers and influenced their style of potting. At the end of the last chapter we saw that much the same thing had happened further to the east at Playden (Sussex).

One of the commonest sights on the downs of southern England until wartime and subsequent ploughing destroyed so many of them, were the Celtic fields. The system of agriculture that produced these small, squarish plots was first introduced by the Deverel-Rimbury people and it continued to function in some areas down to the end of the Roman occupation.

These fields were formed by ploughing; the use of a hoe, the implement used until the end of the Middle Bronze Age, could not move sufficient soil to produce the banks, or lynchets, which delineate the fields. A plot of about four acres is the maximum size normally attained, and they are squarish, oblong or of the shape of a broad diamond. Their opposite sides are seldom parallel and rarely curved though the shape is very largely determined by the slope of the ground. In normal lights the lynchets are not often clearly visible, but when the sun is low in the morning or evening, a whole system of fields with associated tracks, and more rarely, the farmstead site, will appear etched in shadow on the hillside.

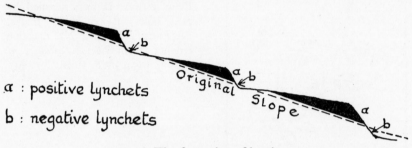

a : positive lynchets

b : negative lynchets

FIG 8 The formation of lynchets

The formation of the lynchets began as soon as the ground was broken by the plough (Figure 8). If the turf were first stripped off and piled at the edges of the field, soil would slowly accumulate up-slope from the turf boundary. The movement of soil by the plough and the action of rain, wind and frost constantly move clods and crumbs of soil downhill so that in time the upper part of the field would be denuded of humus and show up as a chalky white; and at the foot of the slope the soil would steadily accumulate against the turf barrier, thus forming a positive lynchet. The first furrow at the top of the field would gradually cut into the slope, and, as the earth slipped away, a baulk of unploughed soil would be left as an upper edge to the field forming a negative lynchet. Where plots are contiguous a positive has been formed above a negative lynchet roughly doubling its apparent height. Field boundaries running up and down a slope are hardly affected except where it is canted with a fall in two directions. Then the strongest lynchet was formed on the boundary running athwart the steeper slope. The field ways also often run across a slope between two fields so that a positive lynchet was accumulated on the upper edge of the track and a negative on the lower. As the tracks themselves were not ploughed there was no build-up of soil on their lower verges; and where they run along a ridge, or up the spine of a chalk spur so that the ground slopes away on both sides, then a negative lynchet was formed on both sides.

The farmstead site, if it shows at all, will be seen as one or more roughly oval or circular patches of gorse, nettles or lusher grass. Such a clue from the vegetation is produced by a greater depth of soil where a hut floor has been cut to below the ground surface. After abandonment, humus is added by natural agencies to the domestic refuse that had been left in it. With a deeper rooting medium, more moisture is available to the plants and they flourish accordingly. Ditches that have silted up, and positive lynchets, afford the same favourable conditions for grass and herbage so that, especially in time of drought, their course can be sometimes determined by such surface signs alone. Probing with a metal rod down to the compact subsoil makes it possible to confirm the existence of a ditch located solely by vegetational clues; or the method of 'bosing', described by Dr. Curwen in *Antiquity*, II, p. 258, and IV, p. 30,

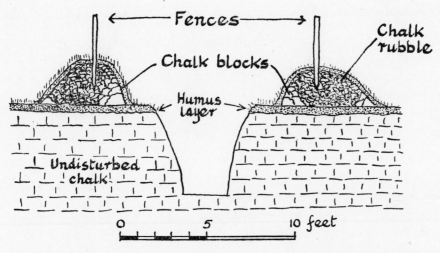

FIG 9 Late Bronze Age ranch boundary ditch. Reconstruction of a section

can also make it possible for the field-worker to plot the course of a ditch of which only the faintest of traces are visible on the surface. Such methods could be used for a rough survey of newly discovered neolithic camps or the surrounding ditches, where present, of round or long barrows. For the much longer boundary ditches now to be described, these methods would be impracticable because of the intermittent destruction of the ditches by later agriculture.

Even in the Late Bronze Age arable farming probably remained subsidiary to stock-rearing. The extensive enclosure ditches of Dorset, Wiltshire, Hampshire and Berkshire, usually interpreted as the boundaries of large cattle ranches, in some instances almost certainly came into use in this period. Besides setting limits to the pastures, they divided them from the arable. Along the flat bottom of the ditches herds could be moved with the minimum of manpower and with no possibility of the animals straying; for on the banks which flanked both sides of one of these ditches, a simple fence was no doubt erected to contain the cattle (Figure 9). Just beyond the

F

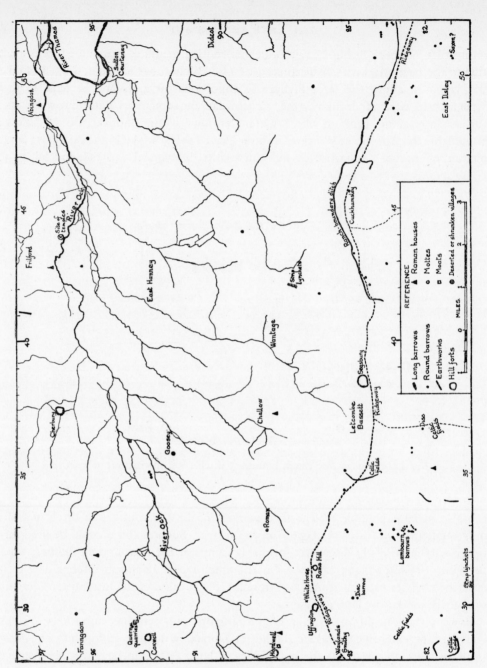

MAP B The Berkshire Downs

Hampshire boundary near Cholderton (Wilts) an almost complete system of these ditches has been mapped. An air-photograph of Quarley Hill (Hants) reveals similar earthworks meeting near the crest of the hill after running beneath the Early Iron Age ramparts which crown its summit. Clearly then the ranch boundaries antedate the hill-fort, though as there is little to distinguish the agricultural methods of the Late Bronze and Iron Ages, it is not impossible that the ranch came into use during the later period but before the construction of the fort, which belongs to the first phase of the Iron Age (Plate 9).

Another long stretch of boundary ditch can be traced running just north of the Berkshire Ridgeway, starting a little east of Wantage and seemingly ending on the Downs above Moulsford (Map B and Map I). There are stretches also near Lambourn (Berks) and Martin (Hants). On Martin Down there is a square earthwork under three hundred yards away from the ranch boundary, here called Grim's Ditch. The enclosure was proved to be of the Late Bronze Age as was a similar one on Boscombe Down East (Wilts), which is also located within a ranch. These enclosures have yielded just enough evidence of occupation to suggest that men and beasts may have sheltered in them during the worst rigours of the winter.

Extensive ranch ditches are not so far known in Sussex or neighbouring counties, but this is probably to be explained by the nature of the terrain; instead of a broad undulating plateau as in Wessex, there are only limited areas on the South Downs where arable farming was possible. Like much of the Chilterns and North Downs, the chalk of west Sussex is in many areas burdened with clay-with-flints, a soil even now largely wooded; and in east Sussex, where the Downs are free from a clay overburden, there are areas of acid soils, now bearing heather and gorse, which would never have been worth the ploughing. Besides this, from the apparent total area of potential arable a considerable acreage must be subtracted for the steeper slopes, especially on the sides of combes, where soil-creep is continuous even where the turf is unbroken. Every acre of basic soil on the slighter slopes was therefore needed for arable; pasture for cattle was limited to the scarpface which, apart from its steepness, faces north, away from the sun; its arable potentialities were therefore negligible.

That the South Downs were intensively cultivated during the Late Bronze Age is suggested by the dozen farmstead sites already discovered; but there is no reason to think that stock-rearing was any less important here than in Wessex simply because of a lack of ranch-boundary ditches and cattle enclosures. Some of the minor Iron Age hillforts, such as Harrow Hill and High Down, both very close to Late Bronze Age settlements, may well overlie the weak palisade-banks of Deverel-Rimbury cattle pounds; and the boundary ditches of Wessex are probably replaced here by the structurally comparable but much shorter cross-ridge dykes, which are still to be seen at intervals along the scarp-crest of the Downs (see Map D). They would have assisted herding from winter quarters on the warmer arable dip-slopes to the summer pastures on the scarp face. In times of danger the cattle could the more easily be brought to the neighbourhood of the farmstead by the same route. The ditch of the cross-ridge dyke on Glatting Down, Sutton (W. Sussex) actually yielded sherds of Late Bronze Age pottery, but there is otherwise scant evidence for the date of these earthworks. Some of them were probably constructed later to serve as barriers or even toll-points, limiting alien movement along the ridgeway which follows the crest of the Downs. But their main purpose, in this or the following period, was to canalize the movement of cattle. In this they are comparable with the far more extensive boundary ditches of Wessex.

There is evidence from the study of molluscan fauna (snail shells in particular) that by the Late Bronze Age the primeval scrub and woodland of the chalk country which had confronted the neolithic farmers on their arrival in Britain, had been destroyed largely by grazing. The characteristic species of snails found on neolithic sites are such as may still be encountered in the undergrowth of woodland on a basic soil. They are species adapted to damp conditions. From Iron Age sites, however, have been re-covered snail shells from species whose habitat is open grassland. The occurrence of Celtic fields of this age betokens much deforestation, and the fields no doubt remained fallow in alternate years and afforded pasture for sheep, 'the golden hoof' on down-land. By the Iron Age, sheep had become more numerous than cattle, judging from the relative numbers of bones from the farmsteads; and it is probable that the recession of cattle was already far advanced in the Late Bronze Age. One can see, therefore, that a more balanced farming economy, with arable and sheep interdependent and with cattle as a subsidiary source of food, would have afforded a more reliable supply than in earlier times. It would have made possible yet further expansion of the popu-lation. The great increase in the number of interments of the Late Bronze Age over previous ages is thus to be explained. The influx of new peoples from the fifth century B.C. onwards, practising similar farming methods and closely related in culture, swelled still further the number of mouths to be fed. In the earlier phase of the en-suing Iron Age it is likely that few suitable acres on the chalk uplands or on the lighter soils of the lowlands remained untilled.

BIBLIOGRAPHY TO CHAPTER VII

On the origins of the Deverel-Rimbury culture and Late Bronze Age barrows see *Antiquaries Journal*, XIII, pp. 414 f., and see also *Proceedings of the Prehistoric Society*, volumes I, VIII and IX, and *Antiquity*, IV, 'The Sword Bearers'. On settlement sites and farming, see *The Archaeology of Sussex*, pp. 169 f.; and Crawford's *Archaeology in the Field*, chapter 10, on ranch boundaries, especially those in Berkshire and Hamp-shire. His footnote, p. 198, affords a useful short bibliography on prehistoric agriculture generally, to which should be added, for example, *Proceedings of the Hampshire Field Club*, 14 (1939), pp. 143 f., and *Oxoniensia*, 15 (1950) for further local studies.

The two waterside sites are described in *Antiquaries Journal*, XI (Southchurch, Essex) and *Antiquity*, III ('Old England', Brentford).

CHAPTER VIII

The Early Iron Age

Phase A

THE THREE MAIN phases of the Iron Age have been designated A, B and C for the sake of simplicity and clarity, but it is necessary to emphasize that they are partly contemporary and that the distinctions to be made between them are not only cultural but partly geographical as well. In older works the term Hallstatt is applied to the A culture because at an Austrian place bearing that name the distinctive elements of the culture were first recognized. The B culture is termed La Tène from the Swiss type-site, though frequently it is referred to as Marnian from the region inhabited by the B tribes shortly before their migrations to Britain; and the C culture is often termed Belgic as the majority of those who possessed it belonged to the confederation of tribes known to the Romans as the *Belgae*. It, too, was a La Tène culture and often used to be called Late La Tène or Late Celtic. This varying and somewhat confusing nomenclature is mentioned here because the older terms are still appearing sporadically in local guidebooks, though one cannot always be sure that 'Late Celtic', for instance, has any more precise meaning than the term 'Ancient British', which could be used comprehensively for anything from the neolithic to the end of the Iron Age.

The Iron Age as a whole was marked by a complex series of folk movements from east to west in Europe, some of them originating as a result of pressure from still more easterly tribes of barbarians; but others, mainly the later migrations, were caused by the threat of Roman conquest in Gaul. Caesar's 'Commentaries' provide some of the context for the invasion of Britain by both B and C tribes.

The Iron Age A culture was brought from the Low Countries and from northern France by numerous bands of settlers who made landings on the south and east coasts from Dorset to Yorkshire. These migrations were not all contemporary but, beginning probably in the fifth century B.C., they continued sporadically for a century or two. The westward trend of ideas and fashions was also continuous throughout this period and the later comers brought with them styles of potting and decorative patterns which had percolated through to their continental homelands after the departure of the earlier bands of emigrants. In Britain the same borrowings occurred: the B invaders contributed elements of their styles to the culture of the long-settled A peoples. Eventually in south-eastern Britain, particularly, there is evident in pottery a mingling of the two (A-B) and later of all three cultures in what is succinctly termed the ABC style, though latterly this, as will be seen later, has acquired its own distinctive name.

The virtue of iron as compared with bronze is its wider availability and its greater ease of production and working. It keeps its edge for a longer time and can be cheaply replaced when no longer serviceable. Tin and copper, the two main elements of bronze, rarely occur together as ores and seldom in abundance in easily accessible lodes. In the British Isles it is probable that bronze could be produced only after Cornish tin and Irish copper had been brought together. The wonder is that bronze was so common in the Late Bronze Age and suggests that a considerable surplus of agricultural products was available to pay for implements.

Methods of smelting iron ore had spread to the Hallstatt tribes of Central Europe during the seventh century B.C. and it is clear that iron tools had reached this country some time before the A people had settled here. At the Late Bronze Age farmstead on Plumpton Plain (Sussex), for instance, chemical analysis of the surfaces of whetstones revealed that iron tools had probably been sharpened upon them. Moreover a hoard of the same period from Sompting (Sussex) included bronze axes, on one of which was an accretion of iron rust suggesting that the hoard had originally contained an object made of that metal.

In the earlier phases of Iron Age A iron was not common and it is likely that the implements in use had been brought over by the migrants. In a later phase the Forest of Dean afforded a distant supply of good quality ore. But nearer sources were no doubt exploited even before the main Wealden deposits had been discovered by pioneers who ventured across dense forests on the Weald Clay. For the richest ores were to be found towards the middle of the Weald in the ironstone at the base of the Wadhurst Clay or in the Ashdown Sand. These sources were perhaps little known before the first century B.C. and it was necessary to work ores that occurred nearer to the Downs where the population was concentrated.

It is not unlikely, therefore, that the less rewarding carstone of the Folkestone beds and even the sporadic deposits of ore in the Atherfield Clay were used. Both of these beds are parts of the Lower Greensand between which and the chalk only the minor barrier of Gault Clay intervenes. The Upper Greensand, which outcrops immediately below the chalk scarps and next above the Gault, is a well-drained and easily traversed tract of the Weald.

The actual process of invasion by the scattered bands of Iron Age A settlers is only now beginning to be understood, mainly through the study of pottery. Coming from diverse regions on the Continent and tending for a while to remain isolated from other groups, the invaders of the fifth and fourth centuries B.C. exhibit local individuality in their styles of pottery yet at the same time they clearly belong to the same inclusive Hallstatt culture. Thus one group ultimately from the Marne region of northern France landed soon after 400 B.C. on the coast of Dorset and Hampshire. From there they extended into the hinterland of Wessex, eventually as far as the

Berkshire Downs. Probably the earliest band so far identified came to land at Bindon in Dorset and constructed a dyke to defend their beach-head. Not long afterwards a related group fortified the peninsula of Hengistbury Head at Southbourne (Hants) beside another fine natural harbour (Figure 10). Inland in Hampshire they later settled on Quarley Hill and Meon Hill (Stockbridge), as well as at a number of other places that yielded less informative material. Sites in Dorset, such as Maiden Castle, Chalbury, Kimmeridge and Marnhull, although outside our region, require at least

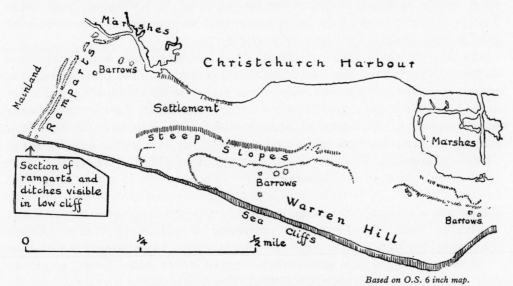

Based on O.S. 6 inch map.

FIG 10 Promontory Fort: Hengistbury Head

a mention to indicate the extent of this invasion. In Berkshire the main sites are at Frilford, Blewburton (Blewbury) and Ram's Hill (Uffington).

A characteristic of these, the Wessex Iron Age A people, is that they coated some of their pottery with a red haematite (iron oxide) slip. They had already been doing this in Normandy and Brittany before the invasion, and continued the practice for some time after their settlement in Britain. It is not therefore, necessarily an early practice though it was not maintained in the later phases of Iron Age A. Outlying sites where haematite-coated ware has been found include several on the upper Thames, as well as in Surrey and along the South Downs. Two Kentish sites, at Margate and Worth, have yielded similar pottery, but the technique of producing the red colouring was different from that used in the Wessex province and its outliers.

An invading band from Artois and Picardy and from the neighbouring regions of Hainault in Belgium made their way along the Thames, possibly in the late fourth century, and settled near its upper reaches. Their occupation sites include Long Wittenham and possibly Frilford and Ram's Hill, all in Berkshire; and two sites in

Dorchester as well as others further afield in Oxfordshire. In the later phases of the period there was some percolation of cultural influence from the Wessex province into this region, especially to the Berkshire sites. It may well be that the presence of haematite coating on pottery at Ram's Hill, Frilford, and Blewburton should be explained as one result of that influence rather than as due to a direct settlement from the south coast. But the latter explanation is not an impossible one; the vanguard of invaders who had landed at Bindon and Hengistbury could have established themselves on the Berkshire Downs before the arrival of the immigrants from down-Thames. The expulsion of the earlier arrivals and their replacement by newcomers is by no means outside the bounds of probability.

The invaders who occupied the South Downs appear to have arrived earlier and in greater strength even than those who settled in Wessex. They probably began to migrate soon after 500 B.C., and their earliest pottery shows closest affinity with that of the Late Bronze Age population of northern France and the Low Countries. Early occupation-sites of these invaders occur at undefended settlements on Park Brow (Sompting), at Findon Park and Kingston Buci. Other sites are the hill-forts of the Trundle (Singleton), Cissbury (West Tarring), High Down (Ferring) and New-haven, besides that on St. Catherine's Hill, Winchester. In east Kent there were similar settlements at Margate, Broadstairs, Richborough and elsewhere. Probably the earliest of all Iron Age immigrants to the south-east were those who settled at Eastbourne. Their painted pottery is unparalleled on English sites. It is most closely matched by that which was in use from c. 700 to 500 B.C. in south-western Germany.

An obvious route of entry into southern England lay along the Thames, and, as we have seen, it was probably used by some of those who occupied Berkshire. From the river-bed numerous early weapons of Hallstatt type have been dredged and along its lower reaches several early settlements have been identified. But there is a curious absence of them from the Kentish side of the estuary, though on the Essex side, at Shoebury, Prittlewell, Southchurch and Walthamstow, for example, sites belonging to the A1 phase have been discovered. Further upstream, in Middlesex, dwellings have been located at Brentford and inland at Harlington. Some of these sites were occupied in the Late Bronze Age and Roman period as well. But in Iron Age A as a whole almost every suitable gravel spread from the estuary as far as the upper reaches of the Thames seems to have been occupied by Hallstatt immigrants.

But most of the other sites on the lower Thames, such as Crayford (Kent), Kingston and Esher (Surrey) and Burnham (Bucks) probably imply a fresh influx of immigrants in the third century B.C. or later and they are roughly contemporary with the many A2 sites lying further back from the river. A large group of them lies on the dip slopes of the North Downs between Croydon and Leatherhead; and there are smaller groups near Guildford and Farnham. Moreover, the evidence from the majority of hill-forts indicates their construction in A2 and there is a dozen of them to take into account from the Darenth valley in west Kent to the Wey valley in Surrey (Map

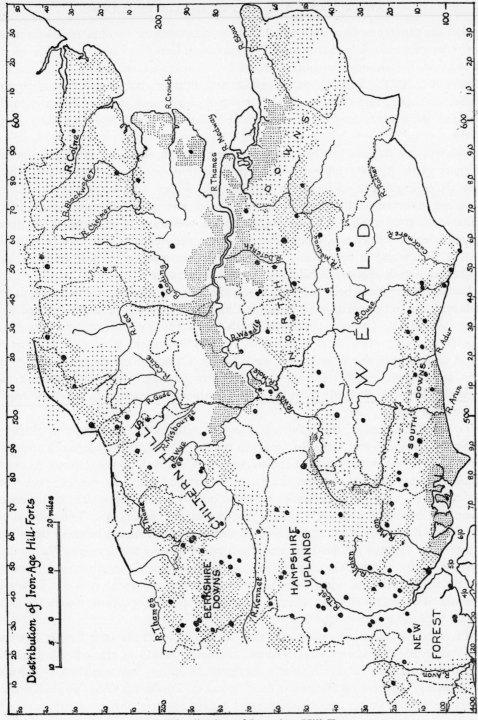

MAP 5 Distribution of Iron-Age Hill-Forts

5), besides numerous sites from which only an odd sherd or two has been recovered. A similar expansion inland from the river may be inferred in Essex, with settlements at Prittlewell, Danbury, Little Baddow and Witham, some of which are forts. The plateau-forts in the parishes of Loughton and Epping should also belong to this phase. Obviously, some of these Essex sites, particularly that at Great Bromley in the north of the county, may have been reached via the estuaries of the greater Essex rivers.

Many of the A2 invaders had remained long enough on the Continent to imbibe Marnian (Iron Age B) influences, most notably those who settled at Esher, which they are believed to have reached *c.* 250 B.C. At Wisley, Clandon and other Surrey sites, the influence of the Marnian culture is also perceptible and the source of that influence is most probably to be sought to the westward in Hampshire. In these instances an A culture was modified locally by a neighbouring AB culture. Further east in Surrey and in west Kent, the A culture continued with little trace of such modification until about the middle of the first century B.C.

Earlier settlers have been located on the chalk of the Chilterns which delimit the London basin to the north-west. A site at Chinnor (Oxon) was probably reached by a movement up the Thames and thence north-westwards along the valley of the Wye. The pottery suggests a date, *c.* 350 B.C., for this settlement which has little or no direct affinity with the sites farther up-Thames. Comparable material has come to light at Ellesborough, Saunderton, and Bledlow (Bucks), where occupation began somewhat later but probably from the same Continental homeland in the Aisne region of northern France.

To the north-east of this Chiltern group of settlements are others of different origins at Pirton, Letchworth, Royston and Willian (Herts), the last situated on heavy clay. The earliest pottery from Letchworth (the Wilbury hillfort) shows a fusion of influences from Central Europe, the Lower Rhine and northern France; that from Holwell (Pirton parish) had similar affinities but with a stronger Central European strain that had arrived via the Lower Rhine in the fifth century B.C. The main route of entry to this area was along the Thames and Lea valley, though some of the immigrants seem to have landed near the Wash and followed the Icknield Way south-westward to the Hitchin Gap. At any rate, some close parallels are observable between the Holwell pottery and some from the early Hallstatt settlement at West Harling in Norfolk. The site at Willian appears to have been first occupied somewhat later, probably in the fourth century.

The thread of continuity is by no means broken between the Late Bronze Age and the Iron Age. The Continental Hallstatt retained features of the preceding phase, especially in pottery; and in southern England the affinity between the two cultures is frequently apparent on the earlier Iron Age sites. Fusion between two such related peoples almost certainly occurred, though evidence for it is elusive. A habitation site at Wrecclesham (Farnham, Surrey) yielded cylindrical loom-weights and potsherds of typical Late Bronze Age character; but with them were sherds comparable with some from the Iron Age hill-fort at Wimbledon and from a site of the same period at Artington (Surrey). As this material was procured only as a by-product of gravel digging the stratigraphical relationship of the two kinds of pottery cannot be determined, and they may well betoken successive occupations of the site. Similar finds on the same spots have been made at Watford (Herts), Kingston (Surrey), Colchester (Essex), and at several places in Sussex, among them Plumpton, Lullington, Ferring and Newhaven. It may be that the identity of settlement sites between the two periods merely reflects the fact that two related peoples with an almost identical economy were attracted to the same kind of locality; indeed, this is in any case very probable; but these similarities of preference would themselves have facilitated fusion between the two peoples.

The earliest earthworks attributable to the Iron Age are comparatively feeble, sometimes four-sided, enclosures not unlike those of the Late Bronze Age. On Harrow Hill (Angmering, Sussex) is such a refuge, little touched by later peoples. Excavation revealed the post-holes of a timber palisade and of a gateway; dating evidence was limited to a small amount of pottery belonging to the earliest phase of Iron Age A1. Similar fortlets exist beneath the later ramparts of High Down (Ferring) (Figure 11, Ia), and Hollingbury (Brighton) and within the ringwork at Thundersbarrow (Shoreham, Sussex). The ringwork belongs to a slightly later phase of the occupation of the hill and is a more obvious precursor of the imposing contour-forts which are the noblest monuments of the period.

A number of these simple forts of the A1 phase have now been recognized. They were originally defended by a wooden palisade set in a trench which often follows the contour of the hill at a constant level. Often, too, the traces of the palisade-ditch were overlaid by the more formidable ramparts which are still visible. Such are Quarley Hill (Hants), Blewbury (Berks) and Wilbury (Letchworth, Herts). The approximate date of the A1 period and its forts may be put in round figures between 350 and 250 B.C. (Plate 9).

Many of the less complex forts that encircle the summit of our southern chalk hills belong to the A2 phase, especially to the earlier part of it (c. 250–200 B.C.), and may well symbolize the reaction of the Hallstatt people to a threatened invasion of their territories by Iron Age B people. The forms of these forts are somewhat variable for the semi-isolation of the different groups since their first settling here had probably resulted in local customs in the making of earthworks as well as of pottery; or it may be that their diverse Continental origins should be held responsible for variations in both (Plates 11, 12 and 13).

In the earlier forts the chalk excavated from the ditch was piled into a bank with as steep a face as possible above the ditch. Larger chalk blocks from among the excavated material might be used as at Ladle Hill (Litchfield, Hants) to revet the bank and hold back the smaller rubble from tumbling into the ditch. The first camp at Bury Hill

(Upper Clatford, Hants) and the visible defences at St. Catherine's Hill (Winchester), the Trundle (Singleton, Sussex), High Down (Figure 11, Ib), and such unfinished forts as Wilbury, Quarley, Ram's Hill (Uffington, Berks) and Ranscombe (South Malling, Sussex) are probably of this period. The uncompleted forts are probably symbols of an invasion scare, such as the impending approach of Iron Age B bands who, in fact, may never have entered the area supposedly threatened. The hastily built strong-points of the A.D. 1940's are comparable with those of the 240's B.C. or thereabouts. For instance, a band of Marnian warriors that had reached the Goring Gap on the Thames would have set off the alarm which prompted fortification of the Hampshire and Berkshire hills to the south and west of the Gap respectively, and of Wilbury and Limlow (Littlington, Cambs) near the line of the Icknield Way to the north-east. But at Wilbury, so far as could be ascertained, the threat passed away, and the occupants of the fort continued their existence much as before. Yet a movement of Iron Age B warriors from Sussex to the north-east coast, such as has been suggested by some scholars, would probably have passed via the Goring Gap northeastwards along the Icknield Way, passing close to the forts at Wilbury and Limlow. Some of these invaders actually settled and were buried in the Cambridge region, but if they approached it along the Chiltern route, they preferred to husband their fighting strength until they reached an area less densely populated or more to their taste in soil and situation. An alternative possibility is that Wilbury and Limlow were begun after the Marnian occupation of the Cambridge region to meet the threat of their expansion south-westward. The unfinished hill-forts of Berkshire and Hampshire might then be the result of a chain-reaction of fear transmitted along the Icknield Way and the Berkshire ridgeway. Or again, there were several Iron Age B invasions of southern Britain and several resulting periods of threat to the Iron Age A population and the unfinished forts need not all be contemporary.

These various alternatives are given not because they are thought valuable, but rather as a warning of the theorizing that is possible when facts are so few.

Two forts of particular interest are Hengistbury (Southbourne, Hants), which commands the seaward side of Christchurch harbour and which was a main point of entry for the Iron Age invaders; and Butser (Langrish, Hants), which guards a wind-gap in the chalk now followed by the Portsmouth road. Both are promontory forts. The Hengistbury defences consist of banks and ditches cutting off a headland which is protected on its other sides by the sea (Figure 10). The builders of Butser relied on steep chalk slopes for a defence and merely entrenched the downland spurs which rise gently from the neighbouring chalk or from the valley. The south spur has a double line of ditches about 200 yards apart and an outer ditch some 500 yards away on Hillhampton Down. These triple earthworks guard the most vulnerable approach to the fort where the ground remains fairly level for some distance at over 700 feet above sea level. The earthworks on Bow Hill (Stoughton, Sussex) are very much like those of Butser in their situation and arrangement (see Map D). Ranscombe Camp

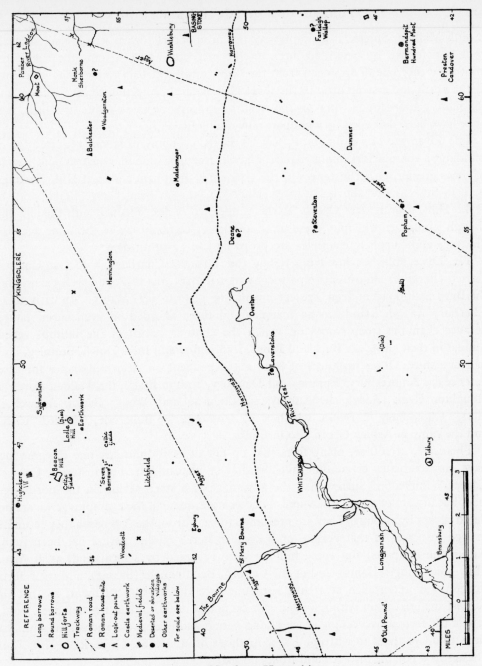

MAP C Northern Hampshire

(South Malling, Sussex) is a simpler type of promontory fort in which a single chalk spur is defended by bank and ditch on the east side where it joins the ridge that affords an easy line of approach from the Caburn hill-fort half a mile away. A combe to the north and a steep drop to the Ouse gave natural protection to Ranscombe, and the more gently sloping spur on the west, in appearance an easy line of attack, may once have been defended by a rampart now obliterated.

The advantage of a promontory fort lay in the economy of labour required for its building; a contour fort might require a labour force, or time for construction, dozens of times greater. Other instances of the type are at Burpham and East Hill, Hastings, both in Sussex; Bransbury, Andover (Hants); Compton Beauchamp (Berks) and the Dyke Hills, Dorchester (Oxon), at the confluence of the Thames and Thame. But though similar in principle, these forts are almost certainly not of the same age; the Hastings and Burpham examples are probably late Saxon in date.

The Dyke Hills are low-lying beside the Thames; Cherbury, a fort at Charney Bassett (Berks) is almost encompassed by its tributary, the Ock, and well exemplifies the third main kind of Iron Age earthwork, the plateau-fort (Map C). In early times Cherbury was an island among marshes and these afforded an even surer natural defence than the steep slopes on which the contour camps of the hilltops relied. Similar in their siting are Buckland Rings, Lymington and Bulls Down, Bramley, both in Hampshire. Other instances of forts not dependent on steep hill-slopes for their defence are Ambresbury (Epping) and Danbury, both in Essex; the Maiden Bower at Houghton Regis (Beds); the Aubreys, Redbourne and Arbury Banks, Ashwell in Herts; Cholesbury in Bucks, which is of Iron Age C; Bulstrode, Gerrards Cross, and the camp at Ashley Green also in Bucks.

There are, of course, many forts that do not fit easily into any one category but have characteristics of contour hill-fort and of plateau-fort. For instance, Caesar's Camp, Wimbledon (Surrey) had the advantage of a steep ravine on the north-west side, but of gentler slopes elsewhere. Furthermore, some of the examples given are not dated except by analogy. They are presumed to be of Iron Age A because they resemble proved instances of that period, or because material of that period has been found within the ramparts. But some hilltops were occupied by a farmstead, as at Meon Hill, Stockbridge (Hants), and at the Caburn, Beddingham (Sussex), and their fortification was undertaken at a time subsequent to the initial settlement, so that the earliest material from within such a site cannot be used to date the defences. Not a few of the forts were occupied over a long period and underwent successive modifications to adapt them to withstand new methods of attack. St. Catherine's Hill, Winchester, is a notable instance and Maiden Castle, Dorset, another.

The various methods employed to hold the ramparts of a fort from falling into the ditch below are more thoroughly described by diagrams (Figure 11, I–IV) as are the complex developments of the entrances to forts. Fuller information on these topics will be found in *Antiquity*, volume V, pp. 70 f., and *The Archaeology of Sussex* (1954), pp. 239 f. Much relevant information will also be found in *Maiden Castle*, pp. 36, 103 and 109.

It is doubtful whether any of the hill-forts were permanently inhabited. Even within the windbreak provided by the ramparts, living conditions would have been very uncomfortable, especially as the Iron Age partly synchronized with a climatic phase that was both wetter and cooler than the present. In the earlier part of the period the occupants of the forts possibly consisted of a few families who could

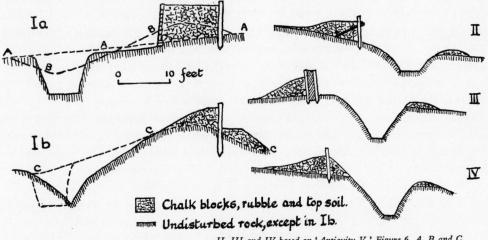

II, III and IV based on 'Antiquity V,' Figure 6, A, B and C.
Ia and Ib based on 'Sussex Archaeological Collections,' 89, Figure 10.

FIG 11 Hill-Fort Defences. Ia High Down, Sussex, circa 500 B.C. A-A-A: original ground surface. B-B: the surface after the decay of the first rampart. Ib High Down, Sussex. The reconstruction, circa 300 B.C. C-C-C: modern outline of the decayed second rampart. Other forms of rampart construction: II Cissbury, Sussex, circa 250 B.C. III Uffington, Berks, circa 250 B.C. IV The Caburn, Sussex, circa A.D. 43 a reconstruction of the first Caburn hill-fort of circa 100 B.C. but see Sussex Arch. Coll. 80, p. 193 f.

gain a livelihood by farming the immediately surrounding slopes; but in times of danger those who dwelt in outlying farms would have come in with their movable wealth in chattels and cattle to seek protection from the palisaded ramparts. In the A2 phase it seems that five of the southern forts, St. Catherine's Hill, Old Winchester Hill (Warnford, Hants), The Trundle, Cissbury and Torberry (Harting, Sussex) remained in occupation for a long period, each the central refuge of a main block of downland which was, perhaps, the territory of a tribe. Except for Old Winchester Hill, so far not excavated, these forts show some uniformity of construction and in the culture of their occupants; only in the area enclosed by the ramparts do they reveal any marked variation.

Eastward of Cissbury and the river Adur no evidence of lengthy occupation of forts has yet come to light. The Devil's Dyke (Poynings), Hollingbury (Brighton) and

Seaford Head were probably built at the end of the A1 phase, or at the beginning of A2, and have defences notably less massive than the group mentioned above. Other points of contrast between the two groups have been noted in their method of construction; and it has been concluded from those contrasts that the Adur formed a main tribal boundary from the third century B.C. between peoples of different traditions and having distinct political loyalties.

As research proceeds it is becoming more evident that the farmstead was the more normal unit of habitation; and that the former belief in numerous villages on the Wessex chalk, for instance, was due to a misconception. Their sites are marked by hollows once termed 'dwelling pits'; but they were in fact storage-pits ancillary to a single farm (Plate 10). This on excavation may appear as a group of buildings difficult to interpret where the site was occupied for long, because successive reconstructions obscure the contemporaneity of any of them. But a single farm then, as today, required outbuildings for several purposes other than the occupation of its owners.

It was the excavations at Little Woodbury, just south of Salisbury, that first made clear the layout of an Iron Age A farm; and although it is situated outside our region, it is probably representative of the many known to occur within it, especially in Hampshire (e.g. King's Worthy, Twyford and Farley Chamberlayne), in Berkshire (e.g. Boxford), and in Sussex (e.g. Findon and Sompting, the latter with a rectangular hut). The dwelling at Woodbury was circular with a double ring of supporting pillars about seven feet apart on the circumference. The doorway was protected by a porch, and the double ring of timbers may have contained stalls where cattle could be sheltered head to tail over the winter. A central hearth was flanked by four massive posts set in a square to provide support for a conical roof. At its apex there was, presumably, a hole from which smoke could escape.

The house was about forty feet in diameter, and with its ancillary buildings was protected by a palisade and ring-ditch roughly 400 feet from side to side of the enclosure. Within it were racks for the drying of hay, threshing hollows and small square timber granaries for seed corn, set on posts out of reach of damp and vermin. Also within the enclosure were some 360 storage pits, mainly used to hold bread-corn which had been roasted in ovens of clay, with flint hearths.

Recently it has been suggested that storage-pits could not have held corn owing to their dampness and that in fact they were made for the storage of dried or salted meat, large quantities of which would have to be held over from the autumn slaughter of cattle. Such a use is probable; but the not infrequent recovery of carbonized grain from these pits (as, e.g., at Park Brow) suggests their more usual function. Certainly their use as dwellings was always exceptional, but the discovery of the burnt remains of three adults and a child in a pit at Casterley (Wilts) may indicate such a use, perhaps in a hard winter and before the pit had begun to be filled with domestic rubbish and the chalk from newly dug pits.

The large number of pits at Little Woodbury, the forms of the pottery and the fact that the supporting posts of the house had often to be renewed, prove a long-continued occupation of the farm, probably for two to three hundred years from the beginning of the A2 phase in Wessex (*c.* 300 B.C.). For only a few of the pits were in use at any one time. Infection by mildew, even of parched grain, rendered a pit useless after two or three seasons and new ones had regularly to be dug.

The term 'pit-dwelling' has sometimes been used to describe the excavated bases of huts, as at Wilbury; but these depressions were seldom more than thirty inches deep and are quite distinct in form and function from storage-pits which may be as much as eight feet deep or more and from three to five feet in diameter. They are to be found on sites of the later phases of the Iron Age and were used also by the Romano-British farmers.

But besides circular dwellings of the Woodbury type there were others of Iron Age A that were oblong in shape. The evidence for this is derived from the disposition of post-holes and, though several rebuildings sometimes make interpretation difficult, a rectilinear plan is reasonably certain for the huts of phase A1 at Long Wittenham (Berks) and Muntham (Findon, Sussex). In some other instances the disposition of post-holes and size of the structure suggest raised granaries rather than dwellings; but it is worthy of note that huts of this period in northern Europe were quite commonly oblong.

Cultural continuity with the Late Bronze Age is evident not only in the generally circular shape of houses, but in pottery styles and in farming methods. Celtic fields may belong to either period or to the Romano-British era; the two-field system whereby cropping and fallowing alternated year by year was probably the common practice, as indeed it remained in most parts of midland England until about the thirteenth century A.D. Barley and wheat were still the main crops in the Iron Age, but oats and spelt also were sometimes grown. The damper climate made harvesting difficult. Before the grain was fully ripe the corn stalks were cut just below the ears, leaving a long stubble which was no doubt cleared by fire. With the grain still in the ear it was roasted in cob ovens, not without risk of rendering it useless by burning. Such carbonized grain has often been recovered from Iron Age sites: and the same practice, with the same attendant risk, was followed in the Late Bronze Age, for complete ears of barley in a heap of a dozen pounds of carbonized grain were found in the farmstead at Itford (Beddingham, Sussex). After drying, the separation of the husks from the seeds by winnowing was much easier. The process of grinding continued as in earlier ages to be done on saddle-querns.

The post-holes indicative of hay-drying racks at Woodbury are symbolic of yet another innovation: the making of hay. In earlier periods winter fodder for cattle had mainly consisted of the leaves of elm and lime. But cattle were no longer the most numerous domestic animals. Sheep had risen to dominance and they are well adapted to thrive on the broad grasslands of the downs. That these were now in many places bare of trees is indicated by the wide extent of Celtic field agriculture on the chalk;

G

and some confirmation of this is to be found in the species of snail-shells found on Iron Age sites. They are of kinds that flourish in open grassland in contrast with those of the neolithic period which are characteristic of a damp woodland environment. The sheep were grazed on the stubbles and fallow, giving not only meat but wool and few farms of this period are devoid of some evidence for the craft of weaving: spindle-whorls, or the triangular loom-weights which replaced the cylindrical form of the Late Bronze Age. Long-handled bone weaving combs and other accessories which become common in the A2 phase betoken a main preoccupation of the womenfolk. Hunting and the breeding of cattle, pigs and small horses all had a place in the economy of the farmsteads and were no doubt chiefly the concern of the men.

Iron Age A pottery clearly derives from traditions related to those of the Late Bronze Age inhabitants of Britain; but rims now tended to become flattened and finger-tip ornament was applied to the body of pots and not only to the rims. Common to all the local varieties is the situlate pot whose prototype was a high-shouldered bucket of sheet bronze riveted at the seams, a vessel much prized among the Hall-statt tribes of the Continent. Among earlier situlate earthenware pots the shoulder is sharp-angled but in the A2 phase the angle becomes more obtuse and is finally lost in a rounded profile.

The finer wares show more of local idiosyncrasies. They include thin-walled bowls of attractive appearance, often angular in outline and decorated with horizontal cor-rugations or with bands of varied chevron designs. Some of them are dimpled at the base, and many were coated with haematite slip before firing in order to produce a pleasing dark red surface.

In contrast with the abundant evidence for funerary custom in the Late Bronze Age that for the Iron Age is remarkably scanty. Cremation burials in flat graves are known from Park Brow and the Caburn (Sussex), and one was found under a barrow at Compton (Hants). In the A2 phase burial of the contracted corpse, unburned, seems to have been customary. Instances of it occurred at the earlier (A2) hill-fort at Bury Hill (Upper Clatford) and at the farmstead at King's Worthy, both in Hamp-shire. But this practice was not unknown among the earliest Iron Age settlers as exemplified by crouched burials of about the fifth century B.C. at Pirton (Herts). On Beaulieu Heath (Hants) immigrants from the lower Rhine had interred one of their number under a barrow that had a core of turves. All trace of the body had been destroyed by the acid soil, but traces of woodwork suggested that a cart may have been buried with the corpse.

The remarkable wartime discovery at London Airport (Harlington, Middx) of a temple of this period awaits a definitive report; but enough has been published to make clear its importance for a fuller understanding of ritual structures in Iron Age and Roman times. An oblong area was delimited by a bank and ditch within which were hut-sites marked by post-holes in the northern part, and in the western was situated a rectangular wooden building surrounded by a colonnade. The plan closely resembles that of the Romano-Celtic temples of which several are known in south-eastern England. The pottery at London Airport was confined to types current about 300 B.C. and this structure, so far unparalleled in Iron Age A, is probably one of the prototypes of the later brick or stone temples.

It was beneath a Romano-Celtic temple at Frilford (Berks) that the other known sacred site of Iron Age A was found. This earlier Frilford temple has closest analogy with the secondary neolithic henge monuments in that it consisted of posts set within a broad ditch interrupted at one point by a causeway. Nearby was the site of an Iron Age A2 farmstead that contained pottery showing B influence. In its plan the Frilford temple belongs to the same category as sites I, IV, V, VI and XI at Dorchester. The Middlesex temple looks forward, the Berkshire one backward; and there is little that they share in common and nothing yet known to narrow the gap between their conceptions.

The end of Iron Age A came at different times in different places, and in many respects its replacement or modification by the B and C cultures is obscure. In some areas, such as the Thames valley, the purer A culture was submerged by that of later invading Hallstatt bands who had acquired some of the fashions, especially in potting, of the Marnian tribes. The latter soon afterwards followed in the wake of those whom they had influenced and displaced. But to distinguish between the two series of migrations is not easy. If the Marnians came over mainly in fighting bands, as is normally assumed from the panoply of war sometimes buried with their dead in Yorkshire, then they must, in Britain, have been dependent on native women for their pot-making, and their traditional styles would necessarily have become much modified by the forms and decoration of the A2 culture which was that of the women. Therefore the material evidence would be much the same whether it be relics of A tribes influenced in their culture by B or whether the relics were those of Marnian warrior groups migrating without their women. Of Marnian objects other than pottery—horse-bits, brooches and other metal goods—we cannot be sure when they occur in the south-east whether they represent the traditional culture of their final owners or whether they had been acquired as exotic goods by trade from the Continent.

BIBLIOGRAPHY TO CHAPTER VIII

A work of primary importance for this period is 'St. Catherine's Hill' (1930) by Hawkes, Myres and Stevens in *Proceedings of the Hampshire Field Club*, XI. A recent controversial paper is 'The Chronology and Origins of Iron Age A in Southern and Midland Britain' (1952) in the *8th Annual Report of the University of London Institute of Archaeology*, which is a study of regional variations in pottery with an up-to-date bibliography. It is by Dr. Kathleen Kenyon. A. W. G. Lowther, 'Excavations at Caesar's Camp, Wimbledon', in *Archaeological Journal*, 102; the *Third Report of *the Research Committee of the Society of Antiquaries, Excavations at Hengistbury Head* (1915); 'Hill-Forts' in *Antiquity*, V (1931), pp. 60 f., by Professor Hawkes; 'Rams Hill, Uffington, Berks', in *Antiquaries Journal*, 20 (1940); 'Excavations in the Trundle' in *Sussex Archaeological Collections*, vols. 70 and 72; and 'Butser Hill' in *Antiquity*, IV (1930), pp. 187 f., are all relevant to this chapter. Professor Sir Mortimer Wheeler's *Maiden Castle* (1943), the 12*th Report of the Res. Comm. of the Soc. of Ant.*, has much that is of importance concerning our region and this period; Crawford and Keiller's *Wessex from the Air* (1928) includes fine aerial photographs of forts and other sites in Hants. G. Bersu's 'Excavations at Little Woodbury' in *The Proceedings of the Prehistoric Society*, IV and VI, are papers of great significance in their enlargement of our understanding of life in Iron Age A. For the Frilford temple, see *Oxoniensia*, IV.

* An inexpensive work.

CHAPTER IX

The Early Iron Age

Phase B

IN MANY RESPECTS this is one of the most complicated phases of prehistory and conclusions about it are likely to undergo some revision in the next few years. Several separate incursions of Marnian tribes affected our region between the middle of the third and the middle of the first centuries before Christ. None of them was necessarily an immigration of large numbers of people, though the first, as we have already seen, was sufficiently great to cause widespread alarm among the native Hallstatt people in about 250 B.C.

These immigrants from the Marne region of northern France succeeded in establishing themselves in east Yorkshire in some numbers; in Lincolnshire and the eastern counties smaller lodgements were made. East Kent was occupied at about the same time and their settlement sites have been found at Worth, Manston and Margate. In mid-Sussex they established themselves at Park Brow (site II) and at Findon Park. At both sites typical Iron Age B pottery, including vessels with pedestal bases, were recovered and from Findon came a brooch with flattened bow which is also distinctively Marnian.

The invaders were warrior aristocrats of the same stock as the Hallstatt peoples whom they conquered in Britain, but their culture had been much modified and enriched by trading contacts with the more advanced civilizations of the Mediterranean. Their occupation of the Marne district soon after 450 B.C. had set in motion the earliest Hallstatt invasions of Britain; and their expansion had dislodged further groups already tinctured by the superior Marnian (La Tène) culture. These dislodged AB peoples were probably responsible for scattered settlement along the lower Thames valley in about 350 B.C.

The Marnian influx of the mid-third century stimulated the peaceful Hallstatt tribes to build many of the hill-forts that remain such dominant features in the landscape of England; but in areas such as central Sussex this vast labour was of no avail, for the Marnians established themselves there as overlords, possibly dependent on food-tributes levied on the native farming communities. Their success came principally because of their superior armament and mobility. They attacked in light two-horse chariots and struck down their enemies with swords whose mountings bear the utmost skill of the metalworker's craft. Even the currency of kindred tribes in south-western Britain consisted of iron bars that represent the first stage in the forging of sword-blades. In contrast with the Marnians' warlike panoply there are few weapons found in Britain that can be attributed to the Iron Age A peoples in the settled phase that followed the turmoil of their invasions. The fine series from the Thames, of swords and daggers especially, belong to the beginning of the A1 phase during the actual immigration of the Hallstatt tribes.

The two Sussex sites, at Park Brow and Findon, are situated in the block of downland that is bounded by the rivers Arun and Adur; between the sites lies the great hill-fort of Cissbury, which seems to have been occupied from phase A1, when the ramparts were constructed, into A2, when their outer faces were revetted with timber in response to the invasion of the B people. From this time pottery from the fort shows an infusion of La Tène decorative motives, textures and shapes. Pots with pedestal bases and others of saucepan shape bearing simple curvilinear patterns characterize the 'Cissbury' culture which seems to have spread westwards as far as mid-Hampshire where similar vessels are found; eastward expansion apparently did not begin until somewhere about 100 B.C.

By this time much of Hampshire and Berkshire had been penetrated by La Tène influence, though Hallstatt traditions still remained strong. In part this intermingling of A and B styles may represent an infusion from Sussex; but the Marnian culture of east Yorkshire had spread as far as Hunsbury in Northamptonshire and it is possible that Wessex was affected from that direction as well as from the south-west where La Tène peoples had begun to exploit Cornish tin. Their distant kinsfolk had been attracted to Hunsbury by its supply of iron ore. However, pottery representing a fusion of the A and B cultures has been found at such Hampshire sites as Balksbury (Andover), a fort originally built in the A2 phase, and at Bury Hill (Upper Clatford), which has much the same history. At Meon Hill (Stockbridge), a few miles to the south, a farmstead of the A1 phase exhibits a similar AB culture by about the first century B.C. In Berkshire the AB fusion is apparent at Uffington, Blewburton and Charney Bassett, all hill-forts, and at open settlements or farmsteads such as those at Long Wittenham, Frilford and Hatford, and just across the Thames at two sites in Dorchester (Oxon). This region on the upper Thames was vulnerable to influences emanating from either the north-east or south-west along the Jurassic ridgeway of the Cotswolds and its continuations. It is also likely that B influences were brought up the Thames by immigrants that had remained long enough on the Continent to absorb La Tène styles; traces of those styles have been noted on even the earliest Hallstatt pottery of this region. During this earliest phase the influence of the Wessex Iron Age is, however, more clearly apparent, and it would not be surprising if some of the La Tène tincture had been derived from that quarter as well as from north-east or south-west Britain.

Julius Caesar's campaigns in western Gaul in 56 B.C. dislodged several tribes which crossed the Channel in order to escape Roman rule. Among these were the Veneti, who had inhabited the southern coast of the Armorican peninsula, and who are said by Caesar to have been engaged in trade with Britain, for which purpose they had a fleet of seaworthy ships. In Britain they, or a neighbouring tribe, probably seized Maiden Castle near Dorchester (Dorset) and the country around it. There they intermarried with the Hallstatt people and rebuilt and strengthened Maiden Castle producing the enormous earthwork much as we see it today. The hybrid culture thus established appears not to have penetrated beyond the Hampshire Avon. Stray sherds at Armsley (Fordingbridge) on the east bank of that river are all that is certainly known of them in our region. But it is not unlikely that the refortification of Bury Hill (Upper Clatford) was the work of these people in marking their eastern frontier. Other multivallate hill-forts such as Danebury (Nether Wallop) may represent part of the same process, in which case the Wessex B frontier was pushed forward to the line of the river Test, perhaps in a vain attempt to halt the westward drive of the Belgae in the later part of the first century B.C.

The multiplication of hill-fort ramparts was also, no doubt, a response to developments in the skill of slingers. A single rampart and a ditch, combined with an uphill slope, afforded reasonable protection against a throwing-spear; but the range of a sling was much greater and hill-fort defences had to be reorganized accordingly if the forts were to continue in their function of refuges. It is likely that the majority of those with a single rampart ceased to be used for defence after about 50 B.C.

It is probably no coincidence that the Veneti were formidable with the sling. The enormous hoards of sling-stones at Maiden Castle and the multiplicity of its defences can hardly be unconnected. In small quantities flint sling bullets have been found on Late Bronze Age sites such as that on Itford Hill; a few occurred in the A-culture levels at Maiden Castle and in Sussex hill-forts; but in large numbers they are found only in the subsequent B levels. Beach pebbles for this purpose occurred most commonly at the Trundle (Singleton, Sussex) in just those horizons where B-culture pottery was most frequent; and a hoard of pebbles was discovered at Cissbury. The hill-forts of Chanctonbury (Washington, Sussex) and the Caburn (Beddingham, Sussex), had flat-topped mounds as part of their defences which have been thought to have afforded vantage-points for slingers guarding the gateways. If this was indeed their purpose, they are comparable with the platforms (or towers) that were included in the great reconstruction of Maiden Castle by the Veneti.

This tribe was not the only one to take to flight as a result of Caesar's Armorican campaigns. Pottery from the fort at Hengistbury Head (Southbourne, Hants), with dimpled bases and cordon-ornament (class B in the *Report*), matches what has been found near Avranches in south-west Normandy. This is dateable to the middle of the first century B.C. The same variety occurred at the Glastonbury lake village, suggesting that some of the refugees settled there also. And it may well be that the typical Glastonbury ware, so beautiful in shape and decoration, that was found at Hengistbury, represents a maintenance of contacts between the two bands of refugees. At

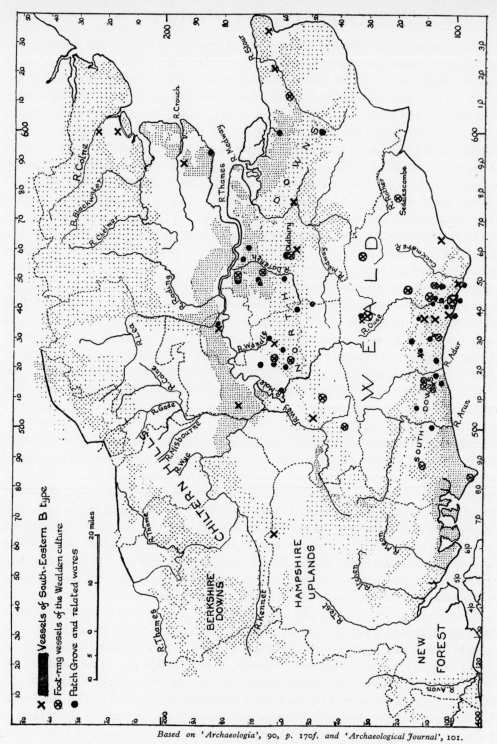

Based on 'Archaeologia', 90, p. 170f. and 'Archaeological Journal', 101.

MAP 6 The Distribution of South-Eastern B and related pottery

both places the cordoned ware precedes the Glastonbury pottery by a comparatively short length of time. The latter kind of pottery has closest analogies with Breton wares of this period and a direct influx to Hengistbury, as well as to Glastonbury, is quite probable. Indeed the Hampshire fort is far more easily accessible from Brittany than from the Somerset levels.

In the same decade, and probably for the same reason, Sussex experienced a new invasion of B peoples, and these, too, it seems, were from Brittany. Though otherwise unlike the Hengistbury class B pottery, the wares of the South-Eastern B people had a concave (omphalos) base in common with it, but in their more typical forms they are decorated with incised arcades of eyebrow motives or with small circlets. This culture spread far inland (Map 6) across the Weald and in its later forms is found on the Essex coast, in Kent, and in Surrey as far west as the river Wey. Besides the Essex finds (at Colchester, Canewdon, Langenhoe and Shoebury) it occurred in London at Silchester (Hants) and at Harlington (Middx). It is seldom found in either the eastern or western Belgic areas, but it was not unaffected by Belgic styles, and even, in its later forms, retained some of the old Iron Age A motives such as finger-tip impressions on bands round the pot. The main concentration of finds from this 'South-Eastern B' culture is in the area first conquered, namely central-southern Sussex from the river Cuckmere in the east to the river Arun in the west, but thinning out between Adur and Arun. Of the local varieties of pottery that emerged, the one that is known as 'Patch Grove' is perhaps the commonest. This is limited in its distribution to Surrey and mainly west Kent; it survived in use as late as the second century A.D. especially in ritual use for the holding of a cremation. The same is true of the other local wares such as those named after Asham (in Beddingham, Sussex) and Ashford (Kent).

But it is necessary to turn back in time to about 100 B.C. to consider the emergence of the 'Wealden Culture', which also contributed something to the heritage of the South-Eastern B peoples. It was itself a composite culture incorporating a considerable element of Iron Age A and, in addition, the Marnian culture which had been established round Cissbury by an invasion of the mid-third century B.C. About 150 years later these Marnians began to spread eastward and northward, moving across the Weald to exploit its resources of iron ore (Map 6). Traces of their settlements have been found in several areas which had probably never known permanent occupation before. They eventually reached the northern confines of the Weald in Kent and Surrey. At Horsted Keynes (Sussex), for instance, they produced pottery on a scale that suggests a minor industrial centre catering for those such as the iron-workers who could not provide for themselves. And here and at Seddlescombe (Sussex) they mingled with the South-Eastern B people. In their eastward expansion along the downs the Wealden Folk captured Castle Hill (Newhaven) and the Caburn (Beddingham) and succeeded in holding the latter against the South-Eastern B people, little of whose pottery was found in it. Later these two peoples were to offer bitter resistance to the Roman conquest.

Some of the Sussex iron-working sites show their earliest use in this, the ultimate Iron Age of the Weald. Fortified settlements are known at Kirdford, Rotherfield and West Hoathly (Sussex) and among a number of undefended sites those at Dallington, Ticehurst and Crowhurst, in the same county, are worthy of mention.

The finds of coins on sites of the Wealden culture such as the Caburn suggests that the produce of the iron bloomeries may have been traded over a wide area of the south-east. These coins, usually termed 'tin' but actually two-thirds of copper, have come from many places in our region, particularly round London and in east Kent. In this connection the La Tène ancestry of the dominant element in the Wealden culture has to be borne in mind, for trade seems often to have afforded an outlet for the energies of the Iron Age B tribes. The Veneti of Brittany, the Glastonbury lake-dwellers and the occupants of Hengistbury were all noteworthy for their commercial activities.

The most distinctive feature of the Wealden culture, as with so many others, is to be seen in its pottery. The foot-ring and shallow S-profile of the sides of its vessels afford the most easily recognisable criteria in differentiating this from South-Eastern B and from Belgic wares, both of which are partly contemporary. But influences from the styles of the latter peoples may be detected in pottery of the Wealden Folk, and the foot-ring is itself probably a development of the pedestal that occurs on some Iron Age B pots.

Outside south-western Britain little is known of the types of houses in use among the B peoples. Evidence from Maiden Castle and from the Devil's Dyke (Poynings, Sussex) indicates that the circular hut was probably still normal, sometimes with a central hearth with an opening above it as at Woodbury, and sometimes with a central roof-support, with the cooking-place presumably outside the hut. At the Dyke the hut was twenty-five feet across. The walls were sunk in a shallow bedding trench but the floor was not cut below turf level. Two small storage-pits had been dug within its limits.

In personal adornment, brooches of safety-pin type tended to replace the pins which had been usual among the Hallstatt tribes. But life in general can have changed little in most parts of the Home Counties between the fifth and first centuries B.C. Upland farming from lone steadings probably continued with little interruption except for changes in ownership as new immigrants displaced the natives. There may have developed a tendency to seek the less inhospitable lower slopes of the downs as at Park Brow, where the AB farmstead was moved further down the hill to a new site. But, on the whole, the valleyward movement did not get under way until Iron Age C, for the Marnian peoples had neither the traditions nor the equipment for cultivating the richer and heavier soils of the lowlands. Though the upland Celtic fields may several times have changed master, the old methods of farming remained much the same; and the breeding of stock and hunting were important still in supplementing the food supply.

One innovation, ultimately from the Mediterranean, was the rotary quern which seems to have been gaining favour steadily from about the beginning of the first century B.C. The upper stone revolved on a wooden spindle secured in a central socket in the nether stone. Let into the circumference of the upper stone was a groove to take a handle by means of which the mill could be turned to grind grain to flour. In the earliest forms the nether stone has a steeply conical profile but by Romano-British times it had generally become flatter. Quarries from which suitable stone could be extracted are known in a few places in southern England. The most famous are the Pen Pits, near Wincanton in Somerset; but in the Greensand formation near Faringdon (Berks) is a series of pits which may possibly have been in use in the Iron Age. A quarry on the same geological formation may have existed in the parish of Farnham (Surrey), and another in the same county at Worm's Heath, Chelsham. North of the Thames similar quarries have yet to be found, but quern-fragments of pudding-stone found at the Maiden Bower (Houghton Regis, Beds) suggest that the conglomerate of the Reading beds, especially in Hertfordshire, may have been a source of raw material for querns in this area.

Much of the south-east remained unaffected or only superficially modified in culture as a result of the Iron Age B invasions. Essex, inland from the coastal areas, has revealed little indication of their effects, and Hertfordshire, Middlesex and Buckinghamshire with much of northern Hampshire and eastern Berkshire probably continued in their old Hallstatt ways where they were inhabited at all. The New Forest, too, remained unaffected. Indeed, it has yielded very little that can be confidently dated to any period between the Late Bronze Age and the Dark Ages, to which a few linear earthworks may be attributable. The Weald saw little change until the last century before Christ, and, in the culture to which it gives its name, the Hallstatt element is almost as strong as the La Tène. Of the three main phases of the Iron Age, the B phase was least enduring in its effects. The Hallstatt tribes and the Belgae made an altogether larger contribution to the amalgam of peoples who eventually formed part of the Roman province of Britain.

It may be helpful at this point to give a brief summary of the folk-movements which affected our region in the Iron Age B period. In the mid-third century there was probably a Marnian conquest of a part of Sussex and of east Kent and a later influx of related people to Sussex in the mid-first century who were originators of the South-Eastern B culture. On the Hampshire coast La Tène incursions may have occurred about the beginning of the first century B.C., but were more certainly under way, perhaps as a resumption of the migration, half a century later. From the Sussex area there was a diffusion of the earlier B culture northward and eastward giving rise eventually to the Wealden Culture. Over the Home Counties as a whole, Iron Age A2 gave way gradually to a mixed AB culture though the change-over was mainly a superficial one and the long-established Hallstatt peasantry probably continued in their old modes of life until displaced by the Saxons and Jutes in the fifth and sixth centuries A.D.; for even the Roman occupation brought them little besides greater security which, no doubt, they paid for dearly in corn taxes.

BIBLIOGRAPHY TO CHAPTER IX

No general study of this period has yet been published though some aspects of it have come into sharper focus in recent years. The Wealden Culture is defined by Ward Perkins in his report on the Oldbury excavations in *Archaeologia*, 90 (1944); and see also the *Proceedings of the Prehistoric Society*, IV. Relevant also is Hawkes's paper on the pottery from the Caburn in *Sussex Archaeological Collections*, 80 (1939). See also volume 87, pp. 77 f., of the same series and *Archaeological Journal*, 101 (1944), pp. 50 f., 'Some Aspects of Iron Age and Romano-British Culture in the Wealden Area,' by S. S. Frere. For the metalwork of this period and later see *The Heritage of Early Britain* (1952), chapter III, by J. M. de Navarro, which has a useful select bibliography appended.

The Maiden Castle report (see above, p. 100) and Curwen's *Archaeology of Sussex* (1954), pp. 232 f., contain much that is relevant to the Home Counties as a whole, and their footnotes afford many further references to sites within the region.

CHAPTER X

The Early Iron Age (Belgic Settlement)

Phase C

ALREADY IN THE preceding Iron Age phase we have seen recorded history impinging on prehistory. Caesar's campaigns in Gaul had affected southern Britain even before the Marnian incursions of the mid-first century. Yet there is a vital difference between the Belgic invasion of *c.* 75 B.C. and those of the Marnians, for the Belgae came *en masse*, men, women and children; the Marnian invaders appear to have consisted of men only, and the archaeological record registers comparatively minor changes of culture, at any rate in the south-east. But with the coming of the Belgae there is an almost complete change, reflecting a revolution in the mode of living wherever they settled; outside their territories, however, the old ways of life continued with only superficial modifications right down to the time of the Roman conquest and even beyond.

The origin of the Belgae is largely a matter of history. The pressure of migrating German tribes had already forced La Tène Celts westward to the invasion of these islands in the middle of the third century B.C. In the latter part of the second century the Germanic tribes of the Rhineland moved forward into the old Marnian districts of which the natives either fled, were exterminated or merged with their conquerors. Eventually the mixed Celtic-Germanic confederacy of Belgic tribes thus formed occupied the whole of the region bounded by the river Seine on the south, the Channel on the north-west, the Rhine to the north-east and the Ardennes to the south-east.

The burial rite changed from the normal Teutonic custom of inhumation to that of cremation and interment of the ashes in flat graves; and the potter's wheel was introduced for the first time into the region. But Marnian traits remained strong in the new hybrid culture, suggesting a considerable survival of Celtic women. It was strong enough to ensure that the Celtic strain did not become subordinate to the Germanic. Though pots were turned on the wheel, their forms were obviously derived from Marnian prototypes; and Celtic speech and Celtic personal, tribal and place-names prevailed.

Alone among the tribes of Gaul the Belgae were successful in beating off the attacks of the Cimbri at the end of the second century B.C. and thereby gained a well-deserved reputation for their valour; and they were alone, too, in their cultural self-sufficiency, notably resistant among the Gauls to the process of Romanization which so often

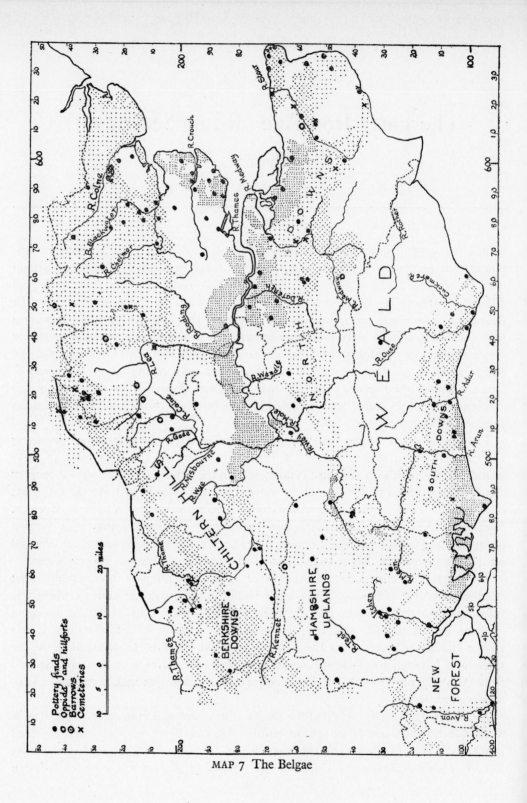

MAP 7 The Belgae

opened the way for Roman conquest. And when Caesar began his first campaign against them in 58 B.C. he soon discovered that their warlike reputation was not an empty one.

The Belgic invaders of Britain came from the southern part of the confederacy, that is from the Marnian region from which had issued the Iron Age B tribes who had settled in Sussex and elsewhere. From about 75 B.C. the Belgae began occupying Kent, especially its eastern parts where settlement sites or their cemeteries have come to light in some numbers. Among them may be mentioned Deal, Faversham, Folkestone and Walmer (Map 7). At the beginning of the invasion they appear to have conquered the northern part of the region up to the line of the Medway beside which, at Aylesford, one of their most notable cemeteries was found. At the same time as the first invasion of Kent, landings were made in south-east Essex, as for instance at Shoebury, Southminster and Southend, from which places their typical pedestal urns of the first half of the first century B.C. have been recovered; but otherwise the (Hallstatt?) Trinovantes of Essex, little affected by the earlier La Tène invasions, remained undisturbed until about the first decade of the Christian era.

Not long after the landings in Kent the Belgae had penetrated into Hertfordshire and constructed a fortified oppidum at Wheathampstead (c. 70 B.C.). This was defended by enormous earthworks (Figure 12B) of which the V-shaped ditch at its greatest width was 130 feet and its depth 40 feet. Commanding two fords across the upper waters of the river Lea, the oppidum defences enclose an area of about 90 acres (cf. Maiden Castle, with an internal area of 45 acres). It is now held to be the stronghold which Cassivellaunus vainly defended against Julius Caesar in 54 B.C. Its position on the fringe of the older settled areas to the north and north-west is similar to that of the contemporary earthwork, the Beech Bottom Dyke, which spans a lightly forested tract of chalk country between Wheathampstead and St. Albans and which was probably intended as a traffic barrier rather than as a line of defence. It has been called 'the largest of its kind in Britain', having a width of 100 feet and depth of 30 feet excluding the banks on each side; and the original dimensions would have been even greater before silt had accumulated in the ditch.

So far as present information goes, the Iron Age A2 fort of Wilbury (Letchworth, Herts) was taken over by the Belgae not long after 50 B.C. The Wheathampstead oppidum was abandoned in favour of a new and less heavily defended settlement now covered by Prae Wood (parish of St. Michael's) and the Hitchin, Welwyn and Baldock neighbourhoods were apparently first occupied at about the same time. There was also an expansion into southern Bedfordshire where Belgic cemeteries of the late first century B.C. have come to light, at Arlesey and Stotfold, for instance.

In the primary phase of settlement it seems that occupation was limited to eastern and north-eastern Kent, to the northern and southern shores of the Thames estuary and, within a decade, to Hertfordshire. At first there was little movement from the primary regions of occupation in east and north-east Kent. Although no doubt they dominated it, the Belgae did not until much later occupy Kent west of the Medway, though recently it has been conjectured that the fort at Cobham (west Kent) was a Belgic tribal centre. South-westward expansion was made difficult by the more heavily forested tracts of the Weald which had, however, already been penetrated by the Wealden Folk and by the South-Eastern B people. They were mainly iron-workers whose produce was probably soon diverted to Belgic use. But normal settle-ment by any of the Iron Age peoples was not attempted beyond the fringes of the Weald even though in other regions clayey loams were now being tilled for the first time by Belgic farmers.

In the west of our region, in west Sussex, Hampshire, Berkshire and west Surrey, the course of the Belgic settlement is rather less clear. It does not appear to have begun before the middle of the first century B.C. and was no doubt in part the result of Caesar's conquest of Gaul. The exodus from Brittany of the Veneti and neigh-bouring peoples who occupied the more westerly parts of Wessex and central Sussex was broadly contemporary with the flight of irreconcilable Belgic groups from the north-east of Gaul. The Atrebates (cf. Artois and Arras in their ancient homeland) emigrated first to Normandy and thence in sufficient strength to give their name to a kingdom set up in northern Hampshire and Berkshire and probably taking in the western part of Sussex. Landings were perhaps made on Selsey Bill (which extended several miles further to the south than it now does), at Hengistbury Head, to which so many earlier refugees from the Continent had made their way, and possibly in the many inlets in between. But the sour gravels of the New Forest were avoided as was the heavy clay of the Forest of Bere to the east of Southampton Water (Map 7).

It is known from Roman historians that a certain Commius, an ally of Caesar and made by him king of the Atrebates, turned against the Romans in 52 B.C. Defeated and marked down for assassination, he fled to Britain. He avoided the Belgic pro-vince in the south-east, where he was already hated as a former ally of the Romans, and betook himself to the culturally backward regions further to the west. There coins inscribed with his name (or his son's) appeared, and the bead-rim pottery which distinguishes the western Belgae from the eastern; for the latter produced characteris-tic pedestal urns among many other forms.

In a route book of the third century A.D., the Antonine Itinerary, there is refer-ence to a *Calleva Atrebatum* (the woodland town of the *Atrebates*) which coincides in its location with the Roman town of Silchester (Hants) (Map J). An inscription *Callevae* from the town itself confirms the identification. But direct evidence for the existence of a Belgic oppidum before the Roman conquest is limited to Belgic coins with the inscription EPP / REX CALLEV and EPI / CALLEV (Epillus / Calleva). Eppillus was a son of Commius and presumably king of the Atrebates with their capital at Calleva. There is also a wide flat-bottomed ditch with internal rampart which, on recent excavation, yielded Belgic pottery of pre-conquest date. Moreover, coin-moulds, similar to those from pre-Roman Colchester, reinforce the argument for a Belgic foundation of the settlement at Silchester.

An incursion into the western parts of our region in about 50 B.C. may be inferred also from the stratified evidence on a number of other excavated sites. St. Catherine's Hill, Winchester, was sacked about this time and soon after there began the Belgic occupation of the site of Winchester and of Chilbolton to the north-west. A group of the same people took over farmsteads on Twyford Down to the south of Winchester, at Stanmore to the south-west, on Worthy Down and at Odiham to the north. Traces of their occupation have also been found at Gorley (Fordingbridge) and at Armsley (Godshill) on the Avon, beyond the New Forest to the west.

In western Sussex the position is even more obscure. Numerous finds in the neighbourhood of Selsey suggest a considerable settlement there, and coins of the Morini, who had occupied the region round Calais, may betoken cross-Channel trade or that some of that tribe joined their neighbours the Atrebates in the migration to Britain. The Roman attribution of the generic name Belgae to the settlers of parts of central Hampshire (*Venta Belgarum* was the Roman name for Winchester) and parts of Wiltshire suggests that these areas too were occupied by groups from a number of distinctive tribes, in contrast with the Atrebates further to the north who, it seems, remained tribally intact with their old name.

Much of the Belgic material from Selsey came from the foreshore, having been washed out of the low cliffs; and it is likely that the main Belgic habitation centre has been eroded by the sea. Numerous coins inscribed with the names Tincommius or Verica (sons of Commius, the Atrebate, and brothers of Eppillus) may indicate that they ruled successively from this lost oppidum. If the linear earthworks near Chichester (Map D) are indeed Belgic like those defending pre-Roman Colchester (Map E), then it may well be that the Sussex town originated in this period; but positive evidence of this is so far lacking. Traces of Early Iron Age A habitations have been found within and just outside the walls but there is a temporal gap in the occupation until Belgic material of the mid-first century A.D. appears. This, of course, is contemporary with the earliest years of the Roman occupation.

The nearest Belgic site to Chichester seems to be at Idsworth (Rowland's Castle), just over the Hampshire border, where bead-rim pots and a coin from a ditched enclosure indicate a settlement early in the first century A.D. This site continued to be occupied in the Romano-British period.

In Sussex, west of the Adur, hill-forts such as Cissbury, Torberry (Harting) and the Trundle were suddenly abandoned at about the time of the Belgic irruption of 50 B.C. and the defences on Beacon Hill (Harting) were re-cut; the settlements of the A-B culture in Findon Park and at Park Brow were deserted and then re-established on the lower slopes of the Downs, a valleyward movement typical of the Belgae. This, however, was an area influenced, and possibly ruled, but not settled by them. It has been asserted that the abandonment of the Trundle was probably followed by

H

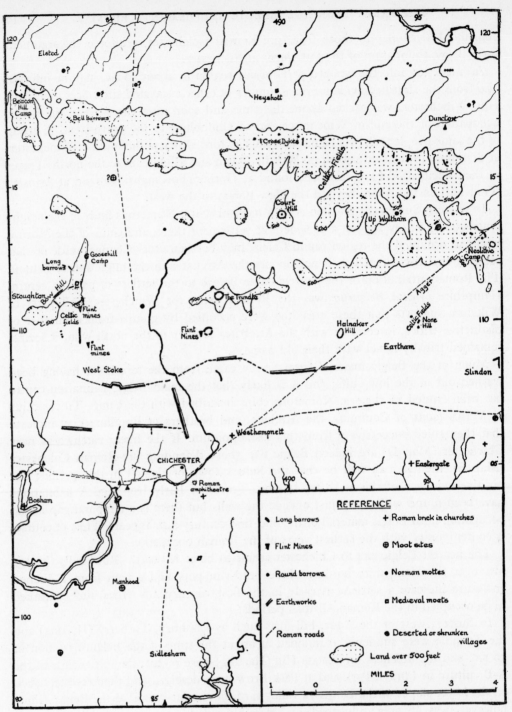

MAP D The Chichester Region

settlement at Chichester, known as *Noviomagus*, which may be interpreted as 'new city on the plain'; but, as we have seen, proof is lacking. A later alternative name for the Roman city was *Regnum*, from the tribal name *Regni*, which was applied to the inhabitants of western Sussex.

In Sussex east of the Adur Belgic influence was slight, for there, as noted in the previous chapter, an Iron Age B population had probably migrated from Brittany soon after 56 B.C. They extended northward and eastward merging with the Wealden Folk; only the Caburn people, so far as we know, retained their culture and their independence down to the Roman Conquest.

To the west of their new kingdom the Belgic tribes made slow progress in their expansion. At approximately the time of Commius's death in 20 B.C. they appear to have reached the river Test. Bury Hill (Upper Clatford) was occupied from about fifty years before the Roman conquest, with displacement of the AB natives. The hill-fort had been strengthened in vain in the face of threatened Belgic encroachment. Danebury, the finest hill-fort in Wessex after Maiden Castle, probably had a similar history; its complex entrance and massive ramparts seem to betoken a similar attempt at stemming the Belgic tide. The farmstead at Meon Hill (Stockbridge) was also remodelled during the AB phase of culture about 50 B.C. But before the Romans called a halt to their westward drive the Belgae had reached eastern Devon and the Bristol Channel.

In Surrey most of the Belgic material dates from after the Roman conquest. At a few sites in the west of the county, such as St. George's Hill camp (Walton-on-Thames) Farnham, Carshalton and Wimbledon, pre-conquest Belgic pottery occurs. Belgic influence is to be seen in some from Wisley and Cobham; but at many sites, for example West Clandon, Waddon, Malden, Ewell, Ashtead and Fetcham, South-eastern B, Wealden, and (in its latest form) Patch Grove ware occurs unmixed with, and hardly influenced by, Belgic styles. In some places native occupation, untouched by the invaders, continued until the first quarter of the first century A.D. At Epsom. for instance, Iron Age A vessels of degenerate form were still being produced as late as the beginning of the first century B.C. At Wisley an original A2 culture was modified by B influences and later still by Belgic styles.

This complexity of Surrey archaeology in the Iron Age is probably exceptional only because of the more intensive research carried out there by many skilled workers in the last few decades. Similar work in other regions might well reveal a similar complexity.

On the middle Thames, in Berkshire and Oxfordshire, we come nearly to the limits of Belgic domination, but there is little evidence of mass settlement; its extension to this region was perhaps halted by the Roman conquest. Information derivable from coins indicates that the southern invasion barely reached the line of the Thames which, with its tributary the Cherwell formed a boundary, in part, between the two main Belgic regions of the west and east, and between them and unconquered natives.

The Atrebates were to the south-west of the line of the Thames between Goring and Oxford. Traces of their occupation have come from such places at Rams Hill (Uffington), Lowbury (Aston Upthorpe) and Alfred's Castle (Ashbury) behind the chalk scarp; and from the great northern loop of the Thames at Radley and Appleton.

East of the Cherwell and on the left bank of the Thames in southern Oxfordshire were territories subject, from the end of the first century B.C. at any rate, to the Catuvellaunian dynasty represented by Tasciovanus and Cunobelin. Few Belgic finds have, however, been made in this area and it retained its AB culture with little modification. On the opposite side of the Thames the majority of the coins came from Atrebatic mints and were inscribed with the names of Tincommius or Eppillus. Not long before A.D. 43 the meagre evidence suggests an extension of the Catuvellaunian dominion beyond the Thames into Berkshire.

Just as the Marnian invasions prompted a wave of fort building among the A2 natives, so fear of the Belgae stimulated the AB population to take active measures for their own defence. The Wealden people of the neighbourhood constructed a strong refuge for themselves on Oldbury Hill (Ightham, Kent); Dry Hill camp (Lingfield, Surrey), and others further to the west on the Greensand, may represent a similar local reaction to further Belgic expansion westward, for Oldbury was in fact seized and later, in A.D. 43, the Belgae themselves had to set to work to strengthen the defences in the vain hope of repelling the Romans. Saxonbury (Rotherfield, Sussex), on the central Wealden ridge, a fortified refuge of iron-workers, which had consisted of an oval stone enclosure, was superseded by a hill-fort perhaps in about 50 B.C. Thereafter pottery made at the site was of the AB variety with signs of Belgic (C) influence. In the Roman period Belgic bead-rims were in use there.

On the northern fringe of our region in Hertfordshire, at Wilbury and Arbury Banks (Ashwell), and beyond at Vandlebury, near Cambridge, there seems to have been similar re-fortification as the Belgae advanced northward from Kent. It was at Wheathampstead, as we have seen, that the Belgae established their capital. Bigbury (Harbledown), which is situated close to Canterbury, was one of their earlier oppida and like Wheathampstead it may be identified with one of the forts stormed by Caesar. Later the Belgae built other forts after fanning out from central Hertfordshire; among them are Cholesbury (Bucks) and Bulstrode (Gerrards Cross, in the same county). Bulstrode had existed in simpler form in Iron Age A and, like some of the other forts mentioned, was merely adapted by the Belgae.

Belgic forts tend to be simpler than those of the Iron Age B tribes. Entrances are not elaborated and the ditches are sometimes flat-bottomed as at Oldbury, at Silchester, and at several points in the defences of the oppidum immediately north-east of the Roman and medieval city of Colchester. But the Beech Bottom Dyke at St. Albans, the Wheathampstead oppidum and that in Prae Wood have V-shaped ditches, though usually of a more obtuse angle than those of the preceding phases of the Iron Age. Furthermore, both Cissbury and the Caburn, for instance, have flat-bottomed ditches, and they cannot therefore be taken as characteristic of Belgic defences. The Repell Ditches at Saffron Walden (Essex), which enclose a rectangle of more than twenty acres, guard a ford on an important route between the Thames and Cam valleys. It is, moreover, a lowland site and the ditches are flat-bottomed. All this may, by analogy, suggest a Belgic settlement.

From their oppidum at Wheathampstead the Belgae moved southward about five miles and re-established their capital at Prae Wood on a plateau above the river Ver and guarding an important ford. The evidence from the pottery found there indicates a date roughly between 15 and 10 B.C. for its first occupation and, in general, the Prae Wood pottery is later than that from Wheathampstead. At the latter site there are none of the wares imported from Gaul which imitated the products of Arretium in Italy. These were entering Britain for at least a generation before, as well as after, the Roman conquest. They are found sporadically throughout our region apart from Middlesex, Buckinghamshire and Oxfordshire, and they occur outside it to the west and north.

The Prae Wood settlement was situated in a clearing of primeval forest which throve on a varied soil of clays, loams, sand and gravel. Apart from bronze-founders and ironworkers, neither of whom had made permanent or normal settlements in forested tracts, this siting of the Prae Wood oppidum is representative of the beginning of a new era in man's conquest of his environment.

In its present state the Prae Wood settlement is a mere jumble of banks and ditches, some of which may be of much later date than those investigated. The woodland earthworks cover only a quarter of the area of the whole Belgic complex, for beyond the fringes of the wood much has been obliterated by the modern plough. The eastern boundary ditch of the settlement, which runs parallel to the ramparts of the Roman city in the valley below, was proved to extend for nearly a mile from north to south. Within Prae Wood itself the ditch is double, and at one point it bounds a roughly rectilinear enclosure of about two acres which was no doubt used for the corralling of cattle. Rubbish tips containing animal bones, ashes and pottery dating from the end of the first century B.C. were found to the south of the enclosure, and in the same area were numerous shallow drainage ditches that had made the site habitable. All signs of huts had been destroyed by tree-roots, but oval ovens with clay walls, similar to those found at Hengistbury and at Tilbury (Essex), suggest cooking-places; the huts cannot have been far distant.

There were indications that the earliest boundary ditches had been greatly strengthened and that this had probably been undertaken in face of the threat of Roman conquest. After A.D. 43 the ditches gradually filled up. The settlement had moved downhill to beside the river and astride a main Roman highway; the Prae Wood plateau was deserted except for the plough-teams that came up from the first Roman city of Verulamium.

But before the Roman conquest the main centre of Belgic power had shifted from

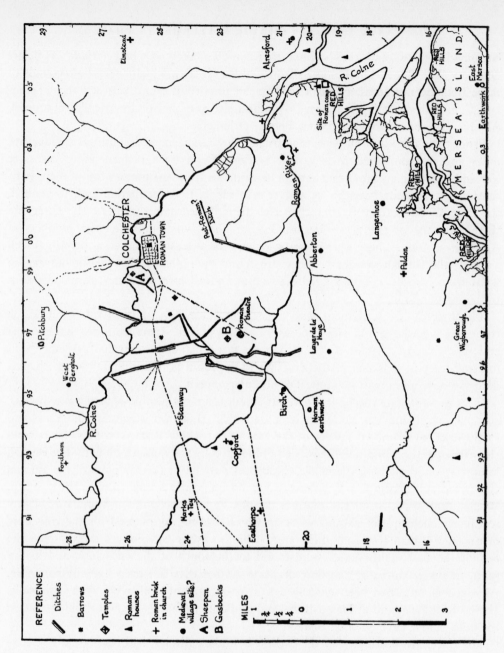

MAP E The Colchester Region

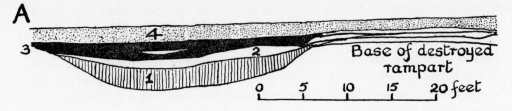

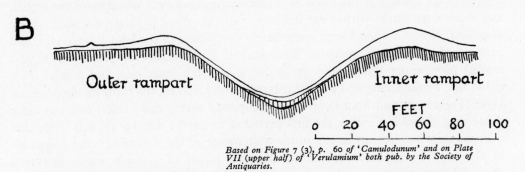

Based on Figure 7 (3), p. 60 of 'Camulodunum' and on Plate
VII (upper half) of 'Verulamium' both pub. by the Society of
Antiquaries.

FIG 12 Belgic Dykes. A. Sheepen Dyke defending the Belgic oppidum of Camulodunum (Colchester) of circa A.D. 10. Section showing: 1 silt; 2 material thrown into
the ditch when the rampart was destroyed; 3 subsequent occupation layers; 4
plough soil. B. Devil's Dyke, Wheathampstead, defending an oppidum of about
half a century earlier than Camulodunum. The ramparts are probably much reduced from their original height

central Hertfordshire to north-eastern Essex, in the territory of the Trinovantes, a
non-Belgic tribe. The Catuvellaunian king, Tasciovanus, from his base at the Prae
Wood oppidum, harried the Colchester region from about 15 B.C. and established
himself there for long enough to mint money locally. But the Belgic dynasty of Kent
under their king Dubnovellaunus seems to have ousted his rival temporarily in the
first decade A.D. and his coins have been found in some numbers near Colchester.
However, his main strength lay in Kent, much further away from the scene of operations than Prae Wood, and it was Tasciovanus's son, Cunobelin, who eventually
(c. A.D. 10) gained possession of the coveted region and set up in it a new capital
from which to rule a unified kingdom. This finally came to include most of south-
eastern Britain. Meanwhile, to the south of the Thames, the house of Commius was
pushing forward its frontiers towards the west.

On a plateau of well-drained gravel resting on stiff London Clay, bounded to the
north by the river Colne and to the south by its tributary the Roman river, Camulodunum was well sited for communication by sea with the Belgic settlements in Kent

and easy of access by land along the gravel terraces of the river valleys and the open chalk belt to the west, so that central Hertfordshire, now a region of dense occupation, provided a reservoir of manpower and a source of food during this new phase of expansion. The large promontory of land between the two rivers was cut at its base by an elaborate system of linear earthworks which controlled access from the west. The outermost dyke extends from north to south for three and a half miles; one of the inner lines of defence reaches beyond the two rivers and its extreme points are four and a half miles apart (Map E).

The area of about twelve square miles that is bounded by the dykes and the two rivers was not densely settled; as at Wheathampstead and Prae Wood there was arable, and pasture for cattle, within the defences, and the round or oval huts were widely dispersed. Near Sheepen Farm, immediately north-west of the later Roman city, and near a ford and springs, was the 'inner kernel' of the settlement. Here was built a smaller promontory fort, similar in all but size to the outer one, and protected on either side by the Colne and a small tributary brook and on the third by the Sheepen Dyke (Figure 12A and Map E, site A). Occupation within this smaller fort was more dense than elsewhere, and in the first period of its use (c. A.D. 10–43) it is likely that a Belgic mint was set up in the south-west corner of the defended area; fragments of coin-moulds, unstruck coin-flans, slag and pieces of crucible were discovered there. This mint appears to have been destroyed by the Romans.

But the earliest phase of Belgic occupation in the Colchester area is probably represented by a contour work, the Cheshunt Dyke (Stanway parish), the course of which is closely related to the lie of the land in the manner of the previous phases of the Iron Age. The later Belgic dykes of the neighbourhood are cut across country in straight alignments. Within the Cheshunt Dyke there was a square sacred enclosure bounded by a large ditch. Within it a Romano-Celtic temple and a theatre were constructed in the Roman period (at Gosbecks Farm. See Map E, site B). Little is visible of all this above ground, but the whole complex is likely to add to our knowledge of both periods when it has been fully explored. Indeed, vestiges of pre-Roman buildings on this large site suggest the possibility of its being the nucleus of the first local Belgic capital. The eastern defences of this nucleus may be the Berechurch Dyke which extends from the ford at Abberton to within a mile of the Roman city.

Even earlier than the Cheshunt complex are Pitchbury Ramparts (Great Horkesley), an unfinished plateau-fort more typical in size and situation of Iron Age A than C. The dykes mentioned earlier were designed to defend a large area from penetration by war chariots, a weapon highly developed by the Belgae. Pitchbury suggests that it may have been built as a protection by an early band of Belgic warriors, perhaps intent on the conquest of the region and safe in the knowledge that the native Trinovantes were not strong in chariotry. The rivalries presumed to have existed between the Belgic kingdoms, all so armed, would explain the need for the linear dykes of Colchester as well, perhaps, as those of Chichester and Silchester.

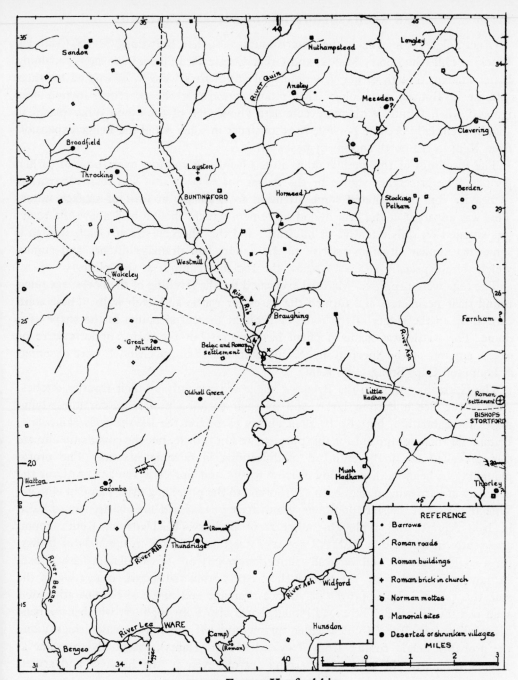

MAP F Eastern Hertfordshire

Other Belgic settlements in the eastern counties, such as Braughing (Herts) (Map F), Brockley Hill (Stanmore, Middx) and Great Chesterford (Essex), are now becoming better known, though earlier generations of antiquaries were so consumed by their interest in Roman archaeology that much concerning the preceding period was ignored when found. With more complete knowledge of these and other places it should eventually become possible to reconstruct in some detail the Belgic expansion from Kent to the north and north-westward.

The dwellings of this period show little advance in comfort over those of earlier periods. The preference shown by the Belgae for riverine sites and their occupation of heavier soils necessitated some attention to drainage, at least of surface water. This was apparent at the Prae Wood settlement which, though well above the river, was situated on soils retentive of moisture; and the Sheepen site at Colchester, in a somewhat similar situation relative to the Colne, had drainage ditches and sumps which were especially necessary below the 100-foot contour at this place.

The huts were primitive. Material excavated for the levelling of the floors was piled round their perimeters and formed the bases for wattle and daub walls. These were carried up to the ridges of the roofs or brought to central points in the shape of a dome. The wattle was made of pliant hazel wands but the main supports were of oak, at any rate on the Sheepen site. Similar huts and drainage channels were observed at Dumpton Gap (Broadstairs, Kent).

The Germanic strain in the Belgae is suggested not only by their frontier ditches, such as the Beech Bottom Dyke, and by their seeming preference for lower-lying places for habitation, but also by their ability to exploit the heavier soils of lowland Britain. Of their equipment for this purpose we know little, but the cool damp climate that prevailed no doubt enforced modifications in farming practice. The cross-ploughing of fields with a shallow furrow to stir and pulverize the soil, without the necessity of harrowing it, had been appropriate to the preceding drier phase of climate. With the onset of moister conditions, grain-drying ovens had already been introduced in Iron Age A, and a plough-coulter from Bigbury (Harbledown, Kent), found apparently in association with AB pottery, suggests a change in methods of tilling; for a coulter cuts the soil vertically immediately in front of the ploughshare which, in moving forward, turns the furrow-slice. Apart from the increased aeration of the soil, this process also improves its surface drainage and makes the preparation of a seed-bed much easier. The broad ploughshares also from Bigbury, which have been assigned to Iron Age C, cut a wider furrow and left the soil in wider ridges; and the probably Belgic coulter from Twyford Down (Hants), essentially the same as a modern one, would have cut a strong furrow even in the heaviest and stiffest soils.

It is unlikely, however, that wheels were fitted to Belgic ploughs. The discovery of a flint-paved road at Willbury and of one with a gravel surface on the Sheepen site suggest the use of wheeled vehicles in this period even if there were no literary references to chariots. But a wheeled plough is less handy implement than a wheel-less on sticky soils, and there is no evidence to suggest the use of the former by Belgic times.

No doubt the Belgae in some places took over the Celtic fields of the uplands (as at Twyford, Odiham and King's Worthy (Hants)) and perhaps continued with the old agricultural practices. But on much of the South Downs and on the chalk of Hampshire and Berkshire the natives may have maintained their former way of life little affected by their new masters; even the Romans caused few changes in their existence. As a lowland people it is unlikely that the Belgae greatly coveted the down-land farms and in some areas it would have been possible for the two peoples, the AB and the C, to coexist with little competition between them. On Twyford Down long strip fields, hardly to be distinguished from those usually assigned to Saxon and medieval times, have been shown to be of Belgic date and may have been cultivated by the people who in about 50 B.C. seized the originally Iron Age A farmstead nearby. The development of strip-cultivation was a consequence of the abandonment of cross-ploughing, which is more conveniently done where the field is a square. The strip had the advantage of requiring fewer turns of the ox-team, thus economizing in time and effort.

That Belgic agriculture produced a surplus, at least to basic needs, is clear from the volume of trade carried on with the Continent. The Greek Strabo speaks of exports of cattle, corn and leather, besides slaves, whose manacles have been found at Big-bury and in the Belgic levels at Park Street (St. Stephen's, Herts). In exchange manufactured goods, especially pottery, and luxuries such as brooches, and wine in great amphorae, were imported. The fine coinage of the Belgic kings in gold, silver, tin and bronze facilitated trade and continued to be held in esteem for a considerable time after A.D. 43.

The first large-scale production of pottery for market had begun in Iron Age A when the fine haematite-coated wares had stimulated a widespread demand. South-eastern B wares were produced in quantity at Horsted Keynes (Sussex). Almost contemporary with the latter industry, in the century before the Roman conquest, there was a considerable expansion of the potting industry; output was much in-creased and some standardization was achieved by the use of the potter's wheel. One of the largest centres of production was at Colchester. Alongside the coarse hand-made pottery that every housewife could fashion, there was much use in the eastern and south-eastern Belgic areas of the fine pear-shaped pedestal urns and of flagons, plates, beakers, bowls, storage-jars and cooking-pots, almost all of them of a shape attractive to the modern eye. Some were grooved or cordoned with pleasing regularity; others were combed horizontally as they spun on the wheel or were striated off the wheel in patterns not quite regular. Rims were given every conceivable form, and when fired, pots might vary in hue from a dull orange through brown to grey or black according to the materials and processes employed.

The repertory of shapes was much influenced by Roman or Roman-provincial models imported in quantity before the conquest; and Belgic styles continued in use for long after the first mass importations from Italy and Gaul. The importation of these Arretine and Gallo-Belgic wares affords some criterion of date for a deposit according to whether they are present or absent, though lack of them may obviously be due to a cause other than that the deposit was formed before the earliest years of their importation. In archaeology as in all other branches of study it is unsound to argue from negative evidence. However, these imported wares first make their appearance in south-eastern Britain in the last quarter of the first century B.C., as for example at Prae Wood; and, as their forms and fabric can be matched on closely dated Continental sites, they sometimes provide a relatively fixed point in the time-scale for Britain. Their stratified position on any south-eastern occupation site is therefore always a matter of importance in working out its chronology.

Another industry that expanded greatly in Belgic times was salt-making. Evidence for it in Iron Age A has come from the coasts of Norfolk and Lincolnshire; in Iron Age C there are abundant indications of it in many coastal parishes of Essex (Map E). The 'Red Hills', so called from the briquetage and reddish burnt earth found in and near them, are most reasonably explained as sites where salt was extracted from sea-water by boiling. Further signs of this industry have been discovered on both sides of the Thames estuary. It is possible that the curing of fish was carried on at the same sites.

Salt-making had a vital importance for peoples deprived of fresh meat for almost half the year. It certainly continued in Roman times, for pottery of that period has been recovered from Red Hills in the parishes of Burnham and Goldhanger in Essex; and in Saxon times there is documentary allusion to it at least from the early eighth century onwards, culminating in the many references in the Domesday Book (A.D. 1086) to holdings of land responsible for saltpans. Moreover place-names such as Salcott (Essex) and Saltcote (Playden, Sussex) afford clues to the location of some medieval brine-boiling sites. The Gazetteer notes many similar place-names.

Evidence of iron-smelting has come from many domestic sites of all the three main phases of the Iron Age, but large-scale extraction of ore and its processing does not seem to have occurred before about the middle of the first century B.C. The bloomeries were situated near streams and close to deposits of ironstone; and in the Weald good local supplies of wood for charcoal fuel were readily available. Sites are normally revealed by the scatter of iron-cinder on ploughed land. The deeper ploughing of recent times may be expected to afford indications of new sites, especially those more deeply overlaid by soil washed down to the lower slopes of valleys where the blooming often took place.

The Weald was scarcely penetrated by the Belgae, and the South-eastern B sites noted earlier (e.g. Kirdford and Saxonbury, Sussex) were mainly contemporaneous with Belgic occupation of Kent and west Sussex. No doubt the newcomers eventually laid the natives under tribute of which iron formed a part; and it is certain that Belgic influence, at least in potting styles, had penetrated to some of the bloomeries (e.g. Bynes Farm, Crowhurst) by the first century A.D. Finished products in iron were of high artistic quality. Apart from sword-blades, the tires of chariots, ploughshares coulters and other tools and implements of common use, fire-dogs with finials wrought into stylistic bulls' heads were made from the product of the bloomeries. The fire-dogs gave opportunity for an expression of the delight taken by Belgic craftsmen in animal forms. Usually these forms are much stylized as in the insect-like horses on the bronze bucket-mounts from the cemetery at Aylesford (Kent) or the White Horse cut in the turf on the chalk-scarp at Uffington (Berks) or the bronze boars from Hounslow (Middx).

Much of our knowledge of Belgic pottery and metalwork comes from cemeteries; settlements were so often overlaid by Roman or later occupation that much material of this period had been found and removed long before modern investigators could get to work. The burial-rite was almost invariably cremation. Among the rare exceptions were inhumations on Battery Hill, Winchester, and a doubtfully Belgic instance at Eastbourne (Sussex). The latter was accompanied by an imitation Belgic beaker of barrel shape (a 'butt-beaker') which does not necessarily imply that it was interred with a Belgic corpse. It was more probably a burial of one of the South-eastern B folk.

The custom of cremation suggests an inheritance from the Germanic forebears of the Belgae; inhumation was the normal practice among the more purely Celtic tribes of Iron Ages A and B. The ashes of the dead were placed in shapely urns, often in the south-eastern counties with a pedestal foot. Usually no mound was put over the burial-place though some kind of marker was probably used, otherwise later interments would have disturbed earlier ones. As, however, at Aylesford (Kent) some of the urns were arranged in irregular rings, and since it is unlikely that all in each ring were buried at the same time, some mark of the position of each must have been used.

More sumptuous interments, almost certainly members of the Catuvellaunian princely family, are exemplified by the two burial vaults discovered at Welwyn (Herts). They were made in the second half of the first century B.C. Among the funeral furniture were three pairs of fire-dogs and an iron frame which had probably been part of a sacrificial table. There were also imported vessels of bronze and of silver, some of them already antique at the time of their deposition. Six *amphorae* (large storage vessels) had contained wine or oil and were ultimately of Mediterranean origin. Six *amphorae*, fire-dogs with ox-head terminals, and many vessels now lost, were discovered in a triangular vault at Mount Bures (Essex). Extensive rectangular vaults with these and other furnishings such as roasting spits, came to light at Stanfordbury (Beds), outside our region. Among the vessels were Samian dishes which point to a date for the interment about A.D. 50; and they illustrate the persistence of Belgic customs after the Roman conquest.

One such custom was the erection of a large tumulus above a princely interment;

and this, too, persisted among the native nobility into the first and second centuries A.D. The most notable instance is that at Lexden (Essex), perhaps that of King Cunobelin himself (obit. *c.* A.D. 40). With a diameter of about 100 feet and 9 feet high, the barrow was surrounded by an irregular ditch. Near the centre was an oval grave, 30 feet by 18, and 7 feet beneath the old land surface. The large vault was probably necessitated by the inclusion of a chariot of which iron fragments survived. The funeral furniture included chain-mail, bronzes from Italy, and figures of animals, among which is a realistic boar in the classical, not the usual Belgic, style. Most interesting of all was a Roman coin minted in 17 B.C., bearing the portrait of Augustus, which had been mounted in a disc.

In the western areas nothing so elaborate has yet come to light. Single cremation burials occurred at Bitterne and Winchester (Hants), contained in bead-rim bowls; and others have been found in Dorset and Somerset. More comparable with the princely burials of the eastern areas was that found at Hurstbourne Tarrant (Hants), beneath a barrow 27 feet across and only 40 inches high. The burnt bones were contained in a wooden bucket bound with bronze and iron strips, some of them bearing dot-and-ring patterns. A fragmentary thistle brooch of the late first century B.C., of a kind rare in Britain, and over a dozen pots, including imports from Gaul, were the chief objects found. One of the vessels has a pedestal added to a more normal western-Belgic shape, producing a very ugly form, but indicating influence from the eastern region. This cremation interment is almost contemporary with that at Lexden (*c.* A.D. 40).

These funerary deposits suggest that Belgic princes looked forward to an afterlife in which feasting had no small part. Kitchen equipment, stores of food, drink and table utensils were buried with them in the expectation of their future use. But Belgic religious sites afford no further clues to their beliefs. Indeed, only one structure has so far been certainly identified, namely that underlying the Romano-Celtic temple on the Gosbecks Farm site (Cheshunt Field) at Colchester (Map E, site B). Elsewhere, as at Worth (Kent), Belgic wares and pottery of the earlier phases of the Iron Age were found beneath a Roman temple, but continuity in the religious use of this site is hypothetical. Where such continuity is probable, as at Frilford (Berks), Belgic material is absent. A ritual pit, probably of the first century A.D., has more recently come to light near Sandwich (Kent), but the contained potsherds and animal remains afford no information concerning its significance.

The movement of refugees into Hampshire and Berkshire could have resulted in little displacement of the native AB population; but, as had happened to so many earlier peoples, they merely changed their masters. Their bead-rim pots could now be turned on a fast wheel, though many domestic vessels continued to be shaped by hand. New forms made possible by the wheel were, however, added to the potter's repertory. The native chieftains had gone westward and north-westward, themselves refugees.

In south-eastern Britain, on the other hand, one would have expected the mass immigrations of the Belgae to have caused a widespread displacement of the natives. But this did not occur everywhere, even in areas densely settled by the Belgae. In east Kent, for instance, 'pottery of native character appears along with the Belgic fabrics at Broadstairs, Margate, Walmer and other places'. The same is true of the oppidum at Bigbury (Harbledown). But, it must be added, in no single instance is it certain that A and C pottery was in use at the same time; that remains no more than a possibility. Northern Middlesex (the Brockley Hill settlement) and southern Hertfordshire (Prae Wood, Wheathampstead, Braughing and Welwyn) seem to have had no permanent occupants before the Belgae. The sherds of the A2 phase from the Park Street villa site are the only vestiges of previous occupation in the St. Albans neighbourhood known to me; and by themselves they are of minor significance. Indeed, this region, with its extensive primeval woodland, was not likely to have attracted tillers of light soils like the Hallstatt tribes; and the Belgae no doubt found an almost empty countryside when they reached it. Here then was no competition for living-space and no displacement of natives.

On the Sheepen site (Colchester) the last settlers before the Belgae had been a Hallstatt group of the Late Bronze-Early Iron Age transition period. After them, in spite of extensive excavation, there is a blank in the archaeological record until Belgic times. The Trinovantes of Essex were no doubt conquered and absorbed, but there was probably no displacement of them from what was to become the Belgic capital.

It is most likely, then, that the Iron Age A and AB peoples were little disturbed after the first impact of the invaders. The two could live side by side and ultimately merge because their traditional ways of life led them to inhabit different types of country. The Weald, East Sussex, much of Surrey and of west Kent preserved their modified Iron Age AB culture with only superficial borrowings from the Belgae. The Germanic strain in the latter was probably responsible for this difference between the economies of the two peoples, but that strain was not so strong that it had changed the Celtic speech of the Belgae; and, though their dialect may have diverged from that of the natives, there was sufficient community of language, if not of ideas and institutions, for the two peoples to coalesce. So the basic continuity of population asserted itself as it seems to have done after every immigration from the Late Palaeolithic onwards.

And there can be little question at all that the bulk of the population of the south-east remained unchanged in all essentials after the Roman conquest. There were refugees, no doubt, who willingly lost their identity as enemies of Rome among the hill-tribes of the west and north; there was heavy mortality among the Britons wherever they put up a fierce resistance to the legions. The war cemetery at Maiden Castle affords clear evidence of this as probably do the numerous burials after battle at Sutton Walls (Herefordshire) and Bredon Hill (Worcestershire).* The Belgae, ever

* At Oldbury in west Kent, Belgic resistance to the legions is indicated by remodelling of the defences and an unsuccessful defence is betokened by the burning down of the north-east gate.

the most bitter opponents of Rome, suffered more heavily even than the western tribes, though the Regni of Sussex and the non-Belgic Iceni of Norfolk, as Roman allies during the conquest, gained materially at first from their loyalty to the Roman cause.

Time-expired legionaries were established in the Colonia of *Camulodunum*, and merchants and administrators settled there and elsewhere in Britain; but few of these were Romans in the more limited acceptance of the name. They were in any case a tiny minority in the land at any one time. The peasants and the villa proprietors were natives, of whom the richer acquired a thin veneer of Mediterranean culture including Latin speech beside their own Celtic dialects. But even as late as the second century A.D. the country gentry were still being buried beneath large barrows like some of their Belgic forefathers; and the upland peasants maintained their old farming practices little touched by Roman custom.

It seems likely that some of the villas were direct successors to Belgic farmsteads. In Hertfordshire the villas at Park Street and Lockleys (Welwyn) overlay Belgic huts. Their pottery was found on the villa site at Ashtead (Surrey). A dwelling of the South-eastern B people preceded the Otford villa in Kent; at Lullingstone nearby there was a hiatus in the occupation of the villa site between Belgic and Romano-British times. A Belgic homestead and a villa occurred near together at Twyford (Hants); and at Headbourne Worthy and Odiham in the same county the farmsteads show a sequence of occupation from Iron Age A through AB and C to Romano-British. Moreover, Belgic relics occurred beneath the Romano-British hamlet at Hambledon (Bucks).

Such evidence, mainly from pottery, does no more than demonstrate that these sites were inhabited in both periods; continuity of settlement is another matter and one difficult to prove. In many instances it may mean no more than a similarity in choice of a place to live and work; and as the population remained basically the same such a similarity should cause no surprise.

BIBLIOGRAPHY TO CHAPTER X

C. F. C. Hawkes and G. C. Dunning, 'The Belgae of Gaul and Britain', in *Archaeological Journal*, 87 (1931), is fundamental to a study of this period. R. E. M. Wheeler in *Maiden Castle* (1943), pp. 58 f. and 237–8, seeks to modify the belief in a second Belgic invasion, resting his case mainly on a further study of the western Belgic pottery. D. Allen, 'The Belgic Dynasties of Britain and their Coins', in *Archaeologia*, 90 (1944), throws new light on political events and on tribal boundaries. The Prae Wood and Wheathampstead oppida are described in Wheeler's *Verulamium* (1936), the 11*th Report of the Research Committee of the Society of Antiquaries*; and *Camulodunum* (1947), the 14*th Report* of the same body, by C. F. C. Hawkes and M. R. Hull, describes the earlier discoveries at Colchester. Both of these reports are finely illustrated and are of the greatest value and interest. The Aylesford urn cemetery is described in *Archaeologia*, 52, part 2 (1890), and that at Swarling in the *5th Research Report* (1925), by J. P. Bushe-Fox. On the princely burial vaults see *Archaeologia*, 63 (1912). A short account of Belgic metalcraft is to be had in *The Heritage of Early Britain* (1952), chapter III, by J. M. de Navarro. See also the general and local works cited in the general bibliography for further details.

* An inexpensive work.

I

CHAPTER XI

The Roman Occupation

THE ARCHAEOLOGY OF Roman Britain is such a vast topic that it can here be touched upon only lightly. In recent years several good and inexpensive books have been produced by acknowledged authorities, and from these it should be possible to obtain a clear notion of the relationship of south-eastern England to the rest of Britain during the period. Their titles are given at the end of this chapter.

Already before the Claudian invasion Romanization had been going on apace, and the Roman commanders of A.D. 43 must have had fairly accurate information concerning the topography of the land and of prevailing political conditions. Ample intelligence was to be had from merchants and from exiles who had been ousted in Cunobelin's rise to power. The landing itself was delayed by the reluctance of the legions to leave the known world of Gaul for what to them was a fearful unknown. The Britons, expecting a longer respite, did not assemble a force to oppose the landing, which was made near Richborough. There shelter was found from storms such as had brought Caesar near to disaster during his British campaigns; and this safe anchorage afforded a base from which operations could be conducted in the knowledge that the supply-lines to Gaul were relatively safe.

With Cunobelin recently dead and his sons Togodumnus and Caratacus not yet securely in control, the Roman forces were not long in advancing to the Thames and beyond, thus driving a wedge between Caratacus' territory in Essex and Hertfordshire and that of Togodumnus in Hampshire and Surrey. The advance to Camulodunum and its capture were achieved under the command of the Emperor Claudius himself.

The non-Belgic tribes, who hated Belgic oppression more than they feared Roman domination, made their peace with the invaders, and Cogidumnus of the Regni (west Sussex) and Prasutagus of the Iceni (East Anglia) were among the first to do so. The adherence of these two rulers gave some security to the Roman flanks. But there was one people, the Wealden Folk, who had here and there retained their independence of the Belgae though hemmed in by them on east, north and west. They too seem to have resisted Roman aggression with some pertinacity. They greatly strengthened the Caburn ramparts, but the hill-fort fell to a disciplined attack after the timber gateway had been destroyed by fire. At Oldbury (Ightham, Kent), where the Belgae had only shortly before taken control from the Wealden Folk, resistance was equally vain and the same attempt at defence followed by defeat may have occurred to a group of the Wealden Folk in the hill-fort known as High Rocks in Frant (Sussex).

130

Even of this earliest Roman phase some visible relics remain. At Richborough (Kent) a rampart with two defensive ditches on its western side runs for over 720 yards, curving at its northern and southern ends to reach the seashore. Thus was created a promontory fort with a central entrance through the earthwork. The Iron Age A people had occupied the site several centuries before and their ditches and domestic rubbish came to light over a large area. And here it was that the Romans established a main shore-base. Traces of military depots have been found also at Fingringhoe (Essex), the port for Camulodunum, and at Heybridge (Essex) on the Blackwater estuary (Plate 15).

It has been argued that more than one landing was made in A.D. 43 and that one of them went ashore in the territory of the Regni. From there a rapid westward advance was possible along the ancient trackways on the downs of Sussex, Hampshire, Dorset and Wiltshire. But a permanent line of communication was soon built across the difficult country of the Weald to the crossing of the Thames near London. Unlike other roads in the south-east, the Stane Street had primarily a military purpose. Along its course at Hardham and Alfoldean (Slinfold parish), both in Sussex, and possibly at Dorking and Morden in Surrey, there are minor forts set across its line which, in the first two instances, have yielded much pottery of the mid-first century A.D. The forts were made at the same time as the road and their function was as bases for the troops patrolling it. Later they became posting stations (*mansiones*) each with an inn and ancillary buildings for the use of imperial messengers and presumably for merchants and travellers of all kinds.

The Hardham station was in use from *c.* A.D. 50 to 150, when it was possibly succeeded by a *mansio* near Pulborough, a locality showing many signs of Roman settlement. The Alfoldean station, however, continued to afford protection to its occupants until the fourth century. The sites of other posting stations probably exist at Iping (Sussex), Cheshunt (Herts), St. Mary Bourne and Sherborne St. John (Hants) and Speen (Berks). Some of the minor Roman towns such as Braughing (Herts), Great Dunmow (Essex) and Staines (Middx) may also have served the same purpose. All are on Roman roads and all but the first are conveniently situated for a break of journey between two larger Roman towns.

The Watling Street and its branches which converge on Canterbury (*Durovernum Cantiacorum*) and goes thence to Rochester (*Durobrivae*) to London (*Londinium*), St. Albans (*Verulamium*), Dunstable (*Durocobrivae*) and the north-west, was also built during the course of the conquest as a line of communication for the legions advancing in that direction. It traversed regions densely settled by the Belgae and soon attracted to its line numerous small settlements, at Faversham, Sittingbourne, Northfleet (*Vagniacae*) in Kent, Charlton in the county of London, Brockley Hill, Stanmore (*Sulloniacae*) in Middlesex and others beyond. Some of these no doubt served as *mansiones*, but others (e.g. Sittingbourne and Charlton) grew up beside the road to reap commercial advantage from the traffic passing along it to and from Gaul and

Italy. In some sections the route coincided with clay suitable for potting and areas of forest from which to obtain fuel for the kilns. There, as at Brockley Hill and north of the road near Upchurch (Kent), minor centres of pot-making were established to have the benefit of the road for the distribution of their fragile wares.

Only a few generations after the conquest roads were made across the Weald to afford easy transport of pig-iron from the bloomeries. Access to London and to quays on the rivers Brede, Rother and Ouse in east Sussex, or to the sea near Brighton, was thus made possible. Slag from the bloomeries was utilized in the making of these roads, of which the London-Lewes way via Ashdown Forest has been dated to the later first century. The London-Brighton way and that running south from Rochester to Maidstone and the heads of the east Sussex estuaries have not yet been dated. Older trackways running east and west linked these roads, and in mid-Kent a system of metalled tracks helped to fill out the complex of communications of the Wealden area.

There is little doubt that the North Downs trackway continued in use during the Roman period; and the ridgeway along the South Downs provided local links between one place and another. More important, however, was the Sussex Greensand Way from Barcombe near Lewes to Streat and Hassocks and thence via Washington to the Stane Street near Pulborough. This ancient trackway was metalled for most of its length and may have served primarily for the transport of farm produce. Along the coastal plain from Brighton to the Stane Street near Chichester extended another metalled road which connected the numerous Roman farming estates (villas) of the plain with their market for produce at Chichester (*Regnum*).

Silchester (*Calleva Atrebatum*), Winchester (*Venta Belgarum*) and to a smaller extent Colchester (*Camulodunum*) became route centres with metalled roads radiating from them in five or six directions. Braughing (Herts), where there had been considerable Belgic occupation, developed into a minor centre and posting-station at the convergence of six roads (Map F). To the east, in Essex, a network grew up scarcely inferior to that of the extreme south-east and necessitated by the numerous villas and hamlets of the Romanized natives which covered much of the region. Some of these roads were probably constructed during the first century in order to render commercial exploitation easier; but the Boudiccan revolt of A.D. 61 demonstrated the necessity of good communications for policing the province.

The small Roman town at Dorchester-on-Thames functioned as a market for farm produce and for locally manufactured pottery and also, it seems, as the headquarters of a Roman official to whom was delegated the duty of policing the land and river routes which here converge. Besides the rivers Thames and Thame and a north-south road, the Icknield Way and the Berkshire ridgeway all meet in this locality; and it is probable that older, unmetalled tracks maintained their value, at least for local journeys, especially along the scarp-foot of the chalk in Berkshire, Oxfordshire and Buckinghamshire, where Romano-British settlement-sites occur in some numbers.

The beginnings of the major towns are obscure. The sites of Colchester, Rochester, Chichester, Winchester and probably Silchester had attracted Belgic settlers, and in some instances (e.g. Canterbury, Chichester, Colchester) may have been continuously occupied from Iron Age A onwards; and Belgic Verulamium (Prae Wood) was very near to its Roman successors. But the site of London, so far as present evidence goes, had few if any permanent inhabitants before the Roman occupation. Pottery of the South-eastern B Folk has indeed turned up in small quantities, but this and Belgic wares from the city were probably in use after A.D. 43; the South Gaulish pottery found there need be no earlier. But, even if London was not settled before Roman times, it certainly became the major route centre very early in the period. During the earlier phases of the conquest it served as a military supply-base for the armies advancing in separate columns to the north, north-west and west; and the fort recently discovered in the Cripplegate area of the city may well have originated at this time as an earthen camp. A century later, or thereabouts, it was strengthened with stone walls.

The major towns began to develop quite early as instruments of Romanization, but to some of them came a severe setback at the time of the Icenian rebellion in A.D. 61. At Colchester both the Sheepen site, which had become an industrial area, and the new undefended *Colonia*, were destroyed before hasty attempts at defence could be made effective. The same fate befell the *municipium* of Verulamium and the villa at Park Street nearby; and great slaughter and destruction were wrought also in London. But reconstruction and revival were rapid. London soon supplanted Colchester as the chief city of the province, and by the end of the first century it had become a garrison town. As we have seen, by about A.D. 140 the Cripplegate fort was enclosed with a stone wall; and the civilian nucleus, situated along the Wallbrook, steadily grew, though it is unlikely that the whole area within the city wall was ever filled by buildings. The city wall was built in the second century to join up with the north-east and south-west corners of the stone fort, whose strengthened western and northern walls then became one with the city defences. This outer line continued to define the limits of the city almost to the sixteenth century, when the Roman wall-base supported a much-patched and repaired medieval rampart.

The story of Verulamium has some points in common with that of London. It was probably after the disaster of A.D. 61 that the newly discovered fort at Verulamium was constructed and it is likely that it occupied the south-west corner of the earthen rampart which was put round the first of the two Roman cities in the late first century. The western angle of this early rampart is still visible projecting beyond the line of the late second-century wall and bank of the second city. The latter came into being in the second quarter of the second century with a major replanning. The new site was much greater in area and extended along the line of the Watling Street, partly overlapping the area of the first city. The later town wall with its towers and the foundations of a main gateway can best be seen on the short southern side of the town (Plate 17).

Considerable portions of the walls of Roman Colchester also survive and are probably of the same date. The defences of Silchester have a more complex history. An outer ditch visible on aerial photographs may prove to be of a pre-Roman defensive system. Certainly the earlier grid of streets round the forum, in the centre of the town, appears to bear no relation to these prehistoric defences. The later grid, planned *c.* A.D. 90–120, is, however, equally ill at ease within the main Roman defences, most of which are still clearly visible. An inner bank and ditch have been dated by modern excavation to *c.* A.D. 160–170 and the stone wall with its gates and earthen rampart belong somewhere in the decades 190 to 210. Of approximately the same period are the walls of Winchester, Canterbury and Chichester. The wall of Roman London was built about A.D. 120. Of the smaller towns, Great Chesterford (Essex) was not walled before the early third century, no doubt as part of the same military programme that was devised for Silchester and other large towns. *Clausentum* (Bitterne, Hants), on the other hand, appears to have gained its walls as late as *c.* 370, by which time raids by Saxon and Frankish pirates were sorely harassing the province. The town was so accessible to sea-raiders that it is a matter for wonder that it had not been protected before.

Of the *fora*, amphitheatres, temples and houses that existed within or just outside the towns, nothing can here be said, even though the excavated remains of many of these structures are to be seen or are known to exist in our region. Their functions and their relationships to the political and economic history of Roman Britain are described in the general works cited at the end of this chapter; their locations and in some instances the date of their construction will be found in the Gazetteer.

The concept of urban life was as foreign to the Romano-Britons as it was later to the Anglo-Saxons. Their sense of community found expression in membership of a homestead or perhaps of a hamlet whose *raison d'être* was the cultivation of the soil. Even the Belgic oppida, with their hovels scattered over a wide area among pasture and arable, had more in common with the later unnucleated villages characteristic of such forested regions as the Weald, than with a Romano-British tribal centre such as Silchester, or with a medieval country town. Urban life was imposed upon the Britons as part of a deliberate policy of Romanization; the towns did not come into being in response to economic needs. But they came for a time to fulfil such needs, especially as market-places, where goods could be exchanged. They gave shelter to specialist craftsmen, potters and metalworkers, for instance, whose convenience was better served by a concourse of customers; and from the late second century, with increasing danger in the countryside from barbarian raids, they served as safe refuges for wealthy landowners who would prefer heavy municipal taxation to the delights of villa life which might suddenly end in slavery in some Germanic village beyond the reach of the *pax Romana*.

Roman Britain was at heart a rural province and even within the walls of its towns the widely spaced houses set amidst gardens had more of a rural than an urban aspect.

Only in and near the forum, with its monumental basilica, temples and baths, was there any true reflection of the Latin *civitas*. But if Verulamium be typical of the south-east, the blandishments of town life were of little avail. The prosperity it enjoyed in the second century was followed in the later third century (*c.* 275) by a widespread decline of civic pride among the city fathers; and recovery in the fourth century was brief, for it apparently endured no longer than the initial impulse given to reconstruction by the Emperor Constantius after the recovery of Britain from the usurper Allectus. The city defences were overhauled, the theatre was rebuilt and enlarged, new houses were put up and old ones restored. But by the middle of the fourth century much of the town was deserted and in ruins; the theatre had become a rubbish-dump; and the citizens were living as squatters in the shells of the buildings. Something similar may be deduced from the earlier and less scientific excavation of Silchester.

All of this is in striking contrast with conditions in the countryside where the vast majority of Britons lived. Here the veneer of Romanization was even thinner and continuity with past modes of living and thinking much stronger than in the towns. The majority of country folk were peasants dwelling in small hamlets or, more probably, in isolated farmsteads. Their existence was in all essentials similar to that of their ancestors before the imposition of Roman rule; a few of the cheaper mass-produced luxuries such as pottery and trinkets were within their reach, and life for a time was more placid with the enforced cessation of inter-tribal warfare.

The farm on Rockbourne Down (Hants), the best-known example, is situated within a kite-shaped enclosure of ninety-six acres whose southern point takes in a large spring-pond. At the northern end was a mud-walled hut, the farmhouse; and near it, one inside and the other outside the enclosure, were two corn-drying ovens, originally misinterpreted as hypocausts for warming the house. The farm itself was surrounded by a smaller kite-shaped earthwork which presumably functioned as a farmyard, for this was mainly a stock-farm. It appears to have been occupied mainly in the fourth century at which time there appears to have been a change-over from the production of crops to stock-raising, at any rate in Cranborne Chase and the areas bordering it. Three miles to the south-west of Rockbourne Down, in the parish of Damerham, there is another kite-shaped cattle enclosure, smaller but better preserved. This encloses two springs and was made subsequently to the cultivation of Celtic fields whose lynchets may be seen from the air to pass under its banks (Figure 13). Here is visual evidence for the change in farming practice in late Roman times. Probably of this period also is the irregular enclosure at Sloden, near Fritham in the New Forest, where superimposed earthworks of four widely separated periods may be seen.

Not unlike these was the farmstead on Roden Down in the Berkshire parish of Compton, completely destroyed by ploughing. But only three-quarters of a mile to the north-east, on Lowbury Hill (Aston Upthorpe) is a small rectangular earthwork, or rather a ruined flint wall covered with turf. The site had been occupied in the

Iron Age from phase A2 onwards, but the enclosure was not built until the fourth century A.D. when the homestead is thought to have become a cattle farm dependent on an estate in the Thames valley below. This site continued to be occupied for an indeterminate period after the end of Roman rule in Britain. Later a pagan Saxon was buried in a barrow just outside the gateway of the farmyard. With him was placed a hanging bowl which had been looted from a Roman country house, perhaps one of those that are known to have existed in the Thames valley below Lowbury.

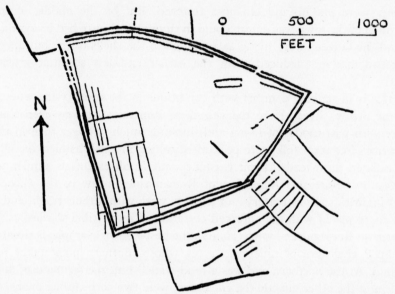

Based on Crawford, 'Archaeology in the Field', Figure 12, originally published in 'Wessex from the Air', O.U.P.

FIG 13 The Soldiers Ring, South Damerham, Hants. A Romano-British pastoral enclosure overlying earlier Celtic fields. This superimposition of earthworks is indicative of the change over from arable farming to stock raising in the late Roman period

Yet further to the north, at Long Wittenham, in a neighbourhood where many vestiges of prehistoric and Romano-British occupation are visible from the air, a hamlet has been excavated. Recent aerial observation has revealed, in addition, a stockaded enclosure which was probably ancillary to this settlement; moreover, near this stockade is a rectangular enclosure with a gateway which is not unlike the earthworks that surround the Ditchley and other villas in western Oxfordshire. On the Berkshire Downs between Streatley and Ashbury over a dozen square miles of Celtic fields are visible, though this is but a remnant that the modern plough has spared. Some of these fields no doubt began to be formed in the Iron Age; but it was in the Roman period that downland arable farming attained its greatest extent.

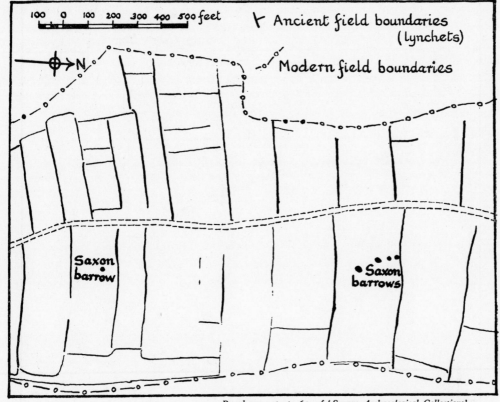

100 0 100 200 300 400 500 feet

Y Ancient field boundaries (lynchets)

-o⁻ Modern field boundaries

Saxon barrow

Saxon barrows

Based on map, p. 64, of 'Surrey Archaeological Collections', Vol. 50.

FIG 14 Iron Age and Romano-British field-system, Farthingdown, Coulsdon, Surrey

In central Sussex alone, on the Downs between the Adur and Ouse, at least thirty-two sites of Romano-British peasant occupation are known; and nearly one-fifth of this area still bears traces of Celtic fields. Here, as in Berkshire, recent ploughing has destroyed large tracts of early cultivation banks and rendered them invisible except from the air. The farm on Thundersbarrow Hill, Shoreham, with its lynchetted fields, cart-tracks, sites of wattle and daub huts, corn-drying ovens and grain-storage pits, is very much like those of the A and B phases of the Iron Age, though it could be shown to belong to almost the whole duration of the Roman era, but not before. And this similarity is certainly indicative of the continuity of peasant life from the fourth century B.C. to the fifth century A.D. That continuity was scarcely broken in many regions in spite of tribal warfare and successive influxes of new peoples from the Continent.

Several other Romano-British homesteads have been investigated in downland Sussex (e.g. at Eartham and Harting); and recent fieldwork in Surrey, especially in the Dorking, Leatherhead, Caterham and Coulsdon areas, has brought to light the

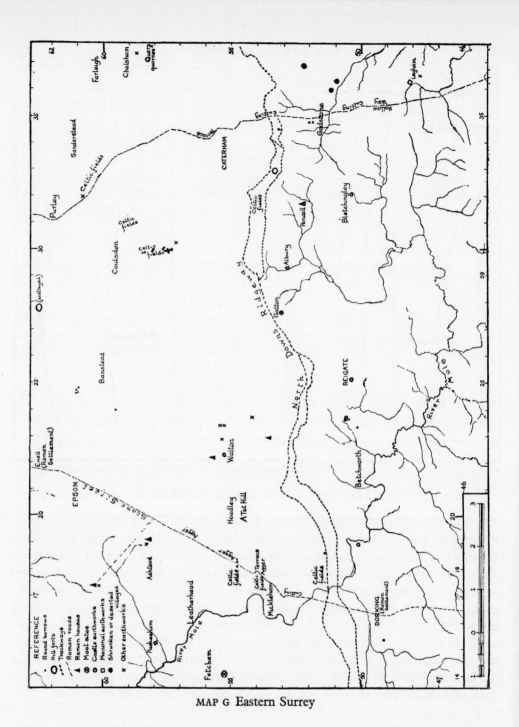

MAP G Eastern Surrey

sites of several Romano-British farms as well as a contemporary field-system on Farthingdown (Figure 14 and Map G). There are indications also of late Iron Age occupation of the same region. In Kent, on the other hand, the evidence for peasant farming is scanty. A kite-shaped earthwork, comparable with that at Damerham, has been largely destroyed in recent years in Mangravet Wood, Maidstone. It is situated in a neighbourhood rich in finds of the Roman period and it was one much favoured by the wealthier Britons whose villas have been located on both sides of the Medway from Nettlestead to Frindsbury. But Celtic fields are strangely rare on the North Downs, even in east Kent where there are considerable areas of chalk free from over-lying clay-with-flints. A few lynchets occur at Godmersham and round Wye; and those associated with Hulberry, the hill-fort of the South-eastern B Folk in Lullingstone parish, no doubt continued in use during Roman times. There are, moreover, several rectangular enclosures which are more likely to be of this period than of any other. There is one at Bishopsbourne near Romano-British barrows and another at Ospringe in an area of dense settlement. Yet others at Coldred, Eastry, Hunton, Farningham and Mark Beech may be further instances, though there is as much doubt concerning them as there is of the fields observed from the air just to the south-east of Chatham.

Evidence for native farmsteads is slight throughout the former eastern Belgic areas and those settled by the South-eastern B Folk. Very many parishes have yielded traces of Romano-British occupation, and throughout those areas, in Kent, Surrey, Essex, Herts and Bucks, the villa-estate, with its headquarters in a building normally suggesting wealthy owners, seems to have been usual. Many of the indeterminate occu-pation sites, or the cemeteries which attest their presence, may represent the flimsy wattle and daub dwellings of people dependent on a villa. But there is still much to be learnt concerning the organization and farming methods of the villa-estates. Probably only aerial photography can supply the information if it is still recoverable.

In the western Belgic areas, Hampshire, Berkshire, west Sussex and west Surrey, villas are numerous also; and here too native farmsteads have been located. Generaliza-tion is hazardous without a detailed investigation of the sites of large numbers of them, but on the face of it, some distinction seems possible between the locations of the two types. The native farms are to be found almost entirely in areas where cul-tivation was practised in the earlier phases of the Iron Age. But the villa-estates were often carved out in virgin territory, avoided by the tribes of the A and AB phases owing to their lack of equipment suitable for tilling the heavier soils. The Belgae, on the other hand, had such equipment as well as a tradition of valley-dwelling, but they had had little more than a century of pioneering before being overtaken by the Roman conquest. It cannot be seriously suggested that all villas had their beginning before the conquest, although it is probably true of several that have been carefully excavated in recent times, a point that was considered earlier. And it must be said that no very clear distinction is possible between the humbler villas and the more prosperous peasant farms.

The status and function of such riverside hamlets as are known to have existed at Tilbury (Essex), Brentford (Middx) and Hedsor (in Taplow, Bucks) is no longer determinable, but their location below high-water mark in the first two instances does serve to demonstrate the rise in water-level since Roman times. The probability is that these settlements were comparable with the one at Long Wittenham and that the livelihood of their occupants was won from riverside fields on the well-drained gravel flood-plain with a top-soil of brick-earth. The Brentford site has a further point of interest in that it was possibly occupied continuously from about the eighth century B.C. to the second century A.D. (Plates 10 and 21).

Whereas the peasantry ploughed the Celtic fields, the villa-owners probably cultivated larger units of arable. In view of the alleged Belgic strip fields at Twyford (Hants) it is possible that the villas in former Belgic areas had the same unit of cultivation. But the greatest contrast is that which existed between the larger villas and the upland farms in their buildings. Even the humblest villas, perhaps the houses of bailiffs rather than landlords, show a far higher degree of comfort and prosperity than was known among the peasantry. The simple barn-like building at Clanville (Penton Grafton, Hants), and several generally similar, had a few lower courses of flint, usually bonded with brick, with a timber superstructure. Buildings with a far more elaborate ground plan, such as the Bignor villa (Sussex), might contain as many as sixty-five rooms set round a courtyard, some of the rooms floored with expensive tessellated pavements. Apart from the elaborate heating system of the house there was sometimes a bath-house attached to the villa. In some instances there was a farm-yard to one side of the house, with barns and labourers' quarters set apart from the main building. Another type of villa had its rooms arranged along a corridor, as for instance that which is now on the cliff-edge at Folkestone. But the plans of these houses are very varied and their function, at least in later Roman times, might also vary from the production of tiles, as at Ashtead (Surrey), to the processing of cloth by either fulling or dyeing, as at Darenth (Kent) or Titsey (Surrey). It is likely, however, that the great majority of them were the headquarters of large farming estates whose owners were local notables descended from a British aristocracy.

Although villas were here and there established on the heavier loams and on the margins of clay tracts, the main forest regions appear to have been avoided. Little or no indication of their former existence has been found in southern Essex or southern Hertfordshire, in Middlesex, western Berkshire or the Weald. In the Thames valley, from Maidenhead eastwards, vestiges of them are similarly lacking, probably because this was a region already in the hands of peasant cultivators. The small group of villas in south-western Essex is located on brick-earth and gravel beside the rivers Lea and Roding and not upon the London Clay.

The tall conical burial mounds of these people are to be seen here and there throughout the south-east (Map 8). The most remarkable group, the Bartlow Hills (Ashdon, Essex), in a locality rich in contemporary remains, were of the second century. They

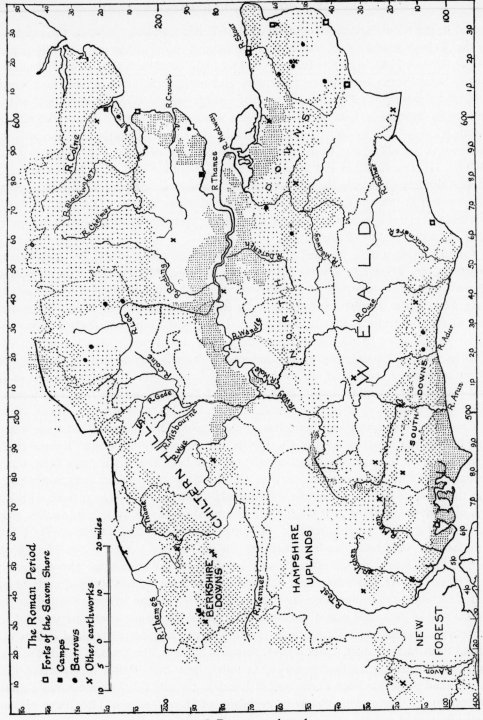

The Roman Period

□ Forts of the Saxon Shore
■ Camps
● Barrows
✕ Other earthworks

20 miles

MAP 8 Roman earthworks

reveal in the tomb furniture some survival of Belgic traditions as seen, for example, in the Welwyn burial vaults which were built about two centuries earlier. The largest of the Bartlow Hills, which is forty-seven feet high, contained a glass urn full of cremated bones, with other vessels of pottery and bronze, including an *amphora* which also held a cremation. The charred wick of a lamp suggested that it was alight at the time of its deposition. Like the Welwyn and Stanfordbury tombs, this one contained sacrificial vessels of bronze, but unlike them, the funeral furniture at Ashdon was enclosed in an oak chest. Romano-British tumuli may be seen near Kingston Lisle (Berks), Hitchin, Standon and Stevenage (Herts), Foulness and West Mersea (Essex), Upper Beeding (Sussex), Bishopsbourne and Canterbury (Kent). One was recently destroyed at Snodland (Kent) after excavation had shown it to be of the third century; but most of the others just mentioned have been provisionally dated by their appearance and location only (Plate 20).

Circular brick tombs, perhaps a development of the tumulus and less laborious to construct, are known in several places, such as West Mersea (Essex) and Keston (Kent). The latter occurred in a walled cemetery of which a number are known to have existed (e.g. Borden, Sutton Valence, East Barming, etc., in Kent; Colchester and Great Chesterford, Essex; Harpenden, Herts, and Compton, Berks). In several instances the ashes of the funeral pyre have been discovered within the walled enclosure, and at Plaxtol (Kent) an inhumation burial surrounded by cremations occurred under a barrow. A walled cemetery at Langley (Kent) contained one large and two small rectangular tombs built of Kentish ragstone and one that was circular. Within the walls were at least five cremations in urns, as well as traces of the pyres.

Cremation cemeteries are numerous in the region. One or more has been found just outside the limits of each of the Roman towns, usually beside the Roman roads that issue from them; many other cremations have been found wherever there was a settlement. Quite often a burial consisted simply of a pottery urn or glass bottle holding the ashes of the deceased; not infrequently additional pots were placed with the burial. During the third century the rite of cremation gave way to inhumation, perhaps as an indirect consequence of the Christianization of the province. Yet a few inhumations were being made as early as the first century A.D., as for example at Toppesfield (Essex) or Chilham (Kent). Inhumation cemeteries are almost equally widespread though less numerous; but single or multiple burials are constantly being found throughout the more densely populated areas of Roman Britain. Sometimes the occurrence of iron nails round the skeleton indicates its former enclosure in a coffin; sometimes a stone sarcophagus held the interment; and decorated lead coffins are found from time to time. Elaborate tombstones, some in the form of a Roman altar and others with human figures carved in relief, have been found incorporated into late Roman structures such as the wall of London. Usually they commemorate legionary officers or high civil officials or members of their families. They have seldom been discovered *in situ*.

In all the larger Roman towns—Colchester, Verulamium, London and Silchester—grandiose temples were built in furtherance of the policy of Romanization. They represent a transplantation of Mediterranean notions to Britain with only a nominal grafting of them on to native beliefs. But in the countryside smaller shrines existed which suggest a pertinacity of religious beliefs and practices, apart from Druidism, which was ruthlessly extirpated by the Romans. The Iron Age temple at Harlington (Middx) was the direct ancestor of the Romano-Celtic temple, at least in ground plan; and at Frilford (Berks) there was continuity in the religious use of a site, ranging from the unique circular shrine of Iron Age date down to a normal native temple of the Roman period. Moreover that at Worth (Kent) was superimposed upon a layer containing Iron Age pottery, including Belgic wares, together with votive offerings that had survived from an earlier religious sanctuary of some sort. At Woodeaton (Oxon) continuity in the religious use of a site is also possible, though earlier vestiges than of the Romano-British era were few. Coins indicated that at any rate during the latter period there had been almost continuous resort to the shrine, especially no doubt at festival times when a fair was probably held within the wall of the enclosure (*temenos*) bounding the temple. The same may be true of the temple on the Gosbecks Farm site at Colchester. The enormous walled enclosure was here preceded by a large boundary ditch of Belgic date. Nearby was built a theatre of distinctively classical plan. To the north, on the Sheepen site, was another Romano-Celtic temple with a *temenos* (Map E). At Richborough (Kent) an amphitheatre and two temples occur in close proximity.

Some of these shrines are found in remoter spots, occasionally, as at Bow Hill (Stoughton, Sussex) (Map D), or Chanctonbury (Washington, Sussex), making use of prehistoric earthworks for their enclosures, and situated on hilltops. The foundations of such a temple have been clearly marked out on Farley Heath (Albury, Surrey) and appear as a larger square enclosing a smaller. The outer wall-footing supported a verandah; the inner wall was carried up to roof height, forming a room which had a hearth in the middle. It is possible that an Iron Age shrine preceded the Farley Heath temple, for British and Belgic coins have been found near the site and the square enclosure of the Roman period replaced an earlier polygonal *temenos*. A hoard of votive objects with dedicatory inscriptions from Barkway (Herts) suggests the possibility of a temple in that neighbourhood also.

Of Christianity there is very little evidence in Britain. A small church of the fourth century was excavated close to the forum at Silchester; but only its plan, consisting of nave and aisles, implied its purpose. Even more doubtful is the small, isolated basilica in the southern quarter of Verulamium. The Chi-Rho monogram and the fish symbol such as occur on the pewter dishes from the villa at Appleshaw (Hants) do not necessarily prove that either their owner or manufacturer was a Christian. But the Lullingstone villa (Kent) revealed that a wealthy landowner of the mid-fourth century might avow his Christianity by having a room decorated with wall paintings of figures in devotional attitudes and with the Chi-Rho emblem; and it is a reasonable assumption that this was a private chapel. There are a few historical references to Christianity in Britain that make it certain that the faith had taken root here; but in the later Empire there was a strong resurgence of paganism even though it had never yielded much ground to Christianity. The purely archaeological evidence for either is, however, of their very nature, all too slight.

It was during the nine years from A.D. 287 to 296 that the most imposing Roman remains of our region began to be built. This period covers the usurpations of Carausius and of his murderer Allectus, who were both much exercised in the repelling of piratical raids by Saxons and Picts. To this end the great memorial at Richborough, whose concrete foundation (c. A.D. 85) forms a conspicuous feature within the walls, was converted into a look-out post and surrounded by triple defensive ditches. The monument itself, possibly commemorative of the conquest of Britain, had already been shattered before the later decades of the third century, no doubt by a piratical band. The triple ditches were filled in again soon after 273, presumably when the stone fort was built. The latter was girt by two ditches and the walls were built of stone with bonding courses of tile. Fragments of the marble casing of the great monument may still be seen where they were incorporated in the walls. At each corner was a solid circular bastion and there were rectangular towers at intervals along the outer face of each side of the fort (Plate 15).

This is but one of a series of fortified bases that guarded the south and east coasts from the Isle of Wight to the Wash. Within our region the forts at Portchester (Hants), Pevensey (Sussex) and Richborough (Kent) are the best preserved, but fragments of walls remain at Reculver and Lympne (Kent) and at Bradwell-juxta-Mare (Essex). The site of the fort at Dover lies beneath the modern town; St. Mary's church stood just within the northern rampart (Map 8). The large ruin of a Roman lighthouse still exists within the precincts of the Castle and a fragment of another, called the Bredenstone, may be seen on the Western Heights.

No two of these forts are identical in plan or construction, and it is unlikely that they are all exactly contemporary though not many years separate them. In spite of present appearances to the contrary, all, including Richborough, Dover, Pevensey and Lympne, stood beside inlets of the sea which have subsequently silted up. They served as bases for naval squadrons as well as for mobile military forces. The considerable distances intervening between them may have been filled by signalling stations sited on vantage points, though only one (at Hadleigh, Essex) is known in the south-east to correspond with those on the Yorkshire coast or on the southern shore of the Bristol Channel. But these gaps in the defences are largely illusory for much of the Essex and north Kent coasts were naturally protected by marshes, and the wide interval between Lympne and Pevensey consists of the seaward end of the Weald which, thinly populated by ironworkers, had little attraction for plunderers. But according to present knowledge the rich coastal plain of Sussex was very much

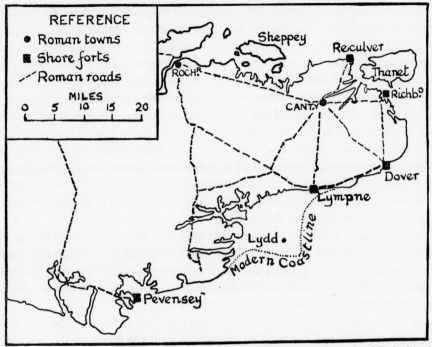

Based on Figure 9 of 'Historical Geography of England', pub. Methuen.

FIG 15 The coast-line of the South-East in Roman times

at the mercy of raiders who may have been responsible for the burning of the farm-steads at Preston and Park Brow *c.* A.D. 270. But houses could be destroyed by fire, then as now, through the carelessness of their occupants, and the risk of it was greater then than now.

Among the commonest finds of the Romano-British era are the traces of industries that flourished in suitable localities in the south-east. Allusion has already been made to the many sites in Wealden Sussex, where iron was mined and smelted; but far more widespread was the manufacture of pottery. Kilns were found in the seventeenth century in London when St. Paul's Cathedral was rebuilt. Colchester had a flourishing industry continuing from the Belgic period and the same is true of the Brockley Hill settlement (Stanmore, Middx), situated by the Watling Street. This manufacturing centre continued busily for much of the Roman period and its products were popular in London and were sold as far away as the military zone of the north. Other kiln sites have been found at Elstree (Herts) and at Radlett (Herts), both of them on Watling Street also. To the south-west of London, at and near Farnham (Surrey) and within the bounds of the neighbouring Alice Holt Forest (Hants), there appears to have been much activity ranging from the first century B.C. to the end of the Roman period (parishes of Binsted and Kingsley). Large areas in

K

the Forest are said to be covered by a deep layer of broken pots which had become misshapen during firing. The market for these wares was mainly local.

The New Forest potteries, of which many remains have come to light in the Fritham and Burley areas (Map H), were most active in the third and fourth centuries A.D. Their products were widely distributed in southern England. In contrast, those of the industry located in the Medway marshes, formerly called Upchurch wares, were limited in their distribution. What seems to have been pottery from this source reached London and across the Thames to the Romano-British hamlet at Tilbury (Essex). The Upchurch kilns flourished in the first and second centuries and, in spite of doubts concerning the existence of a production centre in this neighbourhood, recent investigation tends to confirm that they did in fact exist. The very great quantities of sherds formerly to be seen on the mudbanks of several of the Medway channels can hardly represent domestic refuse only.

The processing of cloth, an industry that probably expanded with the late Roman change-over from mainly arable to mainly pastoral farming in southern Britain, was carried on at an Imperial weaving-mill at Winchester; and Silchester apparently had a dye-works. Fulling, or some similar process, was done at the Darenth (Kent) and Titsey (Surrey) villas as well as at Chichester.

Another villa industry was tile- or brick-making. The output of flue-tiles from the villa at Ashtead (Surrey) was sold to customers in many parts of the south-east as well as in the northern Midlands and the West Country. Their distribution can be traced by the distinctive patterns impressed upon them. This industry was active for about a century from c. A.D. 80. The products of the Plaxtol villa (Kent) were less widespread in their distribution, but they are equally easy to trace because of the trade-mark which they bore: 'Cabrianus made this brick.' Other tileries are known to have existed in the parishes of Cranleigh (Surrey) and Pamber (Hants).

Reference to the manufacture of salt from sea-brine was made on p. 124.

The decay of civilized living, with a steady relapse into prehistoric barbarism in the latter days of Roman Britain, and the ensuing sub-Roman phase, have left little for the archaeological record. The number of villas that have been scientifically excavated is very few; and the majority were 'dug into' before sub-Roman material was recognized. But if a generalization is hazarded from the unsatisfactory evidence, it would be that most Romano-British country houses were abandoned during the two decades after 350 and that a few, such as that at Park Street (Herts), were possibly destroyed in the great barbarian raids of A.D. 367–8. Undoubtedly some of the others were deserted at about this time because of the insecurity of the countryside. This insecurity existed not merely because of the frequent presence of raiders but also, if contemporary Gaul afford a true analogy, because of the even greater danger of a rebellious peasantry.

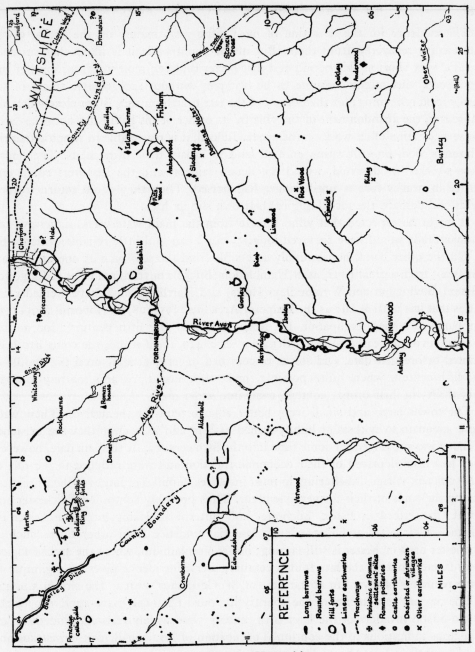

MAP H Western Hampshire

The evidence for the desertion of most villas rests mainly on the dating of the latest coins recovered from them. But in the countryside it is likely that currency became very short at this period and that barter replaced money transactions. If this were so, a villa might continue to be occupied without recognizable traces of the final period remaining; for the pottery of the late fourth century is not closely datable. Moreover, the abandonment of the villa by its owner or his bailiff did not necessarily cause a cessation of all work on the estate. Indeed, it is reasonable to suppose that the labourers went on cultivating enough land to satisfy their own needs. The house, once wrecked or deserted, would not detain raiders; and the labourers could take refuge in nearby forests until danger had passed. Then they could return to their fields and perhaps the rebuilding of their own simple huts.

It might be expected that villas remote from the main waterways, ridgeways and Roman roads would have survived longest; but I can find little reliable evidence for it. On the other hand, houses easily accessible from the sea, such as one at Bosham (Sussex); from a great river, as at Hambledon (Bucks); or from roads, as at Ridgewell (Essex), Bovingdon and Wymondley (Herts) and Hartlip (Kent), have yielded coin-series that last until as late as the Emperor Arcadius (395–408) or Honorius (395–423), implying continued occupation for some time into the fifth century; for normal Roman currency ceased to reach Britain after c. 412, or, if it did, the coins had been minted before that date. Old stocks of coin had to serve at least until the middle of the fifth century when, quite possibly, make-shift imitations and the tiny minims, very thrifty in their bronze content, came into wider use.

The towns large and small were better able to fend for themselves. Their walls were adequate to withstand lightly-armed raiders and it is clear that the existence of many was prolonged for some time into the fifth century. At this late date, however, they had been deprived of their economic function and were reduced to the rôle of self-sufficient villages, sheltering, in most instances, families of impoverished squatters among the ruins of their former splendour. Thus probably continued Colchester and Great Chesterford in Essex, Silchester and Bitterne in Hampshire, Dorchester on Thames, Chichester and Canterbury. Material evidence from other towns such as Rochester or Winchester is still lacking; but at Verulamium, where the archaeological record peters out in the late fourth century, literary evidence gives us a glimpse of some remnants of civic life at the time of St. Germanus' visit to the city in A.D. 429

The peasant settlements of the countryside must obviously have survived, for the Anglo-Saxon invaders of the later fifth century were widely resisted. And there are numerous indications of the continued occupation of Romano-British farmsteads and hamlets until at least the earlier part of that century. This is especially true of the Abingdon region and its fringes. Dorchester, Elsfield, Shotover, Horton and Sandford on the Oxfordshire bank of the Thames have all afforded such evidence; and in Berkshire, settlements at Reading, Wallingford, Lowbury (Aston Upthorpe), Stanford-in-the-Vale and Uffington were all probably occupied after A.D. 400. But the

Romano-British material cannot yet certainly be regarded as extending beyond the earlier decades of the fifth century; and the earliest Saxon relics, possibly excluding those from Dorchester, were not deposited until after *c.* 450, though some of them were undoubtedly made somewhat earlier.

The settlements at Greenwich (London) and at Chobham (Surrey) seem to have prolonged their existence after the traditional date for the withdrawal of the legions. Thundersbarrow (Shoreham, Sussex), Thatcham (Berks), Ashdon (Essex) are similar. The temples at Woodeaton (Oxon), Waltham St. Lawrence (Berks) and Farley (Albury, Surrey), as well as the supposed shrine at Barkway (Herts), have all yielded late Romano-British material, suggesting that the old gods still retained their hold.

Just as the walls of the towns afforded security in the troublous times of the fourth and early fifth centuries so did some, at any rate, of the forts of the Saxon shore. The only two in our region to be excavated, Richborough and Pevensey, yielded indications of continued occupation after the end of the fourth century; and the coin evidence from the Kentish fort even suggests the maintenance of trading contacts with the Continent until *c.* A.D. 430. Within that portion of Britain roughly to the south and east of the Roman Fosse Way (Exeter–Bath–Cirencester–Leicester–Lincoln) a number of late Roman coin-hoards have been discovered. In many cases the coins are so worn with use that they must have remained in circulation for long after their minting in the reign of Theodosius (392–5) and of his sons Honorius and Arcadius. In our region these hoards have come to light in all counties except Buckinghamshire. This fact, together with the Richborough evidence, has been taken to imply a civil and military reoccupation of south-eastern Britain for about a decade from *c.* A.D. 417. But the evidence hardly warrants such a conclusion; a continuance of cross-Channel trade, which is in no way surprising, would explain all the archaeological evidence that needs explaining.

In the next chapter this problem of a continuing Romano-British population is considered from other standpoints. It is, in some respects, the most crucial in the early history of England and, in the dearth of information about it, one of the most disappointing; yet recent studies have afforded a few interesting details that cast a faint but possibly deceptive light on the period.

BIBLIOGRAPHY TO CHAPTER XI

General works on this period are more abundant. Chapters I–XIX of volume I of the *Oxford History of England* (2nd edition, 1937), by R. G. Collingwood, and his *Archaeology of Roman Britain* (1930) are invaluable and should be supplemented by the *Guide to the Antiquities of Roman Britain* (1951), published by the British Museum. Also inexpensive and highly authoritative are I. A. Richmond's *Roman Britain

* Inexpensive works.

(1947, pub. Collins) and *Roman Britain (1955), which is volume I of the *Pelican History of England*. Both are illustrated and the latter has an up-to-date bibliography. F. Haverfield's contributions to the *Victoria County Histories*, though half a century old, retain their value, especially that in *Hants*, vol. I. More recent are *Kent*, vol. III (1932), *Sussex*, vol. III (1935) and *Oxfordshire*, vol. I (1939). Much information about Roman sites, known or presumed, may be had from the publications of the Royal Commission on Historical Monuments, which are listed in the General Bibliography, section C. on p. 229. R. E. M. Wheeler's *London in Roman Times* (1930), Catalogue No. 3 of the London Museum, has a wider significance than its title suggests. The *Journal of Roman Studies* (1911 onwards) has each year since 1921 a summary of the previous year's work in excavation and discovery. See also the periodicals listed in the General Bibliography, section D, p. 229-230.

Studies of separate sites are very numerous and only those with wide implications can be listed. The *Reports of the Research Committee of the Society of Antiquaries*, nos. *6, *7, *10, and 16, record the lengthy and important excavations at Richborough; and no. 11 on Verulamium and no. 14 on Camulodunum are essential sources for a study of the period. The Silchester excavations are described in *Archaeologia* from 1864 onwards, vols. 40, 46, 50, 52–62 inclusive, and 92 (1938–9). Monographs on this town and its neighbourhood may be found in *Antiquity*, 17 (1943) and 22 (1948), the former concerned with the prolongation of the life of the town after A.D. 400 and the latter with the town plan and with its houses.

For the Roman towns of Kent see *VCH*, vol. III, and, in addition, on Canterbury see *Antiquity*, 23 (1949), and *Illustrated London News* for 27 December 1952. The Cripplegate fort and other London discoveries are described in *Buried London* (1955), by W. T. Hill. For Brockley Hill see *Trans. Middx. and London Arch. Soc.*, vol. 10 (1947) and following issues.

On cemeteries see *Research Rep. of the Soc. of Ant.*, no. 8: *Ospringe*; and on walled cemeteries, *VCH*, *Kent*, vol. III, p. 94, and *Archaeological Journal*, 101 (1944), pp. 68 f. (Colchester). For the temple at Harlow, see *Antiquaries Journal*, 8 (1928), and for that at Frilford, *Oxoniensia*, 3 and 4. The Gosbecks site near Colchester is reported in the *Jour. Roman Studies*, 40 (1950). On Roman barrows, see *Antiquity*, 10

Books on local pottery-kiln sites include Heywood Sumner's *New Forest Pottery Sites* (1927) and Wade and Lowther's *Alice Holt Forest* (1949). The Upchurch (Kent) sites are discussed in *VCH*, *Kent*, III, pp. 132 f.

On the agriculture of this period see *Arch. Journ.*, 104 (1947), pp. 26 f. and 82 f. Peasant farmsteads are described in Heywood Sumner's *Excavations on Rockbourne Down* (1914) and in *Trans. Newbury and District Field Club*, 9 (1948): the Roden Down site. D. Atkinson's *The Romano-British Site on Lowbury Hill in Berkshire* (1916) is relevant for this and other periods. Agricultural sites of several kinds are discussed in Crawford and Keiller's *Wessex from the Air* (1928). The Celtic field

* Inexpensive works.

system round Brighton is described in *Antiquity*, 9 (1935), on the Berkshire Downs in *Oxoniensia*, 15 (1950), and that near Leatherhead and Coulsdon in *Surrey Archaeological Collections*, 50 (1949).

Some of the best accounts of villa excavations will be found in *Antiquaries Journal*, 18 (1938), Lockleys; *Archaeological Journal*, 102 (1945), Park Street; and in the book *Lullingstone Roman Villa* (1955) by its excavator, G. W. Meates. A number of papers on various aspects of the villa are collected in *Archaeological New Letter*, 6/2 (1955).

All earlier works on Roman roads have been superseded by I. D. Margary's *Roman Roads in Britain*, vol. I (1955), vol. II (1957); but for methods of research in tracing them see his *Roman Ways in the Weald* (1948).

The Ordnance Survey Map of Roman Britain (third edition, 1956), with an explanatory booklet, is essential to a study of this period.

CHAPTER XII

The Anglo-Saxon Settlement

AT LEAST TWO centuries before the Anglo-Saxons began to settle in Britain their forbears and people of other Germanic tribes were entering the country, some of them to stay; and although they found a Celtic-speaking native population with a tincture of Latin, they must also have found some familiar elements in the life of the south-eastern countryside where the half-Germanic Belgae had been dominant. The legionary reinforcements of the late second and early third centuries had been recruited almost entirely from Germany, and some, no doubt, had settled on the land as time-expired veterans, married British wives, and remained here. To them other Germanic peoples were added, Burgundians and Vandals in the third century and Alemanni in the fourth, transplanted here by Roman Imperial decree.

Yet in spite of this infusion, the skeletal remains of the Romano-Britons, both in town and country, are surprisingly uniform in type when, by the third century, the rite of cremation gave way to unburnt burials, and skulls become available for study. But Romano-British skulls are little different from those of the Anglo-Saxons; for the invaders were probably of hybrid type like the people whom they conquered. For instance, Saxon skulls from the Abingdon (Berks) cemetery are of the same shape as those of the Britons and even of the present inhabitants of the area. Quite exceptional were a number of skulls from Spitalfields (London), truly 'Roman' in shape. They were possibly the remains of Italian merchants who fell victims to the savagery of the Iceni in the Boudiccan revolt of A.D. 61. But there were never sufficient numbers of Romans in Britain to affect the racial type.

The story of Vortigern's invitation to the Anglian or Saxon mercenaries to settle in Britain is a familiar one; and it probably contains an element of truth. There is increasing evidence, however, that his invitation was not the first and that, while Britain was still part of the Empire, the defences of the Saxon shore were partly manned by legionaries or auxiliary troops recruited from among Germanic barbarians. In Rutland, Norfolk, Suffolk, Essex, Hertfordshire, London and Kent, counties that border the Saxon shore or lie immediately behind it, pottery has been found that partakes of the characteristics of Saxon and Frisian on the one hand and of Romano-British on the other. The shape and decoration are Germanic and the fabric and technique of manufacture are native. Some of it can be shown to belong to the end of the third century; most of it that can be dated by associated finds is of the fourth century; and none of it can be attributed to the Anglo-Saxon settlers of the mid-fifth or later. It was a part of the output of Romano-British commercial potters and is never hand-made like normal Saxon pottery.

Within our region this hybrid ware has been found at Colchester, including some from Romano-British cemeteries outside, as well as from places within, the walls. The Roman towns of Great Chesterford (Essex), Verulamium (Herts) and London, and native settlements at Sawbridgeworth and Baldock (both in Herts), Broadstairs, Faversham and Sittingbourne (Kent) have all yielded examples of this pottery. Moreover, the Roman forts at Burgh and Felixstowe (Suffolk), Bradwell (Essex) and Richborough (Kent) have produced similar finds. Further to the north, the Roman towns of Caistor-by-Norwich and Caister-next-Yarmouth have yielded these pots and a fragment has come from Brundall which is situated between them. West Norfolk, West Suffolk and Cambridgeshire, with a stray find from Cowley (Oxon), complete the distribution. A significant aspect of these find-places is that the majority of them have also yielded pagan Anglo-Saxon material indicative of settlement after the mid-fifth century.

It is to the latter period that another category of hybrid pottery belongs, for almost all of it has come from pagan Saxon burials. It is hand-made ware showing Romano-British influence in its shape or decoration or even, in some instances, a borrowing from Belgic forms, especially in the provision of a pedestal. It is probably the product of Romano-British women who were members of Saxon communities; and their casting back to Belgic times for hand-made prototypes has much in common with the recrudescence of Celtic art as seen more especially on the decorative escutcheons of metal hanging-bowls, most of which have come from Saxon graves, though they are clearly among the latest products of Romano-British craftsmen. The later hybrid pottery has come from the sites of Roman buildings at Wingham and Hartlip, from Roman cemeteries at Preston-next-Wingham and at Worth, and from Deal, where there was a native settlement. All of these places are in Kent. Other instances of these pots have been cited from Limpsfield (Surrey), where there was occupation in Roman as well as in early Saxon times; from Frilford (Berks), where the archaeological gap between Roman and Saxon is unusually narrow; from the Anglo-Saxon cemetery at Abingdon (Berks), near which traces of a Roman settlement are known; and from other pagan graveyards.

The reverse process, of Germanic influence on Roman pottery, is exemplified by the sherds stamped with Teutonic rosette motifs that came from the Park Street villa (Herts), from the Lullingstone villa (Kent), from Frilford, Silchester and elsewhere. This kind of pottery, like the bulk of the earlier kind of hybrid ware, is of the fourth century and some of it was produced in the New Forest and at Silchester.

Yet another kind of pottery, a Saxon rusticated ware, has been found in Roman contexts. Sherds of this type occurred with Romano-British house rubbish at Northfleet and Gilton (Kent), at Sutton Courtenay (Berks) and at three places in West Suffolk, all of which are in regions of primary Anglo-Saxon settlement; and the closest Continental parallels for this ware are to be found in the fifth-century dwelling mounds (*terpen*) in Frisian Holland. In both Berkshire and Kent urns and brooches of Frisian ancestry occur in small numbers.

Now the curious thing about the bulk of the hybrid Romano-Saxon pottery consists in its occurrence in just those places or near them, that were specially designed to keep the Saxons out; and the pots belong to a period before the mass migrations which are implied by the large amount of Jutish and Saxon material that has come from the cemeteries of the later fifth and sixth centuries in Britain. It has been assumed, therefore, that Saxon and Frisian mercenaries (or Saxons who had tarried for a while in Frisia and had acquired some of the local cultural traits) were employed as auxiliary forces to repel their own kin as well as the Picts and Franks who were harassing Britain in the fourth century. With the loss of regular Roman forces and command at the end of the century it may be that the Saxon mercenaries, who had married native women, had a sufficient stake in the land to continue in its defence. At any rate, it was nearly half a century after the end of Roman rule before large-scale English settlement was begun. The earliest English traditions are at one on this point; and in so far as Saxon and Jutish objects can be dated, particularly by reference to similar goods on the Continent, the archaeological evidence concurs in a mid-fifth-century date for the first mass immigrations of the English.

We have already seen in the last chapter that the first half of the century is poorly represented in the archaeological record. It is a reasonable assumption from the coin evidence that a number of sites in the south-east continued to be occupied for a few decades after A.D. 400; and to that evidence may be added coin-hoards from Bermondsey (London), Richborough, Verulamium and Dunstable, which are considered to have been buried as late as the middle of the fifth century. On the other hand, the Roman coin minted in 440 which was found on the site of a villa at Houghton Regis (Beds) may well be a stray lost centuries after it had ceased to be current.

The impact of the Saxons on the Romano-Britons left few, if any, permanent signs. It was probably during the period of barbarian raiding rather than at the time of the Saxon settlement that the old hill-forts of the Caburn, Cissbury and Highdown were again put into a state of defence; but it is just possible that the inhumations and cremations from the oblong and figure-of-eight mounds to the east of Uffington Castle (Berks) represent the slain on both sides in a Saxon foray of the late fifth century. Similarly, the hundred or so skeletons hastily thrown into graves scooped in the sides of an Early Bronze Age barrow on Dunstable Down (Beds) may be relics of a massacre of Saxon prisoners during the course of the invasion. The few objects found with the burials are probably too late in date to belong to the time of raiding. Both these groups of burials were made beside one of the main arteries of early communication, the Icknield Way, and its continuation, the Berkshire Ridgeway, which afforded Saxon immigrants a ready route from the Wash south-westwards to the middle Thames and beyond.

Probably during the earlier phases of local Saxon settlement the vast northward-facing linear earthwork called the Wansdyke came into being. Excavation in Wiltshire has shown it to be very late in the Roman period or post-Roman. An outlying portion of the Dyke occurs in the parish of Inkpen (Berks); but this and the four other disconnected sections across the county boundary in Wiltshire have not been proved coeval with the main length of the Dyke. As a whole, Wansdyke suggests an attempt by the Britons to resist a southward extension by the Saxons of their territory

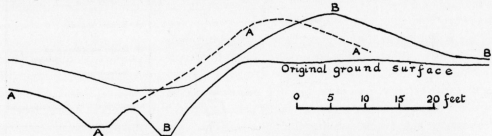

Based on Hawkes, 'Arch. Journ.', 104, Figure 15, 1.

FIG 16 A late Romano-British defensive earthwork, Bokerly Dyke, Martin, Hants. This section shows two phases of construction: A-A dated by coins to circa A.D. 367, when there were widespread barbarian raids; and B-B, which, in the absence of positive evidence, is thought to be of about A.D. 405. Probably among the last defensive works planned by Roman engineers in Britain. The older theory, that Bokerly was reconstructed in the mid-sixth century to hold back the Jutes (or Saxons) settled in the Salisbury neighbourhood, is hardly less probable

in the middle Thames region. Broadly contemporary with it is Bokerly Dyke, in its final phase of reconstruction. The only function that can reasonably be suggested for it is that it was refortified in order to limit Saxo-Jutish penetration south-westwards from the Salisbury region, which had been conquered by the middle of the sixth century. Bokerly extends for three sinuous miles along the boundary common to Dorset and Hampshire in the parish of Martin. It is the most imposing earthwork in our region (Figure 16, Map H and Plate 19).

Possibly of this period also are the linear earthworks at Basildon, Streatley and Aldworth (Berks) and at Mongewell (Crowmarsh, Oxon) (Map I). The three sections of ditch on the Berkshire side of the Thames face northwards, barring the Ridgeway as it approaches the important ford at Pangbourne, but apparently leaving uncovered the more vital crossing at Goring. The Mongewell ditch faces southwards, astride the two prehistoric routes, the Icknield Way and the Chiltern Ridgeway. It was obviously designed to meet a threat from Berkshire or from the Thames itself. It is difficult to believe that the ditches on both sides of the river were intended as parts of a single, coherent system of local or regional defence.

Equally obscure in date and purpose are the other Grim's Ditches further to the north-east along the line of the Chilterns in the parishes of Lacey Green, Great

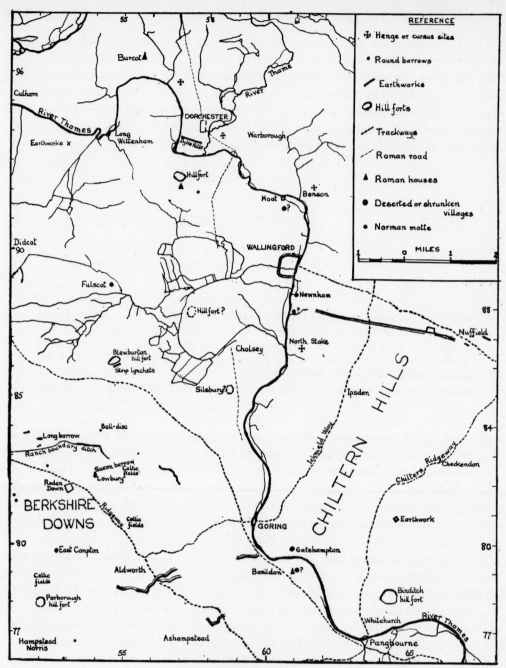

MAP I The Goring Gap

Hampden, Great Missenden, Lee, Wendover and Wigginton (all Bucks) and Berk-hampsted (Herts) (Map K). This series is in four sections facing south and south-east and leaving unguarded both the Icknield route and the natural lines of communication through the Wycombe, Missenden and Berkhampsted gaps. There has been much inconclusive speculation concerning them, but only the spade may decide. The excavation of a somewhat similar earthwork at Bexley (Kent) did not, however, afford any useful clues. Up to the present, the best analogies are those of the Cam-bridgeshire dykes which, like those round Goring, bar a main line of communication. One of them, the Devil's Ditch, near Burwell, was probably constructed by East Angles in the fifth century as a boundary and line of defence between themselves and the Saxon communities in southern Cambridgeshire. The other ditches of this region are probably of later date. (Plate 25).

Another system of linear earthworks exists in eastern Hampshire, in the parish of Froxfield. They run from north to south for about two miles and were designed against encroachment from the west. If they are of Dark Age date, they may mark an early frontier between the kingdoms of Sussex and Wessex.

The earthworks near Silchester in the north of the same county had a different purpose. The Grim's Ditch at Padworth (Berks) is clearly related to two Roman roads issuing northward from a town which may well have continued to be lived in after A.D. 400, but which was deserted in early Saxon times. It is not too hazardous an assumption that the Padworth ditch was made at some time after Roman security had been lost and while the region was being threatened by pagan Saxons expanding their tract of settlement southward from the Reading area. In other parishes around Silchester, namely Ufton Nervet and Stratfield Mortimer in Berkshire and Mortimer West End in Hampshire, there are further linear earthworks which may be con-temporary with that at Padworth (Map J). West of Silchester, on Greenham Com-mon (Berks), there was a dyke of proved sub-Roman date; and others, on Crookham Common, were apparently intended to reinforce the one at Greenham. South of Sil-chester in the parish of Pamber (Hants) are yet other earthworks, and the whole group round the Roman town may be a contemporary sub-Roman delimitation of the area over which the town claimed authority and from which it could draw nourishment.

It is possible that the complex of earthworks round Chichester (Map D) are of the same period, but evidence is lacking; and some think it more likely that they are Belgic and so comparable with the earthworks protecting Camulodunum. There are also within our region a number of comparatively short sections of ditch which have been supposed to belong to one period or another from the Iron Age to the Saxon period; but without positive evidence from excavation little is gained by discussing them, though they are included in the Gazetteer.

The main influx of Saxon settlers began soon after the middle of the fifth century and probably continued intermittently for at least a hundred years. The greater part

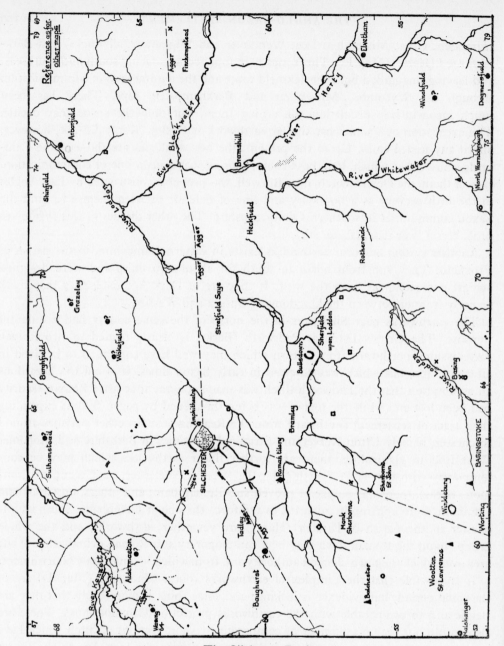

MAP J The Silchester Region

of the evidence for this migration comes from burial grounds (Map 9), the earliest of which have been found in east and north Kent, in north Surrey and in a cluster near Abingdon. There are two showing use before A.D. 500 in coastal Sussex. Just before and during the migrations the rite of burial was undergoing a change from cremation, which is almost universal in the Continental homelands of the Saxons, to inhumation which, in this country, was in use even among the earliest settlers. The Jutes rarely, if ever, cremated their dead; the few exceptions known from east Kent were not associated with objects of Jutish type. But, though cremation was the earlier rite, it by no means follows that it is a criterion of an early interment, for some of the latest princely burials by cremation, such as that from the Asthall barrow in western Oxfordshire, are probably referable to the early part of the seventh century, subsequent even to the local acceptance of Christianity which forbade the burning of corpses.

It is, however, from the metal goods that often accompany interments, and to some extent from pottery, that the date of burials may be postulated. The absence of a dated currency of the early Saxon period deprives us of a precise chronology; the few Roman coins found with interments had been minted and lost long before the migrations and have no chronological value. It may be possible to date a burial to within about half a century of its deposition; but in doing so we are dependent upon a relative chronology deduced from the study of the evolution of metal goods, especially of bronze brooches; and a considerable margin of error must be envisaged in doing so. A brooch may have been in use for many years and in the possession of several owners before it reached its last resting-place with a corpse. Many show signs of long wear, and a few were repaired during their period of use. Moreover, the typology of a brooch-form is determined by an insecure initial dating for the type and the final disuse of the type can be delimited only very broadly. Further complication is introduced by the probability that some craftsmen or their customers may have been conservative in taste; a simple, early form of a brooch might conceivably be reproduced long after the style had gone out of fashion. Generally speaking, however, the earlier styles of jewellery come from cemeteries which, for reasons other than the styles of their brooches, may fairly be regarded as early; and the presumed development in styles is largely borne out by the occurrence of the simpler varieties in areas of primary settlement and of the more evolved and ornate forms in areas of later and secondary settlement.

More reliable information is to be had from early Saxon traditions than from archaeology. These traditions were preserved orally by the West Saxon court poets and were not as a whole put into written form before the end of the ninth century. They are usually referred to as *The Anglo-Saxon Chronicle*. There are good reasons for believing that its earliest entries relating to Wessex were based on still older written material as well as on the obvious source, Bede's *Ecclesiastical History*. But even the written traditions had been preserved for so long by oral transmission that they had undergone some blurring of detail and much had fallen into oblivion. Moreover, only

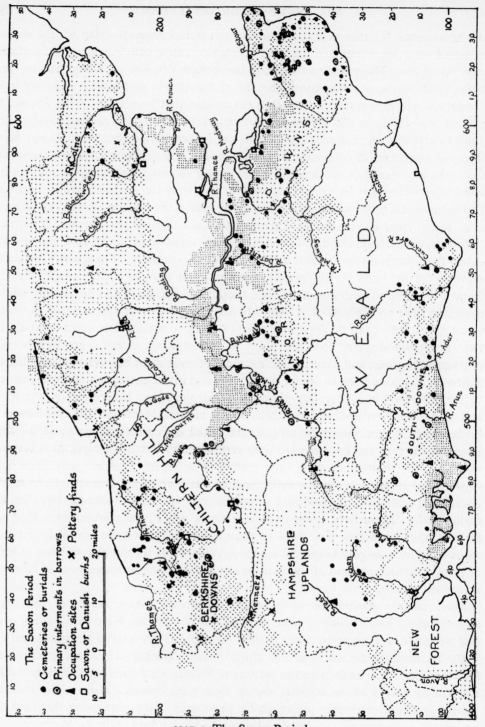

The Saxon Period

- ● Cemeteries or burials
- ⊙ Primary interments in barrows
- ✖ Pottery finds
- ▲ Occupation sites
- ☐ Saxon or Danish burhs

20 miles

MAP 9 The Saxon Period

that which was of interest to an aristocratic audience was thought worthy of permanent record. However, the dim outlines of the course of events during the Saxon and Jutish invasions can be discerned in the earlier annals of the *Chronicle*; and here and there a vivid detail survives.

Under the year 449 we are told of the invitation by a British king Vortigern to Hengist and Horsa to assist him against the Picts and Scots. The barbarian forces landed in east Kent, but later turned on their paymaster. We hear then of battles fought between the mercenaries and the Britons at places which may possibly be Aylesford and Crayford in Kent and of further British defeats at places no longer identifiable. After the battle of Crayford in 457 the Britons are said to have fled to London in great terror. These events are described in five entries attributed to years ranging from 449 to 473 and, in so far as their location is determinable, their action moves westward from the Isle of Thanet to the river Cray.

The next three annals are concerned with the conquest of Sussex, beginning in 477 with the invasion of the region at a place off Selsey that was long ago engulfed by the sea. After an initial defeat, the Britons fled to the shelter of the Wealden forest. A second battle was fought at an unidentified stream and was followed in 491 by a siege of the Roman fort at Pevensey and the annihilation of its British defenders. This campaign covered the length of Sussex except for the Hastings region, which was occupied by a different tribe in an unrecorded invasion. It maintained its existence separate from both Sussex and Kent as late as the eleventh century.

The account of the conquest of Wessex is far more complex. A landing at an unknown place, probably on Southampton Water in 495 was followed by battles at Netley Marsh in the New Forest, at Charford-on-Avon, which is further to the west, and at another place close by, probably in Fordingbridge. These places are on, or close to, an ancient route across the north of the New Forest, a route that continues beyond the Avon on its right bank to Old Sarum (Wilts). This British fortress was captured in 552 after an interval of twenty-five years since the second battle on the Avon. During that interval in the northward advance, the Isle of Wight was conquered. But there were two other landings of English invaders, the first at the same place as that of 491 and the second at Portsmouth, presumably to seize the Roman fort of Porchester; but these landings had no outcome that need detain us.

In A.D. 556, four years after the capture of Sarum, the same force is represented as fighting a battle at Barbury near Swindon in northern Wiltshire; and in 568, successors to the original leaders made a foray against the kingdom of Kent. By this time the invading band of 491 were established in Thames-side Berkshire and had sufficiently consolidated their position to be able to turn their attention to the conquest of territory down-Thames. In 571 a battle was fought against the Britons at Bedford prefacing a campaign that secured the Chiltern scarp-foot zone from southern Bedfordshire to the Thames in Oxfordshire. Thereafter, events moved far to the westward, outside our region.

L

A further source of evidence, which partly confirms the general picture afforded by the archaeological and literary evidence, is place-names. Roughly during the first half-century of the settlement, names ending in *-ingas* were given to small regions occupied by a chief and his following. Usually the name of the chief is preserved in a modified form in the first syllable of the place-name. For instance, Goring in Oxfordshire and Sussex was originally the name given to an area occupied by the people of *Gāra*; it was not at first the name of a village. Neither name is on record before the Domesday Book (A.D. 1086), wherein both appear in the form *Garinges* or variants of it. In modern usage some of these names retain the original plural '*s*', as for example Hastings, but the majority lost it long ago.

Rather later in date are the place-names ending in *-ingham* (e.g. Effingham, Surrey, and Wokingham, Berkshire); and during the period before the tribes were converted to Christianity, pagan place-names came into use, many of which still survive. Some of them contain the name of one of the Saxon gods such as *Thunor* (e.g. Thursley, Surrey; Thurstable Hundred and Thundersley, Essex), or *Woden* (e.g. the lost name *Wodnesfeld* in Widdington, Essex, or the surviving Woodnesborough, Kent); and in Tuesley, Surrey, or *Tiwle*, which formerly occurred in Stanstead St. Margaret, Hertfordshire, it is possible that the name of the god *Tiw* is commemorated.

Another kind of name that may indicate the site of a heathen shrine is that which incorporates *hearg* (a temple) as in Harrow, Middlesex, and Harrowdown in Woodeaton, Oxfordshire, and possibly in Longworth, Berkshire. Words related in meaning, *wēoh* or *wīg* (holy place, sanctuary), occur in the place-names Weedon, Buckinghamshire, Willey in Farnham, Surrey, Whiligh in Ticehurst, Sussex, and in Wye, Kent.

All of the kinds of place-names so far mentioned are indicative of local settlement by about A.D. 650; but the pagan names may also have an archaeological interest, for they probably locate sites where the post-holes of timber structures, representing the original sanctuaries, may be found by excavation. On Harrow Hill, Angmering (Sussex), some tantalizing clues of another kind came to light. A few cuttings into the turf of the Early Iron Age enclosure revealed large numbers of ox-skulls; it was estimated that the earthwork contained well over a thousand. The name of the hill points to the former presence of a Saxon shrine, almost certainly within the earlier enclosure; the skulls suggest that the autumn slaughter of cattle took place here and that the heads of the animals were offered at the shrine. In A.D. 601 Pope Gregory the Great, in a letter to Abbot Mellitus, who was one of the first missionaries to the English tribes, speaks of their 'custom of sacrificing many oxen to devils', which must refer to the pagan gods; and Bede records that November had been termed *Blōtmōnath*, which means 'the month of sacrifice', when the cattle that could not be carried over the winter for lack of fodder were slaughtered and offerings were made of them to the gods. It is reasonable to assume that the slaughter took place in the immediate vicinity of the temple, and that the heads of the beasts, the least suitable part for salting down, were allocated as offerings. The custom of dedicating the heads of animals to the gods is known to have been practised among other Germanic tribes on the Continent; and it may be that place-names such as Eversheds (boar's head) in Ockley, Surrey, or Broxhead (badger's head) in Headley, Hampshire, may commemorate this heathen custom.

It is clear from the archaeological evidence that the settlement in all south-eastern regions was made piecemeal by comparatively small bands of immigrants, men, women and children together. Evidence of a settlement before about A.D. 500 has come from cemeteries such as Sarre, Westbere, Faversham, Bekesbourne, Milton Regis and Sturry in east and north Kent and from Northfleet beside the Thames in north-west Kent; and almost all of this evidence points to occupation by Saxon or mixed Saxon and Frisian communities. It is usual to speak of Frisians in this context, and it is clear from a number of place-names in east and north-east England, as well as from a contemporary Byzantine historian, Procopius, that the Frisians did in fact have a part in the colonization of Britain. But it is possible that in Kent the objects of Frisian origin were brought over mainly by Saxons who had for a time dwelt among the Frisians, though some of the latter could easily have joined the migrants.

The principal criteria of early date and of tribal origins are to be seen in the pottery and brooches interred with the earliest burials; and for Kent, the Westbere cemetery may be given as an example, though, like so many others, the site was not excavated and the finds came to light casually, so that associated groups of objects from any one grave are not known. An early Saxon element is to be seen in much of the pottery, including urns that held cremations and those that had been deposited beside unburnt corpses. No two pots have more than a general resemblance in shape, of which the variety is greater than would be found among a prehistoric people with a common culture. In this we may perhaps detect the effects of a mingling of Saxons drawn from a wide area of north Germany and coastal Holland, each bringing her own local tradition of potting. But the fabric of these pots is similar, so it may be inferred that the same raw materials and methods of manufacture were used by all the potters. Many of these vessels can be matched among the Saxon communities who in the later fifth century dwelt in the region watered by the rivers Elbe and Weser of north Germany. The so-called window-urns, which have a piece of glass let into the base or side of the pot before firing, may have been made by people from the same region, or equally from Frisia. The distribution of this kind of vessel is, at any rate, limited to those two Continental regions and to a few sites in eastern and south-eastern Britain.

Similarly, a fragmentary brooch of cruciform shape from Westbere, belonging to the earlier part of the sixth century, could as well be derived from Frisia as from Old Saxony; and the Kentish burial grounds have yielded more than a dozen of these brooches ranging from the date of the initial settlement to about A.D. 525 or somewhat later.

From the middle of the sixth century, on conventional dating, objects of distinctively Jutish type begin to appear at Westbere. These include a small circular brooch set with wedge-shaped garnets of *c.* A.D. 550; a buckle of a type traded over a wide area of Saxon and Anglian Britain which is a little later in date; and pendants and bracteates of the seventh century. This material is called Jutish because it is found also in the Isle of Wight and to a small extent in southern Hampshire which, with Kent, were all said by Bede to have been colonized by the Jutes. The closest Continental parallels to these goods are found in Frankish territory on the middle Rhine where, presumably, the Jutes sojourned for a while before their further migration to Britain. This period in Frankish territory, together with the close political ties that grew up between the kingdom of Kent and the Frankish kingdoms of Gaul in the seventh century, go far to explain the increasingly Frankish character of Kentish culture from the late sixth century onwards. We know of the political ties from documentary sources; the fact that these sources make no allusion to a Frankish migration to Britain render such an event unlikely, though one scholar has assumed its occurrence in an attempt to explain the strong Frankish element in Jutish culture. But it should be noted that the refutation of his belief is based on negative evidence, which is not the strongest of arguments.

It is possible that some of the Jutes did in fact come direct from Jutland to Britain without the presumed temporary sojourn on the middle Rhine. Gold bracteates, such as came from graves at Westbere and several other cemeteries of east Kent, some of the cruciform brooches and some of the larger square-headed brooches, can best be paralleled in Jutland, but not all elsewhere; and it is significant that, at the time of the earlier migrations to eastern and south-eastern Britain, Danish archaeology, both in Jutland and farther south, reveals a steady depopulation. The settlements represented by large cremation cemeteries down to the migration period died out and burials ceased. It is clear, too, that the void was filled by immigrants from southern Sweden who spoke a northern Germanic dialect as opposed to the west Germanic spoken hitherto throughout the Danish peninsula. Bede's statement that the old home of the Angles remained deserted down to his own day is to some extent borne out by archaeology, which adds that the region north of Angel, in which he seems to have placed the Jutes, became deserted at about the same time or soon after. The appearance of Jutish culture in Britain after that of the Saxons and Angles is quite probably to be explained by their halt on the Rhine.

Of the other two Jutish regions, the Isle of Wight has yielded a considerable quantity of jewellery of middle Rhenish affinities; but there is little from southern Hampshire that can be connected with the first English settlers. The burial ground at Droxford on the river Meon contained a few objects similar to some from Kentish cemeteries, but also some Saxon goods suggestive of cultural influence from Sussex. Otherwise the archaeological evidence for the Jutes in Hampshire is limited to a few jewels recovered from isolated burials at Exton and West Meon. But the place-names of southern Hampshire, especially those ending in -ing (singular), like Swaythling, Chilling and Nursling, have much in common with names of a similar origin in Kent, as well as with a few in Berkshire, which may represent a penetration of settlers from the Hampshire coast to the middle Thames. Elsewhere, as noted earlier, the original ending of such names was -ingas (plural). Moreover, medieval documents refer to the New Forest as Ytene, which means '(land) of the Jutes'; and they show also that the customary land-use of this region was much like that of Kent and quite distinct in certain features from that prevailing in the Saxon and Anglian regions of England.

Quite apart from the information given in the Anglo-Saxon Chronicle it is evident that parts of Sussex had been occupied before the year 500. Some of the pottery found in the High Down (Ferring) cemetery and some of that from Alfriston belongs to an early phase of the English settlement. Sussex, of course, implies in its very name a colonization by Saxons; and the graveyards confirm it. Most characteristic among the metal goods are the numerous saucer-brooches, which far outnumber those of any other kind; and it is in the Saxon areas of the Continental homeland that these brooches are mainly found. Not a single cruciform brooch has yet been recorded from Sussex, nor has the south coast yielded any other indication of Frisian settlement.

The early cemetery at Alfriston included only burials of the unburnt body; but High Down had numerous cremations as well as inhumations. Four* other burial places, at Hampden Park (Eastbourne), Hassocks, Moulsecoomb (Patcham) and Saddles-combe (Newtimber) have yielded cremations, a fact that strengthens the impression of an early settlement of the coastal plain and of the scarp-foot zone immediately north of the Downs. And the distribution of early place-names reinforces this belief. Alto-gether there are forty-five names originally ending in -ingas and of them only Fletch-ing is more than a mile or two from the Downs. In other words, all but one are within a short distance of the coast, and the exception, Fletching, is easily accessible along the river Ouse.

Most of the names in -ingham lie a little farther inland, but every one of them is close to a stream. Of the five pagan names, two, Whyly in East Hoathly, and Whiligh in Ticehurst, are situated well into the Weald and their location recalls Tacitus' remark that the German tribes were wont to place their sanctuaries in the remoteness of forests.

But all over England there is a curious and unexplained discrepancy between the distributions of pagan Saxon burials and of the earliest place-names. For instance, although only two cemeteries are known west of the river Adur, two-thirds of the -ingas names occur there; and on the upper reaches of the western Rother seven -ingas names are to be found, but not a single pagan burial. To the east of the Adur the balance between the archaeological and place-name evidence is more under-standable, if proper allowance be made for the effects of time and chance.

This widespread discrepancy is probably due to various causes, none of which will fit all cases. Some of the earliest Saxon villages (e.g. near Selsey, or Sutton Courtenay,

* Five, if Bow Hill (Stoughton) be included.

Berks) bear no obvious relation to the present pattern of settlement and were deserted early in the period; for some reason the inhabitants migrated to another place, or were exterminated. Some of the known cemeteries may have been attached to such abandoned villages of which all trace has since been destroyed or not yet rediscovered. The name of the abandoned village would be lost or transferred to the new habitation site, which has no obvious connection with the cemetery of the abandoned village. Some settlements were extinguished quite early by war, famine, or pestilence, or from economic causes in medieval times. Of some of these the cemetery may be known but the settlement, if not destroyed by ploughing or quarrying, is still to be found. In other instances, where an *-ingas* name survives attached to a modern settlement, it could easily have happened that the medieval church and burial ground long ago obliterated the burials of pagan times; or, where the earliest cemetery was away from the church, medieval or modern buildings or cultivation could have destroyed all trace of it.

In the last hundred years pagan Anglo-Saxon cemeteries have come to light almost annually; and although this has been a period of much soil disturbance for canal and railway construction, for gravel digging and quarrying and for building of all kinds, it is yet likely that in earlier centuries there were many such discoveries even though they were relatively fewer than in the nineteenth and twentieth centuries. Only a sprinkling of the sites discovered since 1850 has been adequately recorded; before that date references to Saxon burials are rare indeed, for there were very few who could recognize them for what they were, let alone make an intelligible record of them. It is not surprising, therefore, that *-ingas* names are seldom matched by adjacent pagan cemeteries and that the cemeteries are sometimes found in no clear association with names indicative of very early settlement. It comes to this: many of the earliest place-names have survived into modern usage, but probably less than a tithe of the burial grounds are known; what with migration of settlement and the destruction of heathen burials where there had been no migration, it is hardly to be wondered at that both aspects of early settlement survive so rarely in association.

We have noticed that north-west Kent was occupied by Saxons and not Jutes. From Northfleet near the Thames estuary to Frilford in Berkshire, we have indications of early Saxon culture little modified by tribal admixture. The evidence is not, however, continuous. Upstream, from Northfleet there is a gap until we come to cemeteries at Mitcham and Croydon (Surrey) and a still longer interval before we reach the main group of early settlements in the Abingdon region (Map 9). The first of these gaps is explained by the probable survival of London into the sub-Roman period and possibly later, inhibiting settlement along the north bank of the Thames; and the south bank, with its undrained marshes, was altogether unsuitable for dwelling or cultivation. We should have expected, nevertheless, that the gravel terraces of the river Lea would invite occupation and it may be that evidence of early settlement there has been lost, or is still to be found. Place-names in *-ingas*, though not necessarily earlier than the sixth century, do suggest quite early penetration of the Lea valley and its tributaries. From Nazeing (Essex) northward along the Lea and Stort there are in all six such names; and in Hertfordshire we have Braughing and Tewin on minor tributaries; but there are no corresponding cemeteries either early or late.

The gravels of the Wandle valley in Surrey have been more productive of the vestiges of early settlement. Besides the large Mitcham and Croydon burial grounds there is the place-name Tooting and a lost name Washingham in Battersea. The tributaries of the Thames farther to the west in Surrey have so far yielded evidence of secondary settlements only, but some of them (e.g. Fetcham and Guildown) were probably not very much later than those of the Wandle valley. Much the same is true of the Middlesex side. Near to London there is almost a complete blank until the seventh century; and the heavy London Clay of north Middlesex bore dense woodland that was not occupied until some time after the initial colonization of the South-East. On the other hand, the loamy brick-earth in the south-west of the county appears highly attractive; yet apart from a cemetery at Shepperton, occupation does not seem to have begun before the sixth century was well advanced, and then it is attested only by the burial ground at Hanwell. The pagan name Harrow in the tribal region of the *Gumeningas* and the names Ealing and Yeading do suggest, however, that the middle and southern parts of the county were well peopled before the beginning of the seventh century.

The longer gap between the early Surrey settlements and the old nucleus of Wessex round Abingdon may be attributed to two causes; unsuitability of terrain and insecurity. Both on the north and the south banks of the Thames there were large tracts of forest, and, in addition, the Chiltern region was almost certainly in the possession of the Britons until late in the sixth century. Their presence would have made Saxon settlements in Thames-side Buckinghamshire or Oxfordshire most unsafe. Early place-names in this region such as Goring (Oxon), Sonning and Reading (Berks)—the latter with a pagan cemetery—may well betoken extensions of the primary settlement area round Abingdon; at any rate, archaeological proof of colonization in the fifth century does not occur downstream beyond Dorchester except beside the lower reaches of the river.

It is in this nuclear region of Saxon Wessex that we find some of the earliest burials in Britain. They are as ancient as any of those farther to the east in Surrey and Kent, and they indicate a deep incursion into the very heart of southern Britain that was going on at the same time as the first lodgements were being made on and near the eastern coasts. Probably the earliest are the few burials made at Dorchester which, apart from an early pot from Osney, comprise all the fifth-century material from the Oxfordshire bank of the Thames. In neither instance, however, do they suggest the burial place of a settled community; more likely they represent the disposal of casualties on one of the earliest forays before the settlement proper had begun.

It is on the Berkshire bank, at Abingdon, Frilford, Long Wittenham, Sutton Courtenay and, farther south, at East Shefford, that the primary settlements of Wessex were established. The invasion from the south coast that is recounted in the *Anglo-Saxon Chronicle*, and the settlements founded as a result of that invasion, contributed a less conspicuous part to the kingdom of Wessex. From the south came the royal house, Cerdic and his line, and the *Chronicle* was originally compiled as a memorial of that line. If there had been traditions of the conquest of the Abingdon region, they have not survived. The leaders of the Thames-side Saxons may, for a time, have been rivals of the house of Cerdic and in competition for the overall kingship; and the winning side did not see fit to perpetuate memories of the exploits of a rival house. History is therefore silent concerning the advent of an important part of the earliest West Saxons and archaeology has to be called in to supply the deficiency.

Some of the graves at Abingdon and East Shefford included objects of Frankish origin; and the very early cruciform brooches from Dorchester and Abingdon could as easily have been brought from the Frisian coast as from the Elbe-Weser district. But the material from the Abingdon region as a whole is predominantly Saxon in character and the earliest pieces can be matched best in the old Saxon homeland.

The cast saucer-shaped brooches with a running spiral pattern found in five of the cemeteries, and the brooches of similar form on which the same decoration was added by the application of an embossed disc—these were, in origin, a Saxon and not an Anglian or Jutish fashion. But even more distinctive are the equal-armed brooches of *c.* A.D. 450 from Abingdon, and of about twenty-five years later from Sutton Courtenay. They have been found only in the Saxon areas of Britain and Germany, and their distribution on both sides of the North Sea affords the most valuable clue to one of the migration routes taken by the first settlers in Berkshire.

On this side of the North Sea they have been found at Little Wilbraham and Haslingfield (Cambs) and at Kempston (Beds). All of this became Anglian territory before the time of the Conversion to Christianity, but there are good reasons for believing that from the Chilterns near Luton (Beds) north-eastward as far as the Devil's Ditch near Newmarket (Suffolk) there was a broad belt of very early Saxon settlement. Its northerly bounds took in the south bank of the Ouse near Bedford and the neighbourhood of the Roman settlement at Cambridge. There are indications of scattered Saxon occupation even farther to the north and north-west; but the evidence consists mainly of saucer brooches, whose presence may be due to trade from the Saxon areas rather than to actual Saxon settlement.

Most telling of all was the discovery that the equal-armed brooch from Wilbraham had been cast in the same mould as one from Dösemoor in Hanover. It is a fair inference that the Wilbraham specimen was imported by a migrant at about the turn of the fifth century; and the location of these brooches in Cambridgeshire, Bedfordshire and Berkshire suggests a migration route across the North Sea to the Wash and thence along the rivers Ouse and Cam to a junction with the Icknield Way in southern Cambridgeshire. The line of the Way leads from there straight to the Goring Gap and the Abingdon region.

But it would almost certainly be an error to suppose that all of the Middle Thames Saxons came by this route; there is a strong likelihood that some of them followed the Thames up from its mouth. The essentially Saxon character of all the settlements along the Thames valley has already been stressed; but there is material from near the estuary, from its lower course in Surrey, and from above the Goring Gap, which suggests the line of the Thames as one important route of immigration. The early cruciform brooches from East Shefford, Abingdon and Dorchester on the one hand and those from Kent on the other, afford one category of evidence. But there is also a rare form of saucer brooch with a low rim and the spiral pattern, as found in Berkshire, Surrey and north-west Germany; and a similar distribution, with the addition of north Kent, for a type of saucer brooch with a floreated-cross pattern. There are also the early belt fittings from Dorchester, Croydon, Milton Regis and from beside the Elbe—these and other objects afford a chain of evidence stretching from north Germany, across the North Sea and along the Thames which is no less complete than that afforded by the Icknield route. These two lines of approach which are suggested by the study of Saxon archaeology, and the route from the south followed by Cerdic and his successors, together emphasize the complexity of the process of Anglo-Saxon settlement. It was a piecemeal process occupying more than a century with bands striking far inland even in the first phase. Subsequently a coalescence of minor regions gave rise to the kingdoms that are familiar from historical sources.

So far we have been mainly concerned with areas south of the Thames; to the north of it the settlement is more obscure. The modern map of Essex still bears over two dozen -ingas names, seven in -ingham and probably more than ten which commemorate heathen worship. But all of these could have arisen at least half a century later than the primary settlements in Kent or Berkshire. Nor does the archaeology of the East Saxons provide any clear indications of colonization before the sixth century. Cremations have been found in and near Colchester and cemeteries at Heybridge, Kelvedon, Feering, Marks Tey, Great Chesterford and Shoebury. But few deductions can be made from the objects found, except that none is comparable in date with those from areas of earliest settlement, and that the East Saxons were a comparatively poor people. The cemetery at Prittlewell shows close affinities with Kent and points to an extension of Jutish culture and power northward across the Thames estuary. A rich, but late, burial from Broomfield in the north of the county and a jewel from Forest Gate in the south have a distant affinity with the sumptuous East Anglian culture revealed in the royal cenotaph at Sutton Hoo, Suffolk. On the whole, however, it may be said that Essex was colonized later than such inland districts as the Abingdon and Cambridge regions and the cause may well have been that unforested tracts of medium loam were too limited in extent and too inaccessible from the coast, except near Colchester, to entice the earlier immigrants to settle.

The same is true of Hertfordshire; cemeteries showing use before A.D. 500 are not known and the two *-ingas* names, as noted above, are not necessarily earlier than that date. But in the Chilterns there are grounds for believing in a relatively long persistence of British life untouched by the Saxon invader. Southern Buckinghamshire and southern Oxfordshire were also occupied late, and though there are early names and several cemeteries in both areas, there is nothing to suggest their colonization before the later sixth century.

In southern Bedfordshire, on the other hand, it is likely that the Saxon settlers at Biscot in Luton had been in occupation for some time before the capture of Limbury (also in Luton), which the *Chronicle* records as having occurred in the year 571. The West Saxon prince Cuthwulf is said to have defeated the 'Brit-Welsh' at *Bedcanford* (which I believe to be Bedford on the Ouse), and to have subsequently taken Limbury, Aylesbury, Benson and Eynsham. This campaign added the Chiltern scarp-foot zone in Buckinghamshire and Oxfordshire to the West Saxon domains adjacent to them in Berkshire and enabled settlement of the newly-won region to proceed without constant danger from the Britons surviving in the Chiltern forests. The archaeological, topographical and place-name evidence in no way conflicts with this theory even though the proposed identification of *Bedcanford* with Bedford be not accepted.

This extension of the West Saxon kingdom found mention in the *Chronicle*; but, though there must have been other minor campaigns in our region after the consolidation of the original settlements, history is silent about them. Nevertheless, the evidence from the graveyards, and to a less extent from place-names, makes it certain that after *c.* A.D. 550 there was a vigorous phase of expansion in which communities hived off from the initial settlements and established themselves in neighbouring districts which had been less attractive to the earlier colonists. No doubt, too, new immigrants were still entering the country in small numbers and some of them would have joined the bands responsible for the new villages.

In Kent, hamlets were founded to the south of the Downs and especially in the neighbourhood of Maidstone, where there is a great widening of the belt of fine arable soils that follow the scarp-foot of the North Downs. Here place-names such as Barming, Yalding and Malling, and burial grounds such as those discovered at Hollingbourne and Harrietsham, attest settlement before A.D. 600. Rather less evidence, but equally valid, is known from the Ashford neighbourhood. And there was movement into the Weald proper, where small groups of cottages gave shelter to swineherds who were in charge of animals owned by villagers as far away as the Isle of Thanet; for the name Tenterden, for instance, which means 'swine-pasture of the men of Thanet', makes it clear that this Wealden settlement was an offshoot from villages in a region that was among the first occupied.

Something of the same sort happened in Sussex and Surrey. In the Weald of the South Saxons are a number of place-names of early type which are known to have belonged to hamlets of swineherds and to have been dependencies of coastal villages. For instance, Poling near Littlehampton seems to have had such dependencies at Pallingham (Wisborough Green), *Palshuddes* (Petworth) and Pallinghurst (Cranleigh, Surrey). Other coastal villages such as Climping and Bognor are known to have had similar Wealden offshoots. The southward extension of the settled areas of Surrey is evident in other ways. Cemeteries like those found at Ewell, Fetcham and Coulsdon, and many scattered burials, suggest that the whole of this section of the North Downs, wherever free of woodland, was being exploited by the end of the sixth century. But apart from pottery, such as that from Farnham, Thursley, Wotton and Betchworth, there is little to show archaeologically that the Weald had been penetrated so early. Yet settlement to the south of the chalk had certainly occurred before the time of the Conversion, for about ten pagan place-names such as Willey in Farnham, Peper Harow, Thursley and Thunderfield (Horley) still appear on the map; and there is an unusual concentration of them in the Farnham-Godalming region where also tracts of good arable occur. A little to the north-east is situated Guildown with a Saxon cemetery, which had probably first come into use in the later sixth century.

Most of the significant evidence relating to Hampshire has already been discussed. The *Chronicle* gives an initial date of *c.* 500 for the conquest of the southern part and there is nothing yet known to gainsay it. The Droxford cemetery does, however, show late Saxon influence modifying or even replacing the primary Jutish culture; and single burials have been found in most parts of the county (apart from the New Forest), which reveal at least that Saxons or Jutes were active here in the pagan period. The Winchester area was certainly occupied before 700, for burials have been found at Winnall and there is a largely unexcavated cemetery in Kings Worthy Park. In the north of the county a few isolated burials and place-names such as Worting, Basing and Poland (formerly Polling, in Odiham parish) afford a few scraps of circumstantial detail.

In the old heart of Wessex on the middle Thames, evidence is more abundant. A secondary expansion of the settled area at least as far southward as the chalk is suggested by such names as Wantage, Ginge and Lockinge; and cemeteries such as that of the latter place, and isolated burials, provide confirmatory evidence. On the other side of the Thames there was little or no settlement before the *Bedcanford* campaign of 571. But soon after it, communities were burying their dead at Wheatley, Cuddesdon and Ewelme; and there is a whole group of burial grounds in the Aylesbury neighbourhood (e.g. Bishopstone, Kingsey and Dinton) which are not very much, if at all, later. Almost contemporary with these Buckinghamshire burials were those at Ashwell and King's Walden (Herts). In Essex, however, the archaeological evidence is too sparse and too inadequately published to allow of any clear differentiation between primary and secondary phases of occupation.

Much of our knowledge of the life of the early Anglo-Saxons has been provided by their dead; of their agricultural economy there is no direct information, and its nature has to be inferred from documents of a much later date. And there is a serious danger that the more evolved system known to history may be inferred to have existed during the pioneering phase of the pagan period, which belongs mainly to prehistory. But the existence of an open-field system among related Germanic peoples who did not migrate suggests that it was a characteristic of the western and northern German tribes, and that it was, in a simpler form, introduced into Britain by the Anglo-Saxons. Yet the three-field system of crop rotation, beloved of textbooks, developed only sporadically from the thirteenth century in the richer agricultural regions such as the Midland plain; elsewhere, a two-field system prevailed in the western parts of our region. In the east, in Kent and Essex particularly, the open fields, if they occurred at all, were exceptional. In Kent enclosed fields and the hamlet are more typical of the countryside as far back as records take us; and it is sometimes assumed that this was a development of Jutish custom. The Middle Rhine, where the Jutish phase in the archaeology of Kent has its closest analogies, is the Continental region where also Kentish agricultural custom may be most nearly matched. The one set of affinities seems to support the other and an immediate derivation of the men of Kent from the Middle Rhine is thus rendered more probable.

In the laws of King Ine of Wessex (c. A.D. 700) there is clear evidence for private property in land, and that not all of it was held or worked communally. It is probably unwise to go further than the assumption that a division was made between individual holdings of arable and the land which was used as common pasture for the herds. From later developments it is reasonable to infer that in areas of Saxon settlement the houses were placed in compact groups, so-called nucleated villages. When, however, forested regions such as the Weald or, possibly, eastern Berkshire were colonized, a more scattered form of settlement seems to have prevailed: within the bounds of a single ancient parish there may be several hamlets, none of which appears to have predominated unless it be that which includes the church. Parts of Hertfordshire and southern Buckinghamshire also show this form of scattered settlement.

Only one nucleated village of the pagan period has been discovered and excavated; otherwise single hut-sites, that may have belonged once to groups of dwellings, are all that are so far known (Map 9). The Sutton Courtenay village, a mile west of the present nucleus, consisted of more than thirty hovels arranged in irregular lines, each hovel excavated down into the gravel for about two feet. Vestiges of post-holes showed that the roof was supported by two uprights which carried the roof-ridge; and it may well be that the walls of mud and straw were built up a foot or so to the low eaves, which allowed little headroom. The huts varied in shape from squarish to oblong, but all had rounded corners. Their average measurements were about twelve feet by ten; but a smithy, with its hearth, slaking tank and scoriae, had dimensions of twenty-one feet by eleven.

Most of the huts had round hearths of stones, some of which were associated with large, crude cooking-pots and many pot-boilers (heated stones which were dropped into the pot to heat the contents. The pots would have cracked in direct contact with the fire). A few of the houses had a pit for cooking outside the main structure. One of these was adjacent to a hut which had two rooms, corner to corner, with a doorway connecting them. These rooms had not been built at the same time, and beneath a blanket of clay that formed the floor of the later one was the skeleton of a man who had died in his prime. Behind a post-hole of the earlier room, the equal-armed brooch, already mentioned, came to light. It had almost certainly been brought over by one of the earlier immigrants from the Elbe-Weser region of north Germany and its date of manufacture was c. 475, which affords a clue to the dating of the village.

The Sutton Courtenay hovels were deep in filth like all the others known from this period; and, like the few examples found elsewhere, most of them seem to have contained a vertical weaving-loom, marked by the post-holes of its upright beams and by clay rings that had been used as loom-weights. These are sometimes found lying in a line amidst the rubbish on the floor. Broken weaving-combs, small bone heddle-sticks, spindle-whorls of clay or bone or of perforated sherds of Roman pottery—these together suggest the importance of spinning and weaving in the home. The finding of a cow-bell, of saws, chisels, awls, knives and nails is indicative of the importance of the crafts of the smith and carpenter.

Saxon huts have also been found at Thakeham, Selsey and Chichester in Sussex—wattle and daub structures in the latter two instances—but they were probably of a date later than the pagan period. Another habitation site came to light at Radley (Berks); and at Farnham (Surrey) a group of huts contained pottery that was comparable with some from the pagan cemetery at Ewell, indicating a probable sixth-century date for the Farnham settlement. A dwelling-site at Canterbury showed occupation by Romano-Britons of the late fourth century, immediately followed by Anglo-Frisians of the fifth; and other material indicated continued occupation in later Saxon times. The site had been chosen by its fifth-century occupants because it was not encumbered by the debris or foundations of Roman buildings, apart from a timber structure of the earlier centuries of the Roman era. By the fifth century this would no longer have been noticeable. Like the huts at Sutton Courtenay, those at Canterbury were half-sunk into the ground; and one of them had a clay floor.

Although archaeology is silent in the matter, it is evident from the Laws of King Ine and from those of Alfred that later homesteads were fenced round. In the earlier laws the explicit purpose was to keep cattle from the toft; but in the late ninth century the enclosure must have been substantial, for it could stand a siege. In Bede's account of St. Cuthbert's hermitage on Farne Island there is mention of the building of a small dwelling with a well in its floor and 'surrounded with a ditch and earth-wall'; after many years of life on the island the embankment was so high that Cuthbert could see nothing but the sky from within its circuit. In all this we may see the beginnings of the moated homestead of which so many medieval examples survive in the Home Counties.

In the countryside there is little visible that can be confidently dated to the period lasting from the fifth to eighth centuries. At Taplow (Bucks) is a large barrow from which magnificent funeral furniture of the early seventh century was recovered; it is now in the British Museum. A century ago a number of barrow-clusters could still be seen in Kent, but today only those on Breach Down, Barham, remain although others are said to survive in the parishes of Bishopsbourne, Bridge, Kingston and St. Margaret-at-Cliff (Map 9). Outside the modern boundaries of Kent a well-preserved group exists in Greenwich Park (London); and in Surrey fourteen Saxon barrows are to be seen strung out along the ridge of Farthingdown (Coulsdon) (Figure 14). This Surrey group is of particular interest because other Saxon graves, but without a mound, were found in close proximity to barrows of the same date, the sixth and early seventh centuries.

The use of older barrows by the Saxons was common, especially beyond the western parts of our region. Usually these are inhumations of warriors, probably those killed on raids. Such an interment with spearhead and scramasax was found in a Neolithic long barrow at Preston Candover (Hants), and at least two such burials have been found as secondary interments in the Bronze Age round barrows of Sussex. At Bledlow (Bucks) an Early Bronze Age barrow contained two inhumations and five cremations of the pagan Saxon period. A double ring-ditch at Broadstairs (Kent), which contained primary crouched burials of, it seems, the Early Bronze Age, was re-used by the Jutes as a cemetery. There was similar re-use of Late Bronze Age barrows at Hollingbourne (Kent). At Dorchester (Oxon) the very early Saxon burials were made in a part of the Iron Age rampart of the Dyke Hills and there were later Saxon burials in a Bronze Age barrow there and in the hill-fort of Iron Age A2 at Blewburton (Berks). Moreover, a sixth-century inhumation was recovered from the bank of the Roman earthwork called Oliver's Battery at Compton (Hants). The use as a cemetery of the Iron Age enclosure on High Down (Ferring, Sussex) has already been alluded to. In this instance the interments appear to have been made within the area bounded by the banks. The very late Saxon cemetery at Saffron Walden (Essex) was similarly enclosed by the ramparts of the Repell Ditches, which were probably the work of the Belgae.

But the most interesting re-use of older sites may have some bearing on the relationship between the Saxons and the Britons. It has often been stated that the Saxons avoided Roman towns and settled almost invariably in the open countryside, but the known exceptions to this are now so numerous that a revision of the older view seems called for. Saxo-Frisian occupation inside the Roman walls of Canterbury has been mentioned earlier; and Chichester was certainly not shunned by the earliest South Saxons. Almost every major Roman site in Kent has produced Saxon or Jutish burials —Dover, Rochester, Richborough, Reculver, Lympne, Northfleet, Milton Regis and Faversham. It is true that in most instances the burials were placed outside the Roman habitation area; but, if this became the dwelling-place of the newcomers, it is understandable that they would have their cemeteries near, but not within, the habitation area. There was also some Saxon occupation within the walls of Colchester and their burials have been excavated in the minor Roman town of Great Chesterford. Bradwell, one of the shore-forts, had interments nearby. In Hampshire the total evidence for early Saxon occupation is scanty, yet numerous burials have come to light in the vicinity of Winchester. The same is true of Dorchester (Oxon).

Nothing that points to early occupation has been found close to Roman London. At the Savoy a dwelling-site of the seventh or eighth century yielded a sherd with Frisian affinities, and an almost complete vessel from Drury Lane has the same ultimate connections. Its sides are fluted in a manner not customary among Saxon or Jutish potters, yet related types have been found in Kent (Canterbury, Westbere, Sarre and Northfleet), in Surrey (Banstead, Guildown and Limpsfield) and in Middlesex at Shepperton. The Drury Lane pot was made late in the pagan period; some of the Kentish examples are relatively early.

Neither Silchester nor Verulamium and their neighbourhoods have produced any sign that Saxons settled there in the primary phase; the absence of archaeological evidence and of early place-names is noteworthy in both areas. We have already seen, however, that there are indications of a late prolongation of Romano-British life in both, and there is an additional factor which has to be allowed for: that these areas were not especially attractive to Saxon agriculturists.

Almost all of the known dwelling-sites of the Saxons were on or very near to Romano-British buildings, and in Kent and the Abingdon region not a few of the earliest Saxon or Jutish graveyards show a continuation in their use from late Roman times into the following period. Yet in spite of this continuity in the use of burial places, there is little archaeological evidence that affords proof that the two peoples lived side by side or intermingled. The skeletal remains from the Saxon cemetery at Frilford (Berks) pointed to a first generation of interments of Saxon men and women, and to a second generation of mixed Saxo-Roman stock. Yet the objects found with the dead did not necessarily suggest such a conclusion. But late Romano-British occupation of the immediate vicinity is undoubted, and the Saxon cemetery of the fifth and sixth centuries was placed directly adjacent to one that had been used by the Britons.

The occurrence of Saxon pottery on the sites of Roman villas is perhaps no more conclusive of living contact between the two peoples than the proximity of their burial grounds. Such finds of pottery have been made at the Wymondley villa (Herts) most notably; and from Totternhoe (Beds). The vessels with both Roman and Jutish affinities from villas at Wingham and Hartlip (Kent) are, however, of more significance because of their mixed cultural features. The many instances of churches on villa-sites, especially in Kent, Essex and Sussex, indicate merely that the first Christian builders chose a place with ready-made materials at hand. But the probable continuity of Romano-British sacred sites into pagan Saxon times is more to the point. The Saxon name *Harowdone* (fifteenth century) for the hill on which a Romano-Celtic temple stood at Woodeaton (Oxon), makes it probable that the spot had not lost its sanctity during the pagan Saxon period; and finds of many late Roman coins there strengthen the probability that the site continued in use from the one period to the other. The *stan erigan* (stone temple) in the bounds of Washington (Sussex) seems to refer to the Romano-Celtic temple within Chanctonbury Ring and indicates, like that at Woodeaton, that at least the Saxons recognized the function of these buildings. The temple at Farley Heath (Albury, Surrey) yielded a scatter of late Roman coins, but there are no pagan Saxon associations with its site; the place-name Harrows-hill (also in Albury) is not on early record and it is, in any case, too distant from Farley Heath to have any relationship with the temple.

There is one other line of approach: place-names that preserve elements of British speech. The matter is too large to discuss in the present context but it is enough to point out that a small number of such names do survive, especially in Hampshire and Surrey. But the most significant example occurs in Hertfordshire. In the *Anglo-Saxon Chronicle*, under the year 913 (which should read 912) there is the statement that King Edward the Elder of Wessex build a fortress (*burh*) at Hertford between the rivers Maran, Beane and Lea. The name Beane is given as *Bene ficcan*, which is Old British for 'Beane little', with the adjective placed after the noun. In other surviving British names, such as Wen-dover (white stream), the adjective precedes the noun, and it is likely that this word order remained customary until the late sixth century at the earliest. Such a name as Beane could only have been learnt from Britons at some time after A.D. 600, and points to a very late survival of the natives in this region. We have already seen that this was probably true also of the Verulamium neighbourhood and it may be concluded that Cuthwulf's campaign of A.D. 571 cleared the Britons from the line of the Icknield Way but not from the Chiltern forests as a whole.

BIBLIOGRAPHY TO CHAPTER XII

Two general works, *Roman Britain and the English Settlements* (1937) by Collingwood and Myres and *A History of the Anglo-Saxons* (1939) by R. H. Hodgkin, are both valuable for their surveys of the period, for their extensive bibliographies and for their maps. On the archaeology of the period in general, see G. Baldwin Brown, *The Arts in Early England*, vols. III and IV (1915); and for the metal goods, N. Åberg, *The Anglo-Saxons in England* (1926). The problem of agriculture, related to its European background, is discussed in *The Cambridge Economic History*, vol. I, edited by Clapham and Power (1942), chaps. I to IV; and the relation of soils to settlement is studied by regions in *An Historical Geography of England* (1951), chap. III, by S. W. Wooldridge. The Ordnance Survey map of Land Classification (Southern Sheet, 1944) is a useful adjunct. J. E. A. Jolliffe's *Pre-Feudal England: The Jutes*, is a study of the origins of Kentish agricultural custom.

1 Long barrow—Grans Barrow, Rockbourne, Hants, a tomb of the Western Neolithic Culture

2 Neolithic burial chamber, denuded of its earthen mound, of the Medway Culture—Kit's Coty House, Aylesford, Kent

3 Cursus, Overy, Dorchester, Oxon, with ploughed-out barrows and enclosures of the Neolithic, Early and Middle Bronze Age. A crop-mark site

4 The Five Knolls, Dunstable, Beds—barrows of the Early Bronze Age re-used for Middle Bronze Age cremation burials and for the interment of raiding Saxons of the fifth century

5 Bell barrows, Bow Hill, Sussex, of the Middle Bronze Age. A cross-ridge dyke is visible below the nearest barrow and a linear earthwork runs beside the left-hand cart-track

6 A Middle Bronze Age necropolis, Lambourn, Berks,—bell, saucer, bowl and disc barrows. Two of the largest are surrounded by relatively modern tree-rings. See Figure 6

7 Ranch boundary-ditch of the Late Bronze or Early Iron Age on Blagdon Hill, Martin, Hants. Compare Figure 9

26 View of the top of the castle mound, Abinger, Surrey, after excavation. The strings outline the post-holes of a timber tower and the post-holes of the surrounding palisade run parallel to the limits of excavation at the top of the photograph

27 Pirton, Herts. A small part of the extensive manorial and village earthworks. The Toot Hill is obscured by trees to the left

28 A deserted village, Hope All Saints, Romney Marsh, Kent, now within the parish of New Romney. Ruins of the church are visible

There is no comprehensive survey of the bearing of place-names on the history of the settlement, but the works by Myres, Wooldridge and Hodgkin cited above contain good summaries of the evidence. F. M. Stenton's *Anglo-Saxon England* (1943) is also valuable.

Few satisfactory accounts of the excavation of cemeteries in our region exist, but the best is *The Anglo-Saxon Cemetery at Abingdon* by Leeds and Harden (1936). The casual finds at Westbere, Kent, are described in *Antiquaries Journal*, 26 (1946). Among E. T. Leeds's many contributions to the subject his *Early Anglo-Saxon Art and Archaeology* (1936) and his excavation of the village at Sutton Courtenay, Berks, reported in *Archaeologia*, 63, 76 and 92, at least should be mentioned.

Brief regional accounts are to be found in the County Archaeologies listed in the General Bibliography and fuller discussions in R. E. M. Wheeler's *London and the Saxons* (1935); *The Oxford Region* (1954), chapter 10, by J. N. L. Myres; *The Archaeology of the Cambridge Region* (1923), chapter 6, by C. Fox, which takes in parts of Herts, Beds and Essex, and *The Conquest of Wessex in the Sixth Century* (1954), by G. J. Copley, which attempts to correlate all the categories of evidence and is relevant for Hants, Berks, Oxon, Surrey and the Chiltern region. Though a little out of date in its detail, the Ordnance Survey map of Britain in the Dark Ages (South Sheet, 1935) is still very valuable, but the indications of woodland on it are incomplete. Many of the contributions to *Dark Age Studies* (1956), edited by D. B. Harden, are stimulating and break new ground, some of it of moderate fertility.

* Inexpensive works.

M

CHAPTER XIII

The Middle Ages

WITH THE COMING of Christianity to Britain in the seventh century the deposition of funeral furniture in graves soon ceased and a main source of evidence concerning our Anglo-Saxon ancestors was lost. The archaeology of the later Saxon period is scrappy and there are many gaps in our knowledge despite the new accessions of information that have accrued from the excavations at Sutton Hoo (Suffolk) and the Saxon towns at Thetford (Norfolk) and Southampton (Hants).

The dark-age port of *Hamwih* (Southampton) had been largely obliterated by the removal of brick-earth in the nineteenth century, so that a large part of the area of occupation had gone. But enough remained to afford valuable information concerning a period that had been archaeologically a blank apart from stray finds and, in our region, fragments of churches. From the pottery and other small finds it appeared that *Hamwih* had been occupied from about the seventh century until the Norman Conquest.

Cut down to the subsoil were what seemed to be the cellars of huts. They were rectangular in shape and a typical example was eleven feet long by six wide and five deep. Burnt wattle and daub occurred in the occupation layers that filled the pits; and they gave a clue to the type of construction and to the way the house above had been destroyed. There were other, squarish pits with central shafts eight to nine feet deep, revetted with planks, whose function is obscure. A lively import trade was revealed by the recovery of wheel-turned pottery of the seventh and eighth centuries which had come from Frankish territory on the Middle and Lower Rhine, and by the finding of fragments of Niedermendig lava, used originally for quernstones, which had also been imported from the Rhineland. Other imports included ninth-century ware from Carolingian Gaul and fragments of glass beakers. Hand-made pottery of local manufacture, including a sherd of stamped ware like that of the pagan period, may possibly indicate occupation of the site before the seventh century.

That there had been some raising of living standards above the squalor of Sutton Courtenay village seems to be suggested by the finds of window glass and of a coarse kind of brick which may have been used as building material. A hoard of coins (*sceattas*) and other stray finds of money did not, apparently, include foreign coins acquired by trade, though it would be unwise to assume from this that there were no exports to pay for the import of the luxuries. It was remarked earlier that almost all hut-sites of the pagan period yielded evidence of weaving. Apart from the post-holes of

178

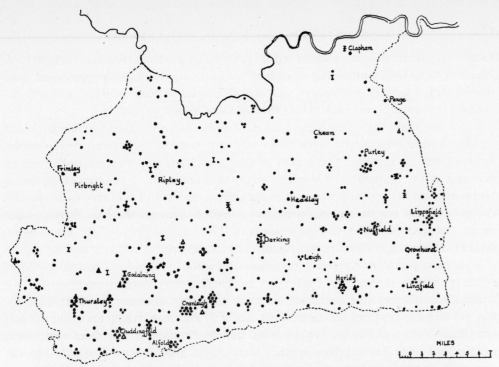

MILES

FIG 17A Ancient woodland in Surrey as indicated by place names. Only those recorded down to the seventeenth century, when deliberate planting began, are plotted. Names probably indicative of a single tree or of small groups of them (e.g. Alderbrook in Albury) are omitted. Symmetrical groupings of dots represent minor place-names that could not be accurately plotted. They are placed near the nucleus of the parish in which they occur

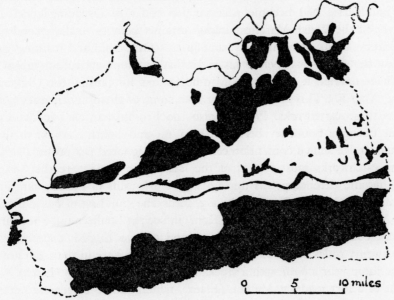

FIG 17B Ancient woodland in Surrey reconstructed on a geological basis

looms, ring-shaped loom-weights afford the main evidence for this industry. At *Hamwih*, as at Leadenhall and elsewhere in London, the loom-weights were bun-shaped with a central perforation; and this difference in form provides a rough distinction between the weights of the early and late Saxon periods.

From the many pits that were excavated came large numbers of animal bones, and these were very wisely collected for later analysis and for a count of the various kinds of animals present. The results of this census shed an interesting light on the economy of the hinterland of *Hamwih*. Cattle accounted for 58 per cent of the bones, sheep or goats for 29 per cent and pigs for only 9 per cent. This latter figure and the 0·4 per cent for red deer is surprising for a town so close to the New Forest, where swine and deer should have been abundant. The total of 87 per cent for domestic hooved cattle suggests much open pasture near the town.

It is here pertinent to notice that some accepted notions concerning the forest cover of Britain during the Dark Ages and before may require modification. Let anyone who doubts this statement compare the maps showing the distribution of the place-name elements *falod* and *hyrst*, and *feld* and *leah*, which are included with the *Place-Names of Surrey* (1934), with the distribution of woodland represented on the Ordnance Survey maps of the 'Dark Ages' and 'Roman Britain'. The discrepancy is immediately apparent (see Figures 17a and 17b). From the place-names it is evident that the local Saxons found wide tracts of forest which the cartographers did not include. The new Ordnance map of 'Roman Britain' does not show the distribution of woodland.

It has already been suggested that some of the linear earthworks of our region may belong to later Saxon times when the kingdoms were expanding and delimitation of their boundaries had become necessary in order to discourage encroachments. Offa's Dyke in the Welsh Marches almost certainly belongs to the second half of the eighth century, as its name implies; and just as Offa delimited his kingdom on the west, so on the south-east, before his realm had attained its fullest extent, he may possibly have defined it against the Middle Saxons by causing the Chiltern ditches to be dug (Map K). This is less unlikely than some of the other theories put forward to explain these earthworks. Possibly also the Froxfield ditches in eastern Hampshire were cut as a boundary between the West and South Saxons; in the present state of knowledge such a contention can neither be ignored nor proved.

But the earthworks most typical of the late Saxon period are the *burhs* built as local rallying and defence points during the Danish raids of the late ninth and early tenth centuries (Map 9). The *Chronicle* records the building of *burhs* by Saxons or Danes at Milton Regis and Appledore (Kent) in 892; at Benfleet and Shoebury (Essex) in 893; the construction of a Danish fort and of two English counterforts on the river Lea twenty miles above London in 894; of yet another in the same area in 912; and in the same year a *burh* with a stockade was built at Witham (Essex). In 919 the annal tells of a fort made at Maldon (Essex), which had to be repaired after a siege

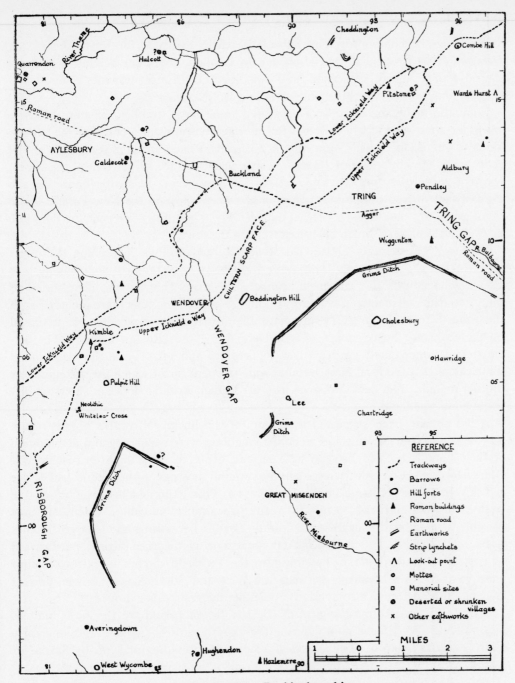

MAP K Southern Buckinghamshire

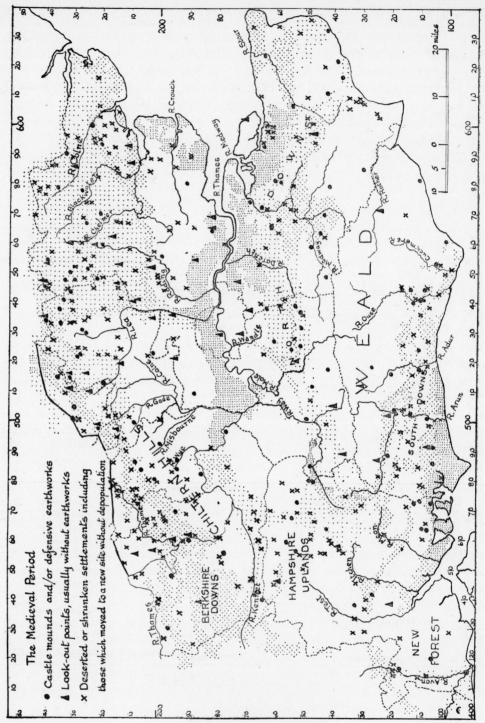

The Medieval Period

● Castle mounds and/or defensive earthworks
▲ Look-out points, usually without earthworks
✕ Deserted or shrunken settlements including those which moved to a new site without depopulation

MAP 10 The Medieval Period

by the Danes in 920. The *burh* at Colchester, presumably the Roman walls, had to
be repaired and rebuilt in the same year. An interesting entry occurs in the Laud MS.
(E) under the year 963. There it is recorded that *Medeshamstede* was renamed *Burch*
(i.e. Peterborough) after a wall had been put round the monastery of St. Peter. In
this part of the *Chronicle* there are a number of references to the Danes or Saxons
encamping at various places within and outside our region; and it is likely that they
built protective ramparts on at least some of these occasions.

A document known as the *Burghal Hidage*, which was probably drawn up in the
late ninth century, refers to some forts other than those mentioned in the Chronicle.
One at Christchurch (Hants) may well have given rise to the place-name Burton, a
mile north of the castle; but those at Southampton, Winchester, Porchester, Chichester, Dover, Canterbury, Rochester, and London probably consisted of the Roman
fortifications rather than of a specially constructed earthen fort. Traces of *burhs*
remain at Lewes and on East Hill, Hastings; and it may be that the existing town
ramparts at Wallingford (Berks) are those referred to in the *Burghal Hidage* (Plate 22).

Fragmentary earthworks at Milton Regis and Kenardington (Kent), the latter
close to Appledore, may be connected with the events of 892. The whereabouts of
the *burh* of 893 at Benfleet (Essex) are now unknown, but the one at Shoebury still
exists in a much-damaged condition. None of the three forts on the Lea near Hertford
has been located, though the name Hertingfordbury may afford a clue; at Maldon
there are faint traces of the *burh* constructed in 919 as well as more considerable
remains at Witham, which is also in Essex. On excavation, however, the latter proved
to be of the Iron Age, and it may be assumed that it was this earthwork that was
strengthened and re-used in 912. It is likely, too, that the *burh* which gave its name to
Burpham (Sussex) was an older work re-used as a local rallying-point during the
Danish raids. It is a promontory fort with a very strong rampart cutting off a long
ridge that is otherwise defended by a river cliff on the west and steep slopes on the
east and south. The evidence so far produced to prove this a work of the late Saxon
period is unconvincing. Similarly, the attribution to the Danes of Ampress Hole at
Lymington (Hants) and of the 'Moat' at Longstock in the same county are intelligent guesses and nothing more. Excavations at Ampress Hole, which is in fact another
promontory fort, produced only medieval pottery, though this neither denies nor
confirms a belief in its Danish origin. The 'Danish dock' at Longstock awaits skilled
investigation with the spade (see *burh*, p. 218).

It was probably during the Danish wars that the many place-names beginning with
the word *tōt* came into use (Map 10). Its meaning is 'look-out hill', and the need for
constant watch from the best vantage point in the parish must have been felt in many
villages so that an alarm could be given in good time. The most interesting instance
of this type of name is Totternhoe (Beds), for the second element, *aern*, means 'house'
and implies some sort of shelter for the watcher. The mound which gave the place
its name was adapted as a castle mound after the Norman Conquest and a rectangular

bailey was added. The Toot Hill at Stanford Rivers (Essex) probably served later as the meeting-place for the Hundred Court of Ongar; the one at Pirton (Herts) survives in the form of a mound with complex associated manorial earthworks (Plate 27).

Ward's Hurst at Pitstone (Bucks), which means 'wooded hill from which watch was kept', is interesting for a sixteenth-century reference to it as *Totehill*. A similar name *weard dun*, 'the watch down', occurs in Crowmarsh (Oxon); in the village name Warborough (Oxon) and in Warborough Farm, Letcombe Regis (Berks), we have a variant *weard beorg*, 'watch hill', with the same meaning. A 'ward-tree' was a feature of Hindhead (Surrey) according to a document of the tenth century. Beacon Hill, Burghclere (Hants), was known as *weard-setl*, 'watch house'. The old phrase 'watch and ward' is called to mind by Wayting Hill in Hexton and in Ashwell (Herts), for the noun 'wait' originally meant 'a watchman' and is related in origin to the words 'wake' and 'watch'. All but two of these instances are on a main route of invasion, the Icknield Way, where peril was much the greater than away from the main natural lines of communication. The number of place-names, usually minor ones, that imply the maintenance of a look-out in our region is very considerable and bears witness to the fearful insecurity engendered by constant Danish raiding. Re-use of the look-out places during the turmoil of Stephen's reign is likely. It should be added that very few of these places are likely to have archaeological significance since most of them are natural hills (see *tōt*, p. 226, and *setecope* in the same paragraph. A number of other instances are given in the Gazetteer).

Medieval earthworks are so numerous and so various that they would require a volume to themselves if adequately discussed; but the fact that they are so common tends to their being easily overlooked. Most frequent of all earthworks in the Home Counties is the medieval moated site, 'The Bury' in several counties. Some perhaps had their origin before the Norman Conquest; a ditch holding water, with a stockaded bank round its inner edge, would have been as serviceable a defence in the ninth as in the thirteenth century; but not one has yet been proved to have been made before the eleventh. They are commonest in Buckinghamshire, Middlesex, Hertfordshire and Essex; six exist in the one parish of Reed (Herts) and there are said to have been five in Arlington (Sussex).

A few of these homesteads have been excavated in recent times. Pachesham Mounts in Leatherhead (Surrey) has been shown from its stratified pottery to have been occupied from *c*. 1200 down to about 1375. The moat was dug *c*. 1290 to surround a hall rebuilt about the same time. Other buildings included a chapel, entrance gateway and a well. Only the moat remains visible. In the same county the Manor of Preston in Banstead has been investigated in advance of its 'development' as a housing estate. Its main feature was an enclosure 700 feet square bounded by a bank and ditch for the corralling of cattle. Their movements were controlled by double-banked roads leading towards Croydon (with its cattle market) and Burgh Heath (the common pasture of the parish). In addition, a north-south road crossed a fishpond by means

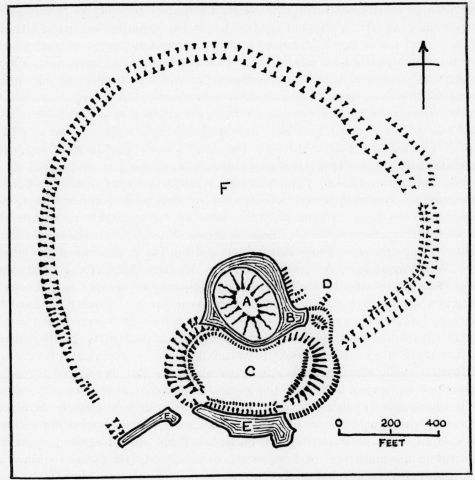

Based on Figure 13, 'Castles', pub. H.M.S.O.

FIG 18 Castle mound 50 feet high (A), moat (B), bailey (C) of about 2 acres, possible remains of a second bailey (D) and fragmentary water defences (E). The outer earthwork (F) protected the village of Pleshey, Essex. The whole complex is of the eleventh or twelfth century

of a causeway at each end of which was a 'guard-point' mound, in shape like a miniature motte-and-bailey castle. These features, hitherto unrecognized elsewhere, no doubt served as places of vantage for the herding of cattle at critical points. An inner enclosure contained a group of manorial buildings whose use could be roughly dated from the late twelfth to the fourteenth century. No medieval site so far excavated has revealed so much of interest concerning a manor and its economy.

Another quite common kind of earthwork is the motte or castle-mound, often with one or more attached courtyards (baileys) protected by ramparts. A few of these were perhaps constructed before the Norman Conquest by Norman favourites of Edward the Confessor. Within our region a few in Essex, notably the one at Clavering, have been said to date from before 1066. But the majority were constructed soon after that time by alien lords who were insecure among a hostile population. A high mound with steep sides and a surrounding ditch, often wet, formed the nucleus of the fortification. At first a wooden tower (*bretasche*) was built on top of it, with a drawbridge over the ditch for access. If the site continued in use, the tower was sometimes rebuilt in stone. The bailey or baileys took various forms, some of which were determined by the lie of the land; but their variety cannot be discussed here. Good examples exist at Pleshey (Figure 18) and Ongar in Essex.

More castles were built in Stephen's reign, symbols of a local tyranny that for a while could defy central authority; but only a few (e.g. Faringdon, Berks, and Abinger,* Surrey) have yet been distinguished from those of the immediate post-Conquest period, for few castle mounds have been excavated. Many later stone castles superseded the primitive mound and bailey fortresses, but the earthworks of the latter, especially the mounds, often remain visible (e.g. Windsor, Arundel and Berkhampsted). Some mottes may be the result of a heightening of barrows (e.g. Caesar's Camp, Folkestone); but a large barrow and a mound without a bailey are hard to distinguish one from the other without digging. At least two hill-forts were adapted for use as adulterine castles in the reign of Stephen: Desborough Castle (High Wycombe, Bucks) and the Caburn (Beddingham, Sussex). In two instances within our region, at Porchester and Pevensey, a Norman stone castle with earthworks was established within a fort of the Saxon shore, the Roman walls providing a ready-made bailey of great strength.

The distribution of castle mounds in the south-east is of great interest (Map 10), for many of them guard ancient lines of communication such as the gaps in the chalk hills round London, or strategic points on Roman roads. Almost all the gaps in the Chilterns to the north-west of London are so controlled, and mounds survive at Wallingford (Berks), dominating the Goring Gap; at Saunderton, High Wycombe, Kimble, Little Missenden and Weston Turville (Bucks), and Berkhampsted (Herts), controlling the Chiltern valleys at one or both ends. The pattern to the south of London is less obvious. The main river route is guarded by the royal castle at Windsor and the Wey gap by Guildford castle. None is known in the Mole gap or at its ends, though Abinger seems to control a minor route across the North Downs to the Weald, and Walton-on-the-Hill another. Reigate, Bletchingley, Godstone and Oxted form a line immediately south of the chalk (Map G), but its eastward continuation near Maidstone and the pattern as a whole in Kent require further study. The river gaps in the South Downs, however, are all guarded: Burlough (Arlington) on the Cuckmere, Lewes on the Ouse (Map L), Bramber on the Adur and Arundel on the Arun. There are, of course, other mounds and later castles in Sussex, most of them on main routes but away from the Downs.

* In fact, this should be dated c. 1100. See Plate 26.

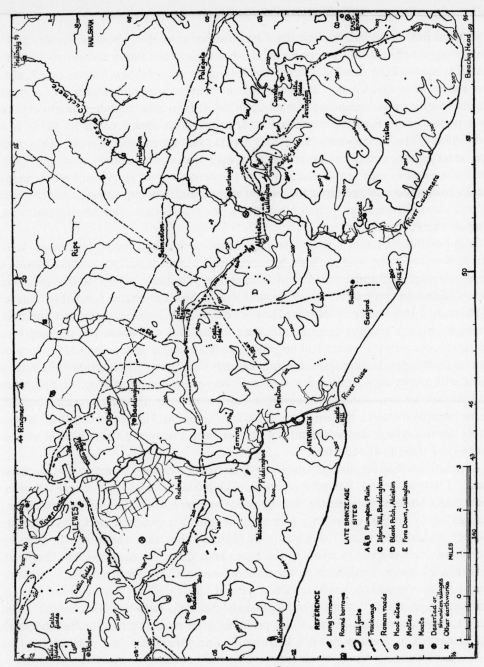

MAP L Eastern Sussex

A good deal of speculative nonsense has been written about hundred-moots and I do not propose to add to the farrago here. The origin of the hundred-court is obscure, but it seems to have developed from the folk-moot of early Saxon times; and when the shires were divided into hundreds in the tenth century or earlier, these small administrative units, consisting of a group of parishes, were put under the jurisdiction of a popular assembly, the hundred-moot, from which appeal could be made to a shire-moot. The former met every four weeks; the latter twice a year. The moot (i.e. meeting; the word has no connection with 'moat' or 'motte') was held in an open place and as near to the middle of the hundred as possible. A point where many tracks converged was preferred for ease of access, and it is not unusual for the spot to be at a convergence of parish boundaries, for these often originally followed the lines of ancient tracks.

It is possible that moots were being held even in heathen times, for one in Kent met at Wye (sanctuary) and in Essex, hundreds were named from *Thunres lau* (Thunor's burial mound) in Bulmer parish and Thurstable (Thunor's pillar). In Sussex there were *Ghidenetroi* (probably 'tree of the goddesses') and Easewrithe (probably 'thicket of the gods'). It is quite possible that Harlow (Essex), which gave its name to a hundred, originally meant 'temple mound', referring to the oval hill where the remains of a Romano-Celtic temple would still have been visible in early Saxon times. It is curious that a field-name Harlow (seventeenth century) occurs in Thundridge (Herts), a name with pagan associations; but the same field-name recurs in Hatfield which has no such known associations. However, if Harlow does, in the first instance quoted, mean 'temple mound', it is in some ways similar to the Harrowdownhill in Woodeaton (Oxon), where also a Roman temple has been discovered. But there is no evidence for a moot at Woodeaton.

A prominent feature in the landscape was usually chosen to mark the meeting-place. Thurstable and Barstable (Essex), Whitstable (Kent) and Staple (Sussex) show that a wooden pillar might thus be used; or a tree, as in Elthorne or Spelthorne (Middx) and Copthorne (Surrey). A prominent stone is a common mark, as in Brixton (Surrey), Maidstone (Kent) or Ossulstone (Middx). But in a number of instances a prehistoric barrow gave its name to the moot and, though it may now be destroyed, its former existence is indicated by the hundred-name. Certainty is not always possible since both *beorh* and *hlāw* could refer to a natural hill as well as a barrow. Flexborough (hill with grass tufts), Swanborough (peasants' hill) and Baldslow (Bald's hill), all in Sussex, indicate meeting-places, in all probability on natural hills; but Bewsborough and Ringslow in Kent may refer to tumuli. The barrow called Cuckhamsley (the *gemote aet Cwicelmes hlaew*, tenth century), in the boundary of East Hendred parish, was the shire-moot of Berkshire. The large oaken stake found in its centre may have been the stump of a *stapol* marking the meeting-place.

The moot could take place at a barrow without the fact being obvious from the name of the hundred. For instance, Thurstable Hundred is known to have met at a surviving barrow in the parish of Tolleshunt Major (Essex), and presumably Thunor's pillar stood on this mound for greater prominence. In the same county at Wendens Ambo there existed a barrow known as Mutlow, which means 'moot hill', and at it the Hundred of Uttlesford gathered. In some instances a prehistoric hill-fort gave shelter to the meeting as at Desborough in High Wycombe (Bucks). Burbeach Hundred (Sussex), which includes the parishes of Upper and Lower Beeding among others, probably met at an earthwork; but as the Hundred is in two detached parts, the meeting-place would be difficult to locate.

Bermondspit Hundred (Hants) came together where the parish boundaries of Nutley, Preston Candover and Ellisfield meet, and the depression (pit) is still visible. The Hundred of Bishops Waltham in the same county met at a wolfpit. From these, and from the instances cited earlier, it may be seen that one effect of locating a moot may be to discover an ancient earthwork; and the hundred-name sometimes affords a clue to its location.

The Old English word (ge-)mōt, 'a meeting', may occur in one of several modern forms, as possibly Mutfords in Hormead (Herts); and it is just conceivable that Mulberry Green, Harlow, may represent a later venue for the Hundred than the one mentioned above, for in the sixteenth century it was called Mudborow Green, which could be a development of the Old English word mōtbeorg, similar in meaning to Mutlow. At Eastbourne (Sussex) the hundred-moot was held near Motcombe, which means 'valley near which the moot was held'. Less probable is the location of the moot of Easewrithe Hundred at Muttons (Farm) on the boundary between Sullington and Thakeham parishes in Sussex. The farm is at the intersection of five ways (as farms are wont to be), but it is not central to the Hundred; and if an eighteenth-century John Mutton did not acquire his family name from the place, then presumably it was named from him or from one of his ancestors, and there need be no local significance in the place-name. A further illustration of the dangers of speculation from the modern form of a place-name is to be seen in that of Mutton Wood near Rochester which takes its name from a castle 'motte'. Motley, in Rainham (Kent), is also suspect.

The minor name Hundredsteddle occurs twice in Sussex, once at Henfield where there is also a Moustows (probably 'meeting-place'), and also at Wittering. Hundredsteddle implies some form of timber structure where the members of the court could gather. Variants of the name Moustows occur in Castle Hedingham (Essex) as Mustow, and in Fulham (London) in the same form in the fifteenth century, but now as Munster (Road). In Bury (Sussex) was situated the Motstowe of the Hundred of Bury, at any rate in the fourteenth century.

The speech that took place at such meetings is commemorated in Littlebury (Essex) as Spelbeorghe ('speech hill') in the tenth century, and in Little Hallingbury as Spellbrook. In Hertfordshire the Hundred of Hitchin met at Sperberry, which is a modern variant of the Littlebury name. The moot of this Hundred was actually held in Ippollitts parish. Tingrith in Eversholt (Beds) means the 'meeting (thing)-brook' of Manshead Hundred; the latter name may possibly imply human sacrifice. Fingest in Buckinghamshire was originally *thing-hyrst* (moot near or on the wooded hill) and near it is Skirmett which means 'shire-moot'. Tinhale in Bersted (Sussex) and Thinglea in Baughurst (Hants) may also contain the word *thing*.

Apart from those already mentioned, a few other earthworks that were hundred meeting-places are known in our region. The Cutted Thorn at Southampton was the moot of the shire of Hampton and a rectangular earthwork still exists there. In Middlesex the moot-place of Gore Hundred narrowly escaped the speculative builder at Kingsbury and may be seen as an artificially raised triangle (gore) of land beside the Gaderbrook (i.e. gathering- or meeting-brook). No earthwork is known at the Edmonton Moot-Plain in the east of the same county, but Mutton Lane and Gate (*mōt-tūn*) are topographically related to it. The meeting-place of Spelthorne (Middx) was on Ashford Common, but the thorn, not apparently an earthwork, marked its site. More moots will no doubt be located by those willing to undertake documentary as well as field research; but there are will-o'-the-wisps of seeming evidence ever ready to lure the unwary away on false trails.

The origins of the parish are as obscure as those of the next larger administrative unit, the hundred; but it is unlikely that many parish boundaries had been delimited much before the tenth century. Nevertheless some, at any rate, were made to coincide with the outer limits of estates, or of the land of a settlement (if there is any real difference between them); and the Old English charters, whose bounds can sometimes still be followed in the field, reveal that parish and estate boundaries were often coincident, thought the charter may antedate the formation of a parish by two or more centuries.

In earlier Saxon times, where wooded waste land surrounded most villages, or on the chalk, where readily identified natural features are sometimes few, existing barrows were occasionally used as boundary points. A good instance of this occurs on the common boundary of Alciston and Alfriston in Sussex, where at least four barrows extending over half a mile were so used. A mile to the west is a mutilated round barrow called Five Lords' Burgh, which is said to have marked the point where five manors met. Today only three parish boundaries intersect there. Even more convenient were trackways, now sometimes highroads, but quite often still mere lanes; and almost any sheet of the one-inch map will show many instances of lanes marking parish boundaries. Lanes or roads thus used may generally be regarded as very ancient, and on some soils confirmation of this antiquity may be found by the manner in which the track has been cut deep by long use beneath the level of the bordering fields. Both Greensand and Chalk country afford very numerous examples of this.

The agger of a Roman road afforded another kind of ready-made boundary mark, and lost sections of road have often been discovered along straight stretches of parish boundary. Many instances occur in our region, among which those at Meesden (Herts) and Litchfield (Hants) may be cited. Pre-Roman trackways were similarly used as, for instance, the South Downs ridgeway at Coombes (Sussex), the Icknield

Way at Lilley (Herts) and the ancient trackway known as Old Street which, for most of its six miles from near Chieveley to near Farnborough in Berkshire, is followed by the boundaries of successive parishes.

Linear earthworks and sometimes hill-forts define the limits of parishes for short distances. Here may be instanced the Grymes' Dyke at Lexden (Essex) and the short cross-ridge ditches at Heyshott and Washington (Sussex). The boundaries of the villages of Mortimer West End and Silchester (Hants) are sometimes said to coincide with the territorial limits of *Calleva Atrebatum*, and they certainly maintain an almost constant distance of a mile and a quarter from the Roman walls. It is possible that a slight ancient ditch was followed when the bounds of the two parishes were laid out, though it is to be noted that the large sub-Roman earthworks of the neighbourhood bear no obvious relation to the English boundaries.

Hill-forts are often ignored by them, or the line goes straight across the fort, as at Ditchling and Wiston (Sussex) or at Blewbury (Berks). However, at Hampstead Norris, in the latter county, the hill-fort of Oareborough, now almost obliterated, is completely engulfed by the parish boundary except for a tiny segment on the northern side.

Much of what has been said of parish boundaries is true also of shire boundaries. Just as the parish was sometimes delimited by the digging of a shallow ditch where landmarks were lacking, so on occasions a shire ditch might be cut; and there are not a few references in old records to these features. Random instances are to be found at Holwell and Thorley in Hertfordshire and at Lingfield in Surrey. The parish of Martin (Hants), as its name implies, lies on the edge of the shire, with Dorset and Wiltshire contiguous to it. The shire and parishes boundaries on the north follow a Roman road for one and a half miles and then Grim's Ditch of the Late Bronze or Iron Age for two and a quarter miles. After this east to west stretch, the bounds follow a lane southward for some distance. The coincident boundaries of Martin and Hampshire then run the full length of the Sub-Roman (or late Roman) Bokerly Dyke for its whole length (Map H). It may well be that some of the other known shire ditches are prehistoric in origin, re-used for convenience as boundaries; but, in any case, the limits of shire and parish are well worthy of the attention of field archaeologists and their continued study cannot but add to our knowledge of both the medieval, Roman and prehistoric past.

In England as a whole there are many vestiges of medieval cultivation, but in our region they are less frequent than elsewhere. The three-field system, by which one-third of the arable lay fallow each year, one-third was sown with spring crops, and the remainder with winter crops, had never been, and never became, the universal system; in England as a whole it was a practice limited to the Midland Plain with extension northward and southward; and even there it was probably normal only in the clay vales, for on other less fertile soils the two-field system continued in use for centuries, and until the thirteenth and fourteenth centuries it is probable that the three-field rotation of crops had not been introduced anywhere. Nevertheless, it is sometimes said to be characteristic even of the pre-Norman manor. By the fifteenth century the open-field system, whether of two or three fields, was being practised in our region only in coastal Sussex, in Hampshire, Berkshire and the Chiltern scarp-foot vale. Surrey, once regarded as following Kentish practice, has much unmistakable evidence of the use of open fields in the Thames-side areas, in later times on the three-field system.

But this leaves large areas of our region unaccounted for. Kent, settled predominantly by Jutes, had a distinctive system which, from the time of the earliest records, involved small enclosed fields; and its units of land measurement were quite unlike those of the Midland Plain. Both in land-use and in the unit of settlement (the hamlet as opposed to the larger nucleated village), Kentish practice spread to the Sussex Weald and perhaps to southern Surrey as well. In Essex and Hertfordshire, on the Chiltern plateau generally, and possibly in much of Middlesex too, the East Anglian system, with some elements in common with that of Kent, showed features in many respects divergent from that of the Midlands. In the early Middle Ages parts of southern Hampshire, originally a Jutish region, also stood outside the three-field system and, so far as the scanty documentary evidence goes, involved some Kentish features.

The commonest relics of medieval agriculture are the strip lynchets still to be seen on many chalk slopes where the steepness made later ploughing unprofitable. Examples may be seen at Sydmonton and Shawford (Hants), Ardington, Blewbury and Lambourn (Berks), Caddington (Beds), Therfield (Herts), and Upper Beeding (Sussex). Not all of these are easy to identify as almost all are overgrown with bushes and trees. It is possible that some strip lynchets first came into use in the earlier phases of Saxon settlement before the valley soils could be cleared and ploughed. The fact that their positive lynchets are, in many instances, quite high, giving the appearance of gigantic steps up the hillside, indicates that they were in use over a considerable period. Indeed, a few are still being ploughed. But most of them are in regions that were turned over to sheep farming in the later Middle Ages, and it may well be that the plough ceased to turn over their soil at that time. Their formation by mainly natural agencies was similar to that of Celtic-field lynchets (Figure 8 and Plate 24).

In the Midland shires the open fields of many villages can still be traced swelling the turf of the late medieval sheep walks; but there are few examples in our region, of which the best is that published by Dr. Crawford at Burghclere (Hants) (Figure 19). Indeed, Chapters 18 and 19 of his *Archaeology in the Field* afford the best introduction to the field archaeology of the Middle Ages. Of especial interest are the parishes of Bygrave, Clothall and Wallington in Hertfordshire, which were not finally enclosed until 1910. Overgrown strip lynchets survive on Bird Hill (Clothall) in a region which is rich in all kinds of medieval earthworks. Faint traces of the medieval fields of Mortlake (Surrey) are perceptible in Richmond Park; and what appear to be faint strip

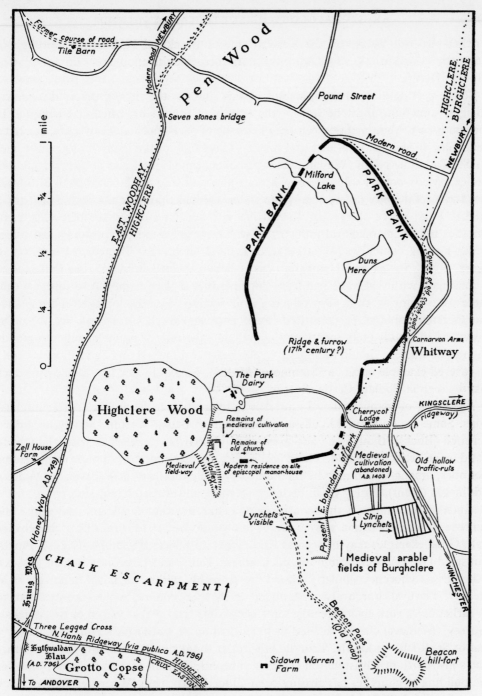

FIG 19 Highclere Park, near Newbury. The original village of Highclere was probably near the old church and was removed to the north-west on empark-ment in A.D. 1403

N

lynchets are just visible on the western side of Brockwell Park in the Borough of Lambeth (London). Vestiges of ridge and furrow cultivation are said to exist at Albury (Herts).

Before passing on to the major topic of this chapter, the sites of deserted medieval villages, something must be said of the variety of other sites which are common in the south-east. Mere mention can here be made of pack-trails, archery butts, marlpits, deneholes, fishponds, mill-leets and mazes. Three only of the latter are known to me: on St. Catherine's Hill (Winchester), at Rockbourne (Hants) and at Saffron Walden (Essex). Many pottery kilns are now known and some, no doubt, are still to be found; and the careful study of 'wasters' from them will make possible the dating of many a medieval site where chronological evidence is otherwise lacking (see below, p. 225). Another important medieval industry of which there should be archaeological traces is salt-making, which was referred to in general on p. 124. The coastal marshes of Essex, Kent, Sussex and Hampshire may all be expected to yield some evidence of it consonant with that to be had from documents and place-names. And in the Weald there were many workshops producing iron or glass. For the location of these sites the Gazetteer should be consulted. Park boundary-ditches are dealt with by Dr. Crawford in his chapters mentioned above; and the related topics of pillow-mounds and rabbit-warrens should be studied in *Antiquity*, volumes II and IV; a more recently discovered example occurs at Stanmore (Middx). Finally in this list, a medieval dock may be seen at Bodiam Castle, Sussex.

The siting of many medieval churches is interesting in its archaeological implications. Some are on natural knolls as at Shillington (Beds), Wotton (Surrey) or Edlesborough (Bucks), though the last-mentioned church has sometimes been thought to stand on an artificial mound. There are, in fact, several churches so built in the Home Counties, among which may be mentioned possible instances at Kingsbury (Middx), Addington (Kent), Farley Chamberlayne (Hants), and Alfriston (Sussex).

Much more common is the occurrence of a church within an ancient enclosure. The purpose of such a location was no doubt to obviate the need for making a churchyard wall. Good examples may be seen at Cholesbury and West Wycombe (Bucks), Finchampstead (Berks), Kenardington and Coldred (Kent) and possibly Chignall (Essex). Other Essex churches similarly placed are probably within medieval defences, as at Pleshey. The oval churchyard at Manuden, in the same county, may be the successor to an earlier earthwork enclosure; the same is possibly true of the church of St. Martha's (Surrey). Medieval chapels so sited included that on St. Catherine's Hill (Winchester); that of St. Roche within the Trundle hill-fort at Singleton (Sussex) and the St. Catherine's just north of Christchurch (Hants). The employment of Roman house-sites for the building of churches has already been alluded to (p. 175). Wherever Roman brick was re-used in medieval structures, the fact is noted in the Gazetteer but with the important exception, made for economy of space, that if a Roman building has already been reported in the parish, then the use of Roman brick in the church is ignored.

This re-use of Roman material affords a useful clue to the one-time presence of Roman buildings in or near the parish; but some of the instances noted in the Gazetteer may well prove to be false clues. For Belgic brick has been found at Verulamium; it is generally reddish-yellow or orange in colour and contains large pebbles, and finger impressions are visible on the surfaces. It lacks the grey core of most Roman bricks, though occasional instances of yellow Roman bricks are known. And the Saxons, too, apparently made coarse bricks. At *Hamwih* (Southampton) pieces were found with a thickness of one and one-third inches; and one fragment had an incrustation of mortar as though it had been used in a building. Ill-fired, like Belgic brick, and coarse in texture, these Saxon bricks are unlike typical Roman work.

The occurrence of so-called Roman brick in many Saxon and early Norman churches becomes, therefore, increasingly doubtful, though in stoneless regions like so much of the south-east, the re-use of the fabric of a Roman building afforded a considerable economy in cost, not so much in quarrying as in transport. The making of thin roofing tiles may have begun quite early in the Middle Ages, but the reintroduction of brick-making cannot yet be put earlier than the thirteenth century. The inner orders of the arch in the second bay of the nave at Copford (Essex) are constructed of bricks which have been dated to *c.* 1300, and they may be directly compared with the Roman brick lavishly used in the outer orders of the same arch. Apparently even earlier (*c.* 1225) were the bricks used in the gate chapel of Little Coggeshall Abbey in the same county. To complicate matters, the fourteenth-century south porch of Thorrington church, also in Essex, has tiled quoins 'on the pattern of the Norman use of Roman bricks'. One-third of all the medieval parish churches of south-west Essex contain some Roman (?) brick in their structures, and there are many instances elsewhere, especially in Hertfordshire and Kent; but the difficulty of distinguishing between Roman and other brick makes the matter very uncertain.

There are in our region a few surviving villages with medieval protective earthworks of great interest. At Sewards End, near Saffron Walden (Essex), may be seen the water defences of a considerable hamlet; three moated enclosures were formed here by diverting a stream. Villages with wet or dry defences are far more common in the Home Counties than is generally realized. Because of their great interest, I give a list, by no means complete, of such defended settlements: Canewdon, Mundon, Hazeleigh, Chipping Ongar, Pleshey (Figure 18), Castle Hedingham and possibly Danbury, all in Essex; Pirton and Therfield in Hertfordshire; Hoggeston, Cublington and Lee in Buckinghamshire; and probably Ruislip in Middlesex. I have not visited all of these places to be sure that the earthworks are easily visible; but even where they still exist, some patient searching with a large-scale map (two and a half or six inches to the mile) is advisable. But most of them contain other medieval earthworks besides the village defences and are worthy of a visit for these alone. For details see the Gazetteer, and see Plate 27.

The economic causes of the desertion of villages (Map 10) in the Middle Ages cannot be discussed except to note that the conversion of arable land to sheep pasture in the later fifteenth and early sixteenth centuries accounts for many instances. It is not surprising, therefore, that villages in chalk country were seldom affected, for they had always been mainly pastoral. Nor would we expect the change to have occurred in forested regions, where swineherding, not arable farming, was the main occupation. These two kinds of countryside account for a considerable portion of the Home Counties. To them we should add the brick-earths of the Thames valley which gave a rich return in crops that could be readily sold in the London market. These may be regarded as negative areas where abandoned villages are unlikely to occur as a result of the change-over to sheep-farming. Positive areas within the Home Counties include the Chiltern vale, parts of Essex and Hertfordshire, the New Forest and Romney Marsh and all marginal land (Plate 28).

In any region a village might have to be abandoned when a great man decided to enclose his house in a park (e.g. Albury, Surrey; Nuneham Courtenay, Oxon). A new village was usually built beyond the park wall. This might happen as late as the nineteenth century. In the Middle Ages a monastery might force villagers to migrate to a new site in order to create sheep pasture (e.g. Balmer, Sussex; Thomley (?), Oxon); or, in medieval or modern times, the nucleus of a village might gradually be shifted across a parish from its original site to the borders of a main highway (e.g. Mountnessing, Essex); or nearer to a railway station (e.g. Fambridge (?), Essex). In the Gazetteer many such abandoned sites are noted, not a few of them with a query mark. One of the criteria for inclusion there was the occurrence of an isolated church, or where it, as well as the village, has disappeared, its site. In addition, many instances of apparent migrations of villages from one neighbourhood to another are noted. In these cases, it is generally assumed that the settlement was originally close to the church, or manor house, or both. There may, however, be instances of settlements whose churches were always distant from the village centre. In many cases the suggestion in the Gazetteer must not be taken as a fact but only as a possibility worthy of investigation on the spot.

Besides sites that were completely abandoned there are many others where it may be presumed that a village has decreased markedly in size. These shrunken settlements may be expected to have deserted cottage and manorial sites in the neighbourhood of the church; but it is possible that some of those noticed in the Gazetteer were always small places with only a few cottages even, sometimes, where the church itself is of some importance. In the forested regions nucleated villages were always abnormal and the church might be built in any one of several small and widely separated hamlets. Deserted sites will seldom be found in such regions.

For the visible earthworks of an abandoned settlement, I cannot do better than quote our foremost authority on the subject, Mr. M. W. Beresford:

'In the village itself—the church apart—the principal surface indications will be the characteristic sunken (that is, worn down) roads and back lanes; the slender banks which carried hedges and palisades round the crofts; the Manor site, often moated or terraced; the fishponds; the windmill; the domestic buildings lightly imprinted in the grass, a length of wall showing in a bank here, and the sharp angle of a corner there. Where rabbits have burrowed or on the banks of ponds and streams pottery can usually be had for the scraping. Erosion may have exposed the old worked stones or a farmer taken them to make a dry way for cattle through a gate. In the nature of the imperfect coherence of an unexcavated site it is often easier to comprehend the plan and relation of the village's parts in an air photograph than on the ground. Where ploughing has risked broken shares the only clue may be in crop marks. . . . The ruined churches of Romney Marsh stand in ploughed land, and their vegetable crops are not the best for showing significant markings.' (*Archaeological News Letter*, volume 5, number 3, p. 43.)

When air photographs are not available frequent visits to a site (of any period) in all seasons and conditions of light will sometimes enable its pattern to be gradually pieced together; and experience of other sites, already elucidated by others, hastens the process even though no two sites are alike. For convenience I give a few examples of the various categories discussed above. They are scattered over the whole region. Map references to these and to many others will be found in the Gazetteer.

Abandoned villages: Fulscot (Berks), Quarrendon (Bucks), Thunderley in Wimbish (Essex), Abbotstone (Hants), Thundridge (Herts), Orgarswick (Kent), Pyrton—three deserted sites (Oxon), Busbridge (Surrey), Balmer in Falmer (Sussex).

Shrunken settlements: Higham Gobion (Beds), Compton (Berks), Bradwell next Coggeshall (?) (Essex), Farley Chamberlayne (Hants), Throcking (Herts), Aldington (Kent), Easington in Cuxham (Oxon), Tatsfield (?) (Surrey), Balsdean in Brighton (Sussex).

Villages that have migrated from the original site: Stoke Mandeville (Bucks), Abberton (?) (Essex), Thorley (Herts), Otham (?) (Kent), Walkingstead (?) in Godstone (Surrey).

Villages moved for emparkment: Eythorpe (Bucks), Dogmersfield (Hants), Pendley in Tring (Herts), Eastwell (Kent), Nuneham Courtenay (Oxon), Albury (Surrey), Binderton (Sussex). In this category some instances may be included where the site is now within the park though the abandonment of the village may have occurred long before emparkment.

A few of the sites above, and many more in the Gazetteer, have not, so far as I am aware, been included in any published list of deserted or shrunken village sites, and should not be accepted without investigation in the field and in documents.

Three sites are of special interest. Tythrop (meaning 'double homestead') in the parish of Kingsey (formerly in Oxfordshire but now transferred to Buckinghamshire) is listed by Beresford as a deserted hamlet. It was large in 1279, though it probably had no church; but by 1712 it had only five houses. It is now a country seat with appurtenant outbuildings none of which are likely to be successors to the medieval hamlet. Somewhere in the park should be vestiges of this settlement which ultimately dates from pagan Saxon times, for in the same park was found a cemetery of that period with grave goods that included saucer brooches of the late sixth century as well as weapons. Moreover, two cremation burials were found. The location of the habitation site and its scientific excavation might result in a valuable addition to our present meagre knowledge of occupation sites stratified perhaps from the sixth century to medieval times.

Similar possibilities exist for Thunderley in Wimbish (Essex) and for Thundridge (Herts), both of which names commemorate the Saxon god Thunor. It is doubtful whether dwellings would have been permitted near his sanctuary before the time of the Conversion, but the deserted settlements could date from the seventh century and offer a more promising line of field research than the great majority of deserted sites so far located.

It is obvious that archaeology does not come to an abrupt halt at the end of the Middle Ages, but increasingly thereafter it becomes dependent on documentary evidence and small finds such as potsherds, coins, tradesmen's tokens, tobacco pipes and so on. Yet all of these, except the coins, can often be dated from the history of the occupation of a site, and similar objects found elsewhere can be used for the approximate dating of undocumented sites. Much of this is, of course, true of the medieval period. But interesting earthworks become few after the fifteenth century and they have not the attraction of those dating from remoter times. However, it is useful to be able to recognize them for what they are rather than ascribe them to an earlier period.

For instance, some traces of earthwork defences constructed in 1588, when Spanish invasion threatened, may still be seen at Tilbury (Essex). There are even more certain traces within the ramparts of the fort of the Saxon shore at Pevensey (Sussex). Here they have an added interest since within a small area may be seen defences against the Saxons of the third century, a Norman castle with later alterations, a fragment of the Armada defences of the sixteenth century, and strongpoints of c. 1940, cunningly contrived to appear as part of the Roman and medieval ruin. Within sight of all this may be seen Martello Towers erected against the menace of Napoleonic invasion. There are few places in Britain where the present and past centuries are brought so close together in time through a similar response to a similar threat. At Greenwich (London) traces of forts of the fifteenth and sixteenth centuries have recently been found.

The civil war of the seventeenth century has left a more durable mark on our landscape than the ruins of slighted strongholds which, without constant work of preservation, would become mere untidy heaps of stones. At Enborne, near Newbury (Berks), are to be seen the burial mounds of some of those slain in the battle of 1643. At Basing House (Hants) are three bastions of the siegeworks constructed by the Cromwellian forces in the same year; and at Quarrendon (Bucks) may be seen trenches,

vallum and gun emplacements made at the time of the Battle of Aylesbury in the previous year. Possible relics of the same period may exist at Banstead (Surrey) and
Bodiam (Sussex).

Traditions concerning plague-pits of the seventeenth century survive in several
localities, including London, but at Twyford (Hants) there are mounds covering the
remains of victims of the plague. Of a very different kind is the course of a sixteenth-
century aqueduct at Caterham (Surrey). The New River, begun in 1609, served a
similar purpose though it is on a far larger scale. It may still be traced for much of
its way from Great Amwell (Herts) through the eastern extremity of Middlesex into
the heart of north London. Several sections of it still remain open in the Borough of
Islington.

Of later kinds of earthwork, and there are many, nothing will be said here; they
are reserved for consideration in the next chapter among the traps for the unwary.

BIBLIOGRAPHY TO CHAPTER XIII

A. Hadrian Allcroft's *Earthwork of England* (1908), chapters XII f., remains a
useful account of medieval earthworks and includes many plans; but Crawford's
Archaeology in the Field (1952), chapters 18 and 19, is valuable for mottes, parks and
cultivation banks. The works of Heywood Sumner, which cover all periods, are of
interest for medieval remains, especially those of south-western Hampshire. See his
Ancient Earthworks of the New Forest (1917) and *Local Papers: Archaeological and
Topographical* (1931). Williams Freeman's *An Introduction to Field Archaeology as
Illustrated by Hampshire* (1915) covers all periods, and is useful for local material of
the Middle Ages.

Crawford's *Air Survey and Archaeology* (1928) and *Wessex from the Air* (1928)
both contain contributions on strip lynchets; and H. L. Gray's *English Field Systems*
(1915) and F. G. Payne's 'The Plough in Ancient Britain', in *Archaeological Journal*,
104, are pioneer studies in vital aspects of early agriculture.

Bruce Mitford's paper in *Archaeological News Letter*, I, 6, gives a concise account
of the problems of medieval archaeology. The *London Museum Catalogues: *London
and the Vikings* (1927) and *Medieval Catalogue* (1940), especially the latter, which is
an authoritative work on small finds, have more than local importance. The first
section of text in *Castles* (1953), published by H.M.S.O.; 'The Excavation of a
Motte at Abinger in Surrey', in *Archaeological Journal*, 107; and the *Transactions of
the Newbury and District Field Club*, volume 6 (1932), on three mottes at Hamstead
Marshall (Berks), should be consulted on motte-and-bailey castles. Various medieval
earthworks are recorded and described in *Transactions of the Middlesex and London
Archaeological Society*, vols. 7, 10 and 11.

* Inexpensive works.

A recent comprehensive work, M. W. Beresford's *The Lost Villages of England* (1954), has a bibliography in the notes and in Appendix III, as well as county lists of lost villages.

Two works, E. Straker's *Wealden Iron* (1931) and S. E. Winbolt's *Wealden Glass* (1933), deal with a region much of which was little touched in earlier times except by these two industries and by the farmer.

CHAPTER XIV

The Study of a Locality

FOR MOST PEOPLE a parish or group of parishes forming a hundred is a convenient unit for study, especially if the neighbourhood is already well known. A wider field necessarily involves diffusion of effort and expense in time and money in moving about; detailed knowledge and the 'feel' of a larger area must remain superficial for a longer time.

A comprehensive knowledge of the geology of the area is a first requisite, and geological maps on the largest available scale must frequently be consulted. A map of solid geology on a scale of one inch to the mile should be available and it should preferably be a permanent possession. If published, the Drift Edition should be bought also since, unlike the Geological Survey maps of solid geology, the drift maps show superficial deposits such as river gravels and terraces, glacial drift (chiefly in Essex), and residual deposits such as clay-with-flints. The distribution of these deposits is important in many parts of the south-east since their occurrence may either give rise to well-drained soils suitable for habitation and farming, or render both impossible.

Whether local drift maps are available or not, some knowledge of natural plant communities is a valuable asset in field work as it enables the careful observer to distinguish between soil types to a degree of refinement that is impossible for the map-maker to attempt. For instance, damp soils will afford conditions suitable for the growth of rushes, sedges, meadow-sweet and willow-herbs (except Rosebay); and such soils, apart from their dampness, are generally too acid to support food plants. But poor drainage may be due to modern disturbance, in which case the soil condition is irrelevant to earlier times. Again, the flora of chalk soils is quite distinctive and easily mastered sufficient for our purposes with the aid of an inexpensive handbook. Knowing the plant communities of the Chalk we would not expect prehistoric occupation on the Downs where we find a predominance of heather and birch, for these thrive on acid soils. Such tracts may, however, have formed the hunting or food-gathering grounds of ancient peoples. Moreover, because of their stickiness and water-holding properties, we should not expect the London, Weald or Kimmeridge Clays to yield evidence of occupation before, at the earliest, the Roman period. But prehistoric potting may have occurred at their edges, and, where they are overlaid by drift deposits, permanent habitation may have been made.

Yet another branch of studies can provide useful clues to the ancient, natural landscape of a region. A distribution map showing the location of all place-names denoting woodland will, as we have seen, give an incomplete but instructive picture of conditions in Saxon times; and it is probable that almost everywhere that was wooded then was not open country from later mesolithic times onwards. Indeed, the extent of pre-Roman woodland was much greater than that shown by such a map; and it will reveal how unreliable are vegetation maps compiled on a purely geological basis. The place-name elements that are relevant to a distribution map of the kind here advocated are listed under 'forest names' in the final chapter (p. 223); and this category includes minor names and field-names, as well as those of villages and hamlets. For most counties they will be found listed towards the end of the Place-Name Survey volumes, but for some (e.g. Hants and Berks) a more laborious method may be necessary. This necessitates combing a large-scale map for all relevant material and then plotting it accurately on a base map, preferably one showing watercourses and elevation. But it should be noted that a minor name on a modern map is not necessarily ancient, and that even a genuinely ancient one could have been so modified that a false etymology is easily adduced if early forms are not available. For example, Bromley Barn, which occurs on the six-inch map which takes in Widdington (Essex), appears from its present spelling to end with a syllable derived from the Old English word *lēah* ('wood' or 'clearing in a wood'). But the name occurs in a document of 1529 as *Bromelowevaley*, which shows that Bromley had developed from *brōm* and *hlāw* ('broom-covered hill'). On the other hand, Great and Little Bromley in northern Essex and the Bromleys in Kent and Hertfordshire have indeed developed from *brōm* and *lēah* ('clearing where broom grew'); and this fact affords a further useful piece of information: that the soil there was acid. Similarly, Fyfield, which occurs in Essex, Berkshire and Hampshire, or Fifield in Oxfordshire, look as though the second syllable comes from the Old English *feld* ('land where trees had been cleared'; related to the verb 'fell), whereas in fact these names are derived from *fīf hīde* ('five hides', the theoretical extent of a thegn's estate). When other sources are wanting, E. Ekwall's *Oxford Dictionary of English Place-Names* is useful, but he gives few minor names, and these are necessary if a satisfactory distribution map is to be made.

Some other uses of place-names in archaeological field work are discussed in the final chapter.

Further steps in mastering the natural background of a region will include careful perusal of the relevant sheets of the Ordnance Survey six-inch map, which, incidentally, provide useful information about finds and earthworks and give minor place-names not to be had from maps on a smaller scale. Old estate maps and even modern farm plans will give disused minor names and quite probably some field-names not listed in the Place-Name Survey volume. The county library and the main library in the nearest town may possess old maps, estate plans, terriers, surveys, charters, perambulations, topographical books that are scarce and out of print, and other documents of relevance. The county record office and cathedral archives may be expected to have similar sources of information. In any case, most public libraries are willing and able to give help to students by obtaining works through the National Central Library.

Membership of the local archaeological society, especially that for the county, will normally bring within reach valuable collections of books, manuscripts, plans and maps directly bearing on the county and in part on the locality which is the special subject of study. The society usually has a museum also, which obviously cannot be neglected. Material in the display cases is generally only a small part of the collection. Much supplementary information is to be had from the museum's accession book.

It is necessary to build up a register of finds and sites; and although a loose-leaf notebook may prove sufficient for a single parish, a larger district will almost certainly require a card-index system. Once the arrangement of this has been decided upon and entries made, it cannot easily be varied without risk of confusion. Probably the best system of recording will be separate registers of sites and finds, with cross-references from one to the other; and within each of these main categories a chronological arrangement by periods and sub-divisions of periods will make for easiest reference. Each site is best given a separate card on which should be entered the national grid bearing, preferably to eight figures; that is, to one-hundredth of a kilometre. The method of doing this is fully explained on the inside of the front cover of the Ordnance Survey one-inch maps. In addition, any old and modern names of the site that can be gleaned from reliable sources should also be entered. A chronological list of name-forms with their dates and sources may eventually prove valuable. Any place-names that may afford a clue to a site, such as an earthwork no longer known, should be given a grid reference also; and the precise location of the site may then be looked for in the field, a matter discussed later in this chapter. A site that was occupied in several periods will have a separate card in the index under each period.

The Gazetteer at the end of this book will provide a starting-point for a local index within the South-East as here understood. But more information than is given in the bare mention of the Gazetteer will be required, and for that laborious task a careful plan of action is necessary if much time and effort are not to be wasted. First, reference will be made to the earlier volumes of the *Victoria County History* (*VCH* for short), though for some counties (e.g. Hampshire) volume one, which includes prehistory, is almost useless. The references to other books given in *VCH* will need to be followed up, and from some of them additional information and, probably, further sites will be gleaned. Then the *County Archaeology*, available for Kent, Sussex, Surrey, Middlesex and Berkshire, should be consulted. Some of them (e.g. Surrey and Berkshire) contain quite comprehensive gazetteers, with references, down to about 1930; others (Kent and Middlesex) are less complete in this respect. In its latest edition the Sussex volume gives much detail about particular sites including their grid references, but it lacks a gazetteer.

It is the next step that may prove irksome. For completeness it is necessary to check right through the many volumes of proceedings published by the local archaeo-logical society. For Hampshire this involves less than twenty volumes, but for Sussex it is not far short of a hundred; and besides checking through the *Collections* there are the fifteen or so volumes of *Sussex Notes and Queries* to be conned. In fact, the task is lightened by the occasional publication of comprehensive indexes to a whole run of volumes. This has the effect of reducing one's labour and leaves only the task of consulting the annual volumes published subsequent to the last general index volume. The annual volumes themselves contain an index to their contents, so that one has not to rely on the contents page alone for the discovery of relevant material.

But besides all this, the proceedings of national societies must be covered by hunt-ing through their indexes for local material. For some counties, however, this needs to be done only for volumes published later than the *County Archaeology*; or rather, from a year previous to the date of publication of the latter. Oxfordshire is fortunate in the late publication (1939) of the first volume of *VCH*. This includes several period gazetteers and a general account of the prehistory and early history of the county; and with the volumes of *Oxoniensia* makes a virtually complete coverage possible of all finds down to the present. Yet even so, *Antiquaries Journal*, *Archaeological Journal*, *Antiquity*, the *Proceedings of the Prehistoric Society*, *Archaeologia*, *Archaeological News Letter* and the *Journal of Roman Studies* will all need to be checked for relevant material on Oxfordshire recorded since 1938, for it will not necessarily be found in *Oxoniensia*. For other counties the check will begin with earlier volumes of county *Proceedings* and national journals. Short-cuts may be found by referring to sections on Periodical Literature and Bibliography regularly included in the *Antiquaries Journal*, and to the *Archaeological Bulletins* for 1940–6, 1947, 1948–9, with its suc-cessor, *Archaeological Bibliography* for 1950–1, 1952–3 and 1954. Both the *Bulletins* and the *Bibliographies* are published by the Council for British Archaeology and are arranged on a county basis. It may be necessary to refer to the pre-war predecessors of the *Bulletins*, namely the *Reports of the Earthworks Committee* (issued irregularly from 1905 to 1939) of the Congress of Archaeological Societies, which was itself succeeded by the Council for British Archaeology. Furthermore, *Archaeological Journal*, from volume 89 (1932) to 92 (1935), contains a valuable summary entitled 'Prehistoric Britain in 1932 (etc.)—A Review of Periodical Publications'. After 1935 reference should be made to a similar section in the *Proceedings of the Prehistoric Society*. For the Roman period recourse should be had to the *Journal of Roman Studies* (1911 onwards), each volume of which contains a summary of discoveries made in the previous year. For Essex the *Annual Reports of the Colchester Museum* are indis-pensable. (See pp. 228–9, Section B.)

The Royal Commission on Historical Monuments has published volumes covering Hertfordshire, Buckinghamshire, Essex, Middlesex and Roman London. These include accounts of earthworks (and sometimes of associated finds) parish by parish. Finally, for counties such as Hampshire, Essex, Hertfordshire, Buckinghamshire and

Bedfordshire, for which there is no *County Archaeology* or recent prehistoric volume of the *VCH*, the work of Kendrick and Hawkes, *Archaeology in England and Wales, 1914–1931*, will fill in many gaps and its footnotes provide a useful bibliography.

The task outlined above will seem unduly onerous, but a careful dovetailing of the sources suggested is better than a vague hunt hither and thither for information. In any case, for a limited area in any one county the labour is not so burdensome. The total number of index entries for any one parish will usually be small and some of them will quickly be discovered as worthless. But obviously such details as are gleaned have to be put into perspective by wide general reading round the subject. The task is clearly impossible unless one has access to a specialist library; and this is available in many counties to members of the archaeological society. The use of the attached museum (in most counties) is also necessary to track down unpublished finds noted in the accessions book. The advice to be had from the curator, the society's librarian, from the staff of the county library and from the county archivist will also be well worth having. Those who live in Kent have the advantage of an archaeological index at the Maidstone headquarters of the Kent Archaeological Society, and students in Essex have the benefit of a gazetteer compiled by the members of the Roman Essex Society. There may well be similar facilities in other counties.

Serious students of prehistory will not be content merely with a compilation of other people's discoveries; they will hope to add some of their own, particularly where there are gaps in the continuity of the evidence. Preliminary work will involve the study of geological and topographical maps, of such air photographs as are available, and of distributions such as are given in some numbers on a small scale in Sir Cyril Fox's *Personality of Britain*. Then will follow fieldwork.

It is useless, however, to seek what is not to be found. For instance, palaeoliths will rarely turn up except in gravel deposits; mesolithic tools are very unlikely on clay, except possibly where it thins out near its margins. Indeed, apart from passing hunters or bronze-founders, little can be expected on clay until the Roman period, and even then only on the fringes. For most periods the chalk, sands and gravels, all soils well drained for habitation and for agriculture, are the most promising. Only the very variable boulder clays of Essex make such generalizations hazardous; but even on them the clay areas that are little modified by chalk, sand or gravel are likely to present a blank until the early Middle Ages.

It is doubtful whether any obvious earthworks still remain unrecorded; but a few denuded ones, especially in woodland, may have escaped notice hitherto. Yet there must be many nearing obliteration still to be found; and even more numerous are the occupation sites that can be located by patient fieldwork.

The best initial training is to be had in the company of an experienced fieldworker. Failing this, no opportunity should be lost in visiting recorded sites and studying them with a plan. Allcroft's *Earthwork of England*, Williams-Freeman's *Field Archaeology as Illustrated by Hampshire* or Heywood Sumner's works provide useful plans for the purpose. The six-inch or two-and-a-half-inch Ordnance maps may often be found better. A conveniently local earthwork should be visited repeatedly at different seasons and at different times of the day. In course of time more and more of it will be perceived, according to the position and intensity of the light. No book can be a substitute for this field experience; at the most it can offer inadequate suggestions.

Little fieldwork is possible in high summer when foliage, tall grass, bracken or crops tend to obscure minor variations in ground level; and these variations will often give the first clue to the presence of an earthwork. The skyline should be constantly scanned for irregularities of surface and for minor breaks in the natural slope. The latter varies according to the geology of the area and only experience can acquaint one with the normal contours of a formation. Clays, gravels, sands and chalk each have generally distinguishable contours which may vary according to the coarseness of the sand or gravel or according to the stratum of the chalk. On the whole the steepest slopes are to be seen in sandy country, especially in the Upper and Lower Greensand formations. In such tracts brooks cut steep-sided valleys and scarp-faces are precipitous. But these formations are far from homogeneous, and an outcrop of 'rag' or carstone will sometimes mark a change in the angle of slope. Where denudation has cut down to clay, the junction of the two beds will usually be marked by a similar change, steeper above on the sand, and gentler below on the clay. A line of springs will obviously play havoc with a slope; and if the spring-line has moved downhill, the total effect may be very confusing; a band of marshiness, clear even in drought periods because of the greenness and nature of the vegetation, should solve the difficulty. Much more of a similar kind, especially about chalk country, might be said; but the printed word is a poor substitute for experience, and the matter is best left there.

Apart from a watch on the skyline, areas nearer to the observer must be carefully watched. In all but the flattest country crouching brings false crests to the eye and greatly increases the horizon seen in silhouette. Moreover, a low 'aerial' view can be had from hilltops; and slopes facing an observer across a valley do in fact give a close-up view comparable with that to be had from the air. It is seldom that a convenient or easily-climbed tree will offer a point of vantage; but it is not to be scorned except perhaps in the neighbourhood of sceptical adults. When the sun is low in the sky, slight surface irregularities are visible even from ground level.

Newly ploughed or reploughed land in suitable localities is well worth quartering, especially after a spell of rain that rinses clean any objects that may have been brought to the surface. The conversion by natural processes of household waste to a dark humus may help in locating a habitation site. Dark patches in a field may have given it a name long before their significance was realized. The name Black Lands was given to a field in Faversham (Kent) where traces have been found of a Romano-British building. The Roman posting-station of Cunetio near Marlborough in Wiltshire is situated in Black Field. Blackpatch Hill in Patching (Sussex) has yielded dwelling sites as well as being the location of famous flint-mines; and Black Patch in Alciston parish (Sussex) has immediately to the south-west of it a complex site where a farm, fields and enclosure of the Late Bronze Age have been recognized. For further occurrences of this type of field-name see the next chapter (see **black,** p. 218).

Dark soil patches will usually show up well on the Downs because of the normal light colour of the soil; and a ploughed-out barrow or earthwork will show as a white area in such a situation because usually both barrows and banks of earthworks are largely of chalk. But not every such patch is of archaeological significance; the charred remains of recent couch-grass fires, or of surplus straw that has been burnt, look much the same as occupation sites from a distance. I have even been misled from a distance by a local spread of manure that had escaped being ploughed in. White patches, too, may deceive: from afar a ploughed-out dewpond looks much like a destroyed barrow. In recent times many hedgebanks have been removed though their line often remains visible and sometimes has the appearance of a destroyed earthwork. The origin of such a soil-mark is, however, normally ascertainable by one's noting the relationship of the mark to surviving hedges.

The presence of flint fragments in ploughed land away from the chalk is a common clue to the location of a site. Very seldom will complete implements be found, but the waste from their manufacture is sometimes abundant. The plough may have carried some of the chips away from the occupation site, but a careful reconnaissance of the field will usually show that they occur in a greater concentration in a somewhat ill-defined area where the actual chipping occurred. Here potsherds, burnt daub and pot-boilers or hearth-flints should be looked for. Quite small scraps of pot may make it possible to date the site, but rims, bases and decorated sherds are the most useful for this purpose.

A scatter of gravel, flints or sand occurring in a band across ploughland may mark the line of a Roman road of which the agger has been ploughed down. In this case the alignment should be noted and search made at both ends of the suspected agger for any signs of its continuation. The grass balk bordering a hedge may rise in a slight hump on the alignment, and the hedge itself may afford a clue at the point where it intersects the road. If the alignment crosses old permanent pasture, there is some prospect of the agger's survival in a denuded state. Metalled roads and drives that were built in the eighteenth century or later have sometimes gone out of use and their superficial appearance when ploughed is not unlike that of a Roman road. Straightness is not a criterion since roads of any period may include straight stretches. Old maps may, however, determine the matter.

The whole subject of Roman roads has been dealt with in some detail by Mr. I. D. Margary and further information should be sought from his works cited at the end of this chapter. Mr. Grinsell's book on barrows and Dr. Crawford's *Archaeology in the Field*, chapter 17 and Appendix 3 on linear earthworks, should also be consulted.

Once crops have begun to grow in the late spring and early summer other opportunities for field research occur. Most plants will grow more luxuriantly where the

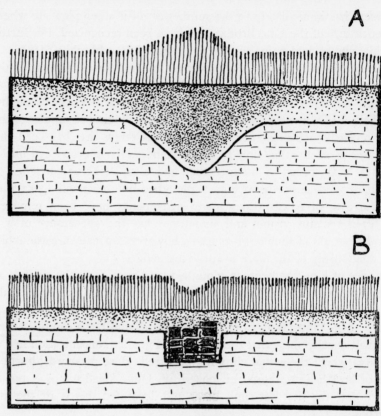

Based on 'Archaeological Journal,' 101, Figures 4a and 4b.

FIG 20 Crop Marks Over Buried Sites. A. Crop growing taller over silted
ditch which affords deep root-run and moister conditions. B. Crop
stunted by lack of moisture and shallow root-run above a buried foundation

humus-layer is deep than where it is shallow; and because they have a better supply
of nitrogenous matter, they are of a lusher green. This will be especially true where
there are filled-in ditches (Figure 20a), storage-pits, refuse-pits or excavations for
the bases of huts. Even from ground level the greater height and greenness of crops
in these situations may be apparent, though where the contrast with normally rooted
plants is slight, some advantage will be had from viewing the site in low sun. Grain
crops that have been nourished with too much nitrogen become weak in the straw
and storms near harvest time occasionally have the effect of laying the corn immediately above filled-in ditches. Here again, however, a knowledge of modern farming
practice, or malpractice, is helpful; for some farmers put excessive dressings of nitrogenous fertilizer on their fields and spread it unevenly, so that later in the season
areas of lodged corn are a common sight. In such instances the flattened areas are
unlikely to suggest buried earthworks, except to the highly imaginative.

A shallow root-system that cannot reach down to adequate moisture stunts growth, and crops sown above the wall-foundations of Roman or medieval buildings suffer accordingly (Figure 19b). In these circumstances nothing will be visible from the ground unless the lines of walls are partly within and partly outside the sown area. A high point of vantage is usually a necessity for the observation of this kind of site. Once one of them has been noted a return to the spot when the stubbles have been ploughed may result in the finding of fragments of wall and roofing material as well as occupation rubbish. But many a barn put up in recent centuries has been demolished and all surface traces of it lost, so it should not be assumed too readily that a crop-site revealing the lines of walls is necessarily ancient. A recognition of the commoner varieties of the plans typical of Roman villas and their ancillary buildings is clearly of some value in this connection. Yet the simplest plan, the basilican, is identical with that of many barns. On this subject of cropmarks, see *Archaeological Journal*, 101.

On permanent grassland the fieldworker must employ different methods of search. Silted ditches will have the same effect on grass as on other plants, and variations in greenness, whether or not they are due only to variations in species of grass, may afford a clue. If such contrasts of colour coincide with irregularities in the ground surface, there is a strong presumption of its having been deeply disturbed at some time in the past. In periods of drought the greater greenness of grass growing in deeper humus is easily visible. Conversely, buried wall-footings will cause parching along their lines sufficient to reveal a complete plan of a building during dry spells. The metalling of a buried road will show as a parched streak across the pasture. Almost the whole street-grid of Roman Silchester has been revealed by aerial photography. Some of the plates in books listed at the end of this chapter illustrate other aspects of cropmarks. (See also Plates 3, 10 and 21 below.)

On permanent grassland the burrowing of rabbits, and the heaps of soil thrown up by moles, offer opportunities for the recovery of small objects. Sometimes rabbit burrows are restricted to the line of silted earthworks where the effort of burrowing is far slighter than in neighbouring consolidated earth. This is particularly noticeable on downland where the unyielding chalk comes to within a few inches of the surface except where man has dug into it. Once disturbed, turf on chalk invariably conveys some indication of the fact to a practised eye; and the activities of rabbits and moles will sometimes confirm it. Other clues may be vouchsafed by local patches of gorse, bracken or nettles. Sometimes they indicate at a glance the shape of an ancient hut-site. In some of the minor river valleys of Dorset, before the plough broke so much permanent pasture, the site of farm, fields and field-ways could be seen across the valley from a facing slope, the hut represented by a patch of bracken or gorse and the rest by earthworks that were just visible under their mantle of turf even at midday. Where such earthworks are almost ploughed away their general layout is revealed not only by low sun, but in shallow flood, when ditch becomes distinguishable from bank by standing water. Light drifted snow and sometimes frost has much the

O

same effect and in many likely situations they are of more frequent occurrence than flooding.

Any cutting into the earth may reveal a section of a habitation site or a barrow. Chalk quarries, gravel pits and the terracing that often precedes building work, present opportunities for examining the face of the unexcavated soil. Ditches intersecting the quarry-face will show up dark against the surrounding soil, as will hut bases or pits To name only two instances, the Sutton Courtenay village of the pagan Saxon period came to light first in the side of a gravel pit; and the long barrow at Badshot Lea, near Farnham (Surrey), was discovered in the face of a chalk-pit through recognition of the side ditches, the northern one in full-length section and the southern one in cross-section. (See Plate VII, *A Survey of the Prehistory of the Farnham District* (1939).) Important information was gained when a water main was laid across Caesar's Camp at Wimbledon (Surrey). The trench was only five and a half feet wide but from the sections it afforded, the method of construction of the rampart could be determined, and from the few sherds recovered it was possible to date it to Iron Age A2. Similarly valuable material was obtained more recently when trenches were cut across the henge monument called Durrington Walls, near Amesbury (Wilts). Whenever trenching of this kind is in progress, even along the sides of roads, the revealed section should be inspected and a sharp eye kept on the spoil bank in case small objects have been thrown up.

Even on the outskirts of the 'Great Wen'—greater and more wennish since Cobbett's spacious days—minor discoveries are possible in territory that is fully familiar. The face of Richmond Hill (Surrey), for instance, was for some years during the last war covered with allotments whose strips ran downhill across the contours. After their abandonment they were ploughed over and sown with grass. But in spite of so much soil disturbance it is possible in some lights from the Middlesex bank of the Thames to detect slight banks running with the contours across the slope. These may be the last faint vestiges of strip lynchets; mere tracks, formed before the road above was metalled and defined, could hardly leave any trace after the recent movements of soil. Not far away, in Richmond Park, may be seen slight traces of field banks that went out of use in 1635 when the common lands of Mortlake were reluctantly sold to Charles I. Very old oak trees grow on the banks attesting their considerable age; and a right-angled re-entrant of bank almost certainly rules out a small dam to hold the waters of a pond.

A few years ago in a combe near Lewes (Nat. Grid ref. 436103), the signs of four different periods of cultivation were visible without movement of the head. The day was January 1st and flurries of snow were frequently whirled earthwards from a leaden sky which produced a diffusion of light completely unhelpful to the detection of faint earthworks. Even so, Celtic fields with strip lynchets partly overrunning them, traces of what had probably been fields of the Napoleonic era and modern arable on the floor of the combe were all visible. The whole of this region is one of great interest in that it exemplifies almost every period of prehistory in its earth-works; and the Barbican Museum is near at hand (Map L).

Another earthwork that I have not seen recorded exists in the New Forest on Setley Plain near Boldre. A well-marked enclosure with bank and ditch almost cuts the edge of the fine double disc barrows which form a figure-of-eight. In part, this earthwork looks like a Late Bronze Age bivallate ditch, but the area is much cut up by more recent tracks and only a detailed survey would enable a reasonable guess to be made about its date and function. The Gazetteer includes a number of minor dis-coveries of this kind, but space does not allow of their description here.

One of the most disappointing aspects of fieldwork to the inexperienced is the absence of small finds of any kind even after repeated visits to well-known sites. One may read accounts written not many years ago of whole hillsides littered with Iron Age or Romano-British pottery; yet a very thorough quartering of the ground and a sifting of molehills and of the earth from rabbit-holes produces absolutely nothing, or at best a few broken flints which are almost certainly due to fracture by frost. It seems that, unless one reaches a site very shortly after its publication, many other searchers arrive there before one. And this kind of frustration may last for some time. Then luck seems to change and a few featureless and undistinguished sherds present themselves as a minor reward for glorious days spent in the open air. But metal goods and flint implements of undoubted human manufacture remain altogether elusive.

In fact, metal goods are rarely found on the soil surface. When they do occur they may easily be overlooked. Iron objects will be deeply corroded with rust and a bronze Roman coin seldom presents more than a small fraction of a protruding edge to the seeker. Like all bronze objects of antiquity (and, indeed, of more recent times, if left for long in the soil) it has a dull green patina of verdigris which does not separate itself easily from a green background of grass or even from the dark soil of an occu-pation layer. The moral is: choose your site carefully and look keenly, or expect dis-appointment. It is of little use choosing one that is well known from textbooks. Rather, seek new ones after gaining familiarity with those already recorded; and if the plough has recently passed that way, only half-hearted searching can result in a complete lack of finds.

Flint flakes, because of their white patina (in chalk country at any rate) are easily visible; but the difficulty there is the sheer abundance of the material. Sometimes it is worth sitting down and picking up piece after piece and examining each under a handglass. When it is not obviously an artifact, look at its edges for signs of minute but fairly regular serrations, for flint saws of small dimensions (a half to one and a half inches) are not uncommon. But do not be surprised when you show your treasures to an experienced fieldworker to be told that most of them, if not all, are natural products. It is, of course, necessary to have studied illustrations of flint implements in excavation reports in order to know what sort of things to look for. Those shown in textbooks of archaeology are usually the more specialized and typical tools but not necessarily those that occur most commonly in the field.

After a while one has no need to be told which are genuine artifacts and they will occasionally be found. Prospects of success are rather brighter in greensand country where the occurrence of flint must be due to human importation from the downs; and the chances are that any flakes discovered away from the chalk are the waste from prehistoric knapping. Even doubtful scraps in such a situation are worth pocketing for later study. Flint often stands out from a sandy background and asks to be picked up, as did quite recently a beautiful implement (a 'fabricator') of triangular section and somewhat pitted by frost, which lay near my path on Farley Heath, Surrey.

Where gravel occurs in sandy country the task of detecting flint is less easy, especially as it does not there acquire the white patina as in chalk country. Moreover chert, a flint-like stone derived from the greensands, was also used as a raw material for implements and its more typical colours of honey or chocolate render it comparatively inconspicuous against a sandy background.

One of the commonest clues to a habitation site are lumps of burnt daub. This was originally the clay that was plastered over wickerwork to form the wind- and rainproof walls of dwellings. Often they were destroyed by fire with the result that the clay was baked to a brick-like consistency. Often it is brick-red in colour. Sometimes it bears the impressed forms of the withies against which it had been smeared. On Romano-British sites fragments of wall-brick and sometimes roofing tiles are quite abundant and it is desirable that one should be familiar with the texture of Roman brick so that it may be distinguished from that of other periods, in so far as that is possible when it occurs in only small fragments.

The subject of pottery is beyond the scope of words and it must be handled in quantity over a long period before any confidence in identifying it can be obtained. The best opportunities for doing this are presented by the numerous excavations undertaken usually by a skilled director who will somehow find time to give instruction in the art of digging and some guidance on the nature of finds to those who are genuinely interested. Museum studies afford further opportunities for gaining familiarity with pottery and other finds, and, although curators are grossly overworked, many pride themselves on their service to students and will go to much trouble in giving help. Courtesy demands, however, that they be sought by appointment rather than by a casual visit.

The townsman has fewer chances than the countryman for fieldwork. As already suggested, the suburban dweller may well find it possible to do research in his immediate vicinity, but those tied for most of the year to the inner parts of large towns are less favourably placed. Yet London, Canterbury and Southampton have shown conclusively the vast amount of information that may lie beneath pavements and buildings. But opportunities are diminishing fast as multi-storied buildings with their deep foundations are erected. Almost any building site is worth watching; and half a crown to stay the bulldozer for a few minutes (in the absence of the clerk of works) may well be worth while so that a bare record may be made of structures or burials. Mithraic temples will always be exceptional; it is, however, the less spectacular discoveries that usually add most to the sum of knowledge.

Other disturbances of town soil may also be fruitful to the patient investigator, and there can be few streets in our towns that do not at some time of the year undergo some form of excavation. This makes possible the search for vestiges of house foundations or of earlier dwelling sites revealed in section in the trench; and the spoilheaps deserve more than a brief glance.

In what follows I offer a selection of instances which enable the fieldworker to study the relative chronology of the commoner types of earthworks. Of necessity, a few of these examples occur outside our region.

(a) At Cissbury (Sussex) none of the shafts of flint mines cut through the lynchets of Celtic fields, which are therefore later.

(b) At Cissbury some of the mineshafts were covered by the ramparts of the Iron Age fort, which must therefore be later.

(c) There is no known instance of a Celtic-field lynchet running beneath (and therefore preceding) a neolithic long barrow.

(d) A ranch-boundary ditch at Shalbourne (Wilts) (N.G. c. 294603) cuts across the encircling ditch of a pre-existing disc barrow.

(e) On Crawley Down (Hants) Celtic fields 'respect' disc barrows.

(f) On Milston Down (Wilts) (N.G. 207450) a ranch-boundary ditch cuts through pre-existing Celtic-field lynchets.

(g) On Quarley Hill (Hants) the Iron Age rampart overlies pre-existing ranch-boundary ditches (Pl. 9). This may now be obscured by ploughing. At Whitsbury (Hants) there is a similar conjunction of Late Bronze Age and Iron Age earthworks.

(h) Celtic fields run beneath the Iron Age rampart of Cissbury

(i) Similarly, they run beneath the enclosure bank of the Soldiers' Ring, Damerham (Hants), which is presumed, by analogy with similar works, to be Romano-British (Figure 13 and Map H).

(j) In South Malling (Sussex) strip lynchets have formed upon Celtic fields (v. p. 210).

(k) An undated circular earthwork in Headbourne Worthy parish (Hants) is cut by the side-ditch of a Roman road.

(l) The Roman Stane Street of c. A.D. 50 cuts through the cross-ridge dyke on Glatting Down, Sutton (Sussex) (Map D). The same thing occurs in West Harting parish (Sussex).

(m) Grim's Ditch in Ufton Nervet (Berks), probably sub-Roman, cuts into the Iron Age promontory fort on Raven Hill.

(n) Flex Ditch (Silchester, Hants) has damaged a Roman road and is therefore late Roman or post-Roman.

(o) Bokerly Dyke, late Roman, overlies a ranch-boundary ditch on Blagdon Hill (N.G. 057180) (see Map H and Plates 7 and 19).

It is important to note that these instances do not logically permit the inference, e.g., that all ranch-boundary ditches are earlier than Iron Age A or that all of them are later than Celtic fields. Large numbers of instances must be recorded before valid generalizations can be made, and it is an unavoidable weakness of prehistoric studies that if any sort of consecutive account of ancient life is to be given there must be some dependence on isolated instances awaiting the confirmation of further similar evidence. Seen from another angle the difficulty may be stated thus: prehistory is much more dependent on slenderly based hypotheses than are most periods of history; but it is also true to say that many of these hypotheses are eventually confirmed. Nevertheless, much that has been said in previous chapters is provisional and subject to radical revision in the light of the fuller knowledge that will come as research in prehistory and related studies advances.

A further point that needs to be stressed is that the use of negative evidence is fallacious. For instance, it is illogical to assert that because no pagan Saxon burials or dwellings have been found in the Hastings region, that no Saxons settled there. Apart from the incompleteness of the surviving evidence in all regions, there is a particular factor in the Hastings region which suggests that the archaeological data is even more incomplete there than elsewhere; and that factor is soil acidity which destroys both skeletal remains and associated metal goods without trace. Moreover, the chance of finding recognizable Saxon dwelling sites in any region is small.

For the unwary fieldworker there are many traps, of which only a few can be mentioned here. Abandoned railways and roads, modern field lynchets and hedgeless hedgebanks, windmill tumps, landscape gardening, old spoil-heaps from quarries, surface gravel-digging and the artificial mounds (cotterels) upon which cattle take refuge when riverside marshes are flooded—any of these may present a specious appearance of antiquity, yet all of them are relevant to the field archaeology of recent centuries.

Old canals, sometimes narrow, have marshy bottoms with a rich growth of rushes; and as they follow a very level course they should be easily identified. In any case, most of them are marked on the one-inch map. So with the embankments and cuttings of abandoned branch railways. If followed for a short way their original function is usually obvious, but at first glance in some situations they may prove puzzling. Abandoned roads are usually overgrown with grass and their true nature hidden. Reference to old maps will sometimes reveal their identity and course.

Modern cultivation on slopes is still producing positive and negative lynchets either separately or together. Very high ones are likely to be quite old and may be the successors of medieval field boundaries. Old hedgebanks sometimes declare themselves for what they are by their bearing an irregular row of hawthorn trees, occasionally interspersed with elms or oaks. It is, of course, possible for ancient banks to have been re-used at the time of enclosure; only local investigation, especially at the two ends of the former field, can decide. Windmill mounds, which are numerous in Essex, may easily be mistaken for barrows, but sometimes a cruciform depression in the top, of fairly regular shape, reminds one of the timber foundation of a mill. The mound could possibly be a prehistoric barrow re-used as at Caddington (Beds); but it would generally be unwise to assume that without evidence.

Landscape gardening, usually of the eighteenth or nineteenth centuries, may mislead. At Boughton under Blean (Kent) some supposed Romano-British barrows have latterly been proved of eighteenth-century date, ornaments on the estate of a land-owner. To the same two centuries may be attributed many of the tree-rings which, when the trees have been forgotten, may easily be mistaken for disc barrows. A tree-ring abuts on the uncompleted rampart of Ladle Hill (Hants); but a nearby disc barrow makes direct comparison possible. Usually such a barrow has one or two tumps in the middle and the ditch is within the bank. A tree ring usually has the ditch outside and is often less regular in construction. But the planting of a clump of trees within a disc barrow is by no means improbable if the area within is large enough. The prominent siting of barrows accords with the preference shown by the planters of clumps of trees as, for example, in the small hill-fort of Chanctonbury Ring. (cf. Pl. 6).

One final point is worth making. Trench-digging practice during the First World War, and the explosion of shells and bombs on former ranges, can suggest various kinds of antiquities to the imaginative; and civil and military earth-moving during the Second World War offers further traps for the unwary. Even earlier, the digging of gravel for roadmaking in the heyday of Macadam, and later, produces an irregularity of surface that may produce fortuitous earthworks. The commons of south-west London all show signs of this surface digging for gravel.

None of these late antiquities is without its historical interest, and they are worth noting because of their apparent air of remote age.

BIBLIOGRAPHY TO CHAPTER XIV

The works cited on pp. 199–200 are relevant also to this chapter, as are those cited on p. 30. See also Crawford's *Man and his Past* (1921), chapters XIV–XVI, concerning the tracing of Roman roads; and the last section on p. 151. *The Ancient Burial Mounds of England* (1953), by L. V. Grinsell, is indispensable to fieldworkers and contains useful local bibliographies confined to his topic. Chapter VIII of E. C. Curwen's *Prehistoric Sussex* (1930) is an interesting discussion on 'The Detection and Mapping of Earthworks'. Covering all aspects briefly but with authority is *Field Archaeology—Some Notes for Beginners issued by the Ordnance Survey* (1951). This affords a quite comprehensive bibliography to all aspects of fieldwork and is valuable out

---

* Inexpensive works.

of all proportion to its small price. *English Prehistoric Pottery* (H.M.S.O., 1952) contains 32 photographs of pottery ranging from the neolithic to the Belgic periods, and is inexpensive. On shadow sites, cropmarks and soil marks see, in addition to *Wessex from the Air* and *Air Survey and Archaeology*, D. N. Riley's 'Technique of Air Archaeology', in *Archaeological Journal*, 101 (1946).

The earlier part of this chapter suggests a number of sources; for local archaeological publications see pp. 229–30; and for place-name studies see the end of the next chapter.

* Inexpensive works.

CHAPTER XV

Place-names and Fieldwork

THE FOLLOWING alphabetical list of words comprises those that are of interest to the field archaeologist and that are of common occurrence. The Old English (OE) period of the language is usually regarded as extending from c. A.D. 700 to 1100, and Middle English (ME) from 1100 to 1450. Thereafter is New English. A date immediately after a modern name indicates the time of its first recorded use, as for example, 11 C. is eleventh century. The name could, of course, have been in use for a long time before the first known record of it.

aern (OE), 'house', usually as a second element in a name. E.g. Seasalter 9 C. (Kent), presumably referring to a building connected with the sea-brine industry; Walkern 11 C. (Herts), 'house for walking (i.e. fulling) cloth'. Crockenhill (Kent), 'building for pot-making'. See also **tōt** below.

ǣwiell or **ǣwielm** (OE), 'river-spring' as in Ewell 7 C. (Surrey), Temple Ewell 8 C. (Kent), Alton 12 C. (Hants), Ewelme 11 C. (Oxon), and Carshalton 9 C. (Surrey), the last of which means 'cress-spring'. These are perennial springs and the two Surrey places attracted to themselves settlers of almost every period from mesolithic to modern times.

balle (ME), 'landmark of earth indicating a boundary'. Occurs occasionally in Oxfordshire, e.g. Chinnor, Pyrton, Aston Rowant, Garsington and Baldon. See Introduction to the *Survey of English Place-Names*, vol. I, pt. 1, p. 159

beorg or **beorh** (OE), 'hill or barrow'. As a second element it sometimes appears as -*bury*, -*berry*, -*burgh*, -*borough*, through confusion with **burh**; e.g. Hawkesbury 12 C. in Fobbing (Essex), Berrylands 13 C. in Kingston (Surrey), Burgh 11 C. in Banstead (Surrey) referring here to a group of barrows and not to a natural hill. Warborough 13 C. (Oxon), 'the watch-hill'. Normally the word would become barrow, as in Barrow Farm 13 C. in Widford (Herts) or Wanbarrow Farm 18 C. in Hurstpierpoint (Sussex). It is of occasional occurrence in field-names and in the boundaries of Saxon charters. See especially *The Place-Names of Oxfordshire*, p. 431; *The Place-Names of Middlesex*, p. 195; and Grinsell, *The Ancient Burial-Mounds of England*, chapter IV. Barrow Field in Teddington (Middx) refers to a barrow that contained a Middle Bronze Age cremation; Barrow Field in Feering (Essex) was used by the Anglo-Saxons for burial but no barrows remained in the nineteenth century.

black-/patch/field/land, etc. See above, p. 206. *Blacklands(s)* occurs in the following Essex parishes: Hatfield Broad Oak, Hatfield Peverel, Great Waltham, Bulmer, Great Henny, Stebbing and Birchanger. The same name occurs in Clifton Hampden (Oxon) and in Thundridge and Walkern (Herts). Pebmarsh (Essex) has a *Black Croft* and at White Notley, Alphamstone and Lindsell in the same county the name *Black Acre* occurs. Other instances are to be found elsewhere.

brick may refer in minor or field-names to a scatter of Roman or later brick indicative of a habitation site. The Park Street Roman villa was found in *Bricket Field*, St. Stephen's (Herts), but may be in some way connected with Bricket Wood in the same parish, which is derived from *beorht*, 'bright'. If so the coincidence is a curious one. At Finchingfield (Essex) there was, apparently, a Romano-British settlement and a villa within the parish. The field-name *Brickstead* occurs there and its relation to the villa-site might be interesting. Usually names compounded with '*Brick*' are fairly recent. They may be derived from words having no connection with the building material. A number of names such as *Brickkiln* are included in the Gazetteer.

burh (OE) is an element of common occurrence in both major and minor names and generally refers to an earthwork of prehistoric or medieval times. In many instances, however, it refers to fortifications in brick or stone, as for instance, Canterbury 8 C. or Richborough 12 C. (Kent), though the word *-chester* is far commoner in this sense. The majority of hill-forts were regarded as *burhs*, e.g. Woolbury, Cissbury, Hollingbury, Danebury, Cherbury, Walbury, etc. The names of some now largely or wholly destroyed are sometimes preserved, e.g. Hulberry in Lullingstone (Kent) or Silsbury in Cholsey (Berks).

The following list consists of names compounded with *burh* with which no earthwork can now be associated and which therefore invite fieldwork. They are taken only from Hampshire and Berkshire as no Place-Name Survey volume has yet been published for those two counties. In the absence of early forms all of these names must be regarded with some suspicion.* The parish name follows in brackets.

Hampshire: Bulberry (Abbotts Ann), Boulsbury—*Bollesborough* in 16 C. (Damerham), Timsbury (Michelmersh), Bigsbury (Ringwood), Luzborough (Romsey), Dunsbury (Rowlands Castle), Burridge (Swanwick), Rowbury—*Widianbyrig* in 10 C. (Wherwell), Rookesbury (Wickham), Linchborough (Woolmer), Burhunt (Selborne), and the parish names Boarhunt and Owzlebury.

Berkshire: the parish name Bucklebury; Rowbury (Boxford), Bury Hill (Buscot), Strattenborough (Coleshill), Youlbury (Cumnor), Coldborough (East Garston and Lambourn), Forbury (Kintbury), Eastbury (Lambourn), Cockleberry (Letcombe Bassett), Sudbury (Longworth), Sowberry (Moulsford), Tilbury (North Hinksey), Stanbury (Shinfield), Limborough (Wantage), Goldbury (West Hendred), Burleigh (Winkfield). There are many other examples from other counties noted in the Gazetteer.

---

* Some, no doubt go back to OE **beorg**.

Sometimes comparatively small earthworks, e.g. Borough Hill in Boxford (Berks) or Holbury, a moated homestead, in Fawley (Hants), are called *burh*; but the word is in fact used indiscriminately for almost any kind of earthwork. Hengistbury (Hants) is a promontory fort; Segsbury in Letcombe Regis (Berks) is a plateau fort; Tunorbury in South Hayling (Hants) is a woodland ringwork; *Padboro*, a field-name in Long Wittenham (Berks), is the site of a Romano-British settlement; Berry Grove in Waltham St. Lawrence (Berks) is the site of a Romano-British house; Egbury in St. Mary Bourne (Hants) is probably the site of a Roman *mansio*; the Borough Field in Great Chesterford (Essex) is the site of a small Roman town; Bury Bank in Greenham (Berks) is a linear earthwork of probably sub-Roman date; Hertingfordbury (Herts) probably took its name from one of the Saxon *burhs* built in A.D. 912; Forbury in Reading should probably be associated with a Danish *burh* built there in 870; Newbury (Berks) is a town founded as late as the 12 C. In the counties of Middlesex, Hertfordshire, Essex and Buckinghamshire, *burh* is widespread in the form *Bury* (see *The Place-Names of Herts.*, p. 243) and is applied to medieval manorial sites many, but not all of them, moated.

The variety of forms that *burh* may assume in NE may be seen from the above lists. Borough is generally from the nominative *burh*; -bury or -berry from the dative -*byrig*.

The name Foxbury probably means 'fox-earth' in most instances (cf. Foxborough in Purleigh (Essex) which was *Foxhole* in 14 C.); but early forms of Foxbury in Crofton (Hants)—e.g. *Forstebyr'* 13 C.—show that it is probably derived from a lost word meaning 'ridge' and that therefore the second element may well refer to an earthwork. See also **burhtūn, eald burh, eorth burh**

burhtūn (OE), 'enclosed settlement (*tūn*) with a *burh* as its nucleus' or '*tūn* near a *burh*'. Blewburton in Blewbury (Berks) clearly takes its name from the Iron Age hill-fort there, and Buriton (Hants) may refer to the promontory fort on Butser Hill. But there is no obvious connection between the following names and recorded earthworks: Bierton (Bucks); Burtonwood in Great Chesterford (Essex); Burton in Thaxted and Stansted Mountfitchet (Essex); Bourton (Berks); Norbelton in Hellingly (Sussex) and West Burton in Friston (Sussex). Burton in Christchurch (Hants) may have taken its name from the Saxon *burh* mentioned in the *Burghal Hidage*; the fort was probably obliterated by the village, though vestiges may still remain. There are said to be earthworks near the site of the lost name of Broughton in Jevington (Sussex). See above, p. 180 f.

byrgen (OE), 'burying place'. At Berins Hill in Ipsden (Oxon) human remains have actually been found; and on Burn Hill in Stone (Bucks) there is a barrow. At Barley (Herts), which also contains the name, Roman remains have been found, possibly including burials. Kinsbourne Green in Harpenden (Herts) means 'Cyne's burial place'. The OE word **byrgels**, with the same meaning, survives in Heathen's Burial Corner in Steyning (Sussex). 'Scores of urns' are said to have been found here. *Haethenan byrgels* 11 C. in Pyrton (Oxon) is a medieval instance.

capelle (ME) and words of similar meaning such as **church** and **minster** are not infrequent in field and minor names. Most of them probably gained such a name from the donation of the land for the upkeep of the place of worship, but it is certain that some were so named because the foundations of a Roman building were visible and these were taken to be the remains of a chapel. Villas are actually known to exist in Chapel Field at Preston Candover (Hants); in Chapel Copse in Appleshaw (Hants); and in Chapel Plat, Bletchingley (Surrey), is an earthwork. A Roman house at Ickham (Kent) was found in Church Field; that at Sarratt (Herts) was in Church Field; and at Hadstock (Essex) in Sunken Church Field. In the parishes of Ashurst and Lyndhurst (Hants) are enclosures known as Church Place, possibly because of their resemblance to the earliest field churches. A villa is known to exist in Minster Field, Abbotts Ann (Hants).

ceastel (OE). Besides its obvious use as in Castle's Farm, Orsett (Essex), where there is a ring-and-bailey castle, or Castle Hill, Bletchingley (Surrey), where a Norman castle once existed, it is applied to manorial earthworks at Great Missenden (Bucks) and at Chessington and Addington (Surrey) and to unspecified earthworks at Horsham and Hartfield (Sussex). At Ashbury and Uffington (Berks) and Newhaven (Sussex) the name is applied to an Iron Age hill-fort. The name Castle Field in Andover (Hants), Wheatley (Oxon), Waltham St. Lawrence (Berks) and Worth (Kent) refers in each instance to the site of a Roman building.

The word Castle with such additions as Green, Down, Hill, etc., is found in the following parishes: Bulphan 15 C. and Great Waltham 14 C. (Essex), Lurgashall 17 C. (Sussex), Chobham 15 C. (Surrey), Caddington 17 C. (Beds), Thorley 17 C. (Herts), Ealing 17 C. (Middx), Britwell 19 C. and Checkendon 19 C. (Oxon). In Inkpen (Berks) there is a 10 C. reference to *stān ceastla*; and Stephen's Castle Down in Upham (Hants) is said to perpetuate the tradition of a 12 C. castle. The place-name Chesham (Bucks) originally had *ceastel* as its first element, but this was later confused with *ceaster*. Other castle-names are included in the Gazetteer. On the probable significance of minor names such as *Owl's* or *Rat's Castle*, see *The Introduction to the Survey of English Place-Names*, pt. I, pp. 148 f.

ceaster (OE), 'fortified place', is usually applied to towns of Roman origin with particular reference to their walls, as in Colchester, etc. But in a few instances it was used of Roman villas, e.g. *Stanchester* in Chilton Candover and *Balchester* in Wootton St. Lawrence, both in Hampshire. *Napchester* in West Langdon (Kent) may be similar, though only a dubious Roman altar has been reported from there. Cheshunt (Herts) contains the same word, which must refer to the Roman camp of which the site is known. Chesterwell in Great Horkesley (Essex) is close to the unfinished hill-fort of Pitchbury, to which *ceaster* presumably referred. Rochester Farm 13 C. in Great Leighs (Essex) probably takes its name from a family that came from the Kentish city; but it is not impossible that the family name was acquired from this Essex place which stands beside a Roman road in a much-Romanized area and on a slope facing south-west, such as was favoured by villa-owners. If villa there were at this place, it is still to be sought.

The old name for the fort of the Saxon shore at Bradwell-on-Sea (Essex) was *Ythancaestir* 8 C., that is, the Romano-British name *Othona* plus *caester*. In this it is like Porchester (Hants) in its application of the second element. Chesterly Piece in Great Milton (Oxon) has no recorded Roman associations (but cf. Little Milton).

ciest (OE), 'chest, coffin', may develop into a form identical with *cheste* (ME), 'strife', which is used in place-names of land in disputed ownership, or with the word for a chestnut tree, *cist-(en)-bēam*) so that it is always difficult to distinguish which word was originally used. Chest Wood in Layer de la Haye and Chisbon Heath in St. Osyth, both in Essex, are on the parish boundary and therefore apt to be in dispute. Other instances may include Chestham in Henfield (Sussex) and Chest-hill in Aston Rowant (Oxon). The latter name in Stonesfield (Oxon), outside our region, is applied to the site of a Roman villa.

cinder in the Weald of Kent, Sussex and Surrey often commemorates Roman or later ironworks. So it is with **forge, furnace, hammer, mine** (i.e. 'ore) and **pit**.

crocc (OE), 'pot, pitcher', in place-names commonly refers to the place where the potter lived or worked (generally the same) or to where sherds were to be found. In some instances the name related to a Romano-British pot-making site or to a dwelling site that had been in use over a long period; in others, medieval kilns are probably in the vicinity. Crockhill near Fritham (Hants) is one of the Romano-British pottery sites of the New Forest and Crockshard in Wingham (Kent) may refer to similar activity, for a Romano-British kiln has been discovered in the parish. Crockfield in Newington-on-the-Street (Kent) is the site of a Romano-British cemetery, and no doubt the name indicates the discovery there of burial-groups with pottery. Compare Panshard, the name of a Romano-British kiln-site in the New Forest. See the Gazetteer under the following parishes for further names including the word **crocc** (or **croccere**, 'potter'): Ardleigh and Greensted next Ongar (Essex); Wymondley (Herts); Fawley and Burnham (Bucks); Nettlebed (Oxon); Fareham (Hants); Dorking and Chertsey (Surrey); Boxgrove, Framfield, Durrington and Horsham (Sussex); Eynsford (Kent). See also **pot** below.

cylen (OE), 'kiln', is quite common in minor place-names but it may often refer to structures of recent centuries for the burning of lime, tiles or brick. Some of these, however, may be of archaeological interest. Only a selection of instances are given: Culham 13 C. in Wargrave (Berks); Limekilns 15 C. in Orsett and Birchanger and Limekiln 16 C. in Widdington (all three in Essex); Tilekiln 15 C. in Earls Colne and 16 C. in Sible Hedingham (both in Essex); Lime Kiln 17 C. in East Dean and Lime Barnetts 14 C. in Ripe (both in Sussex); Brickkiln Wood in Donnington (Berks) is known to have been a place for brick-making in the fifteenth century. *Tyle ostefelde* 15 C. in Send (Surrey) represents the use of *oast* as an alternative to *kiln*.

dead. Field-names such as Dead Churl, Dead Man are occasionally found. Deadman's

Hill in Kelshall (Herts) is the site of a Romano-British cemetery and of barrows; and the group of fields called Deadwife, Deadchild and Deadpriest in Ashwell (Herts) may indicate sporadic discoveries in another burial-place. For other possible instances see the Gazetteer under: Great Coggeshall, Debden, Woodham Ferrers and Writtle (Essex); Hatfield, Flaunden, Berkhampsted and St. Stephen's (Herts); and Benson, Dorchester, Ewelme and Chinnor (Oxon). Some of these may well refer to some medieval tragedy.

dīc (OE), 'ditch', may refer to a linear earthwork marking a boundary, or to a defensive work, to one dug for agricultural purposes such as a Late Bronze Age boundary ditch, or, in riverside and coastal parishes, it may often refer to a drainage channel. Many examples are given in the Gazetteer. See e.g. North Mundham (Sussex), Britwell (Oxon) and Ingatestone (Essex). See also **faesten** below.

eald burh (OE), 'old defensive earthwork' (or occasionally '*Ealda's burh*'), survives as Oldbury in Ightham (Kent)—a hill-fort; as Aubries in Redbourn (Herts)—an Iron Age earthwork; as the parish names Albury and Aldbury (Herts) where the *burh* sites are lost; as Auberry in Aspenden (Herts)—no remains; as Aldbury in Cheshunt (Herts) where it may refer to a Roman camp; and as Olleberrie in Sarratt (Herts)—no remains. Some of these Hertfordshire examples were already regarded as old by the early Middle Ages when their names are first on record; others, however, may refer to manorial sites abandoned early in the medieval period. For further instances see the Gazetteer.

eorth burh (OE), 'earthen defensive work', survives as Arbury in Ashwell (Herts), where it refers to an Iron Age plateau fort; and it was used in the OE period of the Iron Age defended farmstead on Meon Hill, Stockbridge (Hants), rediscovered in 1924 from the air. Oareborough in Hampstead Norris (Berks), which is *Awbury* in 1839, may represent a development of this word, as may the parish name Arborfield in Berkshire. Other instances are noted in the Gazetteer. See **(h)arbour** below.

faesten (OE), 'stronghold', is uncommon. Vasterne (in fact, *faest-aern*) in Reading may, as well as Forbury, be associated with the Danish *burh* built in 870. Brinfast in North Mundham (Sussex) possibly commemorates the outer defences of the Belgic stronghold presumed to have existed but now eroded by the sea. The word may also occur in Holdfast, Haslemere (Surrey). It is applied at least three times to linear earthworks in our region, each time as *faestendic*. These occur in Bexley (Kent) and Eversley (Hants), and it is applied to the Chiltern Grim's Ditches.

flōr (OE), 'floor', is of comparatively rare occurrence. At Fawler in western Oxfordshire tessellated pavements have been discovered which explain why the settlement came to be called 'coloured floor'. Reference to the same thing occurs in a 10 C. charter relating to Gosford (Oxon); for which see Gazetteer under Water Eaton. However, no Roman house is known here; and Fawler, in Kingston Lisle (Berks), has 12 C. forms such as *fage flor* which reveal that it, too, must refer to a Roman pavement. None has so far been found there, but in the same parish is a presumed

Romano-British barrow and there was occupation in the same period on Rams Hill not far away. In a field called Hollyflower at West Dean (Wilts) an extensive villa was found in 1741. It looks as though the name was originally *hālig flōr* (holy floor). Floore (Northants), at one time called Flower, seems to belong to this group of names, as does Flower Farm in Godstone (Surrey) which is recorded as *Flore* in 13 C. A Roman road and cremation burials have been found not far away. See also Pangbourne (Berks), Harpsden (Oxon), Toppesfield (Essex), Bengeo, Eastwick and Redbourn (Herts). Some of these may be worthy of investigation, but the possibility of the family name 'Flower', applied to a place, should be borne in mind.

Forest Names. A map showing the distribution of these names is valuable in giving some idea, however incomplete, of the extent and location of ancient woodland. The following terms imply woodland that was more or less extensive: OE **lēah** (-ley, -leigh, -ly, etc.), which is sometimes confused with **læs**, 'pasture'; OE **feld** (-field), but means 'clearing in forest'; OE **weald** (Wield, wold, etc.); OE **denn** (-den), 'woodland swine-pasture', often confused with OE **denu** (dean). Less extensive areas are implied by OE **fyrhthe** (frith, thrift, etc.), meaning 'woodland'; OE **wudu** (wood); OE **hangra** (hanger); OE **sceaga** (shaw); OE **snād**, (isolated wood); OE **holt** (wood); OE **græfe** or **grāf(a)** (grove). A group of related words, common in field names, denote clearance for cultivation (i.e. ridding the land of trees, etc.): OE **rydding**, **ryden, rīed, geryd, rod, roth**; OE **baernet**, 'burnt' suggest the method of clearance as do OE **stumbel, stocc**, and ME **stubbing, stoccing** ('tree-stumps, place of stumps'). Words denoting enclosures of one sort or another and typical of forest regions are: OE **falod, (ge)haeg** and **tēag**. ME **launde**, 'a glade', occasionally occurs in field-names and OE **haecc**, 'a gate', especially used in wooded areas. See above, pp. 179–80, 201–2.

(ge-)weorc (OE), 'fort', is uncommon. Instances are Southwark (London) and War Coppice, Bletchingley (Surrey), where there is an Iron Age fort. See also Aston Rowant (Oxon) in the Gazetteer.

(h)arbour (ME) occurs quite commonly in the minor name Coldharbour, from the early 14 C. onwards. It probably has no archaeological significance though in a few instances it may represent a development of OE **eorthburh**, as possibly in Arborfield (Berks), and in field-names of Shorthampton and Deddington (Oxon). An earthwork in Maidenhead (Berks) is known as Robin Hood's Arbour and one now destroyed in Harlington (Middx) was called King's Arbour. There is an Oram's Arbour, the site of an earthwork at Winchester; but generalization from these few instances, where there are in fact remains, is unsound in view of the very many instances in which the name has no archaeological significance. See *The Place-Names of Surrey*, pp. 406 f.

heafod (OE), 'head', often refers to the headland where the plough turned. When combined with the name of an animal it may possibly have some significance in connection with pagan Saxon practices. On this see *The Place-Names of Surrey*, pp. 403 f.;

The Place-Names of Essex, p. xxi; and *The Place-Names of Hertfordshire*, pp. 64, 274, etc. See also above, p. 163.

hearg (OE), 'heathen shrine', is, in some instances at any rate, indicative of local Saxon paganism. Of similar significance is OE **wēoh** or **wīg**, 'holy place, idol', and the names of the gods **Thunor, Tīw** and **Woden**. OE **ealh**, 'heathen temple', occurs twice in Kent in the name Alkham, and in the old name of a creek in Graveney. Wyfold in Checkendon (Oxon) and the Berkshire Hundred of that name may mean 'temple in an enclosure'. There is a possibility that structural vestiges may be found by excavation at these sites. See *Transactions of the Royal Historical Society*, XXIII (1941), pp. 1 f., and above, p. 162 f. and p. 175–6. See also under **stān** below.

hlāw (OE), 'burial mound or natural hill' (usually NE 'low'), is often compounded with the name of the person thought to be buried beneath the barrow or on whose land it was situated. Among village names of this kind are Taplow (Bucks), which refers to a Saxon barrow, and Challow (Berks). In Overton (Hants) is or was an *entan hlew* (giant's barrow); in Cuddesdon (Oxon) *eanferthes hlau* (Eanfrith's barrow); and in Wallington (Herts) is a Metley Hill, a tumulus, which appears as *Metelawe* 14 C., showing that the second syllable referred to the barrow. The first syllable may possibly be derived from OE *methel*, 'speech' (cf. *methelstede*, 'place for a council'), in which case Metley may have been a moot-site of Odsey Hundred in the centre of which it is situated. Odsey itself no doubt was the original meeting-place, but it is not now even within the Hundred. Spellow (Lancs) and Mutlow in Wendens Ambo (Essex), the meeting-place of Uttlesford Hundred, both meaning 'moot-hill', are parallel. Sperberry Hill 13 C. in Ippollitts (Herts) from *spel beorg*, 'speech hill', and *Spelbeorhge* 11 C. in Littlebury (Essex) are formations with a similar meaning. See also above, p. 189, and under **beorg**, p. 217. Numerous names of unlocated barrows are given in the Gazetteer.

hlinc (OE), 'bank, rising ground', seems never to provide a clue to the location of lynchets. The latter word appears to be no older than the late 17 C.

hord (OE), 'hoard', especially in the compound *goldhord*, suggests the discovery of coins or other treasure. It has been noted as a field-name in Titsey, Woking, Shere and Godstone (Surrey), Ripe in Sussex, Amport in Hants, Rochford and Colne Engaine in Essex; and *Drakenhord* 13 C. occurs in Garsington (Oxon) and elsewhere commemorating a belief in a 'dragon's hoard'. Hordle (Hants) includes this word. Somewhat similar in significance is Money Pot Hill 13 C. in Roydon, Money Field 14 C. in Takeley and in Nazeing 13 C. (all in Essex) and Money Field 14 C. in Great Munden (Herts); but it should be noted that some of these may have gained their names as did Money Field 17 C. in Therfield (Herts), the rent from which provides bread charity money. The Money Hills at Copythorne (Hants) are barrows beside a Roman road.

Orwell in Kelshall (Herts) is of particular interest, for it probably means 'treasure spring', namely one into which valuables were cast. With a lowering of the water-table the spring now rises farther downhill, but the original spring-pond, now dry, with traces of an abandoned medieval settlement around it, could be excavated. Orwell is not recorded before the 11 C., but Hardwell in Compton Beauchamp (Berks), which has the same meaning, first finds mention in 9 C. Here the spring has been used to supply a moat.

(ge-)mōt (OE), 'a meeting'. See above, p. 188 f.

parke (ME), 'a large hunting enclosure', is a word in living use with a changed meaning. Medieval parks may still retain their great boundary ditches. See Crawford, *Archaeology in the Field*, chapter 18. Smaller enclosures of one sort or another are represented by minor names containing the following words: OE **pearroc** ('paddock'; in ME this often becomes **parke**); OE **haga, penn, pūnd, pȳnd** and ME **pightel** from 12 C. (often in NE 'pickle or pingel'), **close, pundfald**. In some instances the medieval enclosure-bank is probably the boundary of existing fields. The OE **pūnd** (pound) is occasionally applied to earthworks as, for instance, Barley Pound in Crondall (Hants), which is a ring-and-bailey castle; Old Pound is the name of an enclosure in Longparish (Hants) and may be simply the place for impounding strayed cattle. Grimspound and Round Pound are prehistoric stone enclosures on Dartmoor.

pot (ME), like **crocc** above, p. 221, may afford a clue to a kiln- or dwelling-site. The following are instances of the occurrence of these names and of kiln-sites in the same parish: Potter's Field in Ringmer (Sussex) with nearby 13 C. kilns and claypits; Potterscrouch 13 C. in St. Michael's (Herts) with Roman kiln; Potters Heath 13 C. in Welwyn (Herts) with Roman kiln; Potter Row 15 C. and field-name Potsherds 16 C. in Ingatestone (Essex) with 13 C. kilns; Potter Street 15 C. in Sible Hedingham with 13 C. kiln; Potten End 16 C. in Nettleden (Herts) with 13 C. kiln. Numerous examples of names not yet associated with evidence for local potting are listed in the Gazetteer. See Penn (Bucks). See also **cylen** above, p. 221.

stān (OE), 'stone', often in the sense 'made of stone', seems to be associated with a significant number of Roman sites. Stone Grave in Snodland (Kent) and Stanchester in Chilton Candover (Hants) refer to the sites of Roman houses; Stanway (Essex) to Roman roads; Stansted in Stoughton (Sussex) may refer to a villa, and several have been found in the parish of Stansted Mountfitchet (Essex); Stangrove in Harlow (Essex) is the name of the Romano-Celtic temple site; and it is likely that the *stan erigan* (i.e. **hearg**, see above) of a 10 C. charter relating to Washington (Sussex) refers to the Roman temple whose site lies within Chanctonbury Ring. The name and the site appear to come close together in the bounds as set out in the charter. The Stanstead in Godstone (Surrey) was known as *stanstrete* 13 C. and is identical in name with the London-Chichester Roman road. The numerous Stanfords and Stamfords usually refer to a river-crossing on the line of a Roman road, particularly to the paved ford at such a point. The minor name *stan ceastla* 10 C. occurs in Inkpen (Berks) and there is a Stanbury in Shinfield (Berks).

stede (OE), 'place or site', has already been noticed in connection with Stansted

P

(see **stān** above). Brickstead in Finchingfield may also be a villa site; and Alstead 18 C. in Little Waltham (Essex) may have some connection with a Romano-British settlement within the parish. Crockstead in Framfield (Sussex) perhaps has structural significance also.

stōdfalod (OE), 'stud-enclosure', occurs in one major name, Stotfold 11 C. (Beds) and some minor ones. Instances at Farnborough (Berks) and Bighton, Chilcomb and North Hayling (Hants) are mentioned in Saxon charters, but no corresponding earthworks are known in these parishes. There is mention of one at Ashbury (Berks) in a 10 C. charter. Roman houses, which may once have had protective enclosures, have been found at Bighton and North Hayling where this name occurs. It is found also at Westmill (Herts) in the vicinity of an earthwork; and at Braughing (Herts), where there was a Belgic and Roman settlement which was no doubt enclosed with ramparts. But in the latter instance the name could have been applied to one of several surviving earthworks. At Lympne (Kent) the Saxon shore fort is known as Stutfall.

There are other compounds with **falod**, most of which must normally refer to medieval or later enclosures. Commonest is **dēorfald** ('deer fold') of which the first word had already in ME become restricted in meaning to 'deer'. This compound occurs in the parish of Mountfield as Darwell 13 C.; in Warnham as Durfold 14 C. (both in Sussex); in Dunsfold (Surrey) as Durfold 13 C.; and in Lacey Green (Bucks) as Darvills. Alfold in Surrey was already in 13 C. 'the old fold' and this name is recorded from the same period in South Mimms (Middx). Alfoldean in Slinfold (Sussex) is the site of a Roman posting-station on the Stane Street with a protective rampart which is referred to in the English name. A manorial site in Sherfield upon Loddon (Hants) is called Cufaude (presumably 'Cowfold') and in the former spelling it is recorded as the name of the Sussex parish from 13 C. Mention has already been made of Wyfold (see **hearg** above, p. 224).

strǣt (OE), 'paved or metalled road', usually Roman, is found frequently in major and minor names such as Streatham (London), Stratford and Strethall (Essex), Streatley (Beds and Berks), Stratton and Stratfield (Hants), Street (Sussex), etc. It may rarely be applied to a medieval road.

tōte (ME), 'look-out hill', has little if any purely archaeological importance though in a few instances, e.g. Totternhoe (Beds) meaning 'look-out house on a ridge', some structure was present. In this example, however, any vestiges of it will probably have been destroyed by the Norman motte on the site.

In at least twenty parishes of the Home Counties, and especially in Herts and Essex, field-names such as Seed Cups, Seed Cobs, etc., occur. These are derived from ME **setcoppe**, meaning 'seat, camp or entrenchment on a hill-top', a situation in which all are, in fact, found. All known instances are listed in the Gazetteer since there is a possible association with surviving earthworks. Sidcup (Kent) is a major name of this kind (*setecoppe* 14 C.). See above, pp. 183–4.

tigel (OE) originally meant either 'brick', 'tile' or even 'pot'. Tilehurst (Berks) is recorded in 12 C. and thereafter in most counties minor names such as Tilekiln and Tilehouse (usually from 'tile oast', i.e. 'kiln') are found here and there. Usually the reference is to a medieval or later kiln-site; but it is just possible that such a name may afford a clue to a Roman site on which there was seen a scattering of building debris. For instance, Romano-British tombs made of tiles were found at Tileplace Farm, Old Windsor (Berks). But some names beginning with Tile- may be from an OE personal name: e.g. Tilbury (Essex). See also **brick**, p. 218, and **cylen**, p. 221.

tūnsteall (OE), usually Dunstall in NE, refers to some kind of enclosure and there is the mention of one in a 10 C. charter as being situated beside the Watling Street in Hendon (Middx). This, by 10 C., was already regarded as old. Tunstall in Mountfield (Sussex) is first recorded in 12 C. and in Essex there are a dozen parishes containing this name from the 13 C. onwards. The word **hāmsteall** (NE Hamstell, Homestall), of occasional occurrence, may have a similar meaning.

BIBLIOGRAPHY TO CHAPTER XV

Dr. Crawford's contribution, 'Place-Names and Archaeology', chapter VIII, to volume I, part i of the *Introduction to the Survey of English Place-Names* (1924), and his other writings on the subject, contain much of value and interest to the fieldworker. The raw material is available in the following local volumes of the Place-Name Society: *Buckinghamshire* (1925), *Bedfordshire* (1926), *Sussex*, 2 volumes (1929), *Surrey* (1934), *Essex* (1935), *Hertfordshire* (1938), *Middlesex* (1942) and *Oxfordshire*, 2 volumes (1953–4). The treatment of field-names in the first four of these volumes is not adequate for archaeological purposes. The 'Addenda and Corrigenda' sections in all volumes published by the Society need to be consulted. Membership of the Society at twenty-five shillings per annum gives entitlement to an annual volume and to back volumes at the same price.

J. K. Wallenberg's *Kentish Place-Names* (1931) and *Place-Names of Kent* (1934) omit many minor names. W. W. Skeat and Sir Frank Stenton each produced a volume of *Berkshire* in 1911 which is concerned mainly with village names.

The Oxford Dictionary of English Place-Names (1936 and later editions) is useful for Hampshire and Berkshire, but contains very few minor names. It has a very full bibliography to all aspects of the subject. *English Place-Name Elements*, in 2 volumes (1956), published by the English Place-Name Society, is of great value. Sir Alan Mawer's *Problems of Place-Name Study* (1929) and Sir Frank Stenton's contributions to the *Transactions of the Royal Historical Society*, volumes 21–25, should also be consulted.

General Bibliography

SEE ALSO the chapter bibliographies for works restricted in period or topic. Inexpensive works are marked with an asterisk *.

A. General Works

V. G. Childe, *Prehistoric Communities of the British Isles* (1940) is the standard textbook of British prehistory, and his *Prehistoric Migrations in Europe* (1950), though glancing only occasionally at Britain, provides important background information. Grahame Clark's *Prehistoric England* (1940) and *Prehistoric Europe, the Economic Basis* (1952) are both authoritative and well illustrated. *Stuart Piggott's *British Prehistory* is concise and, like Clark's *Prehistoric Europe*, embodies much new thinking on important phases of prehistory. *Prehistoric Britain* by J. and C. Hawkes (1949) is a pleasant, popular account, as is *The Heritage of Early Britain* (1952), consisting of eight chapters each by a different scholar. *Archaeology in England and Wales, 1914–1931*, by T. D. Kendrick and C. F. C. Hawkes (1932), is an invaluable summary of prehistory down to Saxon times, reviewing material that accrued in the seventeen years stated in the title. The summary was continued year by year in *Archaeological Journal*, volumes 89–92. These sources together provide a useful select bibliography of work published from 1914 to 1935. The *British Museum Guides* mentioned in the chapter bibliographies give an unrivalled body of photographic and line illustrations at very small cost. So it is with *English Prehistoric Pottery* (1952), published by H.M.S.O. The Council for British Archaeology's booklet *A Survey and Policy of Field Research in the Archaeology of Great Britain*, Part I (to the seventh century A.D.) (1948) is an important recent summary of knowledge and of work still to be done.

B. National Periodical Publications

Antiquaries Journal (1921 onwards) with bibliographical sections. This was preceded by the *Proceedings of the Society of Antiquaries* (1843–1920).

Archaeologia (1804 onwards).

Archaeological Journal (1844 onwards).

Journal of the British Archaeological Association (1862 onwards).

Proceedings of the Prehistoric Society (1936 onwards) with a section on current prehistory. This was preceded by the *Proceedings of the Prehistoric Society of East Anglia* (1908–1935).

Antiquity (1927 onwards) with select bibliographies.

Journal of Roman Studies (1911 onwards), with a section detailing new discoveries each year.

Reports of the Research Committee of the Congress of Archaeological Societies (1905–1939) record both discoveries and publications. These were replaced by:

Archaeological Bulletin for the British Isles, three issues: 1940–6, 1947, 1948–9, then by:

Archaeological Bibliography, 1950–1, 1952–3, 1954.

Archaeological News Letter (1948 onwards).

Annual Reports (1937 onwards) *of the University of London, Institute of Archaeology* and its *Occasional Papers* are often important.

There are several journals long defunct and containing little of value.

Other national periodicals such as *Man, The Journal of the Royal Anthropological Institute, Proceedings of the British Academy, British Numismatic Journal, Numismatic Chronicle, British Museum Quarterly, Folklore* and *Nature* occasionally include papers of relevance to our subject and region.

C. Books restricted to Counties or other Regions

The *Methuen County Archaeologies* (see p. 203 above): *Berkshire* (1931) by H. J. E. Peake; *Surrey* (1931) by D. C. Whimster; *Kent* (1930) by R. F. Jessup; *Middlesex* (1930) by C. E. Vulliamy; *Sussex* (second edition, 1954) by E. C. Curwen.

Royal Commission on Historical Monuments (see p. 204 above): *Hertfordshire* (1910); *Buckinghamshire* (1912); *Essex* (4 volumes, 1916, 1921, 1922, 1923); *Middlesex* (1937).

Victoria County Histories, see above, p. 203.

The Andover District (1922) by O. G. S. Crawford.

Sir Cyril Fox's *The Archaeology of the Cambridge Region* (1923) includes in its survey parts of southern Beds, northern Herts and northern Essex.

The Oxford Region—A Scientific and Historical Survey (1954), edited by A. F. Martin and R. W. Steel. Chapters 1 to 11, each by a different authority, cover the natural background of the region and its prehistory and early history in outline.

Prehistory of the Farnham District (1939), a publication of the Surrey Archaeological Society, with important contributions by several scholars, has a wider relevance than its title implies.

Early Man in South Buckinghamshire (1955) by J. F. Head.

D. Local Periodical Publications

Transactions of the Essex Archaeological Society (1858–   ).

Essex Review.

Colchester Museum Reports.

Transactions of the Southend-on-Sea Antiquarian and Historical Society.

Walthamstow Antiquarian Society (occasional publications).

Transactions of the St. Albans and Hertfordshire Architectural and Archaeological Society.

Transactions of the East Hertfordshire Archaeological Society (1899–).

East Hertfordshire Archaeological Society Newsletter.

Hertfordshire Local History Council Newssheet.

Barnet and District Record Society (half-yearly bulletins).

Transactions of the London and Middlesex Archaeological Society.

Bedfordshire Magazine (1947–).

Records of Buckinghamshire (1858–).

Berks., Bucks. and Oxon. Archaeological Journal (1895–1930, THEN AS *Berkshire Archaeological Journal (1931–).*

Transactions of the Newbury and District Field Club.

Oxoniensia (1936–).

Oxfordshire Archaeological Society Reports.

Ashmolean Museum Reports.

South-Eastern Naturalist and Antiquary.

Proceedings of the Hampshire Field Club (1887–).

Hampshire Notes and Queries (1883–).

Proceedings of the Bournemouth Natural Science Society.

Surrey Archaeological Collections (1858–).

Proceedings of the Leatherhead and District Local History Society.

Transactions of the Croydon Natural History and Scientific Society.

Sussex Archaeological Collections (1848–).

Sussex Notes and Queries (1926–).

Brighton and Hove Archaeological Society, Annual Reports.

Transactions of the Eastbourne Natural History and Archaeological Society.

Worthing Archaeological Society, Annual Reports.

Transactions of the Battle and District Historical Society.

Archaeologia Cantiana (i.e. Kent) (1858–).

Proceedings of the Woolwich and District Antiquarian Society.

Transactions of the Greenwich and Lewisham Antiquarian Society.

Deal and District Local History and Research Society, Annual Reports.

PART TWO

Gazetteer

IT IS NOT CLAIMED that this Gazetteer is complete but that the omissions are of minor sites and finds. The finding of a single implement has not been noticed except where, as in the Saxon period, it may be indicative of a burial, or where it may have particular significance as an import like that of a stone axe or a winged axe. Finds of pottery have as far as possible been included since they probably indicate local habitation. Many omissions were made deliberately because there was considerable doubt concerning the nature or period of the objects. Roman brick in a church is noticed where there is no record of Roman structures in the parish. Moated sites are included only for areas where they are relatively uncommon.

The arrangement of the entries under each parish is chronological with undated earthworks (e.g. most barrows) and significant place-names last. Where a name is attached to a site of known archaeological significance, the name and site are placed together. A date after a place-name indicates the period of its earliest known record and not of its earliest use.

National Grid references are given as accurately as possible but the published location is seldom precise enough to allow of anything but an approximate reference. Where no site references can be given, that of the village is included.

References to sources could not be given without extending this Gazetteer to an inordinate length and without resort to a very large number of abbreviations. Material published after the early months of 1955 could not be included.

ABBREVIATIONS

c.	circa: approximate location	Mes	Mesolithic
C.	century	N	Neolithic
EBA	Early Bronze Age	P	Palaeolithic
IA	Iron Age	PN	Place-name
LBA	Late Bronze Age.	R	Roman/Romano-British
MBA	Middle Bronze Age	S	Saxon
Med	Medieval		

BEDFORDSHIRE
Southern part only.

Arlesey. Belgic cemetery; pedestal urns at 189332; R habitation site, c. 185345.

Astwick (213386). R occupation site and burials; S inhumation cemetery.

Barton (080310). N, late burials.

Caddington. P, Acheulian working floor; R habitation site c. 055200; round barrows c. 035216, one used as windmill tump; hut circles c. 035216; strip lynchets 040206 etc.; PN Castlecroft 17C.

Chalgrave. Migration of village from medieval site? c. 008274.

231

Chalton (030265). S inhumations.

Clifton (165390). EBA beaker, A-C type, with burial accompanying skeletons of N type; Med hundred-moot, site?

Dunstable. P; N long barrow (destroyed); N (secondary) burial under round barrow within a ring-ditch, Abingdon sherds in the mound 006210; MBA cremation beneath cinerary urn as secondary interment in same barrow as the previous; R town of *Durocobrivae*, coin-hoard of mid-5C.; S c. 100 burials in barrow as above (N and MBA) at 006210; round barrows, bell, bowl and ?pond at 006210; pillow mound: Pascombe Pit; PN Goldenlow, treasure found temp. Henry III—barrow?; Museum in Church Street.

Egginton. IA pottery 3–2C. B.C., showing IA 'B' influence; IA burial; R occupation at Manor Farm; ancient road, 'Ede Way', c. 966254 etc.

Henlow (180380). R burials and finds including Samian pottery of 1C. A.D.; S inhumation?, pot; PN Henlow (barrow?); PN Bradestrete (R road?).

Higham Gobion. Med fishponds and shrunken medieval village c. 104327; triangular earthwork with central mound, 106333.

Houghton Regis. N causeway camp (destroyed), Windmill Hill and Abingdon pottery, 996225, beneath IA plateau fort, 'The Maiden Bower'; IA farmstead and R earthworks, 003236 with coin of 1C. A.D.; R coin minted 440 A.D.; R habitation c. 005243?

Hyde (Luton). Med earthworks, 'Someries Castle', 119202.

Kensworth. R habitation sites; Med village site? c. 030190.

Luton. P, Upper Acheulian working floor, 100225; N implements; R pottery and coins, widespread; R pottery kiln, 061246; S cremation and inhumation cemetery,

with brooches, weapons, pottery etc., 078240; S inhumations, 058256; Med hundred-moot c. 075244; Med fishponds c. 075244; earthwork, 'Waulud's Bank', 061246 (N, IA and Med occupation).

Meppershall. Med castle earthwork, 'The Hills', 122359.

Shefford. EBA beaker of A-C type and wrist guard; Belgic interments of early 1C. A.D., c. 148405 (Southill parish); R building c. 138380; R settlement, many finds, coins and pottery early 1C. A.D. to early 4C.; S inhumations.

Shillington. Belgic pottery; R occupation c. 125300 and an interment c. 120300; earthwork (moated site?) 119350.

Stanbridge. Moot of half-hundred c. 970230?

Stondon, Upper and **Lower**—Shrunken Med village 151355; PN *stratebrade* 14C., R road?

Stotfold (220365). Belgic cemetery of 1C. B.C.; R occupation; PN Stotfold 11C. suggests an original earthwork enclosure. For Wilbury see Letchworth, Herts.

Streatley with **Sharpenhoe.** Secondary N? henge monument of Class I, mortuary enclosure, avenue of pits, crouched burials, EBA beaker pottery, MBA cinerary urn sherds, c. 094286; round barrows, 903270; round barrow (destroyed?) c. 091260; linear earthwork, Dray's Ditches, barring Icknield Way, 086266; PN Streatley 11C., R road? PN Warden Hill, 091260, 'watchhill'.

Studham. Original village site? c. 015160; PN Bury, 020151, manorial site?

Toddington. LBA bucket urn; R occupation; R pottery kiln c. 030280; S inhumations; Med castle earthwork, 011289; PN Wadlow, c. 021305, barrow?

Totternhoe. N or EBA site; R house, 4C., c. 990200; S sherd from R house; Med mound and bailey castle, Norman, 978222;

PN Totternhoe 11C. 'Look-out house on ridge'.

BERKSHIRE

Abingdon. P, Mid-Acheulian; N settlement 510980, Windmill Hill and 'Abingdon' pottery, Rinyo-Clacton pottery, Langdale axe; EBA beaker burials; EBA handled beaker; EBA food vessel in barrow with cremations and inhumations c. 490983; MBA collared urn; IA 'C' finds; R building c. 497970; R settlement in town; S cemetery, 490963 cremation and inhumation, much grave furniture including pottery with R influence; Med castle mound and moat, 11C., near FitzHarry's house; Med abbey fishponds c. 510980; air sites: BA ring ditches, c. 490963 and c. 495965; PN Burton, 504974.

Aldermaston. R cremation burial; agger of R road 619632 etc.; post-R, Grim's Bank 612640; migration of village from c. 597650? Emparkment?

Aldworth. Ridgeway, 554800 etc.; linear earthwork, Grim's Ditch, 560785 etc.; castle earthwork? 553784.

Appleford. IA 'AB' and Belgic pottery; R inhumations and pottery; circular and rectangular earthwork enclosures, 531937.

Appleton with **Eaton** (445020). Mes implements; IA 'A2' finds; IA 'C' pottery; R finds.

Arborfield. Migration of village? from c. 750680; PN Arborfield derived from *eorthbyrig*.

Ardington. LBA ranch boundary ditch, 425846 etc.; barrows, 433848; Ridgeway, 430847 etc.

Ashampstead. Linear earthwork, 580774 etc.

Ashbury. N long barrow of Severn Culture, 'Wayland's Smithy', 281854; MBA cremation? with ogival dagger of Wessex culture; IA 'A' earthwork enclosure with IA 'A' and 'C' pottery, 'Alfred's Castle', 278823; R building c. 283804; R farmstead, c. 280850; S pottery; S late weapons; Med deserted village, 255879; earthen circles; barrows, 273817 etc. and 276810 etc.; unfinished barrow, c. 258843; Celtic fields, 290830 etc.; strip lynchets, 275811 etc.; earthwork enclosure, R pottery and coins, 285818 etc.; enclosure, Med?, 285808 etc.; PN Stodfald, 10C.

Aston Tirrold. IA pottery; R burials, pottery, coins etc. of 2C. and 3C.; S burials, 545862; Celtic fields, 552825 etc.

Aston Upthorpe. LBA ranch boundary ditch, Grim's Ditch, 540833 etc.; earthwork, rectangular enclosure, Lowbury, 540823, with occupation in IA 'A2' and 'C', in R and post-R; S burial in barrow, with hanging bowl; barrows, 540824 and 542838 (bell-disc form).

Barkham (783664). P, Acheulian.

Basildon. P, Chellean; R pottery, 1C. A.D., c. 600760; R buildings, 609790: linear earthwork, 582773 etc.; Med deserted village? c. 611791; PN Kiln Farm, 591762.

Beedon. MBA cremation, incense cup and riveted dagger, pyre, in ring of posts under bell barrow at Borough (Burrow) Hill, 468787; R building, c. 474790; ancient trackway, 'Old Street', 475770 etc.

Bessels Leigh. S fish-pond, c. 448016; site of village? c. 457010.

Blewbury. N long barrow, 520835; N Windmill Hill and secondary N pottery; EBA beaker sherds with Rinyo-Clacton ware, Churn; MBA riveted dagger from barrow; MBA overhanging rim urn, sherds; LBA globular urn; IA/R barrows, two; LB/IA ranch boundary, Grim's Ditch, 530835; IA 'A2' hill-fort, 546862, A2 pottery, haematite ware, and R. pottery; S burials, 546862; round barrows,

522845, 515838, 523827, 507831, 520833; earthwork, Cucknell Pit, with R pottery, 509837; Ridgeway, 510829 etc.; strip lynchets, 547860.

Bourton (230870). PN 9C. derived from *burhtun*.

Boxford. IA 'A' farmstead, c. 442713; IA 'A' pottery, Basford Hill; IA hill-fort, 'Borough Hill', 440726 (much damaged), pottery including haematite ware and AB ware; R building, c. 440710; R coin hoard; several R occupation sites in the parish; R road, 420704 etc.; round barrow, 445752; PN Rowbury, 438751

Bracknell. PN Borough Green, 872683 (reference to 'Caesar's Camp', Easthampstead?).

Bradfield. N implements? R building? c. 605716.

Bray (900795). LBA founder's hoard; R coins to 400+ A.D.; R building (?) west of Down Lodge.

Brightwell and **Sotwell.** R occupation at both places; R road, agger, 582918; Med hamlet of Clopcote(?), site c. 605915; barrow, 576919.

Brimpton. R road, 560657 etc.; site of R(?) bridge c. 550660 (PN *weala brucge*, 10C.); R brick in church; barrows (including bell?), 570629 and 574626.

Bucklebury. R house, 528717; barrows? 557688; earthworks at Rains*bury* Corner; PN Bucklebury, 11C., derived from -*burh*.

Burghfield (670685). N implements; PN Burghfield 10C. from *beorg*-.

Buscot. PN Bury Hill, 233965.

Caversham (710750). P, Abbevillean, Clactonian and Lower Acheulian; N hut-site (?) and pottery; R finds and cremation of 1C.

Chaddleworth. R house, c. 414763; barrows 410810, and c. 418765?

Challow. R house, c. 373879; PN Challow, 10C., from -*hlāw*.

Charlton. MBA barrow, cremation and riveted dagger; LBA ranch boundary ditch, 416837 etc.

Charney Bassett. IA plateau fort, A2, AB and haematite-coated pottery, 374963.

Chieveley. EBA beaker, c. 490720; IA hill-fort, univallate, 466725; PN Old Kiln Farm, 486724; PN Kiln Farm, 501737.

Childrey. Barrows, 344852 and 351852; lynchets, boundary ditch and farmstead (shadow-site), c. 355840.

Chilton. IA 'A2' pottery, Hagbourne Hill; R cemetery, c. 494866; barrow, 496864.

Cholsey. P, middle Acheulian; EBA beaker, 'B1'; ?BA crouched burial; IA? hill-fort, Silsbury, ploughed out, 587853; IA hill-fort, vestiges?, 573879; linear earthwork, Devils Ditch, 564826.

Cold Ash (510700). N Cornish greenstone axe; ?BA hut.

Coleshill. S inhumations; strip lynchets, 236943 etc.; PN Strattenborough, 238921.

Combe. N long barrow, 365622; IA contour fort, Walbury, 374617; Celtic fields, 376600 etc.; ancient tracks, 369621 etc.

Compton. IA hill-fort, much ploughed, Perborough Castle, 520780; R habitation sites, The Slad and to north of Perborough; R farmstead; R cremating-place within quadrangular earthwork, late 1C. and 2C., 530818 etc.; late R pottery kiln, c. 539789; Med shrunken village, 525796; barrows, 512815 etc.; Celtic fields, 520787 etc.

Compton Beauchamp. IA 'A' and 'AB' pottery, c. 290835; IA? promontory fort, c. 287868; R farmstead; Celtic fields, 290830 etc. and 285810 etc.; PN Hardwell, 9C., 'hoard-spring', 285877 (now a Med moated site).

Cookham. P, Chellean and Acheulian; ?BA cremations in barrows, 887869; LBA urn, c. 877825; S primary inhumation in barrow and S inhumation cemetery, c.

887869; barrow, 907843; rectangular earthwork, Spencer's Farm.

Crookham. Post-R linear earthworks, four, 526645 etc.; Med earthwork, 544653.

Crowthorne. R road, agger, 840643 etc.

Cumnor. Mes implements, c. 490033; PN Iarn Mound, 487023; PN Youlbury, 481031.

Didcot (520905). R pottery, 2C. to 3C. and inhumations; barrow on west side of parish.

Donnington and **Shaw.** MBA overhanging-rim urn, 475683; R cremations, 475683; R pottery, etc., several sites; R road? agger? c. 460685; Med shrunken settlement? c. 475685; rectangular earthwork, 476684; PN Brickkiln, 480695, 15C. brickmaking here.

Draycott. Med shrunken or deserted village? 400990.

Drayton. N (secondary) enclosure and BA ring-ditches, 485935 etc. (air site); EBA food vessel; R inhumation, c. 470940; barrow (destroyed), 477952.

Earley (746722). P, Acheulian; R marble urn.

East Garston. LBA ranch boundary ditch, 365790 etc., and ?367800; R cremations; R road, 358737 etc.; ancient pond, 367803; PN Coldborough, 360776.

Easthampstead. IA? univallate plateau fort, 'Caesar's Camp', with haematite-coated ware, Belgic coin, R pottery and building débris, 864657; R site, 'The Town', 866649; R building, 2C.–4C. pottery, 867646; R road, agger, 870654 etc.; barrow, Bill Hill.

East Hendred. LBA ranch boundary ditch, 460854 etc.; LBA pottery; R finds; S barrow burial? Cuckhamsley Knob, 457850; Shire-moot, 10C., 457850; barrow, Hendred Down.

East Ilsley. LBA ranch boundary ditch, 500834 etc.; S primary and secondary barrow inhumations, 508810; Ridgeway,

500829 etc.; barrows, 492824 etc., and 507831; earthwork, 496825.

East Shefford. S inhumation cemetery, c. 388750; linear earthwork, 'Hug Ditch', 381740.

East Woodhay. Lynchets, c. 400603.

Eaton Hastings. Med shrunken village? 260982.

Enborne. P; N? pottery, Enborne Gate; IA finds; R pottery; S pottery, Enborne Gate; 17C. barrows, 455648 etc.; PN Crockham, 430650.

Englefield (625720). P implements.

Faringdon. IA pottery; Med 12C. castle mound, 298957; ancient quern quarries, 294933.

Farnborough (430820). PN Farnborough from -*beorg*; PN Stodfald, earthwork?

Fawley. R inhumations; barrows, 399804.

Fernham. IA? hill-fort, 289927; PN Barrowbush Hill, 300914.

Finchampstead. R habitation site, c. 770646; R road, agger, 780639 etc.; earthwork round the church, 792638.

Frilford. N, secondary, Rinyo-Clacton and ?rusticated pottery; MBA collared urn; LBA cinerary urns; IA round houses, pottery of A2, AB and haematite-coated varieties; IA circular religious site followed by R circular shrine and Romano-Celtic temple of square form; R cemetery continuing in use? until S times, 438963; R house c. 425970; S cremation and inhumation cemetery, pottery with R influence.

Frilsham (538733). R road?

Fyfield (423987). R house; R coin-hoard buried, c. A.D. 307.

Garford. R house, 438960; barrows, 428954.

Ginge. LBA ranch boundary ditch, 445854 etc.

Goosey. Med shrunken settlement, 357918.

Grazeley. Original site of Med village? 690675.

Great Coxwell. IA? contour hill-fort, 262948.

Great Shefford. MBA barrow, inhumation, urn, incense-cup etc., 374743; linear earthwork, 'Hug Ditch', 381740.

Greenham. Mes implements; R occupation, 508658 and elsewhere; post-R linear earthwork, 'Bury Bank' (destroyed).

Hagbourne, East and **West.** IA hoard of metal goods; LBA–IA burials; Icknield Way, 500869 etc.

Hampstead Norris. N? implements; MBA interment in barrow, 533766; LBA pottery; IA? hill-fort, Oareborough (destroyed), 494752; IA? hill-fort, univallate, 527761; R occupation sites, 494752, 509776; R house and burial vault c. 524750; rectangular earthwork? c. 527763; barrow, 529760.

Hamstead Marshall. R pottery; Med fishponds, 428667; Med park bank, 423668; Med castle mounds, three, 421668; ancient traffic ruts, 421656.

Hatford (338948). Mes implements; IA pottery, 'A2' with haematite and 'AB'; R pottery.

Hermitage. IA? multivallate hill-fort, 'Grimsbury', 512723; R house, c. 520725.

Hinton Waldrist. R linear earthwork; Med, 12C., moated site, 372987.

Hungerford. P implements; S inhumations; barrow, Eddington; PN Brickkiln, 320695.

Hurley. R building, c. 825795.

Inkpen. EBA 'C' beaker; MBA overhanging-rim cinerary urns in barrow, 349621; LBA globular urn, c. 374618; IA? multivallate hill-fort, 'Walbury', 374618; R pottery, c. 349621; S pottery, c. 349621; post-R? 'Wansdyke', linear earthwork, 352635; barrows, 349621; PN stan ceastla, 10C, c. 353632.

Kennington. P implements; IA field system; R occupation site, Bagley Wood; R pottery kiln, c. 510020.

Kingston Bagpuize. BA cremations; R occupation sites; S linear earthwork, 411978 etc.

Kingston Lisle. N Windmill Hill pottery, 314863; IA 'A2' hill-fort, ploughed out, *Hremnesbyrig*, 314863; IA 'C' pottery and rectangular enclosure, c. 314863; R pottery, 314863; R cremations, silver coin-hoard of 4C. A.D. and enclosure, 314863; R? barrow, 329882; barrows destroyed c. 314863; Icknield Way, 320864 etc.; PN Fawler, site of R house with pavement? c. 320882.

Kintbury. N working-floor, c. 391671; R building, 2C. and 3C., c. 391671; PN Forbury, 389652.

Lambourn. N implements; EBA 'A' beaker; MBA barrows (bell, bowl and disc), 328828; LBA urnfield; LBA ranch boundary ditches, 340820 etc., 340810 etc. and 295783 etc.; IA? hill-fort, Membury, 304755; R finds, c. 347772; R building and cemetery, c. 352818; S burial; S pottery from lynchets; earthwork, damaged, Lambourn Park; round barrow with sarsen peristalth, 290807; 'Hangman's Stone'? 320812; barrows 332833 and elsewhere in parish; Celtic fields, 304793 etc. and 293807 etc.; ancient pond and track, 345797 etc.; strip lynchets, 308803 and 332794; R road, 430769 etc.; PN Coldborough, 345776; PN Eastbury, 347772; PN Foxbury, 333807.

Leckhampstead. Alignment of large stones, destroyed, 450765.

Letcombe Bassett. R occupation; disc barrow, 367821; barrow, 360826; Celtic fields and ancient track, 367817 etc.; PN Cockleberry, 362831.

Letcombe Regis. 1A? hill-fort, univallate plateau fort, Segsbury, 384845; R habitation; PN Warborough, 'watch-hill', 384853.

Little Coxwell. IA? hill-fort, univallate, 288928.

Little Wittenham. IA 'A2' contour fort, 569924; R occupation? and inhumations, 564933; R building, c. 570923; Med cultivation, 569924.

Lockinge. LBA ranch boundary ditch, 420844 etc.; S inhumation cemetery, 423872; S burial, 431868; barrows, 421843 418862, 433849 and 423844; strip lynchets, 421872 etc.

Long Wittenham. P implement; EBA beaker pottery; MBA collared urn; LBA urnfield cemetery, bucket urns and habitation site, 537923; IA 'A1' and 'A2' settlement site, rectangular hut; R settlement, Padboro, c. 560956; R occupation, 539923 and elsewhere; S inhumation and cremation cemetery, 558953; barrow circles (air site); Celtic fields, enclosure and palisade, R? (air site). c. 555950.

Longworth. Mes implements; IA 'A2' finds; Med village site? c. 383995; PN Sudbury, 394993; PN Harrowdown, pagan S sanctuary? 389005.

Maidenhead. P, Chellean, Acheulian, Levalloisian, 878807 and 880827; MBA cinerary urns; R house, c. 880810; R building, c. 860797; R tile kiln, c. 860797; R pottery, c. 880860 and 860823; earthwork, circular, R?, 'Robin Hood's Arbour', 852811; earthwork, rectangular, 885828; two earthworks, rectangular, c. 850801; PN Castle Hill; PN Ditton, from –*dic*? 865824.

Marcham (455965). IA pottery, 'A','AB', and haematite-coated ware; R pottery; S occupation, Cothill.

Milton. IA 'A' occupation; R occupation and cremations; S inhumations, c. 490930; S occupation.

Moulsford. Barrow, ?569823; linear earthwork, 'Devil's Ditch', 567825; PN Sowberry, 592833.

Newbury. P, Chellean, Acheulian; LBA bucket urn; IA site, Enborne Gate; R habitation sites in town; R cremations; 17C. burial mounds; Museum, Wharf St.

New Windsor. P, Acheulian; M and LBA hoards; R finds; earthwork, 'Bear's Rails', 974738; PN Burfield, 984738.

North Hinksey. P, Chellean; IA and R settlement, c. 500040; PN Tilbury, 480068.

Old Windsor. R inhumations, Tile Place Farm; S and Med occupation, Kingsbury; 15C. brickmaking, Tile Place Farm.

Padworth. EBA beaker; IA pottery; R road, 634656 etc.; post-R linear earthwork, Grim's Bank, 626660 etc.

Pangbourne. N solitary inhumation, Abingdon pottery; Belgic bead-rim urns; R cremation and inhumation cemetery, kiln, occupation débris, c. 625770; PN Flower's Farm, villa-site reported nearby, 634758.

Purley. P, Chellean, Acheulian; N implements; S inhumation; Med deserted village? 668760.

Radley. N? settlement, 510980; EBA 'B1' beaker, gold earrings; EBA ring-ditch, cremation with food vessel and flint knife; MBA disc barrow with Wessex Culture interment; MBA collared urn; MBA cremation, bronze awl and gold-foil shells; E?BA bell barrow, petit tranchet arrowhead, bronze dagger with inhumation; LBA cremation in urn, disc barrow with double ring-ditch. The preceding BA burials at Barrow Hills, 513984; IA settlement, 'A' pottery, haematite ware and Belgic pottery, c. 520990; late R cemetery; S cremation burial; S hut-site; barrow, 534988; earthwork, 537983; R? rectangular and circular enclosures, air site, 513986; R occupation, 513984 etc.

Reading. P, Chellean, Acheulian, Mousterian; N implements; L?BA cemetery, urns; IA 'A1' pottery, c. 730715; IA 'A', 'AB', 'C' settlement, c. 690718; R finds, much scattered evidence of occupation; late R cemetery, inhumation; R coin-

hoards, two, late 4C; S cremation and inhumation cemetery; late S inhumation
cemetery; earthwork, Danish? of A.D. 871?
Forbury, 725737; linear earthwork,
Coombe Bank, 699748; PN Vasterne
Rd., reference to Danish fort ? of A.D.
871?; Museum, Blagrave St.

Remenham. P, Chellean; N? passage
grave, Park Place; S inhumations, c.
785845.

Ruscombe. P, Chellean, Acheulian, Mousterian; Mes? implements; LBA urn; R
pottery; PN Castle End, 805772; PN
Northbury, 798767.

Shellingford. N Langdale axe; linear earthwork? field-name 'Red Dyke', c. 297929.

Shinfield. P, Chellean; PN Stanbury,
712671; PN Crockers, 737699.

Shottesbrooke (840770.) Med village destroyed on emparkment?

Shrivenham (240890). R silver coin-hoard,
late 4C. A.D.

Sonning. P, Chellean, Acheulian, Mousterian; Med park bank? c. 756750.

Sotwell, (585910). EBA beaker 'B' burial.

South Moreton. P, mid-Acheulian; Med
deserted village, Fulscot, 545888.

Sparsholt. N long barrow, chambered,
with protruding sarsens, 326833; MBA
barrow, cinerary urn and lignite bead,
327838; R pottery, 338852.

Speen. P, Mousterian, Aurignacian; MBA
barrow with concentric ring ditches,
Speen Moor; R posting station and settlement of '*Spinis*', c. 452670; R occupation
sites, 455678 and on Speen Hill; barrow?
Bagmore.

Stanford-in-the-Vale. R occupation, continuing into 5C. A.D., c. 320950; barrows,
350927 etc.; PN Stanford, R road?

Steventon. R pottery, c. 455908.

Stratfield Mortimer. Barrows, including
bell?, 642652 etc.; linear earthwork,
Grim's Ditch, 645647 etc.

Streatley. LBA cinerary urn; IA pottery,
lynchets and field-system, 553807 etc.; R
finds, 553807 etc.; R? building, R pottery
etc., 591820; earthwork? 591820; linear
earthworks, Grim's Ditch, 570789 etc.,
590796 etc., 567790 etc.

Sulham, (645743). P, Acheulian; LBA cremation cemetery, bucket urns.

Sulhamstead Abbots. R occupation, Oak-
field Park; Med village originally at
640685? .

Sulhampstead Bannister (685665). Site
of Med village? Ditches near Kennet.

Sunningdale. R road, agger, 952673 etc.
See Chobham, Surrey, for LBA urnfield.

Sunninghill (935680). BA barrows, destroyed.

Sunningwell. IA, 'A2' and 'C' pottery,
etc.; R occupation, Foxcombe Hill and
Boars Hill; R pottery kilns, c. 500013.

Sutton Courtenay. N Langdale and dolerite axes; N Rinyo-Clacton ware; N cursus
and ring ditches, 487938 etc.; EBA 'B'
beaker burials; MBA habitation site, ring
ditches, 489940; LBA globular urns; IA
'C' pottery; R occupation, 489940 and
elsewhere; S village, destroyed, 489940;
S inhumations, 510945; barrow at Cross
Trees.

Thatcham. Mes occupation of Maglemosean type; IA 'A' pot and 'C' ware of
1C. A.D., c. 525681; R village site, 457675
etc.; R hoard of late 4C.; R road, 530667;
PN Devil's Den.

Theale. EBA 'B' beaker burials; IA 'A',
'AB' and 'C' settlement; R house,
637710; S cremations.

Tilehurst. P, Chellean, Acheulian, Aurignacian; R habitation, 651722 and elsewhere; linear earthwork, c. 677748; PN
Tilehurst, 12C.

Tubney. R cremations; barrow, 448006.

Twyford (790760). P, Chellean.

Uffington. MBA enclosure (air site), 314864;

IA 'A2' contour fort, unfinished, 'A2', 'AB', 'C' and haematite-coated wares, 314864; IA 'A2' contour fort, 299863; hill figure, White Horse, of IA 'C', 302867; R enclosure (air site), 314864; R burials and silver coin-hoard of late 4C., 314864; late R and S? inhumations and cremations in pillow-mound, c. 300865; S inhumations in irregular barrow, c. 300865; disc barrow, 303847; barrow, Idlebush, 303849; Celtic fields, faint traces, 301868 etc.; strip lynchets, 312868.

Ufton Nervet. IA? promontory fort, 628661; late or post-R? Grim's Ditch, 632662 etc.

Wallingford. P implements; LBA barrel urn and two hoards; IA 'A2' habitation sites; R settlement, 1C., A.D. to late 4C.; S cremation and inhumation cemetery; late S town ramparts, 606893 etc.; Norman castle mound and earthworks, 610898 etc.; Museum.

Waltham St. Lawrence. R temple and buildings, Castle Field, 818777; R pottery, 830770; R occupation at Berry Grove.

Wantage. MBA hoard; R settlement, c. 400865; earthwork (destroyed?), Limborough.

Wargrave. R road? from Church Green to the Loddon; PN Kiln Green, 808785.

Wasing. P implements; R road, agger, 580648 etc.; Med shrunken settlement? c. 575643; five barrows, 577626 etc.

Watchfield. R building, c. 256905.

Welford. R burials, c. 423750; R coin-hoard, late 4C.; R road, 410709 etc.

West Hendred. LBA ranch boundary ditch, 450856; barrow, 441891; PN Goldbury, 448880.

West Ilsley. N (secondary) pottery; LBA ranch boundary ditches, 480845 etc., 478842 etc.; LBA pottery; barrows, 486831 etc.; oval earthwork, c. 487830; ancient track, 448830 etc.; PN Bury Down, 480840; PN Kiln Barn, 452816.

West Woodhay. N working-floor, c. 410639; Norman castle mound.

White Waltham. R house, 844792; R occupation, c. 840800 and at other sites; PN Paley St., R road? 870763.

Wickham. R occupation, 395716; R road, agger 378705 and terraceway 366702; S pottery.

Winkfield. R occupation site, embanked, 898650; PN Burleigh, 908697.

Winterbourne. Migration of village from 450720?; linear earthwork, Black Ditch, 460712.

Wokefield. Shrunken medieval settlement? c. 670660.

Wokingham. P, Acheulian; R cremations; IA pottery; barrow? c. 792682.

Woodley and **Sandford.** P, Chellean.

Woolstone. R building, c. 290877; S inhumation, 298883; disc barrow, 303848; barrow, Idlebush, 303849.

Wootton. Mes implements; IA 'C' pottery, 492013; R finds, Boar's Hill and near Fox Inn.

Wytham. EBA beaker; MBA finds, Wessex Culture; LBA pottery; IA, 'A1', 'A2', 'AB' and 'C' pottery, occupation; R pottery; Med deserted village, Seacourt, 486075; original site of Wytham? c. 475093.

Yattendon. MBA barrow, cremation, Rowcroft; LBA hoard, 557747; LBA urns; R house, c. 535744, field-name 'Green Ditch'; barrow, 532742.

BUCKINGHAMSHIRE
Southern half.

Amersham. R finds, c. 950977.

Ashendon. S finds; Med moot of Ashendon Hundred, c. 703140?

Ashley Green. IA? plateau fort, 997040; Med moated site, 986043.

Aston Clinton. IA 'C' pottery; R occupation, c. 864128; Med. moated site, 864128; linear earthwork, Grim's Ditch, 008079.

Aston Sandford. Med shrunken settlement? 756079.

Aylesbury. R coin-hoard; R road, agger, c. 795150; PN Aylesbury, from *burh*; PN Kingsbury, from *burh* (Med manorial site?); Museum, Church St.

Beaconsfield. P implements, c. 925908 and c. 933923; barrow? c. 954909.

Bierton with **Broughton.** Med deserted village? 847136 (Broughton); Med deserted village, 840130 (Caldecote); PN Bierton, from *burh*, 840157; PN Burcott, from *burh*, 843153.

Bledlow. EBA beaker burial under 'The Cop' barrow, with greenstone axe and tanged dagger 773013; IA 'A1' occupation sites, c. 788003? and 766003; R building, c. 769016; R inhumations and pottery finds, several sites; S cremations and inhumations, 773013; S inhumations, c. 777015; Med? cross cut in chalk, 770010; barrows, 788003 and 767005; Icknield Way, 780012; lynchets? c. 793990.

Boarstall. Med shrunken village? near manorial site 623143; PN Boarstall, from *burh*, 11C.

Bourne End. R inhumations, 893878.

Bradenham. Linear earthwork, Grim's Ditch, 830986 etc.

Brill. R building, c. 650145; Med pottery kilns, 13C.–14C. and manufacture of tiles and bricks from 15C.; earthwork, square, Muswell ditch? 13C.; 17C. earthwork of Civil War, c. 140657.

Burnham. P, Abbevillian, Clactonian, Acheulian, Levalloisian, 926819 and at E. Burnham; MBA hoard; IA 'A' pottery, 926819; IA 'C' occupation, 926836; R pottery, 4C.; Med? earthwork, 946856; bell? barrow, c. 930860; IA? plateau fort, 947846; PN Kiln Farm, 945844.

Chalfont St. Giles (990935). P?; R coin hoard, 2C.

Chalfont St. Peter. P implements, c. 007900; N? implements, c. 015925, c. 975900, and c. 989895; earthwork, rectangular, Blacket Grove Wood.

Chartridge. Earthwork, 916050; Med manorial site, 925028.

Cheddington. Strip lynchets, 918165 etc., and 914170 etc.

Chenies. R building, 998986; R occupation, 026989.

Chesham. Mes implements, 983016; Med? earthwork, 926028; lynchets; PN Tylers Hill, c. 983015; PN Brickkiln, 951004; PN Chesham, from *ceaster* or *ceastel*, 10C.

Cholesbury. EIA 'A' and 'C' occupation at plateau fort, Cholesbury, 930073; IA 'C'? pottery, c. 919067; earthwork, 950059; linear earthwork, Grim's Ditch, 910080 etc.

Denham (040870). P, Acheulian, Normer Hill.

Dinton. S inhumation cemetery; Med shrunken village, Aston Mullins, 768084; Med shrunken settlement, Waldridge, 783073.

Dorney (930790). P implement.

Drayton Beauchamp. Linear earthwork, Grim's Ditch, 917086 etc.; lynchets; migration of village? from c. 903120?

Edlesborough. Strip lynchets, 970184 etc., and 934190; original village site? 970191? PN Edlesborough from *beorg*, the natural? mound on which the church stands.

Ellesborough. N stone adze of Scandinavian type; IA 'A' occupation, c. 846065; IA pottery, c. 837061; R house, c. 838085; R building, c. 830050; R pottery, c. 837061 and the Rectory Garden; S inhumations, c. 846065; Med castle mound and two baileys, c. 837061; Med oval moated site, 836081; barrow? used as beacon, 837061; linear earthworks, 836063 and c. 850065; PN means 'ass-hill'.

Eton. R pottery, Barnes Pool Bridge.

Eythorpe. Med deserted village, emparkment? 770140.

Farnham Royal (960830). P implements.

Fawley. Med shrunken settlement? 753868; PN Crockmore, 750859.

Fingest. R 3C cremations; PN *Tingeherst*, 12C. (i.e. Fingest, meaning 'wooded hill of the moot') and cp. Skirmett, 775900, nearby (meaning 'shire-moot'); Med deserted village of Ackhampstead, 805908.

Fleet Marston. R settlement, c. 779155; Med deserted village, 779159.

Fulmer. Belgic pottery, c. 995868; R pottery kiln, 2C., c. 995868.

Gerrards Cross. P implements; N? implements, c. 970892 etc., and 015880?; IA 'A' and 'C' occupation of plateau camp, 995880 (Bulstrode).

Great Hampden. Med deserted village? emparkment? c. 848024; barrows, 856020 and 848021; linear earthwork, Grim's Ditch, 838029.

Great Missenden. R finds; Med (and earlier?) earthworks, 916021; earthwork, 'The Castle', 908004; earthwork enclosures (destroyed?), 900014; earthwork, destroyed, c. 888013; linear earthwork, Grim's Ditch, 890033 etc.

Haddenham. Barrow? c. 736100.

Halton. IA 'A'? pottery, contour hill-fort, 883080; R pottery, R.A.F. Station.

Hambledon. P implements; Mes implements; IA 'C' bead-rim pottery (of R period), 785855; R house, warehouses and corn-drying furnaces, occupation c. 50–400+ A.D.), coin-hoard, c. 320 A.D., etc., 785855, 783854, 776894; PN Burrow from *burh* or *beorg*, 797857; Museum.

Hartwell (795125). R? clay-pits; S finds; barrow, Hartwell Park; PN Culley from *hlāw*.

Hedgerley. N? implements, 982873; R pottery kilns, 2C., 973888; PN Kiln Wood, 967870.

High Wycombe. N occupation, c. 873925, Ebbsfleet ware and beaker ware; EBA? inhumation; MBA cinerary urns and pigmy vessel, Barrow Croft, c. 884915; IA hill-fort, Desborough, 847933; IA? fort, Keep Hill, 874921; Belgic gold coin-hoard; R house, Great Penns Mead, c. 873925; R building, All Hallows Lane; S inhumation, c. 867933; S pot (burial?), Loudwater; Desborough (above) adapted by Normans; Norman castle mound, 867933; Med hundred-moot, 847933; lynchets; earthwork? circular, Malmer's Well; Museum, Queen Victoria St.

Hitcham. P implements; EBA (beaker), and LBA (bucket urn), occupation, Wyn Hill; R occupation, c. 920813; S burial? weapons, Windmill Field.

Horsenden. Med shrunken village? c. 794030.

Hughenden. R building, c. 883951; R coin-hoard; R pot, c. 860955; Med village site? c. 865955.

Hulcott. Med shrunken settlement? c. 853168.

Iver. P, Levalloisian and Mousterian, various sites; Mes implements, Iver Heath; N (secondary) occupation, Peterborough pottery; N greenstone axe; R brick in church, 040812.

Ivinghoe. IA? contour hill-fort, 959168; R occupation, c. 960175; barrows, 959168 and 959164; strip lynchets, 957173 etc.; ancient tracks, 958167 etc.

Kimble, Great and **Little.** R house, c. 827065; R pottery, 832050; R finds, 830064; IA? contour hill-fort, 832050; Norman castle mound, baileys and complex of Med earthworks, 830064; Med manorial site and fishponds, 823060; 17C.? earthwork, west of church; barrows,

Q

836061 and 824060; Icknield Way, 830063 etc.

Kingsey. S cremations and ? inhumations, Tythrop Park; Med deserted village, Tythrop, c. 740070.

Lacey Green. Linear earthwork, Grim's Ditch, 830015; PN Darvills, 835996, Med? park.

Langley Marish. P implements; Med fishponds, 007803.

Lee. Med homestead, 916050; linear earthwork, Grim's Ditch, 890033 etc.; Med village enclosure earthwork; PN Potter Row, 902027.

Little Missenden. P implements; Norman castle mound and bailey, 927997.

Long Crendon, (700090). N pot; R building and cemetery, Cop Hill.

Marlow (850865). P implements; N pottery, Windmill Hill ware; IA 'C' occupation; R finds.

Marsworth (920145). R. pottery.

Medmenham. N? implements, 817845; IA? hill-fort, univallate, contour, 807847; IA? hill-fort, univallate, 817845; Med castle site, c. 807847.

Monks Risborough. N barrow of kidney shape, wooden burial chamber, Windmill Hill pottery of East Anglian type, 822041; IA pottery, c. 822040; R pottery, c. 822040; barrows, 822041: linear earthwork, Grim's Ditch, 838029 etc.; Whiteleaf Cross, 821040; Icknield Way, 817040 etc.

Oakley. R occupation, c. 654108; Med shrunken settlement, Addingrove, 665113; Med hundred-moot, Ixhill, c. 654107.

Penn (915933). P implements, Knotty Green; Med 14C. pottery kilns, Tyler's Green.

Pitstone. R building, c. 935154; S? inhumation; Med village originally c. 943151?; Med moated site, 943152; barrow, Moneybury, 972136; earthwork? 952148; Moot-site of hundred, Yardley;

PN Ward's Hurst (*Totehill*, 16C.), 'look-out hill'.

Princes Risborough. R occupation, 2C.–4C., c. 804025; R pottery, coins, etc., in mound, 'Soldier's Hill', on Downs; Med manorial earthworks, 805035; barrows, 821041; strip lynchets (ploughed), c. 807022.

Quarrendon. Med village site, 800158 etc.; 17C.Civil War earthworks of 1642: trenches, vallum, gun emplacements; PN Quarrendon implies the presence of quern-quarries?; PN Weedon, 807157, pagan S sanctuary; PN Berryfield, 793162, manorial?

Radnage. R cremation, late 1C. A.D., c. 767982.

Saunderton. N (secondary) Rinyo-Clacton ware, 789004; N? implements, c. 804985; EBA 'B' beaker sherds from? bell barrows, 789004; IA 'A' pottery, 797018; IA 'A', 'C' and R pottery, occupation, hut-circles, 796099 etc.; R building, pottery etc., of 1C. to 3C., 797018; R house, 2C.–4C., burials, corn-drying furnace, 797019; Med castle mound and bailey, manorial and ?village site, 797018; barrows (air site, ploughed), 809989; barrows, c. 805986; barrow ring-ditches, c. 805986 and c. 805998; barrow c. 805998; ancient track and earthwork enclosure, 796099; linear earthwork (air site), c. 787004; Med parish boundary ditch, 793000 etc.

Seer Green (965920). P, Acheulian; late N implements, Jordans.

Slough. P implements, Baker's Farm; Med palace site, 952797; mound (barrow?) c. 970803.

Stoke Mandeville. R house, c. 840085; Med village site? 838094: lost site of Hallinges, early S settlement.

Stokenchurch. LBA cremation cemetery; Med settlement, 'Abbefeld', ?787967; barrows (destroyed?), Colliers Lane.

Stoke Poges. LBA cremation, Golf Course; barrow? c. 965825?

Stone. R occupation, kilns, 778121; S inhumations, Cursley Hill and at Stone; Med hundred-moot at Stone; church on ?artificial mound, 784123; barrow with inhumation, 779132; PN Chilborohill, from *-burh-*, 789107.

Taplow. P, Levalloisian; N implements, c. 906821 and elsewhere; greenstone axe; LBA urnfield?; R? pile-dwellings, 903861; R pottery, 924873; S barrow inhumation, 906821; Med deserted village? emparkment? c. 906863; earthwork, 906821, etc.; PN Berryhill and Bury Fields, 907816 (manorial?); PN Taplow refers to S burial above.

Turville. Mes occupation, c. 754891; ?rectangular earthwork, hut-circles, flint implements, c. 733926.

Upper Winchendon. Med deserted village, Beachendon, 759137; Med deserted village? emparkment? 747145; Med '*burh*' ditch mentioned in 11C. charter; Med hundred-moot, c. 758154?

Weedon. PN Weedon Hill, pagan S site? and later hundred-moot, c. 815165.

Wendover. IA 'A' pottery, c. 885062; IA? hill-fort? 860073 (or scarping to form Med castle mound?); Grim's Ditch, linear earthwork, 895067 etc.

Weston Turville. R occupation, c. 858103; R inhumation; Med mound and bailey castle, 859104.

West Wycombe. IA? contour hill-fort round church, 827950; R finds, c. 847933; Med deserted village, Averingdown, 825964; mound, 827946; earthwork enclosure, c. 835970; PN 'Fastendich', 'stronghold-ditch'; PN Tilbury, from *burh*; PN Loxboro, 806967, from *burh* or *beorg*.

Wooburn. PN Kiln Cottages, 909888.

Wraysbury. PN Wraysbury, 000740, from *burh*.

ESSEX

Abberton. P implements; IA or R Red Hills, c. 020163 etc.; Med village, migration from 997195?

Abbess Roding. Mound, c. 572120; site of village, Beauchamp Roding? c. 578097; PN Netherstreet, 13 C: R road?; PN Brickkiln Wood, 553104.

Alphamstone. LBA urnfield; R tile-kiln, c. 878354; R building beneath church, 878354.

Alresford. Beaker, B2, from barrow (destroyed), 063202; LBA bucket urn; R house, 062200; Migration of village from c. 065206?

Ardleigh. P implements; beaker, B2, 052284; IA pottery; PN Fox Street, R road? 030277; PN Crockleford, 'Potters' ford', 13C., 030262.

Arkesden. P implements; LBA founder's hoard, c. 470345; R coin-hoard and other finds; Med mill-mound? c. 467346.

Ashdon. P and N? implements; R house, c. 578435; R building, c. 581445; R tile-kiln, c. 584389; R barrows, four, 'Bartlow Hills', 586448; R? rectangular earthwork, 584450; PN Street Farm, 14C., R road?

Asheldham. IA 'A' pottery; IA? plateau fort round church, 976014 (*Suneceastre?*); R brick in church.

Ashingdon. IA or R Red Hills, c. 842957; R brick in church; Danish earthwork of A.D. 1016? 866936.

Aveley. R brick in church, 567801.

Bardfield Saling. Med deserted village, Black Death? 686265; PN Stamford, 15C., R road?

Barking. P and N? implements; IA 'C' and R pottery, c. 460845; R occupation, c. 440840; field-name, Crickelwood, 13C. probably 'barrow hill wood'.

Barling (930895). IA 'C' pottery.

Beaumont-cum-Moze. IA or R Red

Hills, c. 200245; Med deserted village? Moze, c. 200260.

Belchamp St. Paul. Med fishponds, 797436; Med deserted village? 798435— migration of site?

Belchamp Walter. Med? moated cattle? enclosure, 830408.

Berden. EBA beaker burial; Med? fortified mound, 470289; earthwork, 466292.

Berechurch. IA 'C' pottery; IA 'C' linear earthwork, 997220 etc.; R earthwork, 997207.

Billericay. LBA founder's hoard; IA 'C' pottery; R settlement and kilns etc., c. 680955; R? earthwork enclosure c. 686955 etc.; barrows c. 686955; earthwork, 'Blunt's Walls' (destroyed), 658942.

Birch. Norman castle earthworks, c. 944198, Med deserted village, 951209; R brick in church.

Birchanger (510225). Field-names: Tot Lane, etc., 11C.; Black Lands, 16C.; Limekiln, 15C.; Stansted, 16C.

Birdbrook. IA finds; R cremations and in-humations, and earthwork, c. 707428?; R brick in church; R road?; S pagan sanctuary, 'Harrowdown'?

Bocking. LBA bucket or barrel urn; R brick in church, 757257; Med? moated mound, c. 763278.

Boreham. R cremation cemetery, c. 750120; R brick in church.

Bowers Gifford. R brick in church, 756873.

Boxted. R brick in church, 998332; Med? mill basins and dams, 008334 etc.

Bradfield (140300). PN Street Farm, 13C., R road?

Bradwell-next-Coggeshall. R occupation; R brick in church; Med shrunken village? c. 818220; PN Stratford, 13C., 807232, R ford?

Bradwell-next-the-Sea. R fort of the Saxon shore, coins c. A.D. 250–400,

031082; Romano-Saxon pottery from fort; R road, 026080 etc.; S burials.

Braintree. P implements; IA 'C' pottery; R buildings, 778242, 781242; R occupation, c. 781236; R? camp, destroyed, 766234; prehistoric lake dwellings, c. 760227.

Brightlingsea. R houses, 059188, c. 080170 (built over); PN Aldboro, near R house; PN Salcots, Med salt pans.

Bromley-by-Bow (380825). LBA founder's hoard.

Broomfield (705105). P implements; R tiles in church; S burial in barrow.

Broxted (580270). R finds; R? brick in church; PN Broxted, 11C., 'badger's head', place of pagan S sacrifice?

Bulmer. R? brick in church; PN Thunder-low, 11C., site of moot of a half-hundred, place of pagan S worship? and site of barrow? c. 833403.

Bulphan. Med shrunken settlement? Dunton, 653883; PN Castle's Farm, 15C.

Burnham. P implements; MBA merchant's hoard; IA 'C' and R pottery; IA or R 'Red Hills' with R pottery, c. 980955, 985962; R brick in church; PN Salt Coat Marsh.

Buttsbury. R burials and kiln; Med deserted village? c. 664986; PN Buttsbury not from *burh*.

Canewdon. N hoard of axes; IA South-eastern 'B' pottery; IA 'C' pottery; R building, 897945; IA or R 'Red Hills' with R pottery, 876956 etc.; earthwork surrounding the village, 900957.

Canvey Island. IA 'C'? 'Red Hills'; R pottery, c. 820833.

Castle Hedingham. Med castle earthwork and town enclosure, 787359; Med moot of Hinckford Hundred, Crouch Green, for-merly 'le Motestowe', 13C.; Med deserted settlement of Northwood? 790395.

Chadwell. R pottery kiln? c. 650780; R pottery, c. 651780; R brick in church.

Chelmsford. P and N? implements; MBA hoard; IA 'C' pottery; R town of *Caesaromagus* in the Moulsham district; R road, 708080 etc.; Museum, Moulsham St.

Chickney. Med deserted village, 574280.

Chignall. R brick in church; Med deserted village, c. 669108 (earthworks); Med shrunken village? Chignall Smealey, 670117; earthwork (damaged), 661102.

Chigwell. IA 'C' pottery; R house, c. 457964; R settlement, 457959; R road, c. 446948 etc.

Chingford (380940). IA 'C' pottery, Flanders Weir; Epping Forest Museum.

Chipping Ongar. R building, 553030 (beneath church); R burials; Med castle mound, baileys and town enclosure, 554032.

Chrishall. N? occupation and knapping site, c. 430363; LBA founder's hoard; EBA beaker? primary and IA or S secondary inhumations in barrow, c. 440430; Med fortified mound, 452386; migration of village? from c. 451385.

Clavering. LBA hoard; S? and Norman castle mound and water defences, 470320.

Colchester. P implements; EBA beaker, 'A' type; EBA rusticated ware; MBA overhanging-rim urns holding cremations in flat cemetery; LBA bucket urns; LBA–EIA 'A' transition, occupation site, c. 987257; IA South-eastern 'B' pottery; Belgic oppidum, 985255 etc.; Belgic occupation site, 997207; Belgic cremation cemeteries, c. 975248 etc., with barrows; Belgic barrows, 968248, 975247; Belgic linear earthwork, 986257 etc.; South Gaulish R provincial pottery, imported before the R conquest; R ditch of 1C. A.D. fort? 979246; R town wall and Balkerne Gate, 992252; R cremation and inhumation cemeteries, one walled, 989248 (destroyed); R pottery kilns, c. 995244, c. 985255; R coin-hoards; R temple sites,

982244, 968227 and 001255 (beneath Castle); R centre of pottery and glass production; Romano-Saxon pottery; S pottery on R house sites; S cemetery, Hythe; post-R earthwork, 010236 etc.; S restoration of town walls, A.D. 921; Castle earthwork, partly pre-Norman?; earthwork, rectangular, Brinkley Grove; PN Borough Field, 12C., from *burh* (the R town?); Museum, The Castle.

Colne Engaine. R brick in church, 850303; S pottery; field-name, Goldings (*Goldhord* 14C.).

Copford. R building, c. 932231; R road, 930218 etc.; Med village, migration from 935227?

Creeksea. Belgic pottery; migration of village from c. 930970? PN Creeksea implies a barrow?

Cressing. IA pottery and hearth, 787188.

Dagenham (490840). MBA hoard; R inhumation; Museum, Becontree Avenue.

Danbury. N secondary (Peterborough) ware; LBA hoard; IA 'A' fort(?) and IA 'C' pottery, 794062; IA 'A' fort (*Danbury*), 778047 etc.; R occupation, 778047.

Debden. R finds; Med? moated mound, c. 541332; field-name, Bone Lands, 16C.

Dedham. R brick in church, 057331.

Dengie. R brick in church, 989017; shrunken settlement?

Dovercourt (250310). P, Acheulian; LBA hoard near a globular urn; R house (built over); S burial?; Viking weapons.

Downham (720960). Field-name Grimstead, '*Grimshed*' 16C., place of pagan S sacrifice?

Earls Colne. PN Tilekiln, 863282, cf. *Tilewic*, 13C.; field-name, *Sedcoppe*, 16C., 'look-out place'?

East Donyland (025210). Barrows (destroyed?); Med village site?

East Ham (440840). P implements; R inhumations.

Easthorpe (910215). R brick in church.

East Mersea. IA or R 'Red Hills', c. 040156 etc., and 060158 etc.; Danish? earthwork of A.D. 894? 051142; shrunken Med village? c. 051142.

East Tilbury. P implements; R circular wattle huts; IA or R 'Red Hills'; R brick in church, 689770; earthwork, 'Soldiers' Graves', 687769 etc.; PN Tilbury from *burh*.

Eastwood. R brick in church; PN Westbarrow, 13C., 865896; field-name, Saltreach; field-name, *'Grymesfeld'*, 14C., equivalent to 'Woden's field', suggesting pagan S shrine.

Elmdon. LBA hoard; Med fortified mound in Castlegrove, 461400; Med? moated mound, mill-stead? 466393; field-name, *Setecuppe*, 14C., 'look-out place'?

Elmstead. R brick in church, 064260.

Elsenham. R coin-hoard and other R finds; R? brick in church; migration of village from c. 542259?

Epping. Mes site, Epping Forest; IA 'A' fort, Ambresbury, 438003; R pottery kiln, c. 474030; mounds, c. 448030.

Fairstead. R brick in church, 768167.

Farnham. Med village site? c. 481248.

Faulkbourne (800170). R bricks in a wall (from Rivenhall R settlement?).

Feering (870205). S cemetery, 'Barrow Field'; field-name, Mott Field, 16C.

Felsted. P implements; M? BA hoard; R occupation; Med? mound and moat, 695207; Med? dam, 673214; millponds, mostly dry, along river.

Finchingfield. R occupation (village?); R house, 'Brickstead Field', c. 660330; R building, c. 690320.

Fingringhoe. EBA beaker, A1 type; LBA barrel urn; IA or R 'Red Hills', c. 050190 etc.; R fort of 1C. A.D., c. 049194 (military depot and port); R cremations; R building, c. 050193.

Fobbing (720840). PN Hawkesbury, 12C., from *beorg*.

Fordham (930290). R brick in church.

Foulness. IA or R 'Red Hills', c. 980907; R barrow, cremation, 980905; R occupation, c. 976915; PN Burwood, 13C., 000910, from *burh*.

Frating (090230). R brick in church.

Fryerning. R brick in church; Med 13C. pottery kiln; earthwork, Moore's Ditch, 640016.

Fyfield (570070). R brick in church; LBA hoard.

Gestingthorpe. R buildings, 828388 and 830385.

Goldhanger. IA and R 'Red Hills', 926087 etc.; R occupation, Fish Pit Marsh; S burial(s); PN Barrowmarsh, 16C., mounds formed in excavating brine pits?

Good Easter (626123). Field-names, Great and Little Oldbury, 15C., from *burh*.

Grays Thurrock. P implements; LBA two hoards, including winged axes; IA finds; R? brick in church, 613777.

Great Baddow. N? implements, votary deposit; LBA hoard and bucket urns; R pottery; R brick in church; earthwork, Galleywood; PN Tilekiln, 712040.

Great Bentley (110220). LBA bucket urns.

Great Braxted. R pottery; R brick in church; Med village, original site? c. 851154.

Great Bromley. IA 'A' pottery c. 106257; R pottery; R brick in church, 083263.

Great Burstead (680922). P implements; Belgic pottery and kiln; R kilns, burials, coin-hoard, etc.; PN Burstead, 10C., from *burh* (reference to earthwork in Norsey Wood, Billericay?).

Great Canfield. R brick in church; Med castle mound and baileys (Norman), 594179; earthworks, cattle enclosures? c. 597193.

Great Chesterford. P and N implements;

EBA beakers, 'A–C' type, and handled type, c. 500535; IA 'C' settlement and cremations, 500435; R town (partly destroyed), earlier a fort, 500435; R walled inhumation cemetery; R temple, c. 1 mile east of town; R house, 514436; Romano-Saxon pottery; S cemetery, cremation and inhumation, 500435 and c. 500535?; earthwork, rectangular, 'King's Hedges' in north of parish; barrow and trackway (air site); PN Burton, 13C., from *burhtun*, 533438.

Great Clacton. P, Clactonian implements; Mes, Lower Halstow culture; N pottery, including Windmill Hill, Abingdon, Peterborough and Rinyo-Clacton wares; EBA beaker 'B'. N.B. The preceding finds come from various sites on the foreshore, especially from 153129 and 146128. Elsewhere: EBA beakers, 'A1' and 'B'; IA or R 'Red Hills'; R brick in church; S inhumations; Med parks, Alton (163142) and Clacton Park.

Great Coggeshall. R buildings, c. 840225 and immediately S.W. of church; R cremations; R cremation in brick vault; field-name, Dead Woman's Hill.

Great Dunmow. R posting station at junction of five roads; R ford? 634220; R road? 633220; PN *Stratford*, 13C., R ford?

Great Easton. R brick in church; Norman mound and bailey, 609255.

Great Hallingbury. IA hill-fort, Wallbury, 492178; Belgic pottery, c. 492178; R cremations, c. 492178; R inhumation; R brick in church; Med? moated mound (mill-stead?) in Hallingbury Park; PN Tilekiln Green, 18C., 523210.

Great Henny. Med shrunken settlement? 867379; field-name, Blacklands, 16C.

Great Horkesley. P implements; IA 'C'? fort, Pitchbury, Belgic pottery, 966291; R brick in church; migration of village? from c. 972325.

Great Leighs. R? brick in church; Med shrunken village? 738156.

Great Maplestead. R? brick in church, 808346.

Great Oakley. EBA food vessel; R? brick in church, 194276.

Great Parndon. R occupation, Water Lanes; barrows, 429100.

Great Sampford. R road, 609341, etc.

Great Stambridge. IA or R 'Red Hills', c. 962928 and c. 982935.

Great Tey. R occupation, Warrens Farm; R brick in church, 892258.

Great Totham. R? brick in church; barrows, many destroyed, 876079.

Great Wakering. Belgic and R site, pottery and cremations, c. 969871; PN Oldbury, 15C., 928876.

Great Waltham. R brick in church, 696134; field-names, Black Land, 16C., Castle Field, 14C.

Great Warley. PN Berry House, 602866, *Aldebury*, 14C., from *burh*.

Great Wigborough. IA or R 'Red Hills', c. 975135 etc.; PN Wigborough, 11C., from *beorg*, possibly reference to small barrow, c. 968157; PN Seaborough, 14C., from *burh*.

Greenstead (Colchester), R brick in church, 019250.

Greensted-next-Ongar. Med shrunken settlement? 540030; PN Crockleford.

Hadleigh. R fortlet or signal station, c. 801862.

Hadstock. R house in 'Sunken Church Field', 571462.

Halstead. EBA beaker, 'B2' type; R pottery kiln, c. 820280; R road, 790300 etc.

Harlow. LBA bucket urns; Belgic and R occupation, c. 469124; R temple, 469124; PN Potter St., 13C., 473085; PN Mulberry, 477113, *Mudborow*, 16C., moot-site and barrow?

Hatfield Broad Oak. LBA hoard; IA? fort,

Portingbury, 534204; Med homestead site, 550155; earthwork (destroyed?), 533204; barrow? c. 552205; mill-mounds, c. 522150 and 530211; PN Aldbury's, 17C.; field-name, Black Land, 15C.

Hatfield Peverel (790120). Belgic occupation; field-name, Black Lands, 16C.

Hazeleigh. Med deserted village? Earthwork surrounding manor and church, 836038.

Helions Bumpstead. Med homestead site, 645414; PN Boblow, 653404 from *hlāw*; field-name Tile Kiln, 16C.

Hempstead (635380). Mound at road-junction in village.

Henham (550285). R finds.

Heybridge. Belgic and R pottery; R port on estuary; S inhumations(?); barrows, R?, c. 872076; PN Saltcote, 872079.

High Easter. R building, 649142; field-name, Seedskips, 15C., 'look-out place'.

High Laver. R brick in church, 528087.

High Roding. LBA hoard; migration of village from 593166? mill? mound, c. 600163.

Hockley. Mes site, Hullbridge; IA 'A' pottery, c. 810950; R? barrow (Plumberow Mount) and R pottery, 839938; R brick in church; mounds, débris of Med salt-making? c. 826961.

Hornchurch (545870). P, Mousterian; field-name, Sedcups, 'look-out place'.

Horndon-on-the-Hill. R brick in church, 669833.

Ilford. P implements; IA 'A' pottery, c. 445900; R building near Fern Hall; R burial, Valentine's Park; earthwork (damaged), c. 435860.

Ingatestone. R brick in church; Med pottery kiln, 13C.; linear earthwork, Moore's Ditch, 640016; PN Potter Row, 15C.; PN *Writeledich*, 13C.; migration of village from 654986?

Inworth, 880180. R brick in church; PN

Barrows, 14C., and Barrow Hill, 15C.; PN *Potteresrawe*, 14C.

Jay Wick. P, Clactonian implements, wooden spear and bone implements; N habitation sites, 153129 and 146128 (see Great Clacton).

Kelvedon. Belgic pottery; R pottery, 849173 and burials c. 846170; R house, c. 847197; S cemetery (or Feering); field-name, 'Little Barrows', skeletons found.

Kirby le Soken. IA or R 'Red Hills', c. 213236.

Lambourne. Med shrunken settlement? 479961.

Langdon (Laindon Hills). PN Great and Little Berry, 13C., from *burh*, 671877.

Langenhoe. South-eastern 'B' pottery from 'Red Hills', 015164 etc.; Belgic pottery; mounds, c. 046173; migration of village site from ?c. 013175.

Langford. R brick in church, 838090.

Langham. BA? implements of flint; R brick in church, 034337.

Langley. R barrow (site?), cremation, in Rumburg (Rumberry) 14C., Mead. Rumburg probably means 'three barrows'; R road, 450338 etc.

Latchingdon. IA or R 'Red Hills', 886016; Med deserted village, Snoreham, c. 885995.

Latton. R brick in church, etc.; R cremations, c. 470080; Med deserted village? c. 464110.

Lawford. Barrow (082318).

Layer de la Haye. Belgic dyke, 963205 etc.; migration of village? from 965192; PN Chest Wood, 13C.

Layer Marney. Linear earthwork, 909176 etc.

Leigh-on-Sea (840860). LBA, two hoards; S burial(s)?

Lexden. P implements; linear Belgic earthwork, Gryme's Dyke, 962240 etc.; Belgic barrow, early 1C. A.D. (of Cunobelin?),

968248; Belgic and R cremations. (See Colchester.)

Leyton. P implements; R buildings and burials, 376869 and c. 360870; R? burial vault and coin-hoard, Temple Mills.

Lindsell (640270). IA 'C'? cremation; PN *Hertisheved*, 14C., 'hart's head', place of pagan S sacrifice?; field-name, Black Acre, 15C.

Little Baddow. IA 'A' fort, c. 793062; barrow, c. 793062; R brick in church.

Little Bardfield. R? brick in church, 655308; field-name, Pottershedge, 14C.

Little Bentley. R brick in church, 122250.

Little Braxted. R? brick in church, 836147.

Little Bromley (090280). R? brick in church.

Littlebury. P implements; N working-floor; IA fort, 515380, formerly called *Sterchebury*, 14C.; PN Stretley, 11C., 490385; field-name, *Spelbeorghe*, 10C., 'hill of speech'.

Little Canfield. Med village site? c. 586210; barrows (destroyed), c. 590214; field-name, Seed Cobs, 'look-out place'.

Little Chesterford. Rectangular earthwork, c. 515416.

Little Coggeshall (845225). R cremation.

Little Dunmow. Med Priory fishponds, 655212; PN Tile End, 660210—kilns?

Little Easton. R? brick in church, 604236.

Little Hallingbury. Belgic cemetery; R buildings, 492163 and 499166.

Little Holland. EBA, two beakers of 'A1' type, c. 209168.

Little Laver (545095). R occupation.

Little Leighs (720170). Shrunken Med village?; field-name, *Potterefeld*, 14C.

Little Maplestead (830340). PN *Grimesleye*, 13C., from *Grim*, personal name, or the by-name of the god Woden, and suggesting a pagan S shrine.

Little Oakley. R building, c. 220290.

Little Parndon. Barrows? c. 439103.

Little Sampford. (650340); Field-name, *Castell Downe*, 14C.

Little Thurrock. P working-floor; dene-holes, 630794.

Little Totham. PN Chigborough, 13C., from *beorh*, barrow near 878083; PN Totham, 10C., 'look-out place', probably now Beacon Hill, 853127.

Little Wakering. PN Barrow Hall, 13C., from *beorh* (hill?), 920881.

Little Waltham. R cremation cemetery, c. 707126; R? brick in church; PN Alstead, 18C., 727133 (site of R settlement?).

Little Wigborough. IA or R 'Red Hills', c. 996136 and 985137; Med deserted village? c. 980147.

Loughton. IA 'A' fort, *Sateresbyrig*, 11C., 'robber's camp', 418975; PN *Stanweges hacce*, 11C., reference to R road?; migration of settlement from c. 440965?

Magdalen Laver. R brick in church; Med castle mound? 514085; Med deserted village? c. 513083.

Maldon. P implements; R pottery; R brick in church of St. Peter; barrow in Mountfield, 838072; barrows, 881068 and 887057; S *burh* of A.D. 920 at 843067.

Manningtree (105320). LBA cemetery.

Manuden. Oval churchyard, pre-Christian? earthwork, 491267.

Margaretting. R brick in church; barrow, used as windmill tump in 17C., c. 690017.

Marks Tey. Belgic coin-hoard; R road junction, posting station?; R brick in church, 911239; R cremations; S cemetery.

Mashbury. R? brick in church, 651119; PN Mashbury, 11C., from *burh*.

Matching. Med manorial sites, 539137 and 543123; field-name, Seed Gaps, 13C., 'look-out place'.

Messing. R house, Chapel Field, 890196; barrow or mill-tump, 897183.

Mile End (Colchester). Belgic linear earthwork, 975260 etc.

Mistley (120315). R cremations.

Mount Bures. Belgic burial vault, c. 907323; R brick in church; Med castle mound and bailey, 904326.

Mountnessing. R brick in church; migration of village? from c. 648966; PN Bury Wood, 13C.

Mucking. P implements; earthwork? 687810; PN Seaborough, 13C., 'seven barrows'? 652803.

Mundon. IA or R 'Red Hills' (destroyed); Med deserted village? 880028 (manorial site and church surrounded by earthwork).

Navestock. Rectangular earthwork, 549983; moated mound and fishponds, 554988.

Nazeing (415065). R burials; field-name, Seedcups, 15C., 'look-out place'.

Netteswell. Med shrunken village? 455093.

Newport. P implements; R? barrows, c. 525353; PN Bury Field, 14C.; PN Whiteditch, 13 C.

North Ockendon (590850). R? brick in church; R? cemetery.

North Weald. R brick in church, 495052; R road 498023 etc.

Orsett. P implements; Med ring and bailey earthwork 641822; PN Lime Kilns, 15C.; field-name, Sedecope, 15C., 'look-out place'.

Ovington. P implements; Med deserted village? 763426; lost village site, Belchamp St. Ethelbert.

Paglesham. IA or R 'Red Hills', c. 934927; R brick in church; PN Saltpan Marsh.

Panfield. L? BA hoard; migration of village site? from 738253.

Pebmarsh (855335). Field-name, Black Croft, 17C.

Peldon. IA or R 'Red Hills', c. 000145 etc.; R? brick in church.

Plaistow (405830). P implements; R burials.

Pleshey. R building, 649143; R cremations in vault, c. 649143; Med mound and bailey castle and earthwork surrounding village, 665145.

Prittlewell. IA 'A1' and 'B' earthwork, 890878; Belgic pottery; R settlement, 875875; R burials; S (Jutish?) cemetery; Med fishponds, 877873; Museum, Priory Park.

Purleigh. Belgic pottery; earthwork, 841017.

Quendon. P implements; R finds and burials; R? barrows, c. 515314.

Radwinter. R kiln, c. 590390 and burial; R road, 590386 etc., and 608350 etc.; Med? moated mound, 612353.

Rainham (530820). P implements; R burial; S glass vessels.

Rawreth (780935). PN Tryndehayes, 13C., 'circular enclosure'.

Rayleigh. EBA beaker; Belgic pottery; R brick in church; Med castle-mound and baileys, 11C., 805910; PN Hamborough, from *burh*?

Rayne. BA hoard; migration of village from c. 733232?; PN Street Farm on R road.

Rettendon. PN Buckhatch, *Burgatesfeld*, 14C., 779993; PN Potters Farm, 779984.

Rickling. R finds; Med castle mound and bailey, 11C., 499303.

Ridgewell. R house, 738404; R road, c. 732403 etc.

Rivenhall. R settlement, 830178 etc.; R road, north of presumed line; PN Barrow Field.

Rochford. P implements; PN Westbarrow, 865896, from *beorg* or *bearu*, 'grove'; field-name, *Goldhord*, 13C.

Romford. L? BA hoard; R building, c. 537930; mill? mound, half-mile E.N.E. of parish church.

Roxwell. R finds, c. 658100; barrow? c. 659094.

Roydon. PN Totwell, 405082, nearby look-out place?; field-name, Money Pot Hill, 13C.

Saffron Walden. P implements; N working floor, 542392; BA habitation and burial, site destroyed; IA? plateau fort, destroyed, 547406; R finds and coin-hoard, c. 550395; R cemetery, c. 546412; late S inhumation cemetery, 537384; Med castle mound and bailey, 539387; Med? maze on the Common; strong defensive earthwork (IA 'C'?), Repell, War or Paille Ditches, *Besseldyche*, 15C., 535385; village water defences, Sewards End, 570382; earthwork, Grim's Ditch Wood; PN Grim's Ditch—reference to Woden? and hence to pagan S shrine; PN Bury Hill, 15C.; Museums, near Castle and at Audley End.

St. Osyth. P implements; EBA beaker, 'B1' type; IA or R 'Red Hills'; R building, c. 114168; two ditched mounds in Priory Park.

Salcott. IA or R 'Red Hills', c. 957136 etc.; PN means 'salt-cottages'—Med salt-boiling?

Sandon (745050). IA and R pottery; R brick in church.

Shalford (720290). LBA bucket urns; R pottery.

Sheering. R brick in church, 509137.

Shelley. Barrows, 547051 and ?c. 553050.

Shoebury. P implements; EBA 'B2' beaker; LBA bucket or barrel urn; LBA hoards, two; IA 'A' settlement; IA 'B' (Patch Grove) ware; Belgic settlement; Belgic pottery, c. 940850; R kiln, pottery and burial, c. 940850; S burials; Danish fort, much damaged, of A.D. 894, c. 940847; PN Shoebury—the Danish *burh*.

Shopland. Med shrunken village? c.899883.

Sible Hedingham. EBA handled beakers; R pottery kiln and R minor road, 784333; Med pottery kiln, 13C.; field-names, Potsheds (*Pottesherdes*, 16C.); PN Tile-kiln, 16C.

South Benfleet. Belgic pottery; R brick in church; Danish fort built A.D. 894; earthworks? at 777862 and 793866.

Southchurch (910860). EBA beaker burial; MBA pottery; LBA habitation site; LBA bucket urns; L? BA hoards; IA 'A1' habitation; IA 'B' pottery; R pottery.

Southend (880860). P implements; EBA beaker pottery; Belgic pottery.

South Fambridge. IA or R 'Red Hills', c. 862957; Med deserted village? c. 861950.

South Hanningfield (740980). R pottery.

Southminster. IA 'A'? pottery; Belgic pottery; IA or R 'Red Hills'; R pottery; R brick in church; PN Plumborough, 001990; PN Ratsborough, 14C., 955986.

South Ockendon. Barrows (destroyed?); R road, c. 630830 etc.; manorial earthworks and millponds.

South Weald. IA plateau fort, *Sideburg*, 13C., 578947; PN Ditchleys, 552960; field-name, Willeys, 15C., pagan S sanctuary?

Springfield. IA pottery; R brick in church, 719080.

Stanford le Hope (680820). PN Stanford, 11C., R road?; PN Potter's Farm, 16C.; field-name, *Setetup*, 13C., 'look-out place'.

Stanford Rivers. PN Burrows, 13 C., from *beorg*, 524021; PN Toothill, 17C., 'look-out hill', probably the moot-place for Ongar Hundred, 516025; PN Littlebury, 551012; PN Stanford, line of R road?

Stansted Mountfitchet. P implements; MBA overhanging-rim urn; R house, beneath church, 521242; R house, c. 524238; Med ring-and-bailey castle, 515249; original site of village? 521242; PN Burton, 14C., 530240.

Stanway. P implements; Belgic dykes, 959223 etc., 963220 etc., 962240 etc. (triple); R theatre, 969223; R cremations; Med deserted village, 952221; PN Stanway, 11C., 'the stone ways', R roads.

Stebbing. R buildings, 677246 and 689232

(near Tilehouse Farm); Med castle mound, 658244; field-name, Alberry, 15C., from *burh*; field-name, Blackland, 14C.

Steeple (940030). IA or R 'Red Hills'.

Steeple Bumpstead. R building, c. 695425; R cemetery, c. 694426; earthworks, c. 678427.

Stisted (800250). PN Swanstead, originally 'swine's head', 16C., pagan S shrine?

Stock. R habitation? c. 685975; Med pottery kilns, 15C.; barrow, c. 685982.

Stondon Massey. R? brick in church; original site of village? 573016.

Stowe Maries. PN Wellinditch, 819990; field-name, 'Saltcoats'; barrows? c. 834978.

Stratford (West Ham). (390840). R cremation; S burial, Forest Gate.

Strethall (485400). PN Strethall, 11C., R road, of which the line is lost.

Sturmer. R coin-hoard, late 4C.; R road, line lost; barrow, 688443; original site of village? 690440.

Sutton. Med deserted village? c. 889891.

Takeley. R finds; R? brick in church; original site of village? c. 555215.

Tendring. Barrow, 156249.

Terling (770150). R coin-hoard, late 4C.

Thaxted. IA and R finds; R building, c. 615302; R road? line lost; Med? moated mound, c. 595293; PN Borough Farm; field-name, Burtons, 13C.; field-name, *Setecophell* ('look-out hill'), 14C.

Theydon Bois. R building, c. 442992; Med village site? c. 463980.

Theydon Garnon. R road? 470983 etc.; original site of village? c. 473993; field-name, *Wedynsfeld*, 15C., pagan S shrine?; field-name, Oldbury, 15C.

Theydon Mount. R road? 490010 etc.; site of Theydon Parva, 14C., c. 493993?

Thundersley (790890). L? BA hoard; R brick in church; PN Thundersley, pagan S shrine?

Tilbury-next-Clare. Original site of village? c. 760404.

Tillingham (990040). IA or R 'Red Hills' in S.E. of parish (destroyed).

Tilty. R? brick in church; Med shrunken village? 600265.

Tollesbury. IA or R 'Red Hills', c. 950085 etc., and 968103 etc.; R building?; R brick in church; PN Tollesbury, 11C., from *burh*.

Tolleshunt D'Arcy. IA or R 'Red Hills', c. 930088 etc.; barrows, 921094; field-name, *Sedcope*, 16C., 'look-out place'.

Tolleshunt Knights. R house, 930150; S pottery, c. 930150: linear earthwork, c. 930150 etc.

Tolleshunt Major. Barrow, 907110, pagan S site (Thurstable) and hundred-moot.

Toppesfield. Belgic cremation; PN Harrow Hill, 725368, pagan S site?; PN Flower's Hall (*flowres*, 16C.), 729339, from *flōr*, (a villa pavement)?

Ugley. Belgic pottery; Med shrunken village? 520288.

Upminster. PN Pot Kilns, 565888.

Vange. LBA hoard; PN *tha straete*, 10C., R road? 708865?

Virley. IA or R 'Red Hills'; R brick in church; barrow? c. 948146.

Waltham Holy Cross. N? working-floor, 382006; pillow-mounds (IA pottery), 412983; PN Potkiln (cf. *Pottereshylle*, 14C.); PN *Eldewirche*, 12C., possibly meaning 'the old earthwork' (at Sewardstone Street). For Ambresbury see Epping.

Walthamstow (360890). P implements; N Peterborough pottery; IA 'A1' settlement, with later B influence?; Viking ship-burial; PN Bury Field, 15C.

Walton-on-the-Naze. P implements; Mes occupation, Lower Halstow culture; N occupation, primary and secondary (including Rinyo-Clacton ware); EBA beaker 'B' type—N.B. all the preceding c. 250260; IA or R 'Red Hills'.

Wanstead. P implements; R house, 418874 and other R occupation elsewhere.

Weeley. Migration of village from c. 154214; PN Weeley, pagan S shrine?

Wenden Lofts. LBA hoard; original site of village, 463387?

Wendens Ambo. P implements; N working-floor; LBA urns, cemetery?; Belgic crema-tion cemetery; R house, 508361, and burials; S cemetery; site of Wendens Parva? parish absorbed 17C.; PN Mut-low, 14C., hundred-moot of Uttlesford.

West Bergholt. P implements; migration of village from 952280?

West Ham (410820). P implements; R burials.

West Hanningfield. R brick in church; PN Foxborough, meaning 'fox-earth'?

West Mersea. IA or R 'Red Hills', c. 002134; R house, 008125; R building, 009126; R circular brick tomb, 011125; R barrow, cremation in brick vault, 023144.

West Thurrock. Migration of village from c. 593774?

West Tilbury. R building (site destroyed by dock); earthwork of 1588?, 660776 etc.

Wethersfield. R cemetery; linear earth-work, Devil's Ditch, 698318 etc.; moated mound, c. 738277; PN Tilekiln, 703323, and Brickkiln, 736316.

White Colne. LBA cemetery, barrel and bucket urns; R brick in church, 880300.

White Notley. R house and brick tomb, cremations; PN Littleburys, 14C., 762187.

White Roding. R occupation, c. 555135 and cremations; PN Potters, 18C.

Wicken Bonhunt (500330). P implements.

Wickham Bishops. Belgic pottery; R brick in church, 824112; Med deserted village? c. 824112.

Widdington (540317). R coin-hoard; PN *Wodnesfeld*, 14C., pagan S shrine?

Widford (695050). R house? on site of church.

Willingale Spain and Doe. R brick in both churches, 596073; Med castle-mound and bailey? 600082.

Wimbish. R finds; PN Thunderley, 560361, pagan S shrine?; Med deserted village, 560360.

Witham. IA 'A' fort, 823152 re-used by Saxons in A.D. 913; R and S, 10C., occu-pation, 823152; R brick in church; S? burials.

Wivenhoe. IA pottery; R brick in church, 039215.

Wix (170285). LBA bucket urn.

Woodford. R pottery, South Woodford.

Woodham Ferrers. PN Saltcoats, mounds c. 818978 from Med salt-making; PN *Brox-hedde*, 16C., 'badger's head', place of pagan S sacrifice?; field-name, Bone Croft, 16C.

Wormingford. R brick in church, 933323.

Writtle. R brick in church and cell, 633021; PN Barrow Farm, etc., 13C.; PN Monk's and Barrow's Farm, 15C.; PN *Writele-dich*, 13C., forest boundary earthwork?; field-name, *Dedman*, 14C.

HAMPSHIRE

Abbotstone. IA 'A' fort, 584362; IA settlement, earthworks, 585364; Med deserted village, 565345; barrows, 582366; 'Great Ditch' in Spy Bush Plantation.

Abbots Worthy. IA or R farmstead, Celtic fields, trackway and pond, 493345 etc.

Abbotts Ann. R house in Minster Field, c. 314419; R pottery etc., earthworks, c. 330437; earthwork enclosure (air site) in field called Bulberry, 328433.

Aldershot. Mes occupation, 837502 and 841502; barrows, 822493; IA fort?, 'Caesar's Camp', 838500: anomalous earthwork, Bat's Hogsty, 847516.

Alton. R occupation, c. 715386 and 731392; R graves; Curtis Museum, High St.

Ampfield (400232). R occupation; linear earthwork, Portland Bank.

Amport. LBA ranch-boundary ditches, 250435 etc., and 250444 etc.; R road, agger, 294433 etc.; PN Gollard (*Goldhord*, 13C.), 289422; barrows, 244424.

Andover. N long barrow, c. 374505; LBA hoard; IA 'A2' hill-fort, Balksbury, much damaged—later IA 'B' occupation; R posting-station? at junction of R road and Harroway, many finds c. 372475; R houses, 398484 and 398466 (in Castle Field); R building? c. 373447; R burials near Finkley; R road, agger, 357495 etc.; barrows, 393490; barrow circles and enclosure? (air sites), c. 375445; linear earthwork, Devil's Ditch, post-R,? barring R road and Harroway; Museum, Municipal Buildings.

Appleshaw. R houses, 303475 and c. 302487 (in Chapel Copse); IA? occupation, Redenham.

Ashley. N long barrow, c. 394294; R earthwork, occupation, 395301; R road, agger, 410295 etc.; Med castle earthwork, 385309; disc and bowl barrows, c. 394294; Celtic fields, 400305 etc.; ancient track, 395293 etc.

Ashmansworth. R villages on sites of Ashmansworth and Crux Easton; R inhumation, 424562; barrows, 442567, 431562 etc., and 430574 (destroyed).

Ashurst. Barrows, 336083 etc., 367080 etc. and elsewhere; square earthwork, Church Place, 342097; ring earthwork, 336085; PN Colbury, from *burh*? 349107; PN *Poteresford*, 13C., 328109.

Avington. Celtic fields, ploughed, 524290; cross-dyke, c. 530277; linear earthworks, 530304 etc. (Med park bank?) and 523317 etc.; PN Chesford, 531277, from *ciest*?

Awbridge. R habitation site, c. 330250.

Barton Stacey. N long barrow, 426388; MBA cinerary urn; IA? promontory fort, Andyke (Bransbury), 426425; R road, agger, 424395 etc.; R ford? 411414; bar-

rows, 418389, 437383 and ?c. 430430; Celtic fields, 430370 etc.; earthwork enclosure? ploughed, 438417.

Basing. R pottery; Norman ring and bailey castle earthwork, 663527; Med? linear earthwork, park bank?, 665552; 17C.? earthwork, Oliver's Battery, 668536; barrows, 678517; PN Brick kiln, 663543; Museum, Basing House.

Basingstoke. BA? barrow burial; IA Southwestern 'B' pottery, Wellocks Hill; Belgic pottery; R pottery, Latchmore Green; Viking burial; Museum, New St.

Baughurst. R road, 590594 etc.; barrows? 574624?; PN *Thing lea*, moot-site?

Beacon Hill. See Burghclere.

Beaulieu. Mes sites? 393057 and 404051; EBA food vessel, burial, c. 361007; MBA barrows, mortuary houses, 361007 etc.; IA 'A1' burial, with cart?, 366018; IA? promontory fort, damaged, 415983; S? linear earthworks, c. 420034 etc., and c. 360015 etc. (destroyed); Med? oval earthwork, The Noads, 398057; Med deserted village, Hartford; Med linear earthwork, 409049 etc.; barrows, including twin bowl and bell, 403051 etc.; barrow, intermediate bell-disc, 412031; pond? barrow, c. 342994.

Bedhampton. N long barrow, Bevis's Grave, destroyed, 692065; R house, c. 695073; R road, agger, 687073; PN Bidbury, 701068, manorial?

Bentley. R building, c. 779459; R cremation; Med 13C. pottery kiln.

Bentworth. R pottery, 675383.

Bighton. R house, c. 625363; PN *stodfaldun*—earthwork enclosure?

Binsted. R houses, c. 756388 and c. 774415; R inhumations, c. 785401; Belgic and R pottery manufacture, c. 806408 and 814403; Med? earthworks, 743393.

Bishopstoke. P implements; IA? camp, Hickley and Beach Farms; R burial; Med park boundary banks? c. 480195.

Bishops Sutton. Med park boundary banks, c. 620300?

Bishops Waltham. MBA burial in tree-trunk coffin, Wessex? Culture, in bell-barrow (destroyed); R house, 550163; R coin-hoard; R road, 532194 etc.; Med park boundary banks?; Med hundred-moot at *Wulfpit* (13C.).

Bitterne. Belgic cremations; R town, *Clausentum*, 4C. walls and towers, 5C. re-occupation; R linear earthworks, 437133 etc.; R buildings, burials, coin-hoards, etc.; Med park bank? PN Midanbury, 450143.

Blackmoor. LBA hoard; R habitation, c. 780330; R cremations; R coin-hoards.

Blackwater (850600). Mes site (destroyed).

Blendworth. Med shrunken village? 717137.

Boarhunt. Mes sites, c. 618098, c. 606092, c. 620106 and at North Boarhunt; Med shrunken village? 604084; PN Boarhunt means 'Spring by the *burh*'.

Boldre. Disc barrows, three, 296000 etc. (including twin-disc) and one, Race Plain; earthwork enclosure, 298998 etc.; PN Crockford, 350990; PN Tylers Copse, 395991; PN Salternshill, c. 410990.

Borden. LBA hoard?; R coin-hoard, later 3C.; barrows, 782359 etc., and 774352 etc.

Bossington. R road, agger, 313313; R ford? c. 338312; Med deserted village, 336308; barrow, 320312.

Botley. EBA stone axe-hammer, Danish type; R road-line 510118 etc.?

Bournemouth. P implements; Windmill Hill ware, 118941; N axe from Graig Lwyd; N axe of Pembrokeshire Preselite; EBA rusticated ware, Moordown; MBA double-looped palstave, Iberian; LBA urn-field cemetery, bucket, barrel and globular urns, c. 126928; LBA cremations in oval barrow (destroyed?), bucket urns, c. 118941; IA 'A' haematite - coated pottery, Ensbury and 126928; IA Wessex 'B' pot-tery, Strouden Farm; R pottery, c. 126928; barrows (destroyed?) c. 080923 and c. 117929; PN Grimsbury, 167917; Museum, 39 Christchurch Rd.

Bradley. Med 'Hurst Castle', unfinished Norman work? 644413; ancient pond, 648410.

Bramdean. Belgic pottery, c. 625265. R house, c. 627282.

Bramley. IA plateau hill-fort, Bullsdown, 671583, Belgic oppidum?

Bramshaw. Barrows, 286161 etc.; ancient track, 250183 etc.; original site of village? 265167.

Bramshill. Med fishpond, 758602; Med? bank, 766600 etc.

Breamore. N long barrows, 152198 (ploughed) and 138200; N jadeite Breton axe; LBA ranch boundary, Grim's Dyke, 132210; Med deserted village, South Charford, 167190; migration of Breamore? from c. 153189, emparkment?; barrows, 138207 etc.; ancient track, 173198 etc.; earthwork maze, Miz-Maze, 142203.

Brockenhurst. Mes site, c. 355043; Med park ditch, Bishop's Dyke, 340050 etc.; barrows, numerous in parish; PN Row-barrow, 355043.

Broughton. N long barrow, 330358; MBA pottery; LBA barrel or bucket urn; R occupation, c. 290330; R road, agger, 270323 etc.; S burials, c. 318320: barrows, 290330, 308318 and eight destroyed, 323364; PN Broughton, from *beorg*.

Brown Candover. LBA urnfield; R inhumations; Med shrunken village? c. 575391?

Buckholt. R site; R road, agger, 280321 etc.; Med glassworks; Med deserted village, c. 277320?

Bullington. IA plateau fort, Tidbury, 460430; R house, 463429; R building, c. 460405.

Burghclere. BA barrows, 462553; disc barrow, 479570 (cf. tree-ring, 479568);

IA hill-fort (superimposed on N causeway camp?), Beacon Hill, 457573; R inhumations, Ridge Moor; Med park boundary bank, c. 485625; Med strip fields, 457584 etc.; ancient tracks, 465555 etc.; PN Adbury, c. 485625; PN *weardsetl* (watch-seat), Beacon Hill, i.e. a look-out place; Celtic fields, 456568 etc.

Buriton. IA hill-fort, Butser—see Langrish; R building, c. 724179; R occupation, c. 722197; barrows, 721202; Celtic fields (ploughed), 720196 etc.; ancient tracks, 722200 etc.; pillow mound, 721203; PN Ditcham, 745175; PN Buriton from *burh*.

Burley. MBA merchant's hoard, Shappen; R pottery manufacture, c. 240059 and c. 245065; barrows, 197028; bell barrows, 235027 and 206019; barrows, 189009 etc.; PN Castle Hill, 199040, IA hill-fort and Med castle mound?; earthwork enclosure, 16C., c. 203060; PN Greenberry, 219016.

Bursledon (490095). N dolerite axe from Wales.

Butser Hill. See Langrish and Buriton.

Cadnam. R road, agger, 290135 etc.

Chalton. Mes occupation sites, 716160 etc.

Chandler's Ford. LBA bucket or barrel urn; R road, 430203 and 436207; barrows (destroyed?), Cranbury Common: linear earthworks, Hiltingbury, 435224 etc.

Cheriton. N long barrows, 600290 and c. 589281; LBA ranch boundary ditches, several converging, 552260 etc.; Celtic fields, 553262 etc., ancient tracks, 553263, barrows, 593284; 17C. burial mound, c. 597294.

Chilbolton. N long barrow, 418384; LBA ranch-boundary ditches, 420367 etc., and 425370 etc.; Belgic and R occupation, Chilbolton Common; R barrow interment; R coin-hoard, early 3C.; S hut, c. 383393; Celtic fields, 386388 etc., and 428370 etc.; earthwork enclosures, rectangular, 384389, c. 416383 (air site) and 428370 (ploughed);

irregular earthwork, 423370 (ploughed); strip cultivation (ploughed out?) on Chilbolton Down.

Chilcomb. Barrows, 522282, 516291 and four at 500293; Celtic fields (ploughed), 525288 etc.; ancient tracks, 489277 etc., and 525280 etc.; PN *ealdan falde*, earthwork?

Chilton Candover. EBA beaker burial; R house, Stanchester, 580410; barrows, 605404 and 612400; Med shrunken village? 593401.

Chilworth. IA? circular earthwork, 413170; R road, 427198 etc.; PN Castle Hill, 407169.

Christchurch. N Peterborough ware and Rinyo-Clacton ware; EBA beaker ware; LBA urnfield in MBA barrow, Latch Farm; Belgic pottery; Norman castle mound, 160927; barrows, 146954 etc. (eleven), 145957 etc., 193953; earthwork, oval, 143956; earthwork round site of chapel, 144954; PN Burton, site of S *burh*, c. 158945; Museum, Quay Rd. See also Southbourne.

Clanfield (for Clanville see Penton Grafton). IA? promontory fort, 711200 etc.; R habitation site; disc barrow, 716171; earthwork, 716176; Celtic fields, 712197 etc.; linear earthwork, bivallate, 709195; PN Ditch Acre, 705182; PN Ditcham, 749177.

Colbury (350107). LBA barrow, urnfield, bucket and barrel urns.

Colden Common (480220). LBA hoard.

Colemore and **Priors Dean.** N Peterborough ware, c. 728297; LBA cremation in barrow, bucket urn; Med deserted village? 728297.

Compton. IA 'A' barrow, c. 459278; R? road, 464240; R earthwork, 459278, 'Oliver's Battery', re-used in 17C.; S burial, 459278; barrows, 456270 and 468267; strip lynchets, 470245 etc.?

Copythorne. R road, agger, 350153; barrows, 302157 and 318151; earthwork, 293170.

Corhampton. N Windmill Hill ware; IA 'A' and 'C' and R habitation surrounded by earthwork, c. 570204; R house, c. 579209; barrows, 575209 etc.; PN Sheardley, 636185, finds of pottery?

Crawley. IA or R farmstead and associated fields, 443340: barrows, 442352 and 443362, 440362 (including two discs); Celtic fields and oval enclosure, 442362; Celtic fields, 440365 etc., and 400348 etc. N.B.—The majority of the foregoing are visible only from the air.

Crofton (550045). PN Foxbury, 13C., '*burh* on a ridge'.

Crondall. Mes occupation, 822493; EBA flint implements, 821493; R house, 796472; S coin-hoard, 7C.; Norman ring-and-bailey castle, 796468 (Barley Pound); Norman motte, 802469; barrows, four, 821493.

Curdridge. R building, 521119.

Damerham. IA? hill-fort, 099186; R earthwork, kite-shaped, overlying earlier Celtic fields, Soldiers Ring, 082176; barrows, 077178; prehistoric occupation site, 077178; PN Boulsbury, 079163, *beorg*.

Deane. R house, 558514; Med shrunken settlement? c. 547503?

Denmead (660120). R occupation site.

Denny Lodge. LBA? ranch-boundary ditch? c. 359058 etc.; R occupation, c. 341064; S? linear earthworks, 363047 etc., 360045 etc., 362044 etc., 359058 etc.; Med park boundary ditch, 350053 etc.; barrows, 345057 etc., 385062 etc., and elsewhere.

Dibden. R road, 401070 etc.; barrows, 385062 etc.; linear earthwork, 410060 etc.; PN *Dunshamele*, 13C., 397075, mootsite?

Dogmersfield. Med deserted village, 773516?

Droxford. S (Jutish, later Saxon) inhuma-

tion cemetery; barrow, 581196; PN *thunreslea* (Thunor's wood or clearing)—cf. Dundridge, 580183—pagan S sanctuary?

Dummer with Kempshott. P implements; Mes sites; LBA cemetery, bucket urns, 603460; Med deserted or shrunken settlement? Kempshott, c. 597474; barrow, 590474.

Eastleigh. R buildings, 453163 and c. 465182; R hoard, late 4C.

East Meon. Mes occupation, 675200 etc.; N (secondary) occupation?, 712190 and 672205; LBA urn, Coombe; Celtic fields, ploughed, c. 653207 etc.; cross-ridge dykes, three banks and four ditches, 679193; barrows, 674239 and 682257.

East Tisted. Med village site, 700322; linear earthwork associated with multiple cross-valley dykes, 685320 etc.

East Tytherley. IA? fort, damaged, 285274; R house, 282272.

Eling. R coin-hoard; R coins and pottery, Hounsdown Hill; PN Colbury, manorial?, 349107; PN Bury, 378115.

Ellingham (and **Bratley**). LBA barrow with cremations in bucket urns 218087; IA 'A' pottery, haematite coated, c. 150070; IA? fort? 198089; R pottery manufacture, c. 188100; Med? oval earthwork, 'Pinnick', 198077; Med shrunken settlement? c. 144084; barrows, 219097.

Ellisfield. P implements; Med hundredmoot, Bermondspit, 619439; earthwork, 629453.

Empshott. Mes site, c. 753308.

Eversley. Linear earthwork, *faesten dic*, c. 797590 etc.

Exbury. IA? promontory fort, 419987; prehistoric? settlement earthworks, ploughed, 428992; PN Gilbury, 418005.

Exton. Mes site, 640207; LBA bucket urns from barrow; IA contour hill-fort, Old Winchester Hill, 640207; R coin-hoard, early 4C.; Jutish jewels, Preshaw; barrows,

R

576241, 606224, etc., and 573245 (*Maelan beorh*); ancient pond, 590237.

Faccombe. R settlement, c. 390580, linear earthwork, Grim's Ditch, 377565 etc.

Fareham. Mes site, Cams foreshore; Med park boundary bank? c. 550075; PN Aytesbury, 574097; PN Crockerhill, 14C., 570095.

Farleigh Wallop. Migration of village? from 625475?; barrow, 631478.

Farley Chamberlayne. N occupation, Windmill Hill ware; N long barrow, 401291; LBA? ranch-boundary ditch, 403291 etc.; IA farmstead? earthwork with interior annexe (air site), 402291; Belgic pottery; S burial; Med deserted village, 395275; barrows, disc and others, 401291; barrow? surmounted by church, 397274; barrow surmounted by 18C. monument, 403290; ancient tracks, 401291 etc.; PN Berrydown, 400276.

Farnborough. Mes site, West Heath; PN Farnborough, 11C., 870530, from *beorg* (probably 'hill').

Farringdon (710350). EBA beaker, 'A' type.

Fawley. R road, agger, 422050 etc.; R and Med harbour site, c. 462986 (earthworks, 461989); barrows, 421040 etc.; earthwork, c. 423041.

Fleet. Med fish-pond, 800537.

Fordingbridge. EBA 'B1' beaker burial; IA 'B' (Wessex 'B') pottery; Belgic occupation, 165115; R habitation, 165115; R pottery manufacture, Ashley Rails and Sloden (c. 210140 and c. 214128); Med? enclosures, 164112 and 216125 etc.; earthworks, c. 215130, 164115, 164143; ancient tracks, 164111 and 163142; PN Burgate, 11C. (*burh*), 145160.

Frenchmoor. Med deserted village? 280280.

Fritham and neighbourhood. R road, agger, 255118; R coin-hoard, late 4C., Amberwood; R pottery manufacture, 195145, c. 215130, 214145 (PN Crock-

hill), c. 220150; R? cattle enclosures, 203128 etc., 222160 etc., 211126, c. 215130; Med enclosure, 216125 etc.; Med? iron-diggings, c. 199122; barrows, 422143 and 214156 etc.

Froxfield. R earthwork and habitation, 715250; S? linear earthworks, 70127 etc., 720270 etc., 724269, 703265, 703260, 701250 etc., 703246, etc.; barrows, 693248, 703274, 724268.

Froyle. R building, 770436; earthwork, 776458.

Fyfield. IA 'A' haematite-coated ware, c. 300495; R house, c. 295504.

Godshill. LBA sherds, IA 'A' occupation, Wessex 'B' ware, Belgic and R pottery, all at 164161; IA? hill-fort, *Godmanescap*, 168153 (also 'Frankenbury'); R pottery manufacture, c. 195146; Norman castle earthwork, 167162; barrow, 188136; PN Godshill, pagan S shrine?

Goodworth Clatford. R? farmstead site, c. 352420; Celtic fields, 345398 etc.; PN Barrow Hill, 355417, four ploughed barrows.

Gosport (000610). S occupation site; PN Foxbury, from *burh*, not 'fox-earth'.

Grateley. LBA pottery from bell barrow, 244408; R house, c. 270411; R road, 250413 etc.; barrows, six including disc, one with double concentric ditches, 237407; Celtic fields, 260418.

Greywell. R habitation site? c. 710500.

Hale. Med deserted village? 178188, emparkment?

Hamble. IA? promontory fort, 480060.

Hambleden. R house, 644144: bowl barrows, 661196; PN Bury, 642140.

Hannington. P implements; MBA cremation, c. 567547; R road, 532561 etc.; Med cultivation banks, 568553; Med manorial earthworks, 527567.

Harbridge. Med deserted village? c. 144101; barrows, 110100 etc.

Hartley Wintney. Med deserted village? 783564, Elvetham.

Havant. R house, c. 720052; R building beneath church, 717063.

Headbourne Worthy. Farmstead of LBA, IA 'A2', 'B', Belgic and R phases, 469350; IA 'A2' inhumation in cist; Celtic fields, 455353 etc.; circular earthwork cut by agger and ditch of R road, 453353; crop-marks, c. 469350.

Headley. Mes sites, c. 803380, 808388 and 850378; barrows, 807382 and 803374; PN Kiln Copse, 819384

Heckfield. R road, agger, 740634 etc.

Hedge End. R road, 470118 etc.; barrows, 478117 etc.

Hengistbury Head. See Southbourne.

Herriard. Med shrunken village? c. 664460.

Highclere. Med deserted village, empark-ment A.D. 1403? 446588; Med park boundary bank, 453592 etc.; strip lynchets, 445578 etc.; ancient tracks, 457589 etc. and 460585.

Hinton Ampner. N long barrow, 'Lam-borough', 589281; LBA barrow with cre-mations; barrows, 593284 and 599268 etc.

Holdenhurst. N long barrow (destroyed), Windmill Hill ware, Peterborough and rusticated beaker pottery; PN Berry Hill, 105962.

Holybourne (730410). P implements.

Hook. R building, c. 735540.

Hordle. P implements, Acheulian, Leval-loisian, Mousterian; R? road, Silver St., 277060; earthwork, eroded, 262925.

Horndean. S cemetery, 707154; disc barrow 708154

Houghton. R occupation, c. 340340.

Hurn. N Rinyo-Clacton ware; EBA barrow; barrows, 135967 and 124995 etc.

Hursley. IA fort, Cranbury, 445230; IA? fort adapted as Norman castle, 421265; R road, agger, 420294 etc.; Med park boundary bank, 416249 etc.; Med fish-ponds, 416250; Med dams, 421240; ancient tracks, 419266 etc., 414277 etc., and 405243 etc.; linear? earthwork, 445230; Celtic fields, Cranbury Park.

Hurstbourne Priors. BA hoard; pre-historic habitation site (destroyed), c. 431490; R house, c. 443497; R occupa-tion, 439467.

Hurstbourne Tarrant. Belgic barrow burial, cremation, Blagdon Coppice; IA? fort?, Doles Wood; R pottery; Celtic fields, c. 390552.

Ibsley. MBA bowl and saucer barrows, over-hanging-rim urns, 167100; MBA disc barrow, cinerary urn, 175104; bowl bar-rows, 173103 and 182109; R cremation.

Itchen Abbas. N? megalithic chamber of sarsens, c. 518357; R house, 529343; R occupation, c. 511356; linear earthworks, cross-valley dykes, 532362 etc.

Itchen Stoke. Barrows, 555344.

Kilmeston. Barrows, 599268 and 580243; two dykes mentioned in S charters.

Kimpton. R? building, c. 278488; barrow, 264466.

Kingsclere. N, two Graig Lwyd axes; bar-row, 536569; strip lynchets? 527567.

Kingsley. Mes sites, c. 790380 and c. 775370; IA 'A' pottery, Woodfield; R pottery, Woodfield; R pottery manufac-ture, 802388.

Kings Somborne. P implements, c. 353319; N dolerite axe; IA 'A' pottery, c. 353319; R road, agger, 380298 etc.; Med deserted village, Upper Eldon, 364278; Med fish-ponds and dam, c. 350304; Med park bank, 353320 etc.; archery butt? 360310; earthwork, circular, 382284.

Kings Worthy. R house, c. 481333; S cemetery, c. 450330; barrows, 485355; earthwork enclosure, c. 481333; PN *aenta dic*, 'giants' ditch', 11C. N.B. for Worthy Down see Headbourne Worthy.

Ladle Hill. See Litchfield.

Langrish. Mes and N sites, 717203 etc.; IA 'A'? promontory fort, 712201 etc.; barrows, 714202 (including bell), 694247 and 714208; linear earthwork, 701248; PN Barrow Hill, 701224.

Laverstoke. N long barrow, 498448; barrows (including disc), 504448 and 507444; Med deserted village? c. 497490 (Laverstoke); ancient track, Harroway, 500510 etc.; PN Brickkiln Wood, 485455.

Leckford. N long barrows, 394367 and 413358; barrows, 395364 and 400370; Celtic fields, 412357 etc.; LBA boundary ditch, c. 404367 (air site); reference to dykes and Heardwulf's barrow (*hlaew*) in 10C. charter.

Lee-on-Solent (560010). P implements.

Linkenholt. R settlement, c. 365580: linear earthwork, Grim's Ditch, 375565 etc.; ancient pond, *Throcmere*, 350588.

Liphook. R road? marking parish boundary, 816310 etc.

Liss. Barrow, 802299.

Litchfield. N long barrow, 428545; LBA pottery, 473553; IA 'A2' unfinished hill-fort, 478568, and associated Celtic fields, 473553 (ploughed) and track; bell? barrow, 478568; barrows, 482567 etc.; ridgeway, 470557 etc.; R road, 470527 etc.; earthwork enclosures, 475564 and c. 435542.

Little Somborne. Mes or N pick-factory; IA 'A1' hill-fort, Woolbury, univallate contour fort, 382354; barrow, 395364; S brooches, c. 380355.

Littleton. LBA and IA 'A' pottery; disc barrow, 458320; barrows, 460319 and 449343; Celtic fields, 458334 etc.; PN Flower Down, 462320, from *flōr*?

Lockerley. IA? fort, ploughed, 304260.

Longparish. R pottery, Firgrove; R road, 400430 etc.; earthwork, 'Old Pound', 396446.

Longstock. N long barrow, 335381; IA 'A1' and 'AB' farmstead, fortified (air site),

344354; R house, baths and outbuildings in irregular enclosure, 340364; Celtic fields, c. 340367; barrows, 338376 etc. and 347377 (ploughed); enclosures, 342389 (ploughed); ancient tracks, 324379 etc.; Danish? dock? 362373.

Lymington. P implements; EBA dwelling, beaker 'A' pottery, 292928; IA? plateau fort, 'Buckland Rings', 315968; promontory fort and dock (?), medieval pottery, 'Ampress Hole', 322968; R coin-hoard, late 3C; Med deserted village, Yaldhurst; Med salterns, 318923 etc.

Lyndhurst. Earthwork, 'Church Place', 334069; Med? enclosure, 3 miles in circumference, 310079 etc.; PN Brick Kiln, 293064; Med deserted village, c. 282065.

Mapledurwell. Migration of village? from c. 688510.

Martin. N long barrows, 089199 and 036204, EBA beaker 'B1' burial; LBA pastoral enclosure, Deverel-Rimbury pottery, 043201; LBA ranch-boundary ditch, 058182 etc.; IA or R settlement, 070180; R road, agger, 040208 etc.; R linear defensive earthwork, 'Bokerly Dyke', constructed c. 367 and c. 400 (?), 050187 etc.; barrows, 062184 etc.

Medstead. IA? fort, 658375; R occupation; barrow, 652378.

Meon Stoke. Mes site, 643205; N long barrow, 638196; IA 'A1'–'A2'? contour fort, 'Old Winchester Hill', 640206; R building, c. 618211; R occupation, c. 643205; bowl barrows, 641206 etc.; Celtic fields (ploughed), c. 635200; PN Sheardley, 635184.

Micheldever. IA? plateau fort, 'Norbury', 491401; R house, 531378; R coin-hoard, late 4C.; S cemetery; Med route, 'Lunway', 530363 etc.; barrows, 532368 and 527373; Celtic fields, 500370 etc.; PN in charter of 10C., 'ditch of the Frithelings'; PN Borough Down, 450372.

Michelmersh. N occupation, late Windmill Hill ware, 385261; EBA beaker 'B1' occupation, 385261; Belgic and late R occupation, Timsbury; R building, c. 384260; R coin-hoard; PN Timsbury, 'burh made of wood', 347246.

Milton. LBA barrel urn from barrow, c. 250935.

Minstead. EBA barrows (destroyed); LBA bucket urn; R road (destroyed); S linear earthwork (destroyed—Stoney Cross airfield); barrows, 218087 etc.; oval earthwork, Med?, 198089; earthwork, IA fort?, 278123.

Monk Sherborne. N axe of volcanic rock; R house, c. 603549; PN Kiln Green, 609563.

Morestead. N long barrow, c. 522256?; barrow, 525277.

Mortimer West End. R occupation; R road, agger, 635644 etc.; linear earthwork, 644647; circular earthwork, 627631.

Mottisfont. P implements, Dunbridge and Kimbridge; Med moot? c. 327270; PN Cadbury, 311275.

Mudeford. Barrow, 191929.

Nether Wallop. N long barrows, ploughed, 320383; LBA hoard; LBA? ditch, 326377 (air site); IA contour fort, IA 'B'? reconstruction of an 'A2' fort with subsequent Belgic re-use and occupation? 324377; storage pits? 324378; S? burial; barrow, 327377; oval barrow (ploughed), 323387; Celtic fields, 270360 etc.; earthwork, damaged, 261348; ancient tracks (air site), 326377 etc.; PN Heanbyrig.

Netley (455085). P implements, Acheulian; R coin-hoard, late 3C.

Netley Marsh. IA? fort, Tatchbury, 330144; R road, 330153 etc.: ancient track, 330147 etc.

New Alresford. IA occupation and S burials, c. 587316.

North Baddesley. EBA food vessel; linear earthwork? 390208 etc.

North Hayling. R buildings, c. 729032 and Havant Rd. brickfield; PN studfold.

Northington. Med deserted village, Swarraton, c. 570370; PN Totford, look-out place, 570380.

North Waltham. R house, c. 567458; barrow, 571446.

Nursling. IA fort?—surface indications; R settlement, Onna?; Med ridge and furrow cultivation in woodland at 'The Horns'; earthwork, 'The Walls', 358157.

Oakley. Barrows, 570486 etc., and 569517; Med castle earthworks, 566526.

Odiham. MBA pottery and occupation of IA 'AB', Belgic and R phases, farmstead, 727503; R house, 736526; Norman castle earthworks, 725519; Med park boundary bank, c. 724520 etc.; PN Warnborough, NOT from 'burh'; PN The Bury.

Old Alresford. N long barrow near Longwood House; R building, c. 582333 (at Pinglestone—reference to villa enclosure in Pingle?); R farmstead, c. 620370.

Old Winchester Hill. See Warnford and Meon Stoke.

Otterbourne. EBA 'B' beaker and Belgic pottery, c. 447244; R occupation, c. 460237; R road, agger, 457222 etc.; migration of village from c. 465225.

Overton. N long barrow, 507526; R house; barrows, 503474 and 496524 etc.; PN 'on entan hlew' 10C., 'giant's barrow'; PN Brickkiln, 510490.

Over Wallop. N long barrow, 251386; N flint mine, c. 250388; LBA ranch-boundary ditch, 240400 etc.; R building, c. 300380; R burials, Middle Wallop; barrow, 253404.

Owslebury. N long barrow, c. 534245; R road, agger, 523220 etc.; Med kiln; Med park-boundary bank? c. 510215; barrows, 526278; PN Owslebury, 10C., from burh (cf. Rowhay, 528218—reference to same enclosure?).

Pamber. R tile manufacture, c. 622595; R roads, 600600 etc., and from 595596 to 582540?; Belgic? linear earthworks, 623608 etc.

Penton Grafton. R house, c. 317490; R building, 318478.

Penton Mewsey. R house, c. 334474; barrows, 333473 and 332459.

Petersfield. Mes site on Heath; BA barrows (3 disc, 4 saucer and 14 bowl), 755225 etc.; R house, 725237.

Plaitford. Barrow with secondary and tertiary LBA cremations in Deverel-Rimbury urns, 273178; barrow with LBA cremations, bucket and globular D–R urns, c. 278188.

Popham. R house, c. 558433 and two other R occupation sites near; R building, c. 556428; R inhumations; Med deserted village, c. 558439; barrows, including bell and saucer type with ditch, the latter ploughed, 526439.

Porchester. Pre-Roman or R ditch of promontory fort (c. 620050 etc.?); R fort of Saxon shore, 625046; R inhumations, Paulsgrove; Norman castle earthworks, 625046.

Portsmouth. EBA beaker burial, Portsdown; MBA cremation of Wessex culture, 648066; LBA hoard; IA 'A' pottery, haematite-coated, 648066; S burials, 648066; Museum, Eastern Parade, Southsea.

Preston Candover. N long barrow; MBA cremation urns; R house, in Chapel Field, 598423; S inhumation, secondary, in long barrow.

Quarley. LBA ranch-boundary ditch, 260422 etc. (ploughed); IA 'A1' contour fort (haematite-coated ware), modified in 'A2' phase but unfinished; IA enclosure, c. 272442; R road, 273423 etc.; Celtic fields, 255420 etc. (ploughed).

Rhinefield. Mes site, 252986; LBA urn in barrow (destroyed); barrows, 256033.

Ringwood. Barrows, 182007 etc.; PN Bigsbury, 166078.

Rockbourne. N long barrows, 104204, 102222, 113227 and 090198; EBA barrow burial; LBA ranch-boundary ditch, 107230 etc.; IA 'A2' enclosure, c. 100203; IA 'A' haematite-coated ware; Belgic pottery, Rockbourne Down; R house, c. 118164; R farmstead and enclosure surrounding spring-pond, 107215; R coinhoards, Brookheath; round barrows, 107210 etc., etc. (many).

Romsey. P implements, Acheulian and Levalloisian; PN Luzborough, 375206.

Rowland's Castle. Belgic ditched enclosure, later R occupation, c. 752154; R house, Mayze Copse (c. 738100?); R coinhoard; Med castle mounds and baileys, 734105 and 725122; Med boundary bank, c. 725114 etc.; barrows, 734150; PN Dunsbury, 700098.

Rownhams. IA hill-fort, Toot Hill, 382187, later a look-out point; Celtic fields in Nightingale Wood.

St. Leonard's. Barrows, many, e.g. 127020.

St. Mary Bourne. IA 'A' occupation; R houses, c. 422499 and c. 413495; R? buildings, 418533, 432531 and c. 400501; R posting-station? of *Vindomis*? at Egbury, 439518, where is an earthwork enclosure yielding R occupation débris; R road, agger, 420500 etc.; R inhumations; Med and prehistoric river-crossing, Chapmansford, 430486.

Sarisbury (505087). MBA hoard; PN Sarisbury from *burh*?: earthworks at Sarisbury Green.

Selborne. Mes sites, c. 775368 and c. 773353; R pottery, c. 760333; PN Burhunt, 753328, from *burh*?

Shalden (697420). R sites at Manor Farm and Aylesfield.

Shedfield. Mes site, Sandy Lane Sandpit; R pottery kiln, c. 540129; R road, 560126 etc.

Sherborne St. John. R? square earthwork enclosures, 620561 and 623568; R road, 620562 etc.

Sherfield English. IA? fort, 313231.

Sherfield upon Loddon. R habitation site; migration of village? from c. 673567.

Shipton Bellinger. LBA ranch-boundary ditch, 250454 etc.; Belgic occupation, 244456; Celtic fields, 250460 etc.; ancient pond, 241460.

Silchester. IA South-eastern 'B' pottery; capital oppidum of Belgic *Atrebates*, coins A.D. 10–A.D. 40. Defences excavated at 638628; Belgic? earthwork defensive system, 630605 etc., 627617 etc., 635617 etc., and 635627; R tribal capital, walls surviving and amphitheatre, 644625; R roads converging on town; R kilns, c. 645625; earthwork, 619632; models and finds at Reading Museum.

Soberton. R building, c. 625155.

Sopley. N Graig Lwyd axe (or Shirley, Southampton?); barrows, 188003 etc.

Southampton. P implements, Shirley; R pottery, Freemantle; R road, agger, Freemantle Common; Saxon town, *Hamwih*, 430115 etc., occupation from 6C.? to 11C. Finds of pottery, glass, brick, cellars (?) etc. Med shire-moot, earthwork, c. 418153; PN *Thunres lea*, 11C., near Millbrook, pagan S shrine? Museum, Tudor House.

Southbourne. N occupation, Windmill Hill pottery; N long barrow? damaged, 166911; MBA cremations in urns under barrows (including one of Wessex culture), 179906, 172907, 166910 etc.; LBA bucket urns, secondary cremation interments in MBA barrows; LBA cremation in bucket urn, Iford; LBA bucket urns, Tuckton and Wick Lane; IA 'A1' promontory fort, Hengistbury (*Hednesburia*, 12C.) and prehistoric port, 164910—occupation in IA 'A', 'B', Belgic and R phases to 4C. A.D.,

172909 etc.; round barrow, 164922; PN Grimbury, 167916.

South Hayling. IA? plateau fort, Tunorbury, 732999; S pagan shrine? Tunorbury.

South Tidworth. LBA ranch-boundary ditch, 215486; R building? c. 255477; 'Seven Barrows', 219487.

South Warnborough. R building, c. 727459.

Southwick. Mes site; MBA cist burial, 619069; R road, agger, 654084 etc.; Med deserted settlement? Widley, c. 663070; early Norman earthwork, 640090; Norman castle mound and bailey (damaged), 638073; Med vineyard terraces of Priory, 629084; Med fishponds, c. 628085.

Sparsholt. EBA 'B1' beaker burial; IA site? c. 443316; R house, 414300; R occupation, c. 435297; R road, agger, 420294 etc.; R pottery kiln, c. 413294; Med deserted village? Lainston, 443316; barrows, 414293 etc.

Steventon. R building, Manor Park; Med deserted village? 551472.

Stockbridge. EBA 'B1' beaker burial under barrow; EBA 'B1' (degenerate pot) beaker burial, no barrow; MBA settlement site; MBA Wessex culture burials; LBA ranch-boundary ditch, 381350 etc.; barrows, 375347 etc.; Celtic fields, 382350 etc.; ancient tracks, 380347 etc. For Meon Hill see Longstock.

Stoke Charity. P? implement; Celtic fields, 482365 etc., and 493362 etc.

Stratfield Saye. Original site of village? c. 695615; PN Stanford, 628707 on line of R road, R ford?; PN Stratfield, reference to R road.

Stratton (540400). PN refers to R road.

Stubbington. P implements, c. 540022.

Sutton Scotney. R burial; S burial; barrows, 459369; Celtic fields, 454360 etc., and 442363 etc.

Swanwick. LBA/IA 'A' occupation and hoard, 502097; R occupation; PN Burridge, from *burh*?, 512108.

Sway. Bell barrow, 294986.

Sydmonton. Med village site? 485580— traces of fields; barrows, 482567.

Tadley. R road, agger, 611607 and 608604; migration of village from c. 597600?

Tangley. IA? fort, 'Bevisbury' in Bury Field, damaged and cut through by R road, 325541.

Thruxton. R house, 299461; Med manorial earthworks, 288456; ancient tracks, 290452 etc.

Titchfield. P implements (Acheulian and Clactonian) and Mes site, 530022; Med fish-ponds, 541067.

Tunworth (675485). R building, Sturts Copse.

Twyford. IA 'A2', 'AB' then Belgic farmstead, pond and lynchets (ploughed), 483267; R house, 481242; R occupation, c. 480233 and c. 485270; R road, agger, 505265 etc., and terraced c. 502273; Med parish-boundary ditch, 484273 etc.; 17C. mounds covering plague victims, 485273; cross-dyke and trackway, c. 485267; ancient tracks, 489276.

Upham. R buildings? c. 529205 and c. 540220; R road, agger, 529201; Med castle earthworks? 560210.

Upper Clatford. IA fort and annexe (ploughed) of 'A2', 'AB' and Belgic phases, Bury Hill, 345435; IA 'A1' haematite-coated pottery; IA 'A2' contracted burial; R occupation c. 375440; barrow and enclosures (ploughed), air site, 374439.

Upper Somborne. R building, 406311; Celtic fields, 400308 etc.

Vernham Dean. Ancient pond, *Throcmere*, 9C., 350588.

Warblington. R building, c 735052; Med castle earthworks, damaged, 730055.

Warnford. Mes site, c. 640206; IA hill-fort,

Old Winchester Hill, 640206; R occupation, c. 640206; S pagan shrine, Wheely, 11C., 610247; Med village site? 623226; barrows, bowl and pond (?), 607225 and 639207 etc.; ancient river-crossing, 623233.

Warsash, 495060. P implements; IA pottery.

Weeke. IA or R enclosure, lynchets and earthworks (air site), 458295.

West End (near Southampton). R house, c. 465165; barrows, 475148 etc.

West Meon. N long barrow? c. 646260?; LBA ranch-boundary ditch, 650254 etc.; R house, 632245; barrows, 624260 and 646260; PN Westbury, 652238, from *burh*.

Weston Corbett. Med shrunken village, 688470.

Weston Patrick. Med? square enclosure, c. 697447; IA or R farm, c. 700453 (air).

West Tisted. Barrows, 'The Devil's Jumps', 668633; earthwork, damaged, 668634; PN Brickkiln, 670296.

West Tytherley. R house, 259272; R occupation, c. 278315; PN Owl's Castle, 256326.

Weyhill. R building, c. 303476; R? road, 312470 etc.; PN Weyhill implies pagan S shrine—church on its site, 318467?; ancient route, Harroway, 323467 etc.

Wherwell. IA? rectangular enclosure (air site), 331386; R house, c. 370401; R? enclosure, rectangular, 334387 (air site); R? farmstead, earthworks, R finds, 345393 (air site); R pottery, 391409; Celtic fields, 347398 etc.; PN Rowbury, 347397, *Widianbyrig*, 10C.

Whitchurch. N long barrow, c. 480521; R road, agger, 457520 etc.; barrows, 464508 and 476517; PN Brickkiln, 483457.

Whitehill. Mes site near Woolmer Pond; LBA hoard; barrows, 790343; earthwork, 798343.

Whitsbury. N long barrow, 112227; IA? hill-fort, 128197; LBA ranch-boundary ditch runs beneath rampart of fort, 135187 etc., Grim's Ditch; PN Whitsbury from *burh*.

Wickham. R road, 599103 etc.; PN Rookesbury, 586117.

Wield. R house, c. 615385; earthwork, 623384; PN Godsfield, 600371, pagan S site?

Winchester. LBA bucket urns, St. Giles Hill and Fushfield; LBA ranch-boundary ditch, c. 485278 etc.; IA 'A1' occupation, 'A2' contour fort, 'AB' occupation, St. Catherine's Hill, 484276; IA 'A' occupation (haematite-coated ware) taken over by Belgae, 463283; IA pottery, c. 460293; Belgic extended inhumation and cremations; R tribal capital *Venta Belgarum*, first occupied by Belgae. Fragments of R wall in Med wall. R houses, streets, etc., within ramparts. R pottery, c. 460293; S burials, at various points round sity. Med earthwork, 484276; strip-fields in cultivation, 484278 etc.; earthwork at Oram's Arbour, 475297; barrow, 459280; maze, 485276; ancient tracks, 489277 etc. Museum, The Square.

Winchfield. R occupation, c. 750537; shrunken village? 768538.

Winslade (655480). P implements.

Wolverton. Original site of village, c. 550585?

Wonston. N long barrows, 472361 and 473361, ploughed round barrow between them; barrows, 475401, 495438 and 459369; earthwork, 452367; ancient route, Lunway, 490365 etc.; field-name, Devil's Ditch.

Woodcott.
  See Litchfield.

Woodmancott. R farmstead, Dunley Hill; shrunken settlement? 563425.

Woolmer. Mes sites near Woolmer Pond and near Longmoor; LBA hoard; R coin-hoard, 30,000 coins, deposited c. 300 A.D.;

barrows, 791317, 784323, 798322 etc.; PN Linchborough, 807332.

Wootton St. Lawrence. R house, 'Balchester', 579560; R building, c. 600530; Norman ring-and-bailey castle, 588555; barrow, 588513.

Worting. P implements; N long barrow, 612506; MBA cinerary urns, c. 600500; IA 'A2' plateau fort, Winklebury, haematite-coated pottery, 613528; R house, c. 623523; R cremations; R pottery, 613528; S burial; barrows, 598487 and 609512.

Worldham. IA 'AB' and 'B' pottery; R building and coin-hoard (late 3C.); Med earthwork, occupation from 13C., 756377; Med deserted village, 742361.

Yateley. LBA settlement and cemetery, bucket urns; Belgic cremations; R burial, 837605.

HERTFORDSHIRE

Abbots Langley. P implements, Bedmond; Belgic pottery; R house, 079022.

Albury. R occupation; PN Albury, 435248, from *burh*; traces of Med open fields in field called Dobbin Hall.

Aldbury. R building, c. 971136; earthwork, 956134; PN Aldbury, from *burh*; field-names, Mugborrow, 16C., from *beorg* and Bury, 15C., from *burh*.

Aldenham. R building, c. 151012; R tile manufacture, c. 151012; PN *Lusebyrge*, 11C., from *beorh* or *burh*?; PN Berrygrove, 15C., from *burh*?

Anstey. Med castle mounds and bailey and an enclosure, 404330; R? mound, 412329; PN Bury Farm, 411320.

Ardeley. R road, 320278 etc.

Ashwell. IA 'A' plateau fort, Arbury (*Eorthburh*), later Belgic occupation, 260387; R settlement, 'The Bury', 267400; R occupation, c. 285371; R coin-hoard, c. A.D. 185; S finds; barrow, 286379,

Highley Hill which was originally 'nine-barrows'; ancient track, Ashwell St., 280400 etc.; open fields enclosed 1858; PN Barrowsford Bridge; Museum, Swan St.

Aspenden (355285). Field-name 'Auberry', *Aldebere*, 13C., meaning 'old *burh*'.

Ayot St. Peter. R road? c. 220150 etc.; Med shrunken settlement? c. 213153.

Baldock. Belgic settlement; R settlement, 250340, cremation and inhumation cemetery, 'Walls Field', 253337; R cemetery, Hawthorn Hill; R road intersection, posting station; Romano-Saxon pottery; open fields until 20C.

Barkway. R shrine, 373358; Med castle mound and bailey, 373360; PN Burloes, 19C., from *burh*?; PN Whiteley, *Whitbarough*, 16C., ploughed barrows; field-name, *Farloe*, 15C., from *hlāw* (hill?).

Barley. R finds, 396383 and 400385; earthwork, c. 408371; PN Greenbury, 14C., from *burh*; PN Barley from *byrgen-leah* —'burial-clearing'.

Barnet. Med moated sites, 226975 and 244976.

Bayford (310085). Field-name, Brickkilns (*Brickell* 17C.).

Bengeo (320135). PN Flowersash Wood, 19C., from *flōr*?; PN Albury, 14C. from *burh*.

Benington. R finds, 298235; Med castle mound and bailey, 297237.

Berkhampsted. R occupation, c. 000105; linear earthwork, Grim's Ditch, 010092 etc.; Norman castle mound and bailey, 996083; PN Thunderdell, pagan S shrine? PN Brickkiln, 17C., 992104; field-names, Ditch Field and *Dedmancrofte* 17C.

Bishop's Stortford. R settlement, c. 486220; R road, 490220 and ford? 488220; Med castle mound and bailey, Waytemore, 490216; Med pottery kiln; PN Brick Kiln, 17C.

Bovingdon. R house and burials, c. 039058.

Braughing. Belgic oppidum, huts, coins, pottery, 387240; R town, 387240, and cemetery, c. 390240 etc.; R house and R? earthwork, 390250; R houses, 386256, 393236, and c. 390243; R posting-station at junction of 5 roads; R road, 400234 etc.; Med moot of Braughing Hundred, 391244?; earthworks, 400274, and Gatesbury 396240; field-names, *Studfold* 17C., *Caldbury* 13C., and *Brick Kiln* 17C.

Brent Pelham. R occupation and burials, c. 430310; Med castle mound, 425311; field-name, *Potters Croft*, 19C.

Broxbourne. Mes (Maglemosean) habitation site; Belgic pottery; R road, agger, 347073; R or post-R barrow, 356078; field-names, *Cokkabury* 15C., Low Field 13C., Tile Kiln Field 14C.

Buckland. R pottery; PN Burhill, 348323, probably from *būr* (house), moated site there; field-name, Money Field 13C.

Buntingford (with Layston). R brick in Layston Church, 369301; Med deserted village, Layston, 369301; PN Camp Wood, 19C., earthwork said to exist to west of this.

Bushey. P implements; R building, c. 143193.

Bygrave. R finds; R brick in church; Med manorial earthworks, c. 265355; common fields enclosed in 20C.; PN Bygrave, 10C., 'by the entrenchments', earthworks?

Caldecote. R occupation; R road junction? c. 229377; Med shrunken village, 237384.

Cheshunt. IA 'A1' potsherd, Turnford; R occupation; R road, agger, 344008; earthwork, 355047; linear earthwork? c. 322030; PN Aldbury, at site of R camp? 352030, which is also referred to in PN Cheshunt (*Cestrehunte* 11C.); PN Thunderfield, 18C., 340052—*Grymescroft* also in the parish and Grimes Brook suggest former occurrence of a pagan S shrine; PN Bury Green, 345018, manorial?; field-names, Black Dole 15C., and Sedcups 19C., the latter a look-out point.

Clothall. Belgic pottery; Med shrunken village? 272372; strip lynchets, 267329 etc. (open fields enclosed in 20C.); ancient track, 266320 etc.; PN Swamstey, *Qualmstowe*, 14C., 'place of killing' (execution?).

Codicote. R occupation, c. 238190; barrow, c. 207185; migration of village from 218187 to main road?; PN Houseberry, 19C.; PN Potters Heath 13C., 240183.

Colliers End. R road, agger, 372212 etc.

Cottered and Broadfield. R finds; R road, 320277 etc.; Med deserted village, Broadfield, c. 325310; field-name, Brixbury 17C.

Datchworth. R road, 260180 etc.; PN Bragbury, probably 'bracken hill', 269210; PN Godbury, 13C.; field-name Brickill, said to be an old brick kiln site.

Digswell. Med deserted village? emparkment, c. 238148.

East Barnet. Migration of village from c. 277946 on emparkment?

Eastwick (435117). Field-names, Brick Hill, 16C., meaning 'brick kiln'. In 14C. the village name is *Estwyk atte Flore*—see **flor**, p. 222–3.

Elstree. R finds, c. 195965; R tile-kiln and nearby clay-pits, 178955; R? brick in church; mound, c. 177955.

Essendon. Med moated site, 14C., 273097; field-name, Stamford.

Flamstead. R brick in church, 079146.

Flaunden. Migration of village from c. 009988? PN Shardlowe, 14C.; 'barrow with potsherds' or, better, 'a notched mound'; field-name, Deadman, 15C.

Furneaux Pelham (430280). LBA founder's hoard; R occupation; S burial; Med mootsite of Edwinstree Hundred probably in Meeting Field by the river Ash.

Gilston. Former site of village, c. 440136?; field-name Dunstable, *Dunstalls* 17C.,

from *tūnsteall*, 'farmstead'; field-name, Seeds Cup, 19C., a look-out place.

Graveley. Med deserted village, Chesfield, 246279.

Great Amwell (370125). R occupation; R pottery kiln?; barrow in Barrow Field; PN *Flemdyche* 14C., 'fugitives' ditch', the shire ditch; field-names, Ditch Field 14C., and Low Field 13C., from *hlāw*, 'hill or barrow'.

Great Gaddesden. P implements, Acheulian; R occupation, c. 042097; R brick in church; barrow, c. 050125; earthwork, c. 050125 (N.W. of barrow).

Great Munden. Med shrunken village? 355243.

Great Offley. R burials, 168264.

Great and Little Wymondley. Belgic pottery; R house, 205294; R occupation, 215286; R cremation cemetery, c. 216283; R building? 218271; R road, 205300 etc.; S occupation on site of R house, 205294; Med castle earthworks, 215286; Med castle mound and bailey within (R?) rectangular enclosure, 218271; Med earthwork, 219280; field-name, Crockwell 13C.

Harpenden. Belgic pottery, 143153; Belgic and R occupation, Crabtree Lane; R cremation burials and circular tomb in walled cemetery, c. 130135; R cremations, c. 150150 and S.E. of station; R building, Coldharbour, c. 140160; PN Kinsbourne Green, 114161, 13C., meaning 'Cyne's burial-place' (*byrgen*); field-name, Ditches 15C.

Hatfield (Bishops). R house, 237085; PN Stanborough, probably *beorg* 'hill'; field-name, Nine Hills, barrows?; field-name, Deadman's 19C.; field-name, Bowstrey 15C. from *burhsteall*, 'site of a *burh*'.

Hemel Hempstead. R house, 043059; R cremation; barrow, 072084.

Hertford. R pottery, Mangrove Hall; R road, agger, 349127 etc.; two S *burhs* of

A.D. 912 built, one between Maran, Beane and Lea, to the north of the Lea, and the other on the southern bank of the Lea (hence Hertingfordbury?) 310120; Med castle mound and bailey, 325125; Med manorial (and nearby village?) site, Brickendon, 330105; barrow, 348132; Museum, Bull Plain.

Hexton. Belgic pottery; IA hill-fort, Ravensbury, 100296; R occupation, 104293; PN Burwell, 'spring near the *burh*' (see above); PN Wayting Hill (i.e. watching), look-out point.

Hinxworth. EBA food vessel, c. 235395; R cemetery, c. 235395.

Hitchin. P implements; EBA beaker, 'A'–'C' type?; MBA battle-axe of Jutland type; LBA socketed axes of Breton type; LBA hoard; Belgic settlement, cemetery, c. 198309, and cremation, c. 186307; R settlement, coin-hoard of 2C., pottery kiln, finds 170290, cemeteries 170291 and 198309; R barrow, 205318; R brick in church, 184292; S burial, 7C.; strip lynchets in garden (destroyed?) 186290; PN Fibbery Field—originally 'five barrows'; PN Benslow, 16C., from *hlāw*; Museum, Paynes Park.

Hoddesdon. R settlement, c. 380105; R road, 347082 etc.; barrow near Hoddesdonbury; PN *Flemdiche* 14C., 'fugitives' ditch', the shire ditch.

Holwell. IA 'A1' pottery; R finds, c. 174335; PN *Shirediche* 14C., from 189327 to 201327?

Hormead. Migration of village from c. 400296 to main road?; PN Bummers Hill, R? mound, 399286; PN Mutfords, moot-place (?), 400283; PN Stonebury, manorial; PN Bradbury 17C., 392308; field-name, Albury 19C.

Hunsdon. Migration of village from 418127 on emparkment?; field-name, Moat Field 17C., motte (castle-mound) or moat?;

field-names, Brick Clamps etc., 422118, site of brick-making for Hunsdon Ho. in 1525 (field-name, Brykhill 16C.).

Ickleford. Belgic pottery; R coin-hoard and finds; barrows (3), c. 198320; ancient crossing of river Hiz by Icknield Way, 186317.

Ippollitts. R barrow, 187273; PN Wain Wood, 180255, and nearby Domesday Manor of *Welei* 11C., both probably from *weoh*, 'pagan temple'; PN Sperberry (*Speleburwe* 13C.), 'hill of speech', probably the moot of the Half-Hundred of Hitchin.

Kelshall. R cemetery at Deadman's Hill, barrows (air site), 297372; barrow, Gallows Hill, 301380; PN Orwell (Bury), 'treasure spring', i.e. one into which valuables were cast. This dried-up spring-pond is surrounded by earthworks of a deserted medieval settlement, 328368.

Kimpton (178185). R silver coin-hoard; field-name, Old Bury 19C.

King's Langley (073025). Belgic and R finds.

King's Walden. S cemetery, c. 157244; field-name, Cowditch, 13C.; field-name, Seedcotts 17C., look-out place.

Knebworth. P implements; R finds; R? barrows, 214209 and 217210; R road, 262182 etc.; PN Burleigh from *burh*, 223217; Med hundred-moot of Broadwater, c. 247221; Med deserted village? c. 231210, emparkment?

Letchworth. LBA cemetery, bucket urns; IA plateau fort, Wilbury (largely destroyed), IA 'A1', 'A2', 'AB' and 'C' occupation; IA 'C' ditch-circle, 200325; R posting-station, police post and settlement at junction of 3 R roads and Icknield Way; R barrow, 205318; S burial, 9C.; Museum, Town Square.

Lilley (118265). Field-name, Bury Hills 14C.

Little Amwell. R road, 349125 etc.; field-name, Barrow Field, barrow(s) said to exist here; PN Brickkiln Farm 15C.

Little Gaddesden (000135). Field-name, Streat Meadow, 17C., –R? road.

Little Hadham. R farmstead, c. 448207; moated mound, 453232; migration of village? from c. 447228.

Little Munden. Barrows formerly c. 330214; PN Cottonborough 16C., from *beorg*?; PN Potter's Green 14C., 352207.

Markyate. P implements; R occupation, c. 063166.

Meesden. R road, agger, 438321; migration of village from 439325?; PN Oxbury, 19C.

Nettleden. R building, c. 003019; Med pottery kiln, 13C. (cf. Potten End); shrunken Med village? 020105.

Newnham (245375). R finds.

Northchurch. R occupation, c. 960110; linear earthwork, Grim's Ditch, 953092 etc.

North Mimms. Med deserted village c. 222045; PN Brickkiln 19C.; field-name, Swineshead 14C., pagan S shrine?

Norton (232345). IA 'A2' sherd; R pottery.

Nuthampstead. (400350). Med moated site, c. A.D. 1200, unfinished.

Offley. PN Minsbury, 155275; PN Brickkiln Wood.

Oxhey. N? site; R building, c. 099940; Med track and paved causeway, 098937.

Pirton. IA 'A1' and 'AB'? occupation, 166323; IA 'A1' inhumation cemetery, Danes Field; R pottery; Toot Hill, 146316, later used as castle mound with attached bailey and fortified village (*burgus*, cf. Burge End); Icknield Way, 160304; earthwork (destroyed?) in Tingley Wood, c. 137305, which name probably implies an enclosure.

Puckeridge (387234). R road junction; moated mound, Rennesley Garden Wood.

Radlett. R finds, and pottery kilns, c. 162989.

Radwell (230360). R finds.

Redbourn. IA plateau fort, The Aubries (*Aldebury* 16C.), 095113; barrows excavated in 12C. (destroyed?); PN Flower's Farm, 100110, from *flōr*? (R brick in church implying a R building in neighbourhood); field-names, Burrows 17C., Castle Dell 18C., and Coopers Ditch.

Reed (365360). R occupation; six Med homestead sites in this parish.

Rickmansworth. P implements, Croxley Green; LBA founder's hoard; R building 070930; R occupation 097935 and 099929; Med manorial site c. 075933; field-name, Albury, 13C.

Ridge (213005). Field-name, Tilers Croft, 15C.

Royston. N long barrow, 341402; BA barrow; IA pottery; R settlement and burials; S secondary burial in barrow; S? inhumation cemetery; barrow, 333400; Mile Ditches, triple line across Icknield Way, 333400 etc.; cave, 356407.

Rushden. LBA hoard including winged axe; PN Cumberlow from *hlāw*, 301307.

Sacombe. R road, agger, 346198 etc.; shrunken settlement? c. 336194.

St. Alban's (see also St. Michael's, St. Peter's and St. Stephen's). Belgic frontier dykes, Beech Bottom, 154090 etc., and Devil's Ditch, 124086; R house, Park St. (see St. Stephen's); R city, *Verulamium* (see St. Michael's); R cremation cemetery, near Everlasting Lane; R coin-hoard of ?mid-5C.; Med town defences? Tonman's Dyke (destroyed?); field-name, Black Grounds, S.W. of R theatre.

St. Michael's. Belgic oppidum, Prae Wood, 125070 etc., earthworks with surrounding rampart; Belgic inhumation of c. A.D. 50; Belgic linear frontier, earthwork, Devil's Ditch, 122084 etc.; Roman city walls,

137066 etc.; R city gate foundations, 139067 (model in Museum); R house, wall foundations, pavements and hypocaust, 135068; R theatre, 134074; R kilns (cf. PN Potterscrouch, 13C., 116053, Med kilns?); R inhumation and cremation cemeteries; R road, Watling St., 126085 etc.; Romano-Saxon pottery 135069; Verulamium Museum, 137073.

St. Paul's Walden. R finds c. 185210.

St. Peter's (St. Alban's). PN *Brouneslowe* 13C., from *hlāw*, 197062.

St. Stephen's (St. Alban's). P implements, Clactonian type; EBA food vessel sherd, IA 'A2' sherds, Belgic farmstead (round hut) and R house, 147030 (Park St.) which was destroyed in A.D. 61 and A.D. 367; R cemetery, 142061; R tile and pottery kiln c. 129020; R fort? ditch of 1C. A.D., c. 143063; PN Burston 10C., 'stone belonging to the *burh*' of St. Alban's; PN Bury Dell, 17C.; field-name, Dead Woman's.

Sandon. R cemetery, c. 300330; Med lookout point or castle mound of 13C., later used as windmill tump, 329346; PN *Karkelawe* 13C., from *hlāw*.

Sandridge. P implements; Belgic earthworks; Beech Bottom Dyke, 160094 etc., The Slad, 188130 etc., Devil's Dyke, 183134 (parts of the Wheathampstead oppidum); R brick in church; S? burials.

Sarratt. R house in Church Field, c. 037992; R cemetery, 038984; Med homestead moat with inner rampart, c. 040005; PN Olleberie, *Aldebur'* 13C.

Sawbridgeworth. N secondary Rinyo-Clacton ware, Pishiobury; R settlement, c. 475135; Romano-Saxon pot; PN Spellbrook 'speech brook' 489175, moot-site?; PN Bursteads 478171 and Tednambury 481167; field-name, Potters Croft, 14C.

Shephall (255230). N dolerite axe; field-name Brickle, 19C. (brick kiln?).

Standon. R house and R barrows (see Thundridge); R occupation c. 370225; rectangular earthwork west of Fox Inn; Med castle earthworks, c. 370224; PN Potterscroft 14C.; field-names, Ragborough 13C. from *beorg* and Bustles 14C. from *burhsteall*.

Stanstead Abbots. R pottery; R brick in church?; R barrow, c. 380135; PN *Flemdyche* 14C. 'fugitives' ditch', i.e. the shire ditch; field-name, Moat 17C., moat or motte?; PN *Tyule* 12C.—'*leah* of the pagan god *Tiw*'?

Stevenage. R finds and cemetery (New Town); R barrows, The Six Hills, 237237; R road? 220255 etc.; Med village site, 240262; field-name, Woolwicks, site of farmstead, recorded from 11C. to 14C.

Tewin. Migration of village? from c. 268142; PN Tewin—sanctuary of pagan god *Tiw*?

Therfield. N inhumations in round barrow, 340403; MBA 'Five Barrows', 340403 (eight bowl barrows, in fact), cinerary urns holding cremations; MBA 'Money Barrow' (destroyed), cinerary urns; LBA hoard; R settlement; strip lynchets, 331376 etc.; Med castle mound, baileys and defensive enclosure of village; PN Tuthill Farm, 16C., look-out point.

Thorley. R occupation; Med deserted village: migration from 477189?; PN '*Sheire Ditch*', 17C.; field-names, Litel-aldebury 14C. and Castlecroft 17C.

Throcking. Shrunken medieval village, 338302.

Thundridge. R house, 374176, and barrows, 371177; Med deserted settlement, 368173; PN Thundridge probably means 'Thunor ridge'; a S pagan shrine may possibly be indicated by the field-name Harlow 17C., meaning 'temple (*hearg*) barrow or hill (*hlāw*)'; PN Burleigh, 15C., 385174; field-name, Black Lands, 17C.

Tring. R road, agger, 932112 etc.; linear

earthwork, Grim's Ditch, 930092 etc.;
Med deserted village, Pendley, c. 944117;
PN Betlow from *hlāw*.

Verulamium. See St. Michael's.

Walkern. R occupation and cremations;
field-names, Bury Close (*Eldebery* 14C.),
referring to 13C. castle mound and bailey,
305262; field-names, Low Croft, 16C.
(from *hlāw*?) and Black Land, 14C.

Wallington. BA barrow, Metley Hill (*Metelawe* 14C.) possibly 'hill of discourse'
(*maethel*), the original moot-site of Odsey
Hundred? 286352; R cemetery and coin-
hoard; open fields survived until 20C.;
PN Bury Wood, 19C.

Ware. EBA beaker; R occupation c. 345145;
'camp' by river, 372138. Is this Saxon or
Danish of A.D. 895 or of A.D. 912 (on the
latter, see Hertford)?

Watford. LBA-transitional IA 'A1' occupation; R occupation near Hamper Mills;
R tomb, c. 135003; Med hundred-moot
at Cassio Bridge; Museum, Hempstead
Rd.

Watton at Stone. R occupation c. 320185;
R road, agger, c. 310193; Med manorial?
earthworks, Chapel Wood, c. 307214; PN
Crowbury from *beorg* (hill?); PN Arbury
from *eorthburh*?; PN Blackditch Wood;
PN Loefield, 14C., from *hlāw* (hill?).

Welwyn. LBA hoard; Belgic settlement c.
232165 and occupation on site of secondary school, Welwyn Garden City; Belgic
occupation, round hut on site of R house,
238162 (Lockleys); Belgic princely cremations in vaults with much funerary furniture, 232160; R house, 231163; R house,
229163; R buildings, 232160 and 234164;
R kiln, 232160; R occupation at various
sites; R cremation cemetery, 232164; R
cemetery, The Grange; R cemetery, c.
255186; PN Danesbury, 19C., 233172;
PN Pottersheath, 13C., 238182; R road,
261181 etc.

Westmill. R finds; R road, 350258 etc.; R
brick in church; Med deserted village,
Wakeley, 341268; PN Studfold, 'just west
of an ancient camp'?; field-name Aulbury
(*Aldebere* 13C.).

Weston. N? finds c. 269303; R finds and
coin-hoard, c. 265300; R road, 283301
etc.; PN *Carkelawe* 15C. from *hlāw*; PN
Tilekiln 258282; field-name, White Ditch,
16C.

Wheathampstead. Belgic oppidum and
capital 185132 etc., defended by Devil's
Ditch (*headic* 11C., 'high ditch' and cf.
Dychefeld 15C.); R road, agger, 207142
etc.; S (or Frankish?) burial(s); Med
pottery kilns, 13C.; field-name, *Sette-
coppe* 13C., look-out point.

Widford. R occupation; Barrow Hill, castle
mound? 418169; two barrows 'west of railway'.

Wigginton. R? building, c. 950100; linear
earthwork, Grim's Ditch, 930093 etc.

Wilbury. See Letchworth.

Willian. M? BA inurned cremations; IA
'A2' occupation, Jacks Hill, 235297; R
burials.

Wormley. R road 347070 etc.

Wyddial. Field-name Primlow, 16C., from
hlāw, 374317.

KENT

Addington. Mes site, 652592; N chambered
long barrow, damaged, 653591; N chambered round? barrow, 'The Chestnuts'
653592; LBA founder's hoard; Med
village site? 653589; church on a mound?
653589.

Aldington. R buildings c. 072355; R cremations; R? barrow, 'The Mount',
055372; R? beacon, 071353; Jutish cemetery; Med deserted village, 081351 or
093352.

Alkham. PN Alkham, 256244, from *ealh* 'temple': pagan Jutish shrine?

Allhallows (840775). Two LBA hoards, including a winged axe; R occupation.

Allington. Belgic cremations; R buildings (several) c. 753579; R cremation cemetery; R coin-hoard, late 3C.; Jutish cemetery; Med 13C. yellow bricks in Castle, 753579; Med deserted village? c. 748577.

Appledore (957293). R? Rhee Wall; Danes captured a *burh* here in A.D. 892 (see Kenardington).

Ash (E. Kent). R occupation and burials; R road, agger, c. 292585 etc.; Jutish cemeteries behind Volunteer Inn and at Guilton, 280582.

Ash (W. Kent). R building and walled enclosure 609650; R building c. 606653.

Ashford. Belgic pottery; R (modified South-eastern 'B') pottery with cremations; R cremations and inhumations; R road 995406 etc.; Med kiln, 13C., at Potters Corner, 993447.

Ashurst (510390). Med? iron working.

Aylesford. P implements, Acheulian and Mousterian; N megalithic tombs, all denuded of barrows and usually the chambers damaged: Kit's Coty House 745608, Countless Stones 744604, White Horse Stone 753603, Coffin Stone 740600; large cist (destroyed) 753606; E or MBA cists with contracted inhumations; MBA inhumations of Wessex or related culture; LBA hoard of gold ornaments; IA South-eastern 'B' pottery in Belgic cemetery 729591; R building, 730609; R building c. 720600; R temple 749610; R cremations; R tomb c. 720600; R road 751605 etc.; S? pottery and brooch; rectangular earthwork c. 724565.

Bapchild. P implements, Mousterian, Levalloisian and Aurignacian; R occupation c. 940630; R cremations beside Watling St. (R road).

Barfreston. R burials; Jutish barrow inhumations, 261490 (Golgotha, 'place of a skull').

Barham. EBA beaker of 'B1' type; R finds, burial and late 2C. coin-hoard; Jutish barrow-cluster 206490; R road as terraceway, 223495 etc.; barrows 207514 and 213508; earthwork, lynchet or ancient road, 205516 etc.

Bearsted (800555). R? habitation; R cremations; PN Bearsted from *beorg* 'barrow'.

Beckenham. IA? occupation, Toot Wood; R road, 380680 etc.; PN Toot Wood, lookout point.

Bekesbourne. R burial vaults (originally wells) with cremations c. 185563; Jutish inhumations, Howletts and c. 205552; Jutish barrow burials c. 209553.

Benenden. R roads 812343 (agger) etc. and 802330 etc.; R paved ford 801323; PN Barrow, 844344.

Bethersden. R pottery, 910420; R road c. 950428 etc.; PN Tuesnoad (the god, *Tiw*?), pagan S shrine?, 910420.

Betteshanger. R pottery c. 315525; R road, agger, 311527 etc.; Med shrunken settlement? 312525.

Bexley. P implements, Wansunt; N Langdale stone axe; R? building c. 514745; R pottery near Bourne House; R cremations c. 477745, and inhumations.

Bexley Heath (490747). N hoard of axes; LBA founder's hoard; LBA gold hoard.

Bidborough. PN from *beorg* 'natural hill'?

Biddenden. R? cremations c. 849400; Med? ironworking (cf. PN Hammer Mill 821383); PN Rat's Castle, 843361.

Birchington. LBA settlement, Minnis Bay, submerged; IA pottery; R occupation, Minnis Bay; R cremations and inhumations; R ritual shaft; R pottery c. 310684.

Bishopsbourne. R barrows and enclosure (air sites), Bourne Park; R barrows, cists exposed, 172520 etc.; R cremations and inhumations, 183533; Jutish barrows (air sites), Bourne Park; Jutish barrow burials excavated in 18C. and 19C. elsewhere.

Bonnington. Med village site? c. 057344.

Borden. IA occupation, Babs Oak Hill; R buildings c. 880620 and an inhumation; R walled cemetery, cremations and inhumations beside Watling St. (R road).

Borough Green. IA 'A', Belgic and Patch Grove pottery; Belgic cremation c. 603566; R cremations 609577 and c. 605573; pottery kiln of 16C.; PN Borough Green?

Boughton Aluph. Med shrunken village? 033482.

Boughton Malherbe. R road, 870466 etc.

Boughton Monchelsea. IA hill-fort, much damaged; R bath-house, 779515 and cremations and inhumations; R walled cemetery (destroyed) 776522; R road 780516 etc.

Boughton under Blean. EBA beaker, c. 040590; S? burial.

Boxley. R occupation: cremations 787564, 755584 and c. 747587; R? brick in Abbey; Med shire-moot, Pennenden 778574; PN Tunbury 763622.

Brasted, (470550). P implement.

Bredgar. R brick in church 880603.

Brenchley. Norman castle mound 692428; Med? ironworking, hammerponds 693410 and 660407.

Bridge. R inhumations c. 186537; Jutish barrows? c. 185538 and cemetery? 183546.

Broadstairs (and St. Peter's). N working-floor near Dumpton; EBA? crouched inhumations within double ring-ditch; IA 'A1' occupation, 397666; Belgic settlement, 397666; Belgic and early R cremations together; R settlement c. 390695; R inhumations and cremations; Jutish inhumation cemetery and two single burials.

Bromley. See Keston.

Buckland. MBA hoard; R finds, occupation and burials; original site of village 975627?

Burham. R buildings, 725617 and 714624; R subterranean (Mithraic?) shrine 714625; R burials; R road 747625 etc.; original site of village 717620?; PN Burham from *burh*.

Burmarsh. Deserted village of Eastbridge? 074321 and Orgarswick 084306; PN Burmarsh means 'marsh of the citizens of the *burh*, (i.e. Canterbury).

Canterbury. P implements; N Breton jadeite axe and an axe of Scandinavian type; EBA 'B' beaker; IA 'A' occupation; Belgic occupation; R city, walls and part of gate (153578); R houses and theatre; R coin-hoards; R pottery and tile kilns; R cemeteries, seven known beside roads radiating from city; R burial mounds, one (mutilated) surviving, 148574; S occupation 5C onwards, R influence in some pottery; Anglo-Frisian ware of 5C.; Med pottery kiln, 13C.; monolith at W end of St. Pancras church; Royal Museum, High St.

Capel (W. Kent). Med? earthworks, Castle Hill; PN Tatlingbury, 638450.

Capel le Ferne (250390). EBA beaker 'A' burial; R inhumation.

Chalk. R occupation, inhumations, kilns etc. c. 685729.

Charing. R finds c. 930493; PN Burleigh.

Chartham. R? burials, c. 093560; Jutish barrows, over a hundred (destroyed), 107542 etc.

Chart Sutton. R occupation c. 802495; R cremation; R road, 789500 etc.; PN Dunbury 791463; PN Devil's Den, 800473.

Chatham. R buildings c. 760680 and at Borstal; R inhumation cemetery at 'The Brook'; Jutish barrow burials, 767680; earthwork (air site), Denge Wood; ancient fields (air sites) near Capstone and Hempstead; PN Upbery.

Chelsfield (480640). Mes occupation.

Cheriton (205370). Belgic cremation cemetery, 188360; R finds; Jutish burial.

S

Chilham. N long barrow of Wessex type, Windmill Hill ware and axe of Scandinavian type, 077532; IA 'A', Belgic and R occupation, 077532; R coin-hoard, late4 C.; R occupation 065535; Norman castle mound 065535; circular earthwork 076530.

Chislehurst. R finds c. 437699; earthwork, cockpit, 441706; PN Scadbury, 455703, from *burh*.

Chislet. EBA 'B' beakers, two; R pottery; Jutish burial, Grove Ferry; PN Puddledock 229636.

Cliffe at Hoo (735765). LBA founder's hoard; R occupation, pottery and cemetery; S burials.

Cobham. IA South-eastern 'B', Patch Grove pottery; IA fort, 686694, Belgic tribal centre?; R coin-hoard, mid-4C.; R road, 690696 etc. (beside modern road); R brick in church; Med hundred-moot of Shamwell Hundred at 660697; destroyed megalithic monument, Battle St.

Coldred. R pottery; R? cremations c. 278478; Med hundred-moot of Bewsborough (PN from *beorg*); rectangular earthwork surrounding church, 276476.

Cooling. IA or R Red Hills, R pottery and foundations, c. 765765; R kiln c. 760760.

Cowden. R ironworking c. 445387; R road 454424 etc.; Med ironworking 453399.

Cranbrook. Mes implements c. 797363; R road 799362 etc.; Med or later ironworking; PN Glassenbury, 13C., 750365.

Crayford. P implements including Mousterian; P, Levalloisian knapping site; IA 'A2' occupation followed by South-eastern 'B', Patch Grove, Wealden and Belgic, 513751; R settlement, pottery etc., c. 520756 and 520763 and burials.

Crundale. IA 'A' pottery; R inhumations and cremations, 066495; R building, 086486; Jutish inhumation cemetery, 066495; Med deserted village? c. 086486.

Cuxton. R occupation c. 705664 and elsewhere; R building 709664.

Darenth. R house, originally a farm, later a dye-works? 563707; R cremation.

Dartford. P implements, Abbevillian, Acheulian and Levalloisian, Dartford Heath; P skull, Galley Hill; N? occupation, Dartford Heath; LBA founder's hoard; late IA pottery; R settlement, building c. 546749, pottery kilns c. 504705, cremations at Joyce Green, inhumations at East Hill; R gateway from Farningham re-erected in Central Park; S or Jutish settlement and burials, Littlebrook Walls; S inhumation, Powder Mills; Med tile-making; PN Lowfield St.; Museum, Market Place.

Deal. MBA crouched inhumation with food vessel; LBA occupation, ring-ditch, hearths, daub and pottery c. 365510; IA 'A' occupation c. 365510 and 363510; Belgic occupation, kiln? and cremations c. 360510; R occupation c. 376543 and cremations; R coin-hoards, mid-3C.; Romano-Jutish pottery; Jutish burials, Mill Hill.

Detling (790580). Belgic and R occupation.

Ditton (710580). R occupation; PN Ditton from *dīc*, 'ditch'.

Doddington. R occupation; PN Frangbury 937561.

Dover. EBA beaker 'B' type; MBA? cinerary urn; Belgic occupation; R fort of the Saxon shore and settlement; R cremation cemeteries c. 317412 and c. 315416; R lighthouse and surrounding earthwork, 326418; R lighthouse, fragment, 'The Bredenstone', 314408; R road? 295407 etc.; Jutish inhumations, Priory Hill and Old Park; Dark Age pottery; Dark Age tombstone with runes, St. Martin's; Norman and Napoleonic earthworks, The Castle; barrows 295416; earthwork round church, 327418; Museum, Ladywell.

Dunkirk. PN Fishpond Wood, 090583.

Dymchurch (100290). R occupation near Dymchurch Wall—pottery works? and salt-making.

East Barming. R buildings, 721541 and c. 726540; R walled cemetery, cremations, c. 723543; R cremations c. 726544; migration of village? from 720543.

Eastchurch. PN Berryfields 999722; PN Warden 022719, look-out point.

East Farleigh. R occupation c. 753527, at Combe St. and near Medway; R cremations c. 753527, 729524 and at Bydews.

East Langdon. R pottery c. 340464.

East Malling. Mes site; N Rinyo-Clacton pottery; R building, c. 700560; R cremation cemetery c. 702589; Jutish cemetery.

East Peckham. Site of Med village? c. 662522.

Eastry. R ritual shaft; Jutish burials 310544; Jutish barrow cemetery; barrows 291528; earthwork 287528; lynchets? at 'The Lynch' 314546; PN Statenborough 315556.

East Studdal (320495). R cremation.

Eastwell. Line of ridgeway 014474 and 019471, bordered by lynchets of Med open fields?; site of village? c. 010474, emparkment?

Edenbridge. R cremations c. 433461; R road 452430 etc.; moated site, 'Devil's Den' 438452; PN Stanford, near R road, 450445; PN Greybury 438427.

Egerton. R road 880459 etc.; barrow S.W. of Steed House; PN Potters Forstal 890468.

Elham. P implements, Acheulian; EBA occupation site; R finds, many; Med deserted village? Acrise 195425, emparkment; PN Henbury 196445; PN Greenacre (Grim—13C.), pagan S site?

Erith. EBA beakers of 'B2' or 'C' type; R occupation c. 485810; R brick in church; R dock? c. 480788; Museum, Walnut Tree Rd.

Eynsford. R brick in Castle and Norman earthwork 542658; PN Crocken 505670.

Farnborough. Mes? site; PN Farnborough 444641 from *beorg*, 'hill'.

Farningham. R house and bath-building 545667; R house 548677; R buildings 555674 and 555677; R camp? with occupation débris 547667; R camp? Gills Wood; S (or Jutish burial) c. 557667.

Faversham. Belgic settlement; R settlement (*Durolevum*?) 005618; R building on site of church 018616 and at Black Lands c. 035609; R cremations and inhumations; Romano-Saxon pot; Saxon and Jutish cemetery 013609 etc. (See Ospringe.)

Fawkham (597680). IA? farmstead, crop marks (air site).

Folkestone. N Peterborough pottery; EBA beaker; Belgic occupation (beneath R house) 241370; Belgic cremations 221365 and 241370; R houses 241370; R building and inhumations c. 240369; R cremations 214380; Jutish cemetery 235377 and a Jutish? cremation at The Bayle; Jutish barrow 209380; Norman castle earthwork, 'Caesar's Camp' 214380 on site of earlier burial mound; Museum, Grace Hill.

Foots Cray (480710). P knapping-floor; N? occupation.

Fordwich (180598). P implements, Abbevillian; R settlement.

Frindsbury. P implements, knapping-floor, Mousterian; LBA bucket urns; R house and inhumations c. 749693 and cremations c. 756738; PN Frindsbury from *burh*.

Frittenden. R pottery c. 800400; R? brick in church, 813409.

Gillingham. P implements, Mousterian; R occupation sites; R cremations c. 779697, at Barnsole Lane and Burnt Oak; R coinhoard, late 4C; Jutish? burials; PN Gadshill, pagan Jutish site?; Museum, Woodlands.

Godmersham. R pottery; Jutish finds, Crundale; Celtic fields 055513 etc.

Goodnestone, near Faversham. R occupation c. 030624; Jutish burial c. 032625.

Goudhurst. MBA hoard; Med or later ironworking; PN Kilndown 700350.

Grain (890770). R inhumations, Slough Fort; R kiln, Grain Marshes.

Graveney (055630). R cremations; PN *Ealhfleot* 9C.—pagan Jutish site near?

Gravesend (650740). N? site near New House Farm; late IA pottery; R cremation, King's Drive and other R finds elsewhere; Museum, New Tavern Fort.

Great Chart. R road, 980413 etc.

Great Mongeham (350515). R occupation and cremations; Jutish burial.

Greenhithe (585750). P implements; R occupation and burials in chalk cave (destroyed).

Guston. R inhumations; R road 316446 etc.; barrow 334449.

Hackington. Prehistoric occupation and earthworks c. 137599; R kiln c. 150588; Med pottery manufacture, 13C., near Tyler Hill (N.B.—The PN in this connection).

Hadlow. R occupation c. 635510 and c. 637502.

Halling. Late P site, implements and crouched skeleton; R inhumation cemeteries c. 692642 and c. 707663; ancient track 695650 etc.

Halstead (490610). R occupation.

Harbledown. Belgic oppidum with multiple banks and ditches, Bigbury 117577, traversed by 'Pilgrim's Way'. Pottery with IA 'A' influence, IA 'B' pedestal urns and Wealden foot-ring pots. Many Belgic finds of metal and pottery.

Harrietsham (870530). Late Jutish burial.

Hartley (605670). R house? near Scotgrove.

Hartlip. R buildings c. 827637 with S pot showing R influence and a R inhumation.

Harty. LBA founder's hoard; R occupation 015661.

Hawkhurst. 17C. ironworking; PN Potter's Farm, 764328.

Hayes. N? settlement, hut circles 399652; R building on site of church 405663; R building near Baston Court.

Headcorn. PN Hawkenbury 805451; PN Tattlebury 829455.

Herne Bay. P implements; R fort of the Saxon shore, Reculver (*Regulbium*), 227693, bases of walls; Belgic and R finds from fort; Jutish finds, Reculver; PN Hillborough 210680 (13C. *Halybergh*, 'holy hill or barrow')—pagan Jutish site? Museum, High St.

Hever. PN Harborough 482470.

Higham. LBA founder's hoard; R cremation and inhumations 717741 etc.; S cremation cemetery; PN Barrow Hill 710747; Belgic coin-hoard.

High Halden. R road 900360 etc.; PN Potkiln 899393, recent pottery manufacture.

High Halstow. R pottery manufacture? c. 780790.

Hoath. P implements; R cremations, Ford; Jutish burial.

Hollingbourne (845550). Mes site, LBA barrows and Jutish barrow cemetery, all at Whiteheath.

Holwood. See Keston.

Hoo St. Werburgh. R occupation c. 783713 and cremations c. 790715.

Horsmonden. Med double concentric moats 715392; ironworking, Furnace Pond 695410.

Horton Kirby. R cremation in cist; S cemetery c. 568693; Jutish cemetery, Riseley.

Hougham. R pottery 297403; R burial and coin-hoard; R road? 285404 etc.

Hunton. R cremation; rectangular earthwork, Amsbury, 734509.

Hythe. R burials, North Rd.; R and Med harbour c. 126343; Jutish cemetery?; late S site, *Sand tun*, West Hythe; Museum, Oaklands.

Ickham. R building, Church Oare Field 229581; R occupation and Jutish cemetery 196567.

Ightham. P implements; P rock shelters, 584565; Mes site c. 587544; N knapping-floor, Rose Wood; EBA 'B' beaker burial, Ightham Common; IA hill-fort, Oldbury, 582561, IA South-eastern 'B', Patch Grove ware and Wealden ware—Wealden culture fort seized by Belgae; late IA settlement near Patch Grove c. 583574 with later occupation in R period; R occupation 595569; R cremations 594575 and 587543 etc.; R pottery from many sites in parish.

Ivychurch. R? drainage channel and sea wall (Rhee Wall) 010266.

Iwade. R pottery 881698; mounds between village and Kingsferry, near road.

Kemsing. R building c. 544585.

Kenardington. Earthwork round church 975323, Danish *burh* of A.D. 892–3?

Kennington (030450). R inhumation, Sandhurst Farm.

Keston. P implement; N knapping-floor, greenstone axe; IA contour fort, damaged, 422639; IA? promontory fort, c. 416640, cattle enclosure subsidiary to hill-fort?; R settlement c. 420640; R inhumation cemetery; R buildings and tombs (one circular and one rectangular) in Lower Warbank Field, 413632.

Kingsdown. Pagan S cemetery?; migration of village? from 580634; PN High Castle Wood 560625; PN Goodbury 557607.

Kingsnorth. R road 006400 etc.

Kingston. Jutish cemetery originally with 263 barrows and 45 flat graves 202518.

Lamberhurst. Ironworking 17C.–19C., cf. Furnace Mill 661362 and Furnace Wood 635373.

Langley. R walled cemetery with cremations, tombs and cists 777523; R road 778520 etc.

Leeds (825534). Jutish burial?

Lenham. Ruined megalithic monument? 899522; R brick in church.

Leysdown. R lime kiln c. 053680.

Lillechurch (729730). Originally a village?

Linton. PN Burford 738492.

Littlebourne. LBA bucket urns; R road, agger, 200578.

Little Chart. R bath-house c. 940445 and cremations 943469; site of Med village? c. 934466.

Longfield. IA occupation, Hartley; R pottery in denehole c. 603690.

Loose. R cremations 762537.

Lower Halstow. Mes (Maglemosean) occupation contemporary? with N occupation 870680; Belgic pottery; R house 859675; R buildings c. 860664; R pottery manufacture 860695 and 865685; R pottery 853663; R cremation.

Lower Hardres. R building, Heppington (c. 148538?).

Luddenham. R building near Elverton Lane; shrunken village? 993633.

Luddesdown. R pottery c. 665668.

Lullingstone. IA hill-fort, Hulbury 520659: IA 'A' pottery, South-eastern 'B' pottery, Wealden and Patch Grove wares, Belgic and R pottery; Belgic? cultivation banks centring on Hulbury; R house, 529651, preceded by Belgic occupation. Later, Christian chapel (c. A.D. 350–400); S burials; Med abandoned village (A.D. 1412), site 530651?

Luton. R foundations c. 770660; R cremations.

Lydd (045210). R earthwork, track and 2C. pottery, Lydd Rype.

Lydden. R road as terraceway, c. 272453 and c. 258455.

Lyminge. R building beneath church 161408; Jutish cemetery 169417.

Lympne. R fort of Saxon shore (PN Stutfall, 14C.), wherein are re-used materials from an earlier R building on the site, 117342; R harbour c. 124343?; Jutish burials near fort.

Maidstone. EBA 'B' beakers, Tovil and Lower Fant; IA South-eastern 'B' pottery; Belgic pottery; R settlement; R houses c. 766549 and 758563; R building c. 755547; R cremation and inhumation cemeteries, Westborough and Tovil; R pastoral enclosure, much damaged, 774527; R coin-hoard; Jutish inhumations; Med lathe-moot of Shepway at 774537?; Med kiln site? Week St.; Museum, Faith St.

Manston. IA settlement: 'A', early 'B', South-eastern 'B' and Belgic pottery with traces of huts on airfield extension; R inhumations; Jutish barrow cemetery c. 355652; PN *Thunores hlaew*, 'Thunor's barrow'; PN Ozengelt 357656, pagan site?

Marden (745445). LBA hoard.

Margate. IA settlement: 'A', 'AB' and Belgic pottery; R house c. 350700; R occupation near St. Peter's Church; Belgic and R pottery kiln; R occupation in chalk cave; R inhumations and cremations; Jutish cemetery, Shottendean and Jutish burial, Northdown; Museum, Victoria Rd.

Mark Beech (474428). R? camp near church (destroyed?).

Mereworth. R occupation c. 668533.

Milton Regis. N Peterborough occupation 905666; BA pottery; R posting station?; R house 909656; R occupation 904666 etc.; R cremations and inhumations; R? enclosure round church; S and Jutish? cemetery; Danish *burh* of A.D. 892 at 917659.

Minster in Sheppey. R brick in church 957730; R cremations.

Minster in Thanet. LBA founder's hoard; R brick in church 311642; R cremation cemetery 310656; R coin-hoard, mid-2C.;

Jutish burial? c. 315655; strip lynchets? 323667; Med sea wall 300632 etc.; PN Thunor's Pit c. 311654, pagan S site?

Monkton (290650). Med occupation, Monkton Marshes.

Murston. IA 'A' occupation; Belgic pottery; R cremations and inhumations 922641, c. 923653 and c. 920640; Jutish burials.

Nettlestead. IA hill-fort, damaged, 673507.

Newchurch. Med deserted settlements, Blackmanstone, c. 070296 and Eastbridge 075322.

Newenden. Med motte and bailey, the latter possibly pre-Norman, 853284.

Newington (near Hythe). R? camp near Beachborough 169381; Jutish burial, Milkey Downs; barrows 160384.

Newington-on-the-Street. R occupation, Boyse's Hill; R burials in Crockfield; R brick in church 862654.

Newnham. EBA food vessel? Frith; Jutish? burials c. 955580.

New Romney. Med deserted settlements, Orgarswick 084307 and Hope 049258; PN Crockley 062246.

Nonington. PN Easole 260520—pagan Jutish sanctuary?

Northbourne. IA 'A' occupation, Finglesham; R occupation and cremations 335531; R pottery, Updown; R road 311520 etc.; Jutish inhumation cemetery c. 326535.

North Cray (483717). P implements.

Northfleet. P knapping-floor, Levalloisian; P skull; Mes floors, two, superimposed, Ebbsfleet valley; N Peterborough (Ebbsfleet) pottery; LBA winged axe; R occupation 619725 and 625721; R industrial building, Baker's Hole; R inhumations 623727; R brick in church; S cremation and inhumation cemetery 620740; S rusticated ware and Saxo-Frisian pottery 619738. See Southfleet.

Norton. Jutish burial?; original site of village? before emparkment? 967613.

Oare (005630). R cremations.

Old Romney. Med deserted village? Midley 031232; R brick in church.

Orpington. N pottery of Danish passage-grave type—origin doubtful; IA South-eastern 'B' (Patch Grove) ware; Belgic and R pottery, Bellefield Rd. and? c. 470680; Belgic and R pottery from R house 454658; R cremations Green St. Green and High Field.

Ospringe. P implements?; South-eastern 'B' (Patch Grove) ware from R cemetery; Belgic pottery; R settlement (*Durolevum*?): R square earthwork 994610; R occupation 996611 and 999610; R huts c. 992613; R cremation cemeteries 988607, 002610 and 995612; R road traceable in Park; Med deserted village? c. 000604; Museum, Maison Dieu.

Otford. IA promontory fort, Belgic? in Hillydeal Wood; South-eastern 'B' (Patch Grove) ware from R house 536593, from 512593 and 515593 where there was R occupation; R building and earthwork (destroyed) 539603; R occupation, 515593, 529592 and 523592; barrow? Otford Mount.

Otham. Migration of village? from c. 790540.

Patrixbourne. S and Jutish burials 188549.

Pembury. N hoard of axes; site of Med village? c. 625430; PN Pembury 627406 (*burh*).

Penshurst. IA pottery (late type) c. 505463.

Petham. Belgic settlement and cemetery 130529; R inhumation and cremations; cross-ridge dyke, Deadman's Bank (on line of main ridgeway?) 130533.

Plaxtol. R buildings, tile manufactory, 614533; R walled cemetery, cremations and inhumations, and a barrow, and including a cremation with South-eastern

'B' pottery, c. 610543; PN Rat's Castle 630530.

Pluckley. R road 930438 etc.

Preston-next-Wingham. P implements; R pottery kiln and cremations 238598 etc.; S pot with R influence.

Queenborough. PN Barrows Hill 922720. Q. created a 'borough' in 14C., hence PN.

Rainham. IA settlement; R occupation c. 827680 and c. 820673; R occupation and cremation cemetery c. 815677; Jutish cemetery; PN Meresborough 820642; PN Motley 827684.

Ramsgate. LBA occupation and an inhumation; R occupation c. 373646 and c. 373657; R cremations c. 377643 and elsewhere; R inhumations c. 390655 and elsewhere; R coin-hoard; Jutish burials c. 377643.

Reculver. See Herne Bay.

Richborough. IA 'A' pottery and ditches 324602; R base of A.D. 43, ditch 324600 etc.; R monument c. A.D. 100, surrounded by ditches and converted as look-out tower c. 250 and ditches levelled (though now excavated) c. 273; R stone fort of Saxon shore (*Rutupiae*), c. A.D. 290; R amphitheatre (Littleborough 16C.) 321598; R civil settlement mainly on E. and S.E. sides of fort; Romano-Celtic temples of c. A.D. 300 at 323597; R inhumations and cremations; line of R causeway? 310604 etc.; R coin-hoards including some of post-A.D. 400; Romano-Saxon pot; Saxon and Jutish inhumations; Museum at fort.

Ringwould. MBA bowl barrows, chalk cists, one of Wessex cultural affinity, 365470 etc.; LBA cremation cemetery, bucket urns, Kingsdown; Jutish burials; Med deserted hamlet, Oxney, c. 355469; strip lynchets, The Lynch, 364477 etc.

Ripple. N? knapping-floor c. 360500; EBA beaker, Ripple Bottom; R cremations and inhumations; earthwork 350503.

Rochester. Belgic occupation; R town, *Durobrivae*, 742683; R wall fragments, Eastgate House, Esplanade etc.; R cemeteries: cremation 741686 and Watts Ave., inhumation c. 730670; S or Jutish burials 738689; Danish *burh* (protective siege work) in 884; Norman castle mound 741685; Museum, Eastgate House.

Ryarsh. Migration of village from c. 672591?

St. Margaret's-at-Cliffe. LBA occupation; R cremation cemetery; Jutish burial mounds near South Foreland; Jutish cemetery; barrow 369462.

St. Mary Cray. IA South-eastern 'B' (Patch Grove) ware with R pottery c. 466676; Patch Grove ware c. 470675; R occupation c. 470680; R coin-hoard, mid-3C.

St. Paul's Cray. R brick in church; PN Scadbury 460702, from *burh*.

Saltwood. LBA founder's hoard; R building c. 145358; R cremation; Jutish burial; barrows 159384; castle earthworks 161359; earthworks? 140368 etc.

Sandhurst. R road, 793292 etc.

Sandwich. R pottery and ritual pit; PN Archeslo (*Ercleslawe* 13C.) from *hlāw*.

Sarre. R cremations; S and Jutish cemetery; sea wall, R?, 248643 etc.

Seal. Mes site and BA cremation in barrow near Hillingdon Ave.; R cemetery 561532.

Seasalter. Med village site? c. 093647; PN means 'salt-house by the sea', 9C.

Sellindge. PN Barrowhill 110372.

Selling. Earthwork 042554.

Sevenoaks. Former glassmaking c. 528520; Museum, The Drive.

Shadoxhurst. R road 970385 etc.

Sholden. IA 'A' occupation and ditches, Sholden Bank; R occupation c. 356529; R cremations, Sholden Bank.

Shoreham. R bath-building 523623; PN Dunsteall (*tūn steall*?) earthwork? 535613.

Shorne. R pottery kiln c. 699737 and occupation c. 695700; PN Gadshill, 707707, pagan S site?

Sibertswold. R cremations and Jutish cemetery, many barrow inhumations, 262490; R road 240474 etc.

Sittingbourne. N axe from Northern Ireland; EBA beaker-'B1' inhumation in cist with bracer and dagger; LBA founder's hoard; R settlement: cemeteries c. 905625, c. 893640, c. 917630, at Bexhill and at Highsted (908620) where a Romano-Saxon pot was found; R walled cemetery with circular brick tomb; Jutish cemetery, Bell Rd. and Fair Meadows; earthwork (destroyed?) at Bayford.

Smarden. R pottery c. 898421.

Snodland. P implements 700607 etc.; R house in Stone Grave Field 707620; R barrow, Holborough (destroyed), 699627, primary cremation, secondary inhumations; Jutish burials 699627.

Southfleet. R posting-station of *Vagniacae*? 618725 etc.; R occupation 615725 and 617724 and in One Tree Field; R pottery kiln 614726; R walled cemetery with rectangular stone tomb c. 616725; IA South-eastern 'B' (Patch Grove) ware; S? burial; barrow 598716. (See also Northfleet.)

Speldhurst. PN Crockers Hatch 538389.

Springhead. See Southfleet.

Stalisfield. PN Redborough 955534; shrunken village? 968524.

Staplehurst. R road 785460 etc.; Med castle mound 784406.

Stockbury. Med castle mound and bailey 847616; migration of village from 848616?

Stodmarsh. BA cinerary urn; R pottery c. 221605; Jutish barrow burials 230599.

Stoke. LBA founder's hoard; R pottery; earthwork enclosure c. 820751.

Stonar (335595). R finds; Med port.

Stone (near Faversham). R brick in church 992614; Med deserted village 992614?

Stone (near Dartford). Belgic settlement and cremations 574744; R building 586713; R cremations and inhumations c. 584740; R cremations, pottery including derived South-eastern 'B' type, 567751; R pottery kiln c. 590728.

Stone-cum-Ebony (930280). R occupation; S *burh* stormed by Danes when half built, A.D. 892; Med lost settlement of Ebony?

Stourmouth. R brick in church 257629.

Stowting. R finds; R coin-hoard late 3C.; R barrow c. 130430; barrow (BA?) 128426; Jutish cemetery; Med castle mound 122420; earthworks 120426 etc.

Strood. IA salt industry, Red Hills; Belgic pottery; R occupation, 728678 etc.: cremations in Church Field, inhumations Cage Lane etc.; Jutish burials.

Sturry. P implements, Abbevillean, Acheulian, Mousterian; EBA 'B'? beaker; BA hoard; Belgic cremation cemetery including derived South-eastern 'B' ware; R settlement: cemetery at Oaklands; Jutish burial c. 167613.

Sundridge. R cremation cemetery c. 480557.

Sutton-at-Hone (555705). IA pits, Marshfield.

Sutton Valence. R walled cemetery, cist and pyres 812493; R road as terrace 817490 etc.

Swalecliffe (136675). N (secondary) implements; LBA hoard.

Swanley. R cremation c. 512684.

Swanscombe. P implements from gravel pits: Clactonian, Acheulian, Levalloisian and Mousterian; P skull 596746; LBA founder's hoard; R settlement: buildings 617740 and 617727, occupation c. 608747; kilns c. 595725 and c. 608747; R occupation? of a dene-hole.

Tankerton (120670). N Peterborough pottery; LBA cremation in bucket urn.

Temple Ewell. R road as terrace c. 272453;

Med hundred-moot of Bewsborough 296452; PN Bewsborough from *beorg* or *burh*?

Tenterden. R cremation c. 920310; R road 880353 etc.; PN Ratsbury 888322.

Teston. R house 699532.

Teynham. R building? c. 977627; R cremations, Conyer Creek; Jutish burials; earthwork, Sandown; PN Barrow Green 960630.

Thanington. LBA barrow with 5 cinerary urns 133541.

Thurnham. R building c. 803578; R cremations 808581; Jutish cemetery, 807577; Med mound and bailey castles 808581 and 812602 (Binbury).

Tilmanstone. R occupation c. 302516.

Tonbridge. IA contour hill-fort (much damaged), Belgic? ironworkers' stronghold c. 607443; Med castle mound and earthworks 589466; PN Bordyke, i.e. borough ditch.

Tonge. R occupation, Radfield; R cremations; Norman castle mound and bailey 933636; Med deserted village? c. 935640.

Trottiscliffe. N long barrow, The Coldrum, Windmill Hill? pottery and skeletons: megalithic tomb of Danish type; row of prostrate sarsen stones c. 655604; barrow 638593; R cremation; ancient track, Pilgrims' Way, 654613 etc.

Tudeley. PN Crockhurst 623448.

Tunbridge Wells. Mes site c. 555391; PN Hawkenbury 597385; see Frant, Sussex, for 'High Rocks' hill-fort; Museum, Mount Pleasant.

Ulcombe. R road 844477 etc.; Med moated site and fish-ponds 844488.

Upchurch. P implements; IA salt-making, Red Hills; R wattle and daub huts c. 863703; R cremation cemetery c. 832675 and burials elsewhere; R kiln c. 863704; R pottery manufacture widespread in marshes which have undergone marine trangression since R times: much pottery found 860725, 870705 and 863703 etc.; R coin-hoard late 2C.; Jutish burial?

Upper Hardres. R road, agger, 137500 etc.; PN Atchester 160485.

Walmer. Belgic settlement, IA 'C' and 'A' pottery in contemporary use c. 360510; R cremation cemetery c. 363509; Jutish burials c. 362512 etc.

Waltham. R pot c. 105495.

Wateringbury. PN from *burh*? 685536.

Welling (465760). R cremations, High St.

Westbere. P implements, Abbevillean; MBA barrow (destroyed), overhanging-rim cinerary urns; R settlement with quay 186604; R cemetery, Oaklands; R road c. 188618 etc.; Saxo-Frisian and Jutish cemetery, pot showing R influence, 199614.

Westerham. IA contour hill-fort of Wealden culture 443523; Belgic gold coin-hoard; R road as terrace 440513 etc.; Med 13C. pottery kilns; PN Crockham 445515.

West Farleigh. Med deserted village? emparkment? 715536.

Westgate. IA 'C' occupation, sea front; R pottery, Dene Chapel; R inhumations, Hatton House; Med deserted village? 330680.

West Langdon. BA, Belgic and R pottery 315476; Lathe-moot of Hadling c. 303475; PN Napchester 311470.

West Malling (680580). R cremations.

West Peckham. R? cremations, Hurst Wood; PN Rat's Castle 631530.

Westwell. Belgic cremations c. 970460; R burials and occupation 002470; R cremation, Westwell Down; PN Tut Hill 970464, look-out point.

West Wickham. N? occupation; LBA founder's hoard; R cemetery; R pottery c. 387637; R road 387648 etc.; original nucleus of village c. 389649?

Whitfield. R inhumations c. 316456.

Whitstable. LBA hoard including a winged axe; PN Chestfield 136660.

Wickhambreux. R pottery c. 220588; Jutish burials; Med park banks?

Willesborough (030420). PN from *beorg* (hill or barrow?).

Wingham. R house c. 238575 and bath-house yielding S pot showing R influence; R pottery kiln c. 240595; R burials c. 238592; Jutish cemetery; PN Crockshard 13C.

Womenswold. R road 228486 etc.; R barrows; barrows on Ruberry ('rough barrow'?) Down 247496.

Woodchurch. R road and mound 952381.

Woodnesborough. Romano-Belgic ritual pit c. 292553; R road? 307580 etc.; Jutish cemetery; Jutish burials, Coombe c. 297576; PN Woodnesborough means 'hill sacred to Woden' and suggests presence of a pagan sanctuary; PN Marshborough 305574.

Wootton. R road as hollow way c. 252461.

Wormshill (880575). R occupation; PN Wormshill was *Wodnesell* 13C., meaning 'Woden's hill' suggesting a pagan Jutish sanctuary.

Worth. IA 'A', 'B' and 'C' settlement beneath Romano-Celtic temple, 335558; sub-Roman, R and Romano-Jutish pottery from cremation and inhumation cemetery 337553.

Wouldham. Med castle mound 727653; PN Scarborough 722630.

Wrotham. P implement; R finds 588602; R cremations at a 'camp'; Jutish or S burial.

Wye. IA 'A' pottery and ?earthworks; Jutish burials; Jutish barrow 077456; Celtic fields 'around the village'; barrow 072466; pillow-mound c. 077452?; PN Wye means 'sacred place' or 'idol' and suggests a pagan Jutish sanctuary; PN Spider's Castle 047452.

Yalding. PN Brandenbury 721465; PN Congelow 692493 (from *hlāw*?).

LONDON

including areas formerly in Middlesex, Surrey and Kent. Objects from the river Thames are not listed.

Battersea (275770). P (Abbevillean) and N? implements, Battersea Rise; R inhumations, Battersea Park.

Bermondsey (330790). R burials and a coin-hoard of 5C. A.D.

Camberwell (340750). R coins, Grove Pk.; R pot.

Charlton. R settlement 418787: earthwork much damaged, IA South-eastern 'B' derivative ware, Romano-Belgic and R pottery; R circular huts and burials; R pottery? kiln.

Clapham (290750). P implements, Acheulian; line of R Stane St.; R finds.

Clapton (350860). P implements, Acheulian; R burials.

Eltham. R building and burial; R cremations, Corbett Estate; Med moated site 423751; Eltham Palace 423740 on artificial mound?

Fulham. PN Harboro (from *beorg*?) mound shown on old 6 in. O.S. at 237767.

Greenwich. R building (temple?) c. 393774; R cremations and inhumations, Blackheath; line of R road, Watling St., in Greenwich Park?; R occupation c. 394773, fragment of rectangular earthwork; S or Jutish barrows, 388771; forts of 15C. and 16C. c. 389763; National Maritime Museum: early ships.

Hackney. P implements, Stamford Hill.

Hammersmith. N Peterborough pottery; PN Bradmore 15C. 'broad pond' which resulted from the damming of a brook by the agger of the R road after the culvert had become blocked in post-Roman times?

Hampstead. R burial; barrow 274865; PN *Eldebury* 14C.

Holborn. R buildings, inhumations and cremations; British Museum; Wellcome Historical Medical Museum, 183 Euston Rd.

Kensington. LBA founder's hoard; R burials, Notting Hill; London Museum, Kensington Palace; Geological Museum, Exhibition Rd. (for palaeoliths); British Museum (Natural History), Cromwell Rd. (palaeolithic man); Science Museum, Exhibition Rd. (models in Children's Gallery).

Lambeth. IA 'C' finds, including pottery, near Westminster Bridge; R ship on site of County Hall; R pottery near Vauxhall Gardens; R occupation c. 307793; strip lynchets? faint traces 315742.

Lewisham. R occupation, Senlac Rd.; R road as holloway, 366738 etc.; Horniman Museum, Forest Hill.

London (the City). LBA founder's hoard, near Mansion House; R finds and structures, for which see p. 150 for bibliography. Not mentioned there, are IA South-eastern 'B' pottery, Patch Grove ware and a Romano-Saxon pot, all from R levels. On Saxon London see p. 177. Guildhall Museum, King St.

Peckham (340755). R glass factory?

Plumstead. R occupation in dene-hole and inhumations near E. Wickham church; IA pottery (late type) Shooter's Hill; R pottery 463777; Museum, High St.

Poplar. R masonry and burials 374837.

Putney. R cremation and pottery; barrows (destroyed) c. 237737.

St. Pancras. R? building on site of parish church 298825.

Southwark (330800). R bridgehead settlement (see London, the City).

Stoke Newington (330860). P implements, Clactonian and Acheulian (knapping-floor?).

Tooting. Ditched mound (destroyed) c. 286720. This was probably an artificial look-out point and gave name to the village: 'people of the look-out place'. Totterdown (St.) may represent *tōt-aern-dūn*, 'hill with a watch-tower'.

Wandsworth. P implements, Wimbledon Common, Earlsfield and Clapham; N implements; LBA founder's hoard; R cremation. See also Clapham, Tooting and Putney.

Westminster. P implements, Piccadilly, Hyde Park, Mill Bank, Whitehall; N dolerite axe, Pimlico; LBA founder's hoard, Kingsway; R house, College St.; R burials, near the Abbey; Saxo-Frisian pot, Drury Lane; Saxon huts, 6C.–8C., the Savoy; Ossulstone, formerly near Park Lane and South St., the probable meeting-place of the Middlesex Hundred of O, 11C.; PN Tothill, 12C., probably refers to the *hlāw* of a 10C. charter which was later used as a look-out hill.

Woolwich. R hut site c. 434764; R cremations, Dial Square and the Arsenal; R? ironworking, 470780 etc.; PN Castle Wood 432761; see Plumstead.

MIDDLESEX

Acton. P implements, knapping-floor, Levalloisian and Mousterian, Creffield Rd.; LBA cemetery, bucket and barrel urns, 198797; IA hoard of tin coins; R finds; earthworks (destroyed).

Ashford (075715). LBA cemetery, bucket and globular urns, Sunbury Common; field-name, Spelthorne on edge of Ashford Common, hundred moot-place.

Brentford. LBA occupation (including winged axe), IA 'A' occupation, R occupation in rectangular huts, all at 179770 ('Old England'); mound c. 170770; Museum at Public Library.

Cranford. Med moated site 104784; moated mound 102783.

Ealing (180810). P implements, knapping-floor, Ealing Common; field-name, Potters Field 14C.

East Bedfont. Two circular earthworks with parallel ditches? between them (air site) 075738.

Edgware. Celtic fields and associated track (air site) c. 190945; Med shire ditch? 200954.

Edmonton. R building c. 330940; R road, agger? c. 340930; PN Barrowfield 13C. 347933; PN Tilekiln Farm 18C.; field-name, Tile Barrow Field 13C.; field-name, *Settecuppe*, look-out place.

Enfield. P implements, Levalloisian; N stone axe of Scandinavian type; IA 'A' pottery c. 360960; R occupation and burials; Med homestead moats: 314963, 288982, c. 353967 (nearly destroyed), 353984; earthwork (damaged) 324956; earthwork in Hadley Wood; PN Oldbury 15C.: moat destroyed; field-name Brick Kiln 17C.

Finchley. Med homestead moats c. 274883 and c. 254898 (destroyed?).

Hanwell. P implements, Mousterian; S occupation and S cemetery 160798 etc.

Hanworth. Med moated site 110718; PN and field-name, Low (Farm etc.) from *hlāw*?

Harefield (053906). P implements; N knapping-floor? (and ?Mes site), Colney Farm; Med moated sites at Brackenbury Farm and 350 yds. S.E. of it.

Harlington. P implements c. 090800; IA religious sanctuary and hut sites, IA 'A' and South-eastern 'B' pottery 085767; earthwork (destroyed) King's Arbour 087768.

Harmondsworth. N Peterborough pottery; R finds; Med moated site 057778.

Harrow. S pagan shrine on site of church

153875; Med moat (largely filled) c. 145868.

Harrow Weald. R settlement c. 149930; Med moated site three-quarters mile S.W. of church; linear earthwork, Grim's Ditch, 135924 etc.; PN The Kiln 150930; earthwork (Med park bank?), Bentley.

Hayes. P implement c. 100797; Med moated site (damaged) 090810.

Hendon. Med earthwork? Mote Mount 216941; field-names: Oldberry 16C. and Tuttle (Tothill 17C.), look-out place; PN *Tunsteall* 10C. on Watling St.

Hillingdon. P implements; linear earthwork 069829 etc.; PN Stratford. R ford?

Hornsey (290885). Field-name Tilekiln 17C.

Hounslow (140760). P implements; LBA founder's hoard; Belgic finds; PN Hounslow 11C. from *hlāw*, the original meeting-place of Isleworth Hundred.

Ickenham. Med moated site and enclosure 083853.

Isleworth. Med moats 154788 and 157781 (oval, damaged); PN Smallbury from *beorh*; field-name *Stratfurlonge* 15C., reference to R road.

Kingsbury. LBA cemetery, bucket urns, Brent Reservoir; R buildings, c. 190877 and 206868 (parish church); Med hundred-moot of Gore, earthwork, 191887 (Minor names, *Motehegg* 15C. and *Gaderbroke* 15C. refer to this); ancient sunken track c. 197874; PN Kingsbury referred probably to an earthwork (destroyed) round the church.

Laleham. Rectangular earthwork (air site) c. 053706.

Littleton (070687). LBA cremations; R occupation.

Northolt. Med manorial moat, pottery 12C.–14C., 131842.

Perivale. Med moated site 168842.

Pinner. Med moated site 141897; Med park boundary (mentioned 13C.), double ditches with medial bank 131903 etc.; linear earthwork, Grim's Ditch, 113905 etc.

Potters Bar (PN from 13C.). R kiln; Med moot-site of Edmonton 261008 (Minor names Mutton Lane and Gate refer to it).

Ruislip. R? buildings 091877 and 090878 (R brick in church); Norman castle mound and bailey, 11C., 090878; Med park ditch, Park Wood; Med fishponds to E. of castle; Med village enclosure earthwork (*burgus*) 093867 etc.; Med moated sites 084881 and 106889; mound 091880; PN Bury St., manorial.

Shepperton (080670). S cemetery, cremation and inhumation, under small barrows (destroyed) near Halliford (i.e. 'holy ford').

Southall. MBA founder's hoard; mounds? 118784 and 119784; PN Tentlow 110783, from *hlāw*?

Southgate. Med moated site c. 321943; Museum, Broomfield Park.

South Mimms. Med castle mound and bailey 225028; Med moated sites 233020, 226975 and c. 222001; PN Old Fold (already 'old' in A.D. 1294); PN Mutton Lane, see Potters Bar.

Staines. LBA hoard; R settlement; R bridges (*Pontes* is R name), site c. 032715?

Stanmore. Belgic settlement 173937; R posting-station (*Sulloniacae*) and pottery-manufacturing settlement 173940 etc.; R hoard including coins of late 7C.; R road as a hollow way 177934 etc.; R occupation c. 160930; Med shire ditch, mentioned 16C.; barrow 159939; earthwork enclosure c. 175928?

Stanwell. Med double moated enclosure 057746; Med moated site 031761; ringwork c. 058737 and enclosure? c. 059737 (air sites).

Sunbury. IA tin coin-hoard; PN Sunbury refers to *burh* (destroyed?) c. 106685; PN Stadbury '*burh* by the landing-place' 14C.; early charter names: *Eadbryht's hlaew*, c. 084703 and *clofenan beorh* c. 103691—both probably referred to barrows.

Teddington (160710). N Votive? hoard of axes; MBA barrow (destroyed), Sandy Lane.

Tottenham. Med moated site 325901; Museum, Bruce Castle.

Twickenham. Mes site c. 165732 (Eel Pie Island); moated site 149744; Museum, York House.

Uxbridge (050840). P implements? Mes site; Museum, High St.

Wembley. For Med hundred-moot of Gore, 191887, see Kingsbury.

West Drayton (060800). P implements, Mousterian.

Whitchurch (Little Stanmore) (185915). Field-name, Potters Mead 16C.

Yeading. Med moated site, 109838.

Yiewsley (060805). P implements, Acheulian and Mousterian; LBA occupation and cemetery, bucket and barrel urns.

OXFORDSHIRE
(Southern parts)

Adwell. Barrow 703990.

Albury. PN from 11C., 655051.

Aston Rowant (727990). R cremation, Kingston Blount; old names: *Chesthullesforlong* 14C. (cf. Chesthill in Stonor, site of R house) and *Hemcherwurke* 13C. from *geweorc*?, 'an earthwork'.

Beckley and Stowood. R house c. 568112; R occupation elsewhere; R road, agger, 563103 etc.; PN *Parkemed* 14C., 580117 etc.? park bank?; field-names, *Dycheshend* 13C. and *Myclandic* 11C., both referring to a ditch.

Benson. P core; N dolerite axe; N-EBA *cursus* (air site); R riverside village, huts and burials; R enclosure (air site); S inhumations and S pottery from several sites; earthwork, 'Medlar's Bank'. (Is this Kingsbury 13C?). Field-names: Stanford (R road?), *Burewyke* 16C. (*burh*?), *burhslaedes* and *burhweg* 10C. (*burh*), *Bryda beorh* 10C. (*beorg*), Deadman's Bush.

Binsey. Barrow? 496084, perhaps the *Thorneberg* of 1293 (*beorg*).

Bix. R building c. 730850; Med deserted village? 726870.

Brightwell Baldwin (653950). R burial; R coin-hoard 4C.; PN *straetforda* 9C. (R road?).

Britwell. R burial; line of Icknield Way 671920 etc.; PN Cobditch (*Coppediche* 13C., 'hill by the entrenchment'); PN Castle Hill, 19C.

Burcot. See Clifton Hampden.

Chalgrove (640695). N axe from Westmorland.

Checkendon. PN? Devil's Churchyard c. 654841; PN Wyfold, possibly from *wigfalod*, 'idol enclosure', pagan S shrine? 688817; PN *Oldebury* 14C.; oval earthwork 683810.

Chinnor. IA 'A1' occupation 766004; R house 768017; S secondary? burial in twin barrow 770006; barrows 765003; Icknield Way 760002 etc.; PN *Dedegerde* 14C. ('dead enclosure'); PN *Aldeburi* 14C.; PN Hog Ditch 19C.

Clifton Hampden and Burcot. EBA 'B' beaker inhumation; MBA hoard; R house c. 557965; rectangular and parallel ditches (air site) 535951, R? farmstead; S? burials; ring-ditch with cremation (air site) c. 530950; field-name, Blacklands.

Cowley. IA 'A' finds; R occupation, burials and pottery kilns c. 540040; Romano-Saxon pottery sherd; PN Bury Lane 16C.; PN *Puppelowe* 17C. from *hlāw*.

Crowmarsh. P implements, Acheulian and Levalloisian; N occupation, Peterborough pottery etc., 607877; R settlement c. 612890; Med shrunken village? Mongewell, 610878; linear earthwork, Grim's Ditch 617879 etc.; Charter of 10C. mentions an 'old *burh*', 'heathen burials' and 'the watch down' (i.e. look-out hill).

Cuddesdon. R house c. 599033; S cemetery c. 602030; Charter of 10C. mentions 'at the meeting of the paved roads' (593046?), R?; PN Castle Hill (R house).

Culham. EBA beaker pottery; IA pottery c. 530952; R occupation sites; R? farmstead (air site); Charter of 10C. mentions barrows.

Cuxham with Easington. R occupation, Cuxham; Med shrunken settlement, Easington 662970; PN Burrough Way 18C. and *Buriforlong* 13C.; Charter of 10C. mentions 'Cuda's barrow', 'the old ditch' and probably 'salt-boilers' pits'.

Denton. Med shrunken settlement, Chippinghurst 600010; PN 'Eanfrith's barrow' 10C.

Dorchester. P implements, Acheulian and Levalloisian; N occupation, henge monuments and cursus (two), 570957 etc. (mostly destroyed), Windmill Hill ware, Peterborough, Ebbsfleet, Abingdon, Rinyo-Clacton, 'A' and 'B' beaker wares; EBA 'B1' beaker burial; MBA barrow (bell?) with two cremations; LBA cremation, 583950; IA 'A' (?) promontory fort, 570938 etc. and occupation of rectangular enclosures with pits 578937 (air site); IA settlement c. 574963 and 572950 yielding pottery of IA 'A' (including a haematite-coated sherd), 'AB' and 'C'; R town, ramparts, 577940 etc.; R occupation c. 574963 and 572950 (with pottery kilns); R? farmstead (air site) 590940 etc.; barrow circles 590940 etc. and other air sites 572945, 577952 etc.; S burials of late

4C. or early 5C.? 578937; S burials of 7C.; Med earthwork platform of abbey and castle 579942; field-names: *Ardyche* 16C. (earth-ditch?) and Deadman's Furlong 19C.

Drayton St. Leonard (595963). EBA 'B' beaker burial; field-name, High Ditch 19C.

Elsfield (540100). N. dolerite axe; Mes implements; field-names: *Buryforlonge* 13C. (*burh* or *beorg*), Meredyche 13C., 'boundary ditch'.

Ewelme (647914). P implements, Acheulian; N implements and pottery; R coin-hoards (two) 3C.; S inhumations; Med hundred-moot of Ewelme in this parish: site?; field-names, Old Bury 13C. and Deadman's Orchard 19C.

Eye and Dunsden. P implements; R finds and burial; PN *Reddish* 17C. 'red ditch' 711800 and *Dyckcrofte* 17C. (ditch-).

Forest Hill with Shotover. N dolerite axe; BA ditches and pits: occupation (Shotover); R occupation sites 556065, burial and ?kiln; R coin-hoard, late 3C.; field-name, *Burhill* 17C. (*burh*) later corrupted to Barrow Hill 19C.

Garsington. LBA palstave of Spanish? type and socketed axe of French? type; R coins, numerous 567033; R road 562020; PN Kiln Farm 19C., 572027; field-names, Broken Barrow and Greenditch (both 13C.).

Goring. P implements?; Belgic coin-hoard; Med shrunken settlement, Gatehampton 609798.

Great Haseley. Med shrunken hamlets: Rycote 668045 and Latchford 660015 (earthworks); field-names in '-ditch' of 13C. probably refer to watercourses except perhaps *Langedonesdich* ('long-down-ditch') 650010 etc.?; 11C. reference to a 'broad army path'.

Great Milton (630025). Field-name, Chesterley 19C.

Harpsden. P implements; R house and bath-building 757803; PN Flowercroft Wood (from *flōr?*) and Shard Wood (scatter of potsherds?).

Headington. R house 548087; R occupation, several sites; R kilns; R burials; R road 562091 etc.; S hut and inhumation c. 550078; field-name Toot Hill (look-out point); *Brademore Berewes* 13C. may refer to a grove or to barrows.

Henley. P implements, Abbevillian, Clactonian and Acheulian from an ancient channel of the Thames; P implements 741813; EBA food vessel; a Grim's Ditch is mentioned in this parish in 13C.; linear earthwork or track? 740840 etc.

Hinksey (500050). IA 'B'? pottery; important ancient ford at N. Hinksey.

Holton (600070). R occupation sites and burials; PN Buryhook 19C.; field-name, Mawkin Ditch 19C.; a 10C. charter refers to a *strāet* (R road?).

Horspath. R pottery; S inhumation c. 568050.

Horton-cum-Studley. R village 597118; PN Oberry (earth-bury?); PN The Moat 592111.

Iffley (527034). P implements; MBA cinerary urn; IA 'A', 'AB' and R occupation.

Ipsden. R occupation, kilns and a R? well 653850; Icknield Way 627850 etc.; PN *le Berwes* 13C. (barrows).

Kidmore End. P implements c. 700793, c. 700775 and c. 678796.

Lewknor. Med hundred-moot? 717971; PN Ditchgate 13C.

Little Milton. MBA collared urn; R villa and field-system (air site), cf. PN Ditchend Barn 625002—R pottery finds.

Littlemore (538028). P implements, Acheulian; Mes implements; R pottery, Heyford Hill; R pottery kilns.

Mapledurham. P implements; R building 696762; R occupation near West Dene;

field-name, Hollow Hill, ?*Holeburgh* 13C.; PN Whittles 670784, 'white barrow or hill'.

Marsh Baldon. R road 570980 etc.; Med deserted hamlet? Little Baldon 565985.

Marston, (527087). P implements; IA 'A2' pottery.

Nettlebed. Mes site 705867 etc.; N implements; brick-making from 15C.; linear earthwork? Highmoor Trench (continuation of Grim's Ditch?) 705857; PN Crocker End 15C., 710868.

Newington (610965). Field-name, *Kyngesbur'* 13C., manorial?

North Stoke (610860). Mes implements; N Windmill Hill ware and implements; EBA 'A' beaker burial in mound; MBA collared urn; air-sites, EBA? cursus and ring-ditches, one with three infant cremations.

Nuffield. P implements, Acheulian; R? brick in church 668873; linear earthwork, Grim's Ditch 645874 etc. and 676871 etc.; earthwork enclosure 657874; field-name, Burton 19C.

Nuneham Courtenay. Med deserted village? 540980 emparkment.

Oxford. P implements, Abbevillean, Acheulian and Micoquian; Mes implements; N implements; EBA beakers, four of 'B' type and one 'A-C'; EBA food vessel of Northern type; MBA merchant's hoard; MBA founder's tool-kit; BA ditches and pits, Port Meadow; IA habitation sites, Port Meadow; R building, Port Meadow; R occupation, scattered sites, especially in N. Oxford; S cremation? Osney; S inhumations, Park Crescent and Summertown; field-names: Three Barrows 13C. in Walton and *Walecotesborwe* 13C. in Oxford (from *beorg*); Museums: Ashmolean, Beaumont St. and Pitt-Rivers, Parks Rd.

Pishill with Stonor. [Mes implements

reported here are probably those from Kimble Farm in Turville, Bucks.] Med shrunken settlement? 727898; field-name *Stratfelde* 15C.

Pyrton. Med deserted hamlets: *Standedelf* 650000, Clare 673985 and Golder 666978; field-names: the old ditch 11C. (watercourse?), heathen burials 11C. and stone barrow 11C.

Rotherfield Greys. R cremation; R? brick in Greys Court 14C. and chapel 725834.

Rotherfield Peppard. P implements; N flint-mines and implement factory c. 705815; Med? earthwork 683810; field-names: Barrow Field 19C. and Pit Wood 19C.

Sandford-on-Thames (535015). N axe from Westmorland; R occupation and pottery kilns; field-names, all 13C.: birchbarrowfield, the barrow, chesterway and calves' ditch.

Shiplake. P implements, Abbevillean and Acheulian; S cremations; PN Binfield 740785, meeting-place of Binfield Hundred.

Shirburn (700960). R coin-hoard; Med castle moat 14C.; field-names in ' Strat-' 13C. possibly indicating R metalling of the Lower Icknield Way at this point?

South Stoke (600835). R coin-hoard; field-names of 14C.: crows' hill (or barrow), The Lynch, the boundary ditch and of 13C. Ecgbeald's ditch.

Stadhampton. P implements, Acheulian; Med deserted hamlet, Ascott, 612982; 17C.? fishponds 610980.

Stanton St. John. R house 576106; R inhumation; R coin-hoard; R road 562095; field-name, Enslow 18C. (*hlāw*?); Med deserted village, Woodperry 576106.

Swyncombe. R coin-hoard, late 3C.; Med deserted village? c. 683901; linear earthwork 675916 etc.; square earthwork and annexe, Digberry 692882 (late R defence?);

PN Burial Copse 19C.; field-name, Randlesbury 19C.

Sydenham. S inhumation, 739011.

Tetsworth (690020). Field-names: Old Bury 19C. and *La Lowe* 13C. (from *hlāw*).

Thame (705060). R occupation, Lupton's Land; R cremation.

Thomley. Med deserted village c. 630090?; field-names: *Otewey dyches* 14C., and Roughditchfurlong 13C.

Tiddington with Albury. Deserted Med village Albury 655051 — PN means *Ealda's burh.*

Toot Baldon (568008). PN Toot (cf. *Toteheye* 13C., 'look-out enclosure'); field-names: *Werveldiche* 13C. and Monk Hill Ditch 14C.

Warborough. N/EBA cursus (air site); IA occupation; R industrial site?; R coin-hoard early 4C.; R road 590936 etc.; PN Warborough 13C., 'watch hill' 596946; field-names: *Buryefeld* 16C. (*burh* or *beorg*), *Coppydburye* 16C. (*beorg*), *le Berewes* 14C. ('barrows'), Streteforlonge 13C. (R road as above?).

Water Eaton and Gosford. Mes site c. 516123; R occupation; PN Cutteslowe 508112, the barrow destroyed in 13C. Mention of 'evil doers that lurk in the hollow of the mound' suggests a chambered long barrow; Charter of 10C. includes '*to fagan floran*', 'multi-coloured floor', a tessellated pavement?; also 'by the two little barrows' and 'along the ditch'. Med deserted village, Water Eaton 515120.

Watlington. Med castle earthworks 14C. (damaged); Med? enclosure c. 710925; field-name 'Billa's barrow', 13C.

Wheatfield. Med deserted village 689992.

Wheatley. R house and bath-building 606044 on Castle Hill; R inhumation; S cremation and inhumation cemetery 602046, pottery with R influence; Med hundred-moot at Bullsdown Barn?;

T

Wheatley Bridge: 10C. 'army road ford' 612053.

Whitchurch. IA hill-fort, Binditch, 643783; S? inhumation; square earthwork 647808.

Wolvercote. P implements, Abbevillean, Acheulian and Micoquian; R village site, St. Edward's School; R occupation c. 490110; field-name, 'forked barrow' 14C.

Woodeaton. IA 'A' settlement, 'A' and 'AB' pottery; Belgic occupation c. 533123; R town with bounding earthwork 536125 etc.; Romano-Celtic temple with enclosure, and fair-ground c. 533123 on *Harowdone* 15C.; R occupation 543115; R coin-hoards of mid- and end 4C.; R road 533125 etc.; pagan S site, *Harowdone*? as above.

SURREY

Abinger. P implement, Acheulian; Mes habitation, hut sites, 112459; Mes implements 100467 and 103466; N (secondary) sites 100467 and 103466; IA hill-fort, Holmbury, 104430, Wealden culture pottery; R buildings c. 104475; Med castle mound 114460, 11C. to late 12C. occupation; Med? ironworking (cf. PN Abinger Hammer 17C.).

Addington. LBA hoard, including a winged axe; R road 391630 etc.; S? barrows, 25 formerly visible on Thunderhill (pagan S shrine?); circular earthwork, Thunderfield (cf. preceding PN) Common, Addington Park; barrow 367644; PN Castle Hill, 380635, 13C. fortified manor.

Albury. P implements; Mes sites, Blackheath and c. 060462, c. 040476 and Farley Heath; N (secondary) site, 048472; LBA founder's hoard; Romano-Celtic temple and enclosure 053448; R pottery kilns c. 050449 (cf. PN Kiln Hanger 051442); barrow 047496; circular mound c. 053483; Med? earthwork c. 053448; PN Albury 11C. 'the old' *burh*; Med deserted village

065478, emparkment; PN Harrowshill 050498, not recorded early, pagan S site?

Alfold. Mes site c. 036340; late 16C. glassworks c. 020340 (cf. PN Glasshouse Copse, 17C.); PN Alfold 13C., 'the old enclosure'.

Artington. Mes site, 994483; MBA cinerary urn; LBA/IA 'A' transition, pottery 994483; field-name, *Le Bury* 14C.

Ash. Mes site c. 913527; MBA cremation in overhanging-rim urn, Henley Grove; R coin-hoard, early 4C.; barrow c. 902515.

Ashtead. N, three stone axes (imports); BA? earthwork 176600, BA sherds; LBA occupation, 'The Old Quarry'; LBA/IA transition pottery c. 183576; IA 'A2' pottery, 'Inward Shaw'; IA South-eastern 'B' (Patch Grove) ware, Park Lane; IA 'A', 'C' and R pottery, R building 193581; IA 'A' flint shafts; R house and bath building, tile factory 176600; R? earthwork 193581; R cremation; R by-road? 180598 etc.; Med (and earlier?) track 193582; Med pottery-kiln 13C. to 14C.; field-names: Upper and Lower Bury 19C. near earthwork 193581.

Bagshot. IA 'A1' pottery including haematite-coated ware; R pottery 896650; R cremation cemetery; R? 'camp', destroyed 18C.; R road 910649 etc.

Banstead. P implements; N occupation, 'hut-circles'? c. 235545; LBA founder's hoard; R pottery (including South-eastern 'B' (Patch Grove) ware), Banstead Downs; R occupation c. 262580; R occupation and inhumations, West Burgh; S burials; Med manorial site, Preston (destroyed), 12C.–14C. pottery; Med castle mound (near Castle House 233550?); four rectangular earthworks, 236555, 236554, 230553 and 237536 (air site): 17C. Civil War gun emplacements?; four barrows, Galley Hills (damaged), 250607; originally ten barrows, Tumble Beacon, 243591; field-name *Eldebury* 14C.

Barnes. Mes implements, Barnes Common; mill mound (damaged) 223760.

Beddington. Mes site c. 295653; N implements and BA pottery near Waddon; LBA founder's hoard; IA South-eastern 'B' (Patch Grove) ware; R house 297658; R bath-building c. 293666; R settlement, Woodcote; R inhumation; S cremation and inhumation cemetery c. 297658.

Betchworth. Mes, N (Peterborough pottery), R and S occupation 187503; LBA occupation site; PN The Borough etc., 19C., 196497; PN Bushbury 195479; PN Streetfield 14C. (R road?).

Bletchingley. IA hill-fort, War Coppice (*Raulveswerk* 13C., from *geweorc*) 329533; R bath-building 318521, at Pendell (which name, from *pynd-*, may refer to a R enclosure or to the outline of the R walls); Med castle earthwork, 12C., 322506; earthwork, Chapel Plat, Lodge Farm; PN Brick Kiln 337505.

Buckland (220510). Mes site (destroyed).

Burstow. Mes site c. 320455; PN Burstow 12C.—reference to moated site 312413?

Byfleet. Late IA occupation 059603; IA and R occupation, kiln, 059598.

Camberley (870610). Mes site, Barossa Common.

Capel. Mes site c. 139432, c. 149437 and c. 175405; R road, Stane Street, 154420 etc.

Carshalton. Mes site, 280624; N implements; and at c. 280624: EBA, LBA, IA 'A2' (including haematite-coated ware), late IA (South-eastern 'B' and Belgic-type wares), from site of IA 'A2' camp; LBA hoard c. 280624; R occupation c. 280624; S inhumations; PN Barrows Hedges c. 270620.

Caterham. IA? field-system and farmstead? c. 320540; R road as terraceway, 343557

etc.; 16C. aqueduct, 'Wide Ditch' c. 338585.

Chaldon (310557). Quadrangular earthwork.

Charlwood. Mes site; PN Lowfield 14C. (from *hlāw*?) 273143.

Cheam (245640). S spearheads (burials?); Med 13C. pottery kiln; Med deserted village, Cuddington, first mentioned 7C., destroyed c. 1538 for Nonsuch Park.

Chelsham. N implements; LBA founder's hoard, including a winged axe; R road 401588 etc.; Med deserted village c. 388592? (migration of site?); quern quarries 379578 etc.; earthwork enclosure, Med occupation, 374586; earthwork c. 378592; PN Worm's Heath ('snake's head') 13C., pagan S site?; PN Oldbury 385586; PN Millberry, 19C. 386579.

Chertsey. BA urns; earthworks (rectangular) at Laleham Burway and Burridge Stile (both PN from *burh*), 045680; barrows ('three barrows' 7C, now two) 992657; barrows 992647 and ?c. 983648; PN Knighting Barrow Mead ('Knighton Barrow 16C.); PN *Eldebury* 14C. referring to IA? camp, St. Anne's Hill 027676; PN Ruxbury (from *burh*); PN Crockford, 7C.

Chessington. Mes site; PN Castle Hill, moated homestead, 191635.

Chiddingfold. Mes sites, 932350, 925326, c. 964335 and at Gostrode Farm and Riddingfield; EBA beaker burial in barrow c. 964335 in a field named *Goldhorde*; R house 970360; Med (and R?) glassworks (cf. PN Glasshouse Rew); PN Godley Bridge, pagan S site?; PN Great and Little Burrows, 15C. (from *beorg*); PN Furnace Place, Tudor (and earlier?) ironworking c. 931331 and c. 005355.

Chipstead. N (secondary) site 270577; R pottery, Chipstead Valley.

Chobham. LBA cemetery in bowl barrow, c. 953665, barrel and bucket urns; LBA flat cemetery ?c. 985625, bucket urns; R coin-hoard, late 4C.; Med hundred-moot of Godley c. 958666? (PN Godley suggests pagan S site); PN Castle Green 15C., site? 973610?; barrows 934613; PN Burrowhill 974630 (from *beorg*); PN Albury, earthwork 'Bee Garden' 974644; earthwork c. 954666.

Cobham. MBA overhanging-rim urn c. 114603; IA occupation, c. 114603, 'A2' and 'AB' wares, Belgic (western type) and Patch Grove pottery; R bath-house 088596; R occupation c. 114603 and c. 100614; R coin-hoard, late 4C.; S burial?; Med meeting-place of Elmbridge Hundred c. 099606; earthwork c. 086586.

Compton. N implements; R house 959480; R cremation; barrows? at Budburrow Hill and Rowbury Hill (both PN from *beorh*).

Coombe. LBA occupation; IA 'A2' occupation c. 210710; R building 208703.

Coulsdon. N occupation; N axe from Devon (at Kenley); LBA founder's hoard, including winged axe; IA field-system c. 310590; late IA pit; R field-system 300570 etc. and trackway 300580 etc.; R farmstead c. 288566; R occupation c. 297564; R occupation 295572; S burials c. 292588; S cemetery, barrows and flat graves, 300577 etc.; earthwork 304568; field-name, Black Field 16C.

Cranleigh. R tilery, kiln and clay pits 080409; mound, Broomhall Copse; ironworking (cf. Hammer Farm); PN Underslaw, possibly 'Thunor's barrow'; PN Tothill, look-out point.

Crowhurst (390475). R pottery: ironworking, Copthorn.

Croydon. Mes site, Addiscombe; N (secondary) occupation, Peterborough pottery; LBA founder's hoard; R occupation widespread in town; R cremations and inhumations 325651; R farmstead c. 335635; R coin-hoards: early 2C., South End and

mid-3C. at Pitlake and Wandle Rd.; S cemetery, cremation and inhumation 325651; barrow 337632; earthwork? (hillfort?) 312707; earthwork? much mutilated, 304688.

Dorking. P implements; Mes sites: c. 135483, c. 150455, c. 171491 and at Cotmandene; N or BA occupation, Cotmandene; IA (Wealden Culture?) hill-fort, Anstiebury, 153440; IA field-system, Boxhill; R posting-station? in town, many R finds; S burial? 161493; S coin-hoard c. A.D. 900, c. 150450; barrows 153490 and 185513; PN Bury Hill 14C. 157483; PN Crockers Wood 14C.; PN Goldenlands, probably *Goldhordland* 15C.; PN Tilehurst (*Tileost* 16C.) 179486.

Dunsfold (500360). Ironworking (cf. PN Furnace Bridge).

East Horsley. N (secondary) knapping-floor and Med 13C. flint-mine 097516.

East Sheen (200750). P implements, Abbevillean.

Effingham. N implements; barrow (destroyed) c. 113529; Med earthwork, 13C. and 14C. pottery 108548; PN Kiln Field 105513.

Egham. R building c. 999701; R road c. 999701; PN Tile Hill (probably 13C. *Tighelheld*, 'tile-slope').

Elstead. Mes sites (two) c. 882414; N implements; 'prehistoric' habitation sites, 900454, 910456 and 914450; barrows, triple intermediate bell-disc type, 894449; PN Burford 916435.

Epsom. Mes site c. 216581; N implements, Woodcote; EBA? crouched inhumations 223599; IA 'A1' occupation, haematite-coated ware, 'A2' and Wealden pottery; R finds, Epsom Court Farm; R cremation cemetery 216612; R tile kiln c. 196620; earthwork, quadrilateral.

Esher. Mes site 138650; IA 'A2' occupation 138650; S inhumations 138650; PN Old Ditch 11C.

Ewell. Mes sites 218621, 217623, 219625; N knapping-floor 218621; IA 'A2' occupation c. 230630 and 218621 (at the latter IA 'B' Wealden pottery and South-eastern 'B' (Patch Grove) ware; R settlenent (posting-station?), sites: 218621, 223622, 222625, 217624, 223622, 219624 and 218623; R road, Stane Street and branches 225635 etc. (agger 228640); R burials; S cremation and inhumation cemetery 219624; barrows (destroyed) Longdown and North Looe; earthwork, 'Diana's Dyke' 228634. For Cuddington see Cheam.

Ewhurst. Mes sites c. 088430 and c. 083423; R road 105370 etc.; PN Somersbury 13C., 102381.

Farleigh. R road 396612 etc.

Farley Heath. See Albury.

Farnham. P implements, Abbevillean, Clactonian, Acheulian, Levalloisian and Aurignacian: Mes sites: 851478, 853480, 857477, 867483, 864476, 858473, 861471, 862467, 856468, 830461, 860458; N occupation 854480 with Peterborough sherds; N long barrow (destroyed) 861480; N? flint-mines c. 890480 and 863480 (air site); EBA beaker sherds 861480; EBA food vessel c. 813467; MBA sherds of overhanging-rim urn; LBA cemetery 853463 etc., bucket urns; LBA cremation in barrow (destroyed), lugged urn, 857477; LBA occupation 820447, 832454 (transitional BA–IA); IA 'A' occupation 853480, 861480, 880462 (in the earthwork called 'Soldier's Ring'), 875463 (in Botany Hill camp), 875453 (near linear earthwork), 853464, 833454 and 828447; IA 'A' sherds with inhumation burial 887485; IA 'A' haematite-coated ware at 853464, bowl with cremation; IA 'C' occupation, 854480; late IA occupation 853464; IA? fort 'Caesar's Camp' 835496; IA? fort (damaged) 847497; R house, bath-building

and pottery kilns 851477; R cremations, three sites; R pottery-kilns c. 850460; S occupation, huts, 843465; Med (A.D. 1070) castle mound and earthworks 837474; Med park bank? Farnham Park; meeting-place of Farnham Hundred, 'Lawday House' 833493; quern quarry? c. 876452; barrows, 825493 (damaged), c. 887449, 880462 (at Crooksbury which has *beorg* for its ending); PN Bricksbury (near 'Caesar's Camp') 835496; PN Berry Field 17C. from *burh*; PN Rowledge 13C. 'rough ditch'; PN Willey 815452, pagan S shrine.

Fetcham. IA 'A2' occupation 159557, also Wessex IA 'B' ware, South-eastern 'B', Belgic? and R pottery; R brick in church 149556; S inhumation cemetery 156555; S inhumations (two) c. 153542; S occupation 161563; Med hundred-moot 143553; PN Old Bury Meadow 14C.; PN Hawkesbury c. 159557; PN Potters Field 13C.

Frensham. P implements; Mes sites: c. 865394, c. 838418, c. 844404, c. 846397, c. 863417; N axe from Westmorland; barrows 853407 etc.; ironworking.

Frimley (880580). P implement; R cremations and coin-hoard, Yorktown.

Gatton. Med deserted village c. 275528.

Godalming. P implements; Mes sites c. 945440 and c. 985430; N implements; BA pottery; Belgic pottery (of R period) c. 950455 and c. 967447; R cremations c. 967447, 944440, and c. 967460; pagan S shrine, Tuesley? 963420; S *burh* of 9C. at 947438?; Med deserted settlement? Busbridge c. 980420: Museums, High St. and Charterhouse.

Godstone. Mes site; N implements; R cremations 354504; S? burials; Med deserted village, Walkingstead, c. 360510; Med castle mound and bailey (or promontory fort) Castle Hill 363508; barrows (damaged) 348517; moated site 363480;

earthwork, quadrangular 362408; PN Flower Farm (*Flore* 13C., 'floor'), R house? 357523; PN Stansted 356489 and Stratton 353510 both refer to R road; PN Ouborough 362518; PN Goldhard (gold-hoard?) 363416.

Great Bookham. R coin-hoard, late 3C.; S? burials (found in 18C.); Med hundred-moot at 143553 in 13C., earlier at ?151549 (Horsehead Cross and Furlong).

Guildford. Mes site c. 023486; N implements, The Chantries; N (secondary) site, 013487; IA 'A2' pottery 993482; R? brick in Castle walls; S cemetery, cremation and inhumation, 989488; Med castle mound, 998493; barrow? 021485; PN Burwood, 020494; Museum, Castle Arch.

Ham. Mes site; IA and R pottery 164723; S hut; S inhumation (not Twickenham).

Hambledon. Mes site, Vanmoor; N implements; Med castle mound? 'The Tolt'; PN Burgate 13C. 989384.

Hascombe. LBA/IA pottery, R pottery, Med pottery c. 010430; IA promontory fort of South-eastern 'B' or Wealden cultures?: pottery of Wealden type.

Haslemere. Mes sites, c. 890320; N? pottery and implements, Hindhead; LBA bucket urn; Belgic (late) and R cremation cemetery, Beech Rd.; R pottery kiln; iron-working; PN Holdfast 14C. 921332 (from *faestenn*, 'a fortress'); PN Summersbury 16C.; Museum, High St.

Headley. Mes sites, Headley Heath; R occupation; barrows c. 186547; PN Tot Hill 19C., look-out point 201546; field-name, Potters Field 13C.

Hindhead and Churt. Mes sites: 'Bron Y De', Furze Hills and Barford; earthwork? c. 862372. And see Haslemere.

Holmbury. See Abinger.

Holmwood. R road as terrace 165456 etc.; PN Kiln Wood 190436; PN Potkilns 168474.

Hook (180650.) PN Gosbury 16C.

Horley. Mes site c. 259469; R occupation; Med castle earthworks 300425; Med iron bloomery 13C.–15C., 300425; Med iron mine 14C. near Cinderfield; PN Thunderfield 300425 (from *Thunor*) 9C., pagan S shrine; PN Burford 13C.

Horsell. Mes site c. 986597; bell and disc barrows 014598.

Kew (185775.) EBA 'B' beaker, West Hall Rd.

Kingston. N stone axe of diorite; LBA sherds of bucket urn, Kingston Hill; LBA founder's hoard; IA 'A2' occupation c. 210710; S hut (in fact, Ham?); Museum, Fairfield.

Leatherhead. MBA? cinerary urns c. 183547; BA pottery 167562; R road, Stane St., 186550 etc.; IA and R pottery from Celtic fields (ploughed) 180548 etc.; barrows 183547 and 187547 (damaged); Med moated enclosure, 12C. to 14C., Pachesham Mounts 154578.

Leigh. Bury's Court, 14C., 236474 (cf. Bures and Burfords in Horley parish nearby).

Limpsfield. P implements; Mes site, sand-pit, L. Common; IA? fort, largely destroyed; IA South-eastern 'B' occupation 407493, Patch Grove, Wealden and R wares; R occupation c. 431532; R cremations; R pottery kilns, Ridlands, Watts Hill and Scearn Bank; R road, agger, 428524 etc.; S pot with Frisian and R influence; Med kilns 431515 (11C. and 13C. pottery) and c. 431532; mounds? 397554 and 418516.

Lingfield. IA hill-fort (Wealden culture?) 432417; Med moated site, Starborough Castle (PN from 14C.) 426441; Med shire ditch 433420 etc.; ironworking; PN Potters Wood (14C.) and Kiln Wood 424430.

Malden. Occupation 213663: IA 'A2',

South-eastern 'B' (Patch Grove), late Belgic, R (ditched enclosure), Med 11C. to 16C. pottery.

Merrow. N implements; barrows, Newlands Corner and ?Merrow Downs (air site); R cremations; PN Burpham 11C., 017523.

Merstham. N imported stone axe; R cremations; PN Albury 14C. 295527, moated site; PN Dragberry 14C. (dragon-barrow or hill).

Merton. R finds numerous—posting-station on the R Stane St.? 261694.

Mickleham. LBA/IA 'A' (transition) occupation 160518; IA 'A2' pottery from Celtic fields 180537 etc.; R occupation 182533; R ford c. 172518; R? brick in church 170534; S burials c. 173527; Med pottery kiln c. 170518; barrow c. 187513; earthwork (damaged) Mickleham Downs; mound 178536; PN *Grimesditch* 13C.; PN Norbury 13C., 160538; PN Burford 13C., 173517; PN Foxbury (Foxearth?) 163523; field-name Black Lands 16C.

Mitcham. R burial; S cemetery 270682; S cemetery c. 282660; field-name Black Lands 16C.; Museum? Vestry Hall.

Morden. R occupation; R road, Stane St., 248672 etc. and 259690 etc.; R fort? on Stane St. c. 260687?; castle mound, Morden Park; PN Ravensbury 13C.

Newdigate. Ironworking c. 200448.

Nutfield (310510.) R coin-hoard.

Ockham. Barrow, Ockham Common; mounds (natural?) 080590 etc.; PN Stratford 13C.; PN Brickkiln 101566.

Ockley. R road, Stane St., 134370 etc. and 155420 etc.; Norman castle earthwork 158409; PN Burywood 15C., 153414; PN Potland 17C.; PN Castle Copse 137402.

Oxted. R cremations; Med castle mound, Barrowgreen, 380527; Bursted 13C. is an old name for Oxted and refers to the castle as *burh*.

Peper Harow. P implement (late type); PN P. Harow suggests a pagan S shrine, at ?c. 935441; barrows 911409.

Pirbright. LBA–IA? hut circles? c. 954545; PN Stanford 16C.

Purley. Mes site, Purley Oaks; LBA founder's hoard; IA field-system c. 330600; S burials.

Puttenham. P implement; Mes sites: c. 909455, c. 920460 and c. 912468; N implements; IA? enclosure or fort, Hillbury 912468; R building c. 912468; barrow, Frowsbury, 939477; earth circle 939476; prehistoric occupation 915479.

Pyrford (040580). P and N implements; IA and R pottery; barrow? Woodham Lane.

Redhill. Mes site c. 273497; N implements; R building and Med pottery-kilns, Earlswood.

Reigate. P implement; Mes sites c. 237505 etc.; MBA overhanging-rim urn from barrow c. 234501; R building c. 245520; R glass factory?; Med castle mound 253504; barrows, seven (apparent disc-barrows are tree-rings) 237505; PN Linkfield, lynchets?; PN Blackborough 17C.

Richmond. Mes sites near Pen Ponds; barrows 189722, 190734 (destroyed) and ?186732; strip lynchets (faint) 182739; old field banks 198738.

St. Martha's. Mes sites c. 028484 and c. 022487 etc.; IA 'A2' pottery and kiln, occupation, 021483; IA 'A' pottery 028483 R cremations; S pot; earth-circles 028483; barrow? c. 020487 (see *Surrey Arch. Coll.*, vol. 54).

Sanderstead. Mes site 341614; R pottery, Limpsfield Rd.; S burials; prehistoric occupation c. 337633; barrow c. 337632.

Seale. Mes sites: 887473 etc. and 880462 etc.; N implements 887473; EBA food vessel; LBA hoards, 886458 and 880460; IA 'A' occupation 889483; IA 'A'? earthwork 876463; R occupation, Hampton Pk.; R building 885487; Med building and kiln, Hampton Pk.; barrows 880462 etc. (and IA 'A' pottery) and c. 895457; earthworks ('seven ditches' 10C.) 912480.

Send. N? implements; R building?; PN Aldbury 13C. 041577 renamed Newark at building of Med priory; Med meeting-place of Woking Hundred at Harmes Hatch; field-names: Tilefield (16C. *Tile ostefelde; ost*=kiln); Keep Meadow 13C.

Shackleford (935455). Mes sites; Romano-Belgic cremation urns.

Shalford. P implement; Mes sites, 008468, 995455 and Trunley Common; N implements; R occupation; Med hundred-moot site at Perry Bridge; PN Summersbury, 16C. 004463; PN Tilehouse, 14C.

Shere with Gomshall. P implement; Mes site, c. 105432; N (secondary) site 080499; N hoard of axes, Peaslake; R occupation, Tower Hill Pit; Med? ironworking; PN Goldhard 16C. ('gold-hoard'); PN Kiln Platt 076446.

Stoke (998507). N implements.

Stoke D'Abernon. R building? c. 129585; R? brick in church 129585; R occupation, Oxshott.

Surbiton. IA 'A2', Wealden and R. sherds 202674 etc.

Sutton (260640). N implements.

Tandridge. Mes site c. 380490?; IA? fort 363508; Med meeting-place of Tandridge Hundred c. 370520 (on a knoll, *Hundredsnow* 17C.).

Tatsfield. R road 415560; Med deserted village? 417561.

Thorpe. N (Peterborough), IA 'A' and 'AB' (haematite-coated ware and Marnian pedestal urns) and R (pottery and rectangular enclosure) in successive occupation c. 044687; LBA occupation elsewhere.

Thursley. Mes sites: c. 898407, c. 882405, c. 898386; c. 880414 and c. 896398; N implements; LBA hoard; IA? pottery c. 897383; R pottery c. 897383; S pot; Med

glass works; ironworking; bowl barrow 909409; earthwork, Kettlebury 18C., c. 882405; PN Ward tree 10C. (Hindhead?), look-out point.

Tilford. Mes sites: 869447, 872438, 876431, 885429; N implements: 869447, 872438 and 876431; R occupation 880440; R pottery kilns 880440 and 885436; linear earthworks 890445 etc. (destroyed?) and 875450 etc.; barrows (destroyed?) 890444.

Titsey. N implements 411560; EBA beaker, 'A' or 'C' type; R house, later used as fulling? factory, 404546; R temple (Church Field) 420550; R cremation (South-eastern 'B' derived pot); R? building and R pottery 409550; R road 410561 etc.; barrow c. 404546; earthwork, square, 403557; PN *Goldwhurd* 17C. ('gold-hoard'); PN Streatfield 417534.

Waddon. Mes site 313651; LBA occupation; IA 'A' occupation; Wealden Culture (IA 'B') occupation: subterranean chambers 313651; R occupation, 313651.

Wallington (290640). R and S? occupation: earthwork near Wandle; S? inhumations.

Walton-on-Thames. P and N implements 086618; EBA 'A' beaker sherds 096649; MBA barrow cemetery (destroyed), over-hanging-rim urns 083610; LBA flat cemetery, bucket urns c. 096649; IA 'A' hill-fort (cf. *burhwuda* 10C. and *le Bery* 14C.), IA 'A' and 'C' pottery 086618; IA? hill-fort (destroyed) 082652; R finds 096649; S pottery, Anzac Mount; S? barrows, inhumations 096665 (destroyed).

Walton-on-the-Hill. N implements; IA and R sherds c. 220555; IA Southeastern 'B' and Patch Grove ware on site of R house 223557; R house and ?associated fields 232536 and 232540 etc., respectively; Med castle mound, 221552.

Wanborough (934490). P implements; R building?; barrows? (air site); PN from *beorg*.

Warlingham (360585). LBA hoard; R finds.

West Clandon. IA occupation 044503 with 'AB' and South-eastern 'B' wares.

West Horsley. Mes site; N (secondary) knapping-floor 081500.

Weybridge. P implement; EBA 'A' beaker pottery and MBA overhanging-rim urn sherds c. 082652; LBA flat cemetery c. 082652; IA 'A1' pottery; R coin-hoard of c. A.D. 300.

Wimbledon. P and N. implements, W. Common; Mes site c. 230725; LBA/IA (transition) sherds and IA 'A2' ware from Caesar's Camp (Bensbury 10C.) 223712, a hill-fort of 'A2'; BA and S? barrows (destroyed) 223714; Belgic cremation; R finds; Museum, John Evelyn Club.

Windlesham. R road, agger, 940666 etc.

Wisley. N occupation, Peterborough ware and implements; MBA barrows including bell-type at Cockcrow Hill and c. 079600; IA 'A2' occupation, kilns and haematite-coated ware, AB pottery, 060596; R kiln and pottery c. 060590.

Witley. Mes site, W Common; barrow 919402; PN Borough (from *beorg*, 'hill') 16C. and Rodborough c. 930417.

Woking. R pottery; barrows 017598 (including two bell) and 996538; PN Goldsworth (Goldhord 13C.) and Maybury 19C.; field-name Black Field 16C.

Wonersh. P implements; Mes site c. 035457 etc.; N (secondary) occupation 044442; LBA bowl barrow (destroyed?), primary cremations in bucket urns, secondary in biconical lugged urn in cist c. 039454; LBA/IA cremation in urn, Shamley Green; R occupation, Blackheath; Med hundred meeting-place on Blackheath; PN Streets Field 14C., R road from Farley Heath?

Woodmansterne. N implements; Romano-Belgic pottery from occupation site c. 281589; PN Stagbury (*Statbury* 14C.), 273580; quadrangular earthwork?

Worplesdon. N implements; LBA intermediate bell-disc barrows with primary and secondary cremations in bucket urns 997537 etc.; R house c. 960507; R building c. 001531?; S barrow-cluster, Whitmoor Common; linear earthwork (Grymesditch 17C.?) 995536 etc.; PN Tilehouse 16C.; field-name Black Lands 17C.

Wotton. Mes sites: 142432, c. 135442, c. 135433 etc., 135470 etc. and at Tankard's Pond; MBA barrow, intermediate bell-disc, 118481; R cremations c. 118481; S pottery c. 118481; hoard of late R bronze vessels; mound 480115?; PN Whiteberry 137440.

SUSSEX

(E) and (W) refer to the Eastern and Western parts of the County

Albourne (E). Med shrunken village, migration of site? 257162.

Alciston (E). LBA enclosures, fields and tracks 495035; R minor way 490048 etc.; terraceway 497050 etc.; barrows 500045 etc.; Celtic fields 483051 etc.; strip lynchet? 497053 etc. (or terraceway?); earthworks 481049.

Aldingbourne (W). P implements from 70 ft. to 90 ft. ancient shoreline c. 930070; R aristocratic cist burials; Med castle mound, Totehull 13C., used as a look-out point, 923047; Med park to S. of railway-boundary bank?; PN Oldbury 14C., 920067.

Aldrington (E) (270050). R occupation.

Aldwick (W) (915990). P implement, Acheulian.

Alfriston (E). N long barrows 509035 (one called Long Burgh); MBA collared urn; LBA barrow cemetery, bucket and globular urns, c. 517021; LBA socketed axe of

Breton type; S inhumation cemetery 517038; Med meeting-place of Longbridge Hundred 524036; barrows 497028 etc.; cross-ridge dyke and terraceways 508038 etc.

Amberley (W). Barrows 042125; cross-ridge dyke 050124 etc.; Celtic fields 045123 etc.; Med castle earthworks 028132.

Ambersham (W). Mes implements 900310.

Angmering (W). N open-cast flint mines and hut with track leading to them 081100; LBA or IA 'A1' cattle enclosure 081100; IA 'A' ditches (haematite-coated sherd) on site of R house and cremations 054045; R building? 082044 and 068089; PN Harrow Hill 13C. suggests pagan S shrine; Med shrunken settlement? 068089.

Appledram (W). R settlement and quay? 836029; Med? saltpans.

Ardingly (E). Ironworking (cf. PN: The Furnace and Hammer Wood); PN Berry Farm and Burstow Hill 359291.

Arlington (E). N long barrow 542033; R occupation on site of church 543075; R pottery 525090 and 538069; R building; Med castle earthworks, Burlough, 531043; five Med moated sites, 544083, 558094 etc.; barrows 542033 etc.

Arundel (W). IA 'C' and R occupation with South-eastern 'B' ware also 015085; IA and R (late) occupation, 'Nanny's Croft' in Arundel Pk.; R building, Tarrant St.; S barrow inhumations; Norman castle mound and earthworks 019072; barrow and Celtic-field lynchet, Arundel Pk.; double lynchet road c. 015085; earthworks c. 985075.

Ashburnham (E). Ironworking until A.D. 1828, 687160.

Ashington (W). R building c. 120150.

Balcombe (E). Mes rock shelter; PN Brickkiln Wood 322347; PN Kiln Wood 312333; PN Bury Wood 294298.

Barcombe (E). LBA hoard and R pottery 433150; site of hundred-moot?

Barlavington (W). R pottery; barrows 962158 etc.; earthwork 960153 etc.

Barnham (W) (960044). MBA merchant's hoard; BA? flint implements.

Battle (E). Mes? flint implements c. 741176; R ironworking c. 745140, c. 786140 and c. 765175; Med hundred-moot 710187; later ironworking (cf. PN Blacklands? 760135 and Ash Wood? 727173).

Beckley (E). Med moated site c. 858215; Med ironworking (cf. Brownsmith c. 863243).

Beddingham (E). MBA collared urns c. 440055; LBA '2A' village, huts and enclosures 443053; IA 'A1' and 'A2' open settlement (including haematite-coated ware) until fortified in face of Wealden folk expansion and refortified by the latter against Romans—Caburn hill-fort 444089: pottery of IA 'A', Wealden culture 'ABC' and South-eastern 'B' and its derivative Asham-type pottery; R occupation; S? burials; Med 12C. adulterine castle 444089; Med shrunken village? 445078; barrows 452060 etc.

Bepton (W). R road as terraceway 848184 etc.; barrows 855169; Med shrunken village, Lynch, 849185.

Bersted (W) (928013). PN Tinhale (Barn) from (*thing* = 'meeting')—moot site?

Berwick (E). Mound (S barrow?) in churchyard 519049.

Bexhill (E). MBA merchant's hoard; LBA winged axe; R inhumation; ironworking 747110 etc. (cf. PN Furnacefield); Museum, Egerton Pk.

Bignor (W). N camp, 976126 (much damaged); R house 988147; R pottery, Glatting Down; R road, Stane St., agger and terraceway 970128 etc., and 977133 etc.; barrows, including R type, 969130 etc.; cross-ridge dyke 966134 etc.; double earthwork yielding LBA pottery, breached by Stane St., 973129 etc.; Med pot-making, using clay and flint of R road, c. 993141; Mes implements 993173.

Billingshurst (W). MBA hoard; R occupation 086258.

Binderton (W). Med deserted village (emparkment?) 851108.

Birdham (W). Med deserted village, East Itchenor, c. 816005; linear earthwork, *Brynes dic* 10C., c. 840012 etc.?; PN Manhood 12C., meeting-place of hundred 840010.

Blackpatch. See Patching.

Bodiam (E). R road? 787263 etc.; R lookout platform (or Civil War, 17C., gun-site?) 785260; R harbour? 790264; Med dock 786255; Museum, B. Castle.

Bognor (W) (935990). P implement; MBA merchant's hoard and MBA founder's hoard.

Bolney (E) (260230). S timbered road.

Bosham (W). R buildings: beneath church 804039, 812052 and 812053; S? moated site 804039; field-name, Burfield 13C.

Botolphs (W). R occupation c. 190093; Med deserted village? c. 193093.

Boxgrove (W). P implements from 70 ft. to 90 ft. ancient shoreline, Acheulian, c. 914068; EBA beaker inhumation, Goodwood; IA? hill-fort, 921097; R road, Stane St., agger 925095 etc.; linear earthwork (Belgic defence of Chichester?) 900084 etc.; PN Oldbury 14C., 920067; PN Crockerhill, 13C., 922071.

Bramber (W). R occupation 185107; Norman castle mound and bailey 185107.

Brede (E). R bloomery c. 810210; PN Hundred House, moot of Gostrow Hundred; field-name *Wiacre* 13C. (from *wīg/wēoh*, 'temple'?), pagan S shrine?

Brightling (E) (685210). Ironworking (cf. PN Glazier's Forge); Med hundred-moot of Henhurst probably in N.E. of parish.

Brighton (see also Ovingdean, Patcham, Preston and Rottingdean). N causeway-camp, Whitehawk, 330048: N habitation, Windmill Hill and Ebbsfleet ware; Whitehawk also, EBA habitation, beaker and rusticated sherds; EBA 'A' beaker inhumations, Church Hill (St. Nicholas); MBA hoard; MBA cremations in urns under barrow near Hollingbury; MBA overhanging-rim urn, Kemp Town; LBA, two hoards; LBA winged axe and socketed axes of Breton type (two); IA 'A1' contour hill-fort, refortified in 'A2', Hollingbury 322078: IA 'A2' and late South-eastern 'B' pottery; IA 'A1' occupation, Kemp Town; R buildings: Kemp Town, Round Hill Cres., and near St. Peter's Church; R finds, many in the town; R coin-hoard c. A.D. 250; Med shrunken settlement, Balsdean, 378060; Museum, Church St.

Broadwater (W). N implements; LBA bucket urn; IA South-eastern 'B' pottery; R occupation; R burials 142078.

Burpham (W). BA and secondary R burials in barrow 048113, 'The Burgh' (*beorg*), from which also came an EBA 'B' beaker sherd; LBA barrow; R occupation 055084 etc., and several other sites on Downs; S promontory fort (a 10C. *burh*) 039086; barrow 055106; Celtic fields c. 060100 etc.; linear earthwork, Wepham Down.

Burton (W). Med deserted village (emparkment?) 968175; PN not from *burh*.

Burwash (E). Med ironworking (cf. PN Forge Wood, 700262); PN Burwash 12C. from *burh*-: earthwork c. 675247?

Bury (W). R watering-tank beside R road, Stane St., 998149; Hundred of Bury met at *Motstowe* 14C.; cross-ridge dyke (faint) c. 000121; barrows 990130, 002122 etc., etc.; PN Bury 11C. from *burh*; PN W. Burton means '*tūn* west of Bury'?

Buxted (E). Mes site; late IA occupation; R occupation; Med deer-forest look-out point 474304 (like the two preceding sites); Celtic fields c. 474301; 16C. ironworking; PN Potter's Green 13C., 504231.

Caburn. See Beddingham.

Chailey (E). N implements c. 387214.

Chichester (W). P. implements; EBA inhumation with food vessel; LBA urn; IA 'A' occupation 867046 and St. John St.; late Belgic occupation; R city: walls, bastions, houses, cemeteries, amphitheatre (867046); R occupation 877046; S occupation, wattle structures; Med castle mound 863052; linear earthworks 864061 etc., and 850066; PN Pidborough, from *beorg*, probably 'barrow'; hundred-moot at Stockbridge 859037.

Chiddingly (E). R bloomeries c. 563168; later ironworking (cf. Stream Furnace c. 552158); PN Burgh Hill 17C. 540130; PN Thunder's Hill 15C. 550132 very doubtful pagan S site.

Cissbury. See West Tarring.

Clapham (W). IA or R occupation; Celtic fields and strip lynchets 095074; S burial mounds.

Clayton (E). N hoard of axes and pottery spoons; MBA barrow, cremation with collared urn, pigmy cup, faïence pendant etc. 304135; R bath-house 300139; R occupation 298141.

Cocking (W). R occupation 868167; barrows 863168 and 892166; cross-ridge dyke 894165; strip lynchet? 870172 etc.

Cold Waltham (W). R road, Stane St., 024170 etc.; R coin-hoard, late 3C.

Compton (W). IA? fort 766150; barrows 794163 etc.; lynchet? 797165.

Coombes (W). Med deserted village? 191083.

Cowfold (W). PN Godshill, 202213—pagan S site?; PN Potter's Farm 16C.

Crowhurst (E). Late IA and R bloomery 770127; R bloomery and mining sites 758108.

Cuckfield (E). R cremation; R occupation c. 303258; ironworking (cf. PN Furnacegreen Shaw); PN Harradines (Harrowden etc. 17C.)—pagan S site?

Dallington (E). Late IA ironworking 652184; 16C. ironworking c. 680182.

Danehill (E). Med hundred-moot? c. 403276; PN Kidborough 393263.

Denton (E). MBA collared urn; Celtic fields c. 480033.

Didling (W). R road? 840170 etc.; Med deserted village? 835182; barrow? in square earthwork 834175.

Ditchling (E). LBA founder's hoard; IA hill-fort and road 332130; IA and R pottery; barrows e.g. 319131 etc.; Frag Barrow 330178 (natural hill?); circular earthwork with entrance—Middle Brow.

Donnington (W). R burial; R road? 858027.

Duncton (W). MBA collared urn c. 955155; R bath-house 960167; barrows 962188 etc.; PN Burton (not from *burh*); Med deserted village?, Burton, 968175.

Durrington (W) (120050). R occupation; PN Crockhurst 16C.

Earnley (W). R road? 815984 etc.; R coin-hoard, late 3C.

Eartham (W). Late IA and R open settlement with Celtic fields 947100 etc.; R cremation in barrow 946102; R road, Stane St., agger, 936103 etc.; barrows 948101 etc.

East Blatchington (E). R? cremations 483999; barrows 467010 etc.; PN Camp Hill 495014.

Eastbourne (E). P implements, Clactonian; LBA occupation, Kitchener's Furlong; LBA hoards, four, including a winged axe; IA 'A1' occupation; IA inhumation with imitation Belgic pot; R buildings and burials in the town; R occupation intensive c. 595995; R coin-hoard; S inhumations, 596006, Torfield and Mill Field; Med hundred-moot in Borough

Lane (PN from *beorg*): Motcombe (Rd.) means 'valley near which the moot was held'; PN Moatcroft (Rd.) is near site of Norman castle mound (motte); barrows 592982 etc.; strip lynchet? 590984 etc.; ditch? 588983; Museum, Borough Lane.

East Dean (E). EBA beaker sherd 560959; MBA hoard; LBA bucket urn from barrow (destroyed); IA? hill-fort? 560959; R inhumation 558970; barrows 564958 etc.

East Dean (W). Barrow c. 900140, which may be the 'hill of holiness' of a charter, possibly a pagan S site Christianized; IA? hill-fort? and lynchets 900140; Celtic fields and bivallate track 918152 etc.; barrows (including bell type) 929145 etc.; barrows 935127 and 906118; PN Potcomb 918123.

Eastergate (W). R brick in church 945051.

East Grinstead (E). Late IA and R iron bloomery 369357; R bloomery 390357; R road 360338 etc.; Med, 11C., and later ironworking (cf. place-names in the parish); Med moated site? 361390; PN Crockshed (Cracksherd?) 377373.

East Hoathly (E). Mes site c. 500164; ironworking; PN Whyly (from *wīg*?) 13C., possible pagan S site; PN Crockstead 493179.

East Lavington (W). Barrows 943156 etc., etc.; cross-ridge dykes 937160, 941158 and 947157; PN Bury 13C.

Edburton (W). R cremations; Med castle mound and bailey 238110; barrows 233113; Celtic fields, bivallate and double lynchet tracks 228102.

Elsted (W). LBA hoard (merchant's); IA camp 807183 (see Harting); barrow 807181; linear earthwork 815184 etc.

Etchingham (E). PN's: Burgham 11C., 702280; Burgh Wood 725275; Shoyswell 11C., site of hundred-moot; Pentwood (*Pentotes* 16C.), look-out point; ironworking.

Ewhurst (E). N stone axes; R road 782240 etc. (cf. PN Streetfield 787205, 13C.); PN Staple Cross 12C., 781224, meeting-place of Staple Hundred.

Fairlight (E). Med hundred-moot c. 860119; PN Fishponds Farm.

Falmer (E). EBA beaker 'B' burial; MBA collared urn; R cemetery (R and IA South-eastern 'B' pottery), 362118; R settlement, earthworks and Celtic fields 370111; Med deserted village, Balmer (from *burh*, 11C.) 359100; barrows, 365116 etc.; earthwork, valley enclosure, 361080; bivallate track 360104; double lynchet track 363110; ancient pond 359098; PN Patchway 8C. (from *wēoh*)— pagan S. shrine, c. 328101?

Felpham (W). LBA founder's hoard c. 960010.

Fernhurst (W). Mes site c. 917300; ironworks, closed A.D. 1776, 877284 etc.

Ferring (W). M? BA cremation; LBA '2A' and '2B' settlement, 092044; LBA hoards; IA 'A1' rectangular contour fort, Highdown. Finds include 'A2' and 'B' wares, 092044: refortified in R period; R bath-house 088043; R occupation 094026 and 080043; S cremation and inhumation cemetery 092044; Celtic fields 092044 etc.; windmill tump c. 092044.

Findon (W). N/EBA flint mines 113083 and ?110088; EBA (late) beaker burial with rusticated pottery; BA barrows c. 109089; MBA occupation, overhanging-rim sherds 113084; IA open settlement, 'A1', 'B' and Wealden wares, 142097/8; IA 'A1' rectangular huts 109095; IA occupation site (unexcavated) 144093; R circular shrine and ritual burial of ox-skulls 109095; R occupation 108089 and 148084; Celtic fields 129108 etc., and 110088 etc.; ancient track 122104 etc.; ancient pond 110089.

Fishbourne (W). R buildings 839046 and 843045.

Fittleworth (W). P implements, Acheulian; Mes site, Bedham Hill; PN Street Farm 13C.

Fletching (E). P forgeries (Piltdown) 439217; N? implements, Piltdown; Med hundred-moot 443230; ironworking.

Ford (W) (000036). R burials and building (destroyed).

Forest Row (E). R bloomery 398347; R and Med bloomery 447384 (cf. PN Hammerwood); PN Tylehurst 413340; PN Kilnfield 420387.

Framfield (E). Med hundred-moot (cf. PN Hundred House 515218); 17C. tile-kiln; ironworking (cf. PN Pounsley Furnace 526218); PN Bushbury 525191; PN Crockstead 13C. 493179.

Frant (E). Mes? rock shelters 560382; IA ironworking (PN Colegrove) 591326; late IA and R pottery in iron slag c. 586329; IA (Wealden culture) promontory fort 560382; later ironworking in parish; Med archery butts, F. Green.

Friston (E). N (secondary) pottery sherd; IA pottery c. 545992; S inhumation; barrows 544966 etc.; ancient pond 551982; PN Westburton 11C. c. 545975.

Fulking (E). Mes sites c. 238123 and c. 250130; R pottery, Fulking Corner.

Funtington (W). Belgic? linear earthwork 820066 etc.; R aristocratic cist burials by cremation, 833072; Celtic fields 805102 etc.

Glynde (E). MBA cinerary urns and incense cups from barrows; R minor road 463093 and causeway 462090; S inhumations; barrows 446098 etc. and 446094 etc.; square earthwork, Fore Down?, from which R finds.

Goring (W) (110030). PN Streets Copse 14C. PN Potlands 17C.

Graffham (W). Barrows, including bell type, 914163; Celtic fields 918153 etc.

Greatham (W). R coin-hoard, c. A.D. 350; R cremation cemetery; Med shrunken settlement? 043158.

Hadlow Down (E). Med moated site 519226; ironworking (cf. Huggett's Furnace 14C. 532260).

Hailsham (E). PN Tile Hurst (i.e. tile oast) 16C., 575100.

Hamsey (E). R occupation 393124 and 398113; R road, agger, 392153 etc.; Med deserted village? 414122; Med castle earthworks? (damaged) 404128; barrows 380123 etc.; PN (Mount) Harry 17C., 383123 possibly from *hearg*, a pagan S shrine.

Hangleton (E). M or LBA hoard; R barrow on Celtic field lynchet 268084; R inhumations and cremations; S inhumation c. 270080; Med shrunken village, house-sites of 13C.–14C. excavated 271075, double lynchet track 270080 etc.

Hardham (W). Belgic pottery; R posting-station with defensive bank, 031174 with settlement, cremation cemetery and pottery-making nearby; R causeway c. 040173 etc.

Harrow Hill. See Angmering.

Hartfield (E). Late IA earthwork enclosure 474311; R road (section left open) 461391; local site of hundred-moot?; Med castle mound? 482361 (cf. PN Castle Field); ironworking (cf. PN Furnace Pond etc. 454399).

Harting (W). Mes site c. 783227; IA 'A1'? and 'A2' hill-fort, Torberry 13C. (ploughed out) 779204; IA 'A2' hill-fort, Beacon Hill, 806184, defences recut in Belgic or early R period; IA hut shelters, 'A2' and 'B' pottery, 792185; R farmstead, enclosure bank and lynchets c. 800172; R occupation at various sites, e.g. c. 800190; Romano-Celtic temple 806184; R minor road, cutting through cross-ridge dyke 797187; cross-dykes 797184 and 765185; barrows 786266; S barrow c. 797187; strip lynchets 780202 etc.

Hassocks (E). Mes site 297154; N clay spoons; LBA cemetery, bucket urns 297154; IA South-eastern 'B' pottery from R cemetery 296154 with nearby R settlement; S cremation and inhumation cemetery 296154; Med hundred-moot, Buttinghill 298156.

Hastings (E). Mes site 820095; R settlement 804093 etc.; S? promontory fort (*burh*) 833100 etc.; Norman castle earthwork 821095; Med kilns for pottery and tiles 13C.; earthwork, N.E. of castle; Med hundred-moot, Baldslow 11C. (from *hlāw*, probably 'hill'); Museums: Cambridge Rd. and High St.

Haywards Heath (E) (330240). LBA urn; R pottery.

Heathfield (E). Circular earthwork (ploughed); ironworking (cf. PN Furnace Wood); PN Cade Street 13C., 604210, and PN Street End 13C., 606237.

Hellingly (E) (580123). Hundred-moot of Dill in this parish; PN Norbelton (from north *burhtūn* 13C.).

Henfield (W). Mes site; IA? promontory fort? (much damaged) c. 218159; S? moated site 209133; PN Streatham 12C., 201138 referring to R road; PN Barrow-hill 13C., 218152; PN Chestham (from *ciest*, 'chest, coffin'?) 218180; hundred meeting-place at Hundredsteddle? 228151, and, at another period, at Moustows Manor?

Herstmonceux (E). R cremations 647104; later ironworking (cf. PN Cinderford (Cottages) 14C.); PN Flowers Green (from *flōr*?) 638115.

Heyshott (W). R terraceway; barrows 901194 etc., 901190 etc., and 895166 etc.; cross-ridge dykes 908165 etc. and 894166 etc.

High Down. See Ferring.

Hollingbury. See Brighton.

Hollington (E). R bloomery (destroyed) 784139.

Horsham (W). Mes sites in parish and district e.g. Roffey c. 200320 and Colgate c. 230330; PN The Castle, 198341 (earth-work) and Owlscastle 201337; PN Crock-hurst 10C.

Horsted Keynes. Late IA pottery manu-facture, c. 384262?; products revealing fusion of South-eastern 'B', Belgic and Wealden cultures; ironworking (cf. PN Cinder Hill 379298).

Houghton (W). BA and R pottery 002105; R? cross-ridge dyke 000103.

Hove (E). MBA barrow (destroyed): inhumation with amber cup etc.; BA burial, Lower Tongdean; LBA founder's hoard.

Hurstpierpoint (E). R house 279151; R occupation 279165; R tile-kiln 286155; R road 275153 etc.; PN Wanbarrow 271158 (from *beorg*, 'hill'?); PN Berry-lands 17C. (*burh*), PN Tott Farm, look-out point?

Icklesham (E) (880165). R ironworking.

Ifield (W) (250380). Ironworking.

Iford (E). EBA 'B' beaker c. 404058; bar-rows 401061 etc.; ancient pond 378043; rectangular enclosure, Castle Hill, 378068; Med hundred-moot at Swanborough 11C. 'peasants' hill', 401078.

Iping (W). Mes site; R posting-station with defensive earthwork 843262; R occupation c. 849255 and 852230; R road 849220 etc.; R ford? 850227; barrows 848216 etc. and 847222.

Isfield (E). Mes site; R road 444190 etc.; Med castle mound and bailey 442180; mound? 442182; Med village site? near 444182; PN Owlsbury 460200.

Jevington (E). N causeway-camp, Ebbs-fleet pottery 574022; R pottery and coins 576022 from bell barrow (MBA); disc? barrow 576022; Celtic fields 570017 etc.;

PN Broughton 11C. (from *burhtūn*), earthworks c. 563034; PN Farnstreet and Street Farm—R road?

Kingston Buci (W). EBA 'B' beaker occupation; LBA '2B' occupation, bucket urns, IA 'A1', 'B', 'ABC', South-eastern 'B' and R pottery, *all at 233059 and nearby*; R building 231053; R occupation 225065; barrow 225066; Celtic fields 227082.

Kingston near Lewes (E). S inhumation cemetery, 'Saxonbury'; PN Castle Hill 375073.

Kirdford (W). IA (Wealden culture?) fort, iron-smelting refuse, 979295; R occupation c. 005277.

Lancing (W). MBA collared urns and pigmy cups; LBA '2B' ware; IA occupation site, 'A1' (haematite-coated ware), 'A2', 'C' and South-eastern 'B' (Patch Grove and related ware) 188065; Romano-Celtic temple and burials c. 180067; S inhumations, Hoe Court House.

Lavant (W). N flint mines (R finds) 870098 etc.; Belgic? linear earthworks 845080 etc., 874088 etc. and 862075 etc.; earthworks 873099.

Lewes (E). MBA hoard; MBA overhanging-rim urns; LBA founder's hoard; R burials, Cuckoo Bottom; S? burials: weapons; S? promontory fort (largely destroyed) 414104; Med castle mounds 414102 and 414103; Med salt refinery? 416097; platform and disc barrows (damaged) 402110; barrows 398103 etc.; Museums: Barbican House and Town Hall.

Linchmere (W) (870310). R coin-hoard, late 3C.

Lindfield (E). PN Shotenbury 13C.; PN Kiln Wood 344264.

Litlington (E). P implement; N long barrow 536007; LBA 'A2' to IA 'A1' occupation with associated Celtic fields, double lynchet way and cross-ridge dykes 542019

etc.; Celtic fields 540015; barrows 538011 etc.; PN Old Kiln Bottom (lime kiln?) 540015.

Littlehampton (W). LBA winged axe; R building and burials c. 030020; R occupation, ditches, Wickbourne Estate; Museum Maltravers Rd.

Little Horsted (E). Late IA pottery making (including South-eastern 'B' ware with Wealden culture influence); IA iron-working; R occupation (ironworking?) 462173.

Lodsworth (W) (930230). Med glass-making, Sandpits.

Lower Beeding (W). Mes sites c. 220260 and Beeding Wood; MBA hoard; iron-working (cf. PN's Furnace Pond 230253 and Hammerpond 220290); PN Kilnwood 227355.

Lullington (E). LBA 'A3' to IA 'A1' (transition) occupation 541019; Celtic fields, tracks and cross-ridge dyke 545020 etc.; barrows 544025 etc.; strip lynchets 534028; Med deserted village? 528030.

Lurgashall (W). Mes site c. 917300; PN Barfold 14C. (from *burh*) 934311; PN Castle Copse 17C.

Madehurst (W). Celtic fields c. 985090; bivallate earthwork 979086 etc.; PN Madehurst 12C., means 'speech-wood', referring to moot-site 958133 of the two western rapes of Sussex.

Marden (W), including East, West, North and Up Marden. N long barrow, Bevis's Thumb, 789154; MBA collared urn; R house and R mound nearby, 774126; R house, Up Marden.

Maresfield (E). Late IA ironworking 473304; R ironworking 473304 and 475267; Celtic fields 473304; later ironworking (cf. PN Old Forge 460259); PN Brick Kiln Farm 440322.

Mayfield (E). PN Isenhurst 13C. ('ironwood') 565231, Med ironworking.

Middleton (W) (980000). LBA hoard; R occupation.

Midhurst (W) (885215). P implement; Med castle mound, St. Anne's Hill.

Mountfield (E). LBA gold hoard; iron-working (cf. PN Darwell Furnace 710207).

New Barn Down. See Patching.

Newhaven (E). P implement; N Peter-borough ware; LBA hoard, carpenter's kit; LBA '2B', IA 'A1' and 'A2', IA (Wealden culture), IA (South-Eastern 'B') IA 'ABC' and R occupation on site of destroyed IA hill-fort, Castle Hill 445000; R house; R occupation c. 445003; two R coin-hoards, late 3C.

Newtimber (W). LBA occupation c. 268110; Belgic? occupation c. 268110; R occupation c. 270125; S inhumations and a cremation c. 268110; barrows 270111 and 270120 (ploughed).

North Chapel (W) (950290). Mes site; iron-working.

Northiam (E). Ironworking; 16C. glass-making; PN Dixter 13C., 817253 (from *dic*, 'ditch').

North Mundham (W). R occupation; PN Brinfast 7C., 860998 (from *faestenn*, 'stronghold').

North Stoke (W). PN Camp Hill 036112.

Nuthurst (W). Med earthworks 180270.

Ore (E). R road 818130 etc.

Oving (W) (900050). P implement.

Ovingdean (E). MBA overhanging-rim urn; R cremation; barrow 357046.

Pagham (W). R occupation; S pottery 884975; PN Wada's barrow in 7C. charter.

Parham (W). Barrows 059126 etc.; Med deserted village? c. 059141.

Park Brow. See Sompting.

Patcham (Brighton). Mes site 288081; EBA 'B' beaker inhumation 323087; LBA gold hoard; R house c. 330070; R cremations; barrows (including a disc type?) 313102

(destroyed); Celtic fields 318097 etc.; earthworks and lynchets near Eastwick Barn; earthworks, Ewe Bottom; ancient pond 318088. S cremation c. 330070.

Patching (W). N occupation, Windmill Hill pottery and implements; N/EBA flint-mines, Blackpatch 094089 etc. (ploughed): Beaker burials in shafts; MBA cremations in collared urns under barrows; LBA '2A' farmstead (henge-site? re-used) c. 097103; LBA enclosures, circular huts and fields 092092; LBA enclosures 089097; LBA '2B' farmstead enclosure and fields 084090; LBA, IA 'A' and 'A2' pottery 084092; IA South-eastern 'B' ware; R pottery 092092; barrows contemporary with some flint-mine shafts 094089 (ploughed); ancient track 089073.

Peacehaven (E) (410010). Mes site on Wool-wich Beds (sand).

Penhurst (E). Med shrunken settlement? 695165; ironworking until A.D. 1811.

Petworth (W) (980220). Ironworking.

Pevensey (E). R fort of Saxon shore, occu-pation in 5C., 644048; earthwork of A.D. 1577–8 within fort.

Piddinghoe (E). N long barrow, Money Burgh (*beorg*) 425037; IA pottery, many sites; R burials 415029; Med deserted hamlet, at the Lydds, 439029?; strip lynchets? 427026 etc. and 426038 etc.; ancient track? 432026 etc.

Playden (E). Mes site 921227; M/LBA site, ring-ditch and rectangular enclosure 921226; PN's Saltcote and Saltbarn, medieval saltpans near, 927221.

Plumpton (E). EBA 'B' beaker sherd c. 358122; LBA hoard; LBA '2A' farmstead (Site A) 358122: huts, enclosures and contemporary fields; LBA '2B' farmstead (Site B), hut-sites and ?fields, finds of winged axe, bucket and barrel urn sherds; LBA? enclosures c. 351120; rectangular enclosures 353125; Celtic fields 355114

U

etc.; barrows 370127 etc.; cross-ridge dykes 368126 etc.

Portslade (E). P implement; MBA hoard; IA hoard of bronze objects; R building 259085; R occupation and Celtic fields 245097 etc.; R cremations 251053; barrows 239091 etc.; PN Portslade 11C., 'Port's road', a R or earlier trackway 260067 etc.

Poynings (E). N axe of igneous rock; EBA 'B' beaker inhumation 260103; E/MBA crouched inhumation, 'Black Burgh' (*beorg*) c. 264101; MBA contracted inhumation, 'Blade Burgh' (*beorg*), destroyed c. 256109; IA 'A2' promontory fort 'The Devil's Dyke' 256108 etc.; IA farmstead, 'ABC' and South-eastern 'B' pottery 258108; R occupation near 256108; Med? rectangular cattle enclosure 266113; barrows 258094 etc.; PN Bostal Rd., 13C. (from *burhsteall*, i.e. 'The Dyke'?).

Preston (E). R house 309057; R burials; S burials.

Pulborough (W). Mes site; EBA? flint dagger factory; R house c. 069200; R temple 043188; R mausoleum 066190; R buildings 047187, 057188 and 073187; Norman castle mound? 038189; ancient pond 062188; earthworks c. 077177 and c. 070170; PN Pulborough 11C. from *beorg*, 'hill'; PN Brinsbury 12C., 067223; PN Borough Farm 13C., 069202; PN Toat Hill 14C., 050217, 'look-out point'.

Pyecombe (E). IA 'A1' hill-fort, ditch within bank, Wolstonbury 284138; R settlement, late in R period, 286138; Med deserted village c. 293127; disc barrow 284135; earthwork enclosure 266103; earthwork? 284136 etc.

Rackham (W). Barrows (one of IA) 059126 etc.; cross-ridge dyke and terraceways, 051125 etc.

Racton. Med deserted village? 779093; Med shrunken village, Lordington 783097.

Ringmer (E). R road 431140; S inhumations; Med castle mound 449144; earthwork c. 456112; PN Harrowdown 14C.—pagan S shrine; Ringmer was the meeting-place of a hundred; PN Broyle 13C. 'park', boundary bank? 478128; PN Delves 447126, clay pits? for late 13C. pottery kiln in Potters Field nearby.

Ripe (E). R occupation 506104 ('The Burghs'); R occupation 499109; ditch 501110; field - name, *Goldhord* 15C., 501105.

Rodmell (E). IA or S grave-mound cluster c. 411055; R cremations 395050; barrows 404058 etc.

Rogate (W). PN Brickkiln Copse 801265 (but modern brick-works near).

Rotherfield (E). IA (Wealden culture) hill-fort, Saxonbury (*Sockbury* 16C.) 577329: an oval stone enclosure superseded by small hill-fort; IA and later ironworking (cf. PN Forge Farm and Minepit Wood c. 523335); PN Owlsbury 528281; PN Brick Kiln Wood 580295.

Rottingdean (E). P implements, Acheulian; N long barrow? c. 366026; EBA to LBA pottery c. 378060; MBA merchant's hoard; MBA cremation in overhanging-rim urn; MBA overhanging-rim urn 379060; LBA? hoard; late IA pottery (South-Eastern 'B') c. 385025; R coin-hoard, late 3C.; ancient pond 378043; PN Younsmere 13C., probably c. 355063, hundred moot-site in old pit; barrows, 371054; Museum, Grange House.

Rumboldswyke (W). R finds; R brick in church? 870041; R? road c. 859040 etc.

Rusper (W). Mes site c. 218343.

Rustington (W) (050020). LBA gold hoard; R occupation.

Rye (E). Med 13C. pottery kilns; PN Cadborough 009198 (from *beorg*, 'hill').

St Leonard's (E). MBA founder's hoard.

Salehurst (E). 16C. ironworking, Roberts-bridge.

Seaford (E). Mes site (on sand of Woolwich Beds) c. 487986; EBA? barrow 494978; IA 'A2' hill-fort (eroded by sea) 495978; R occupation and IA South-eastern 'B' pottery 490986; R occupation 495997; R cremation cemetery 494505; Med saltpans on coast; Med deserted village, Sutton, 494997; PN Chesterton (modern?) 499993; PN Camp Hill 495014.

Seddlescombe (E). N stone axes; IA and R iron bloomery c. 772200 (finds included painted South-eastern 'B' and Wealden culture wares); R road 779197 etc.; late S/early Norman pottery, Coombe Wood.

Selham (W). Prehistoric or Med mound 933210.

Selmeston (E). Mes, N (Peterborough), LBA (bucket urn sherd) and IA occupation 514069; S occupation 514069.

Selsey (W). P implements; N occupation: Windmill Hill, Abingdon and Peterborough wares; MBA hoard; LBA '2', IA 'A1', 'AB', Belgic and R occupation 858942; Belgic mint? and oppidum? (eroded by sea); R coin-hoard, late 3C.; R settlement, several sites in parish including 872958 and c. 871957; S village (destroyed) 840934; earthwork 872958; mound? c. 871957.

Shermanbury (W). PN Sh. means 'burh of the shireman' 11C.: site of S domestic burh?; Med hundred-moot 236202.

Shipley (W). R occupation c. 123226; Norman castle mound and moat 163208; PN Brickkiln Farm 158242; Med hundred-moot at Slaughterbridge (i.e. sloetree-bridge).

Shoreham (W). EBA 'B' beaker inhumation c. 223069; IA 'A1' defended farm (ploughed) 229084; IA 'A2', 'B', Wealden and R occupation, R cremations 222069; R farmstead with corn-drying ovens

232083; R burials 222067; R, very late, degenerate hand-made pottery 222083; S inhumations 214067; Med shrunken hamlet? Erringham 205077; Celtic fields 227083 etc.; strip lynchets overlying Celtic fields c. 231084 etc.; PN Thundersbarrow and Thunder's Steps 230080 may represent a development of OE Thunor (as in Thundersley, Essex) and indicate a pagan S shrine.

Sidlesham (W). LBA founder's hoard, including winged axe; R house 854970; R house and ditch, Lamb Lea; R occupation 854984 and 860971; R road? 854000 etc. (cf. PN Street End 17C. 853995).

Singleton (W). N causeway camp, Windmill Hill ware 877111; IA 'A1' hill-fort, 'A1', 'A2', 'B' and 'AB' pottery, 'The Trundle' 877111; earthwork 874114 etc.

Slaugham (E). Ironworking (cf. PN Furnace Pond); PN Ditton 284298 (from dic?).

Slindon (W). P implements from 100 ft. ancient shoreline c. 951083, Abbevillean, Clactonian and Acheulian: Acheulian occupation site on ancient sea beach; R road, Stane St., agger, 950113 etc.; earthworks 979088 etc.

Slinfold (W). R posting-station on Stane St. at Alfoldean (this PN 'old fold' must refer to the R defensive earthwork) 117330; R settlement 116327 etc.; R bridge site 118331; PN Toat Hill 14C., 123298, 'lookout point'.

Sompting. EBA, two 'B' beaker inhumations; EBA 'A' beaker c. 152090; MBA hoard; LBA '2A' farmstead, bucket and globular urns, 153086; IA 'A1' and 'A2' farmstead and fields, inurned cremation; 'B', 'AB', 'ABC' and South-eastern 'B' ware, 154087; R farmstead 154087; R house, wattle and daub 158086; R occupation 151082; R road as terraceway 160055 etc.; IA? terraceway 173068 etc.;

U*

crossridge dyke 168077; circular earthwork used as pond; R finds; LBA hoard.

South Heighton (E). MBA overhanging-rim urn with cremation in chalk cist; LBA hoard; S inhumation; R road, agger, c. 467034; barrow (destroyed?) 448033.

South Malling (E). N long barrow 431110; MBA (Wessex or related culture) barrow, faïence pendant etc., two cinerary urns; IA 'A2' unfinished promontory fort, Ranscombe 439092: South-eastern 'B' and R pottery and occupation débris; R occupation 428093; R cremations; S inhumation cemeteries, 428111 and c. 413110; barrows 434109 etc.; Celtic fields 436103 etc.; strip lynchets 436103 etc.; Med? earthwork enclosures, c. 437101 and ?439097; double lynchet way 435104; early 19C. cultivation 436103 etc.; disused 18C. coach road 423113 etc.

Southwick (W). R house 243055; R farmstead, fields and track c. 245084; Med hundred-moot 248050.

Stanmer (E). R occupation, hut, ditches, inhumations etc., Rocky Clump; barrows 343114 etc.; ancient pond 338095.

Stedham (W). R road 849210 etc.; barrows 853215 etc.; PN Harrowdown 14C. (site unknown), pagan S shrine; PN Tote Hill 864247, look-out point.

Steyning (W). EBA beaker inhumation in barrow 166099; LBA cremation cemetery, secondary interments in a barrow with one MBA collared urn 166099; IA 'ABC' ware; R occupation 179114 and elsewhere; R? terraceways 167102 etc.; cross-ridge dykes 163103 etc.; barrows 159108 etc.; earthwork 153110; PN Heathen Burials 13C. c. 182106.

Stopham (W) (027189). Mes site.

Storrington (W). MBA cremation in collared urn in barrow; LBA farmstead c. 080118; IA? fields c. 080118; IA South-eastern 'B' pottery 079135; R occupation 080126, 078117 and elsewhere; R occupation, Celtic fields, bivallate and double-lynchet road 078117; R road c. 070169 etc.; cross-ridge dyke and terraceway 084126 etc.; barrows 078126 etc.; rectangular earthwork c. 080118.

Stoughton (W). N long barrows 822122 and 824121; N flint mines? 825109; R house c. 738100; Romano-Celtic temple? c. 820110 (R coins, barbarous types); S barrow cluster (destroyed?) c. 820110, interments include a cremation; earthworks including cross-dykes 110818 etc.; bell barrows (including one of twin type) with MBA cremations in overhanging-rim urns—also bowl and pond? barrows 825110; barrows 820112 etc.; earthwork enclosure 826116; earthworks, Gobblestubbs Copse.

Streat (E). Mes site c. 350150; R road, agger, 350154 etc. (cf. PN Streat 11C.).

Sullington (W). MBA barrows (damaged) c. 096145: overhanging-rim urns and others; barrows 108120 etc. and 091119 etc.; cross-ridge dykes 105119 etc. and 095124; PN Easewrithe 11C. 'Thicket of the gods', site of hundred-moot (and earlier pagan S shrine? Cf. PN Mutton 119149 (ge-mōt-tūn?) near intersection of tracks and parish boundaries).

Sutton (W). LBA sherd in ditch of cross-ridge dyke 955135; barrows 962128.

Tangmere (W) (902062). PN Berryfield 15C. (nearby was *Beryhamme* 13C.).

Tarring Neville (E). Barrow 447033; strip lynchet? 440039 etc.

Telscombe (E). EBA 'A' beaker inhumation from barrow (destroyed) 402031; MBA cremations as secondary interments in barrow: overhanging-rim urns, 402031; IA 'A' pottery c. 400043; IA pits, South-eastern 'B' pottery c. 402031; R occupation, 397045.

Terwick (W). Med shrunken village? 819235.

Thakeham (W). R road, agger, c. 100157 etc.; S hut, 8C. and Med 12C. pottery.

Ticehurst (E). Late IA ironworking 663294; R ironworking 663294; later ironworking (cf. Old Forge Farm 680338 and Hammerden 13C. 661271); PN Whiligh (from *wīg*) 11C., 657313, pagan S shrine?; PN Brickkiln Farm 678301.

Tillington (W). PN Rotherbridge 11C., 966203, meeting-place of hundred.

Treyford (W). MBA cremations in bell barrows (six in all), 'The Devil's Jumps', 825173.

Trotton (W). Mes. site c. 843223; R occupation (earthwork?) 836286; PN Dumpford 11C., 830218, meeting-place of hundred.

Trundle. See Singleton.

Uckfield (475215). Ironworking.

Upper Beeding. Mes site c. 220130; IA and R occupation 188115; R barrow c. 213097; barrow 215100; Celtic fields 228102 etc.; strip lynchets 207099 etc.

Up Waltham (W). Barrows (including one of bell type) 947126 and 928145; strip lynchets 942140; Med shrunken village? 942138; for moot-site see Madehurst.

Wadhurst (E). Ironworking (cf. PN Old Forge Farm 16C., 680338).

Walberton (W). R cist burials 977066; R brick in church 972057; Med shrunken village? Binsted c. 982060; PN Avisford 13C., 978066, site of hundred-moot.

Waldron (E). MBA merchant's hoard; Med moated site 544192; ironworking.

Warbleton (E) (610180). Ironworking.

Warnham (W) (160335). Mes site; Med fishponds?

Wartling (E). PN Puddledock 17C. 666107; PN Rat's Castle, Med? cattle refuge against floods in the marshes?

Washington (W). IA hill-fort, Chanctonbury, 139121; R occupation near Owlscroft Barn; R road 125146 etc.; Romano-Celtic temple 139121 (probably the 'stone temple' of a 10C. charter); barrows 132121 etc. and 112121 etc.; four cross-ridge dykes 108119 etc. and 134121; ancient track 122105 etc.; Celtic fields 111118; PN Longbury (*beorg*, 'hill'?); PN's in 10C. charter: *lidgeardes beorg*, Tateman's burial-place; Hatheburg's barrow (*hlāw*), stone hill or barrow (*beorg*) and *bennan beorg* (near Clayton Farm?).

West Blatchington (E). LBA occupation and hoard (including winged axe) 275074; IA 'A1' occupation, pit and ditches, IA 'AB', South-eastern 'B', Wealden culture?, and R occupation, all 275074; R farm 275074, corn-drying ovens, cremations etc. (site destroyed).

Westbourne (W). MBA collared urn; R occupation 766055.

West Chiltington (W). MBA collared urn c. 085165; PN Hardbarrow 094168.

West Dean (E). P implement; barrow 540994; Med deserted village, Exceat, 522992.

West Dean (W). IA settlement 830114 etc.; IA 'B'? multivallate cattle enclosure, 'Goosehill Camp' 830126; R occupation 860122, 842109; R aristocratic cist cremation burial c. 835145; R inhumations; R road 847110 etc. Celtic fields, 833116 etc.; Med hundred-moot of *Ghidentroi* 11C., 'tree of the goddess' (originally a pagan S shrine?), at 847147 or 840152 (Stapleash, the moot marked by a '*stapol*'?); PN Brickkiln 825127.

Westfield (E). R iron bloomery 784176; R harbour? 815177; R road? 815145; PN Owl's Castle 813166.

West Firle (E). N long barrow 487058; MBA cinerary urns and incense cup with cremations c. 486059; LBA hoard; late IA farmstead, Wealden, 'ABC' and South-eastern 'B' pottery, 484055; R farmstead 481049; R causeway 464088; R ways

472048 etc.; R finds in several places; S? inhumations; barrows 462058; Celtic fields 480050 etc.; Med hundred-moot at Totnore 11C. on western boundary of parish; PN Burgh Bridge 477089 (*beorg*, 'hill'); PN Males Burgh 462058, barrow?; PN Stamford 484081, 15C., R? ford.

West Grinstead (W). PN Bowshotts, probably 'shed by the *burgh*', 13C.; PN Pothill 13C. (and Potcommon) 161179.

Westham (E). IA South-eastern 'B' pottery; PN Dittons 14C. 602046 ('ditch farm').

Westhampnett (W). R brick in church 881062; linear earthwork (Belgic?) 874089 etc.; earthwork 875085 etc.

West Hoathly (E). IA (Wealden?) promontory fort 348322; ironworking.

Westmeston (E). IA hill-fort 333130; R road 345154 etc.; R minor way 347153 etc.; barrows 340128 etc.; circular earthwork 335123 etc.; PN Sedlow 343147 (from *hlāw*).

West Stoke (W). N/EBA? flint mines 831096; LBA/IA hut and Celtic fields 822106; IA 'A' farmstead c. 831096; Belgic? linear earthwork 837080 etc.; R? cist grave; barrows 829105 etc.; linear earthwork 826100 etc.

West Tarring (W). N flint mines, 137079, late Windmill Hill pottery; EBA 'B' beaker inhumations in barrows c. 137079; IA 'A1' undefended settlement 140080; IA 'A2' contour hill-fort, Cissbury, 1400080: IA 'A2' and 'B' (Marnian), Wealden, 'ABC' and South-eastern 'B' pottery. The hill-fort was under plough in the late IA: Celtic fields 140080 etc.; R farmstead 140080; late R refortification of Cissbury; barrows c. 141075 and c. 140094; rectangular enclosures c. 140081; strip lynchets 141076 (Vineyard Hill).

West Thorney (W). Med? salt-making sites; PN Stanbury 770031.

Whitehawk. See Brighton.

Wiggenholt (W). R house 064175; R occupation 071161 and 068168; R road c. 060171 etc.; R coin-hoard, late 3C.

Willingdon (E) (590025). IA burial with Belgic pot; S inhumation cemetery, Willingdon Hill; S cremation cemetery, Hampden Pk.

Wilmington (E). N long barrow, Hunter's Burgh 550036; N? flint mines? 544034; LBA founder's hoard; R occupation, Endlewick; barrows 540035 etc. (one of platform type) 545034; Celtic fields (destroyed?) c. 536038; hill figure, 'The Long Man', 543035; Med deserted hamlet? Endlewick (earthworks survive).

Wisborough Green (W) (050260). Early modern period: ironworking and glassmaking.

Wiston (W). IA hill-fort, Chanctonbury, 140120; R building 147135; R tile-kiln 157136; R occupation 148143; barrows 144114 etc. and 139121; earthworks 143117 and 158122 etc.; Med deserted village c. 155124.

Withyham (E) (490360). Med? ironworking.

Wittering, East and West (W). Belgic gold coin-hoard; R cremations c. 775982; R road? Acre St.–Nunnington–Snow Hill (cf. field-name Street Field c. 779986); R gold coin-hoard, late 4C.; PN Hundredsteddle, 816988, probable site of hundred-moot.

Woodmancote (W). PN Bylsborough 13C. (*beorg*) 230163.

Woolbeding (W). Barrow? 876257.

Worth (E). Med hundred-moot, Burleigh 8C. (*burh*) 347364; ironworking c. 316377 and 284356 (Furnace Farm); Med? moat and earthworks 295373; earthwork enclosure? 304353; PN Woolborough 13C. (*beorg*) 280383; PN Kiln Wood 338377.

Worthing (W). LBA pottery 146056; LBA merchant's hoard and founder's hoard (including a winged axe); R buildings 147030 and c. 134022; R cremations and inhumations; Museum, Chapel Rd.

Yapton (W) (980035). LBA hoard.

Index

(SEE ALSO GAZETTEER)

ABBERTON, Essex, 120, 197, Map E
Abbevillian Culture, 21
Abbotstone, Hants, 197
Abbotts Ann, Hants, 218, 220
Abingdon, Berks, 43, 44, 46 f, 49, 52, 56, 57, 59, 62, 148, 152, 153, 159, 167 f, 177, Map B
Abingdon Culture, 46 f, 54, Fig 5
Abinger, Surrey, 39, 42, 53, 186, 199, Plate 26
Acheulian Culture, 21, 23, 31 f
Acton, Middx, 32, 76
Addington, Kent, 49, 194, Map A; A., Surrey, 220
Admiralty, London, 34
Adur, river, Sussex, 95, 96, 102, 105, 113, 115, 137, 165, 186
agricultural phases, N, 43 f, MBA, 72; LBA, 74 f, 78 f; IA, 97 f, 106 122-3, 128; R, 135, 150, Plates 10 and 21; S, 171-2, 176, Plates 23 and 24; Med, 191 f, Fig 19
Albury, Herts, 194, 222; A., Surrey, 143, 148, 176, 196, 197
Alciston, Sussex, 190, 206-7, Map L
Aldbury, Herts, 222, Map K
alder, 27, 58
Aldington, Kent, 197
Aldworth, Berks, 155, Map I
Alfold, Surrey, 226
Alfoldean, Sussex, 131, 226
Alfred, King of Wessex, 173
Alfred's Castle, Berks, 116
Alfriston, Sussex, 165, 190, 194, Map L
Alice Holt Forest, Hants, 145-6, 150
Alkham, Kent, 224
Allcroft, A. H., 199, 205
Alphamstone, Essex, 76, 218
Alton, Hants, 217
amber, 67
Ambresbury, Essex, 94
amphorae, 123, 125
Amport, Hants, 224
Andover, Hants, 25, 94, 102, 220, 229, Map C

Anglo-Saxon Chronicle, 159 f, 165, 168, 170, 171, 176, 180-3
Anglo-Saxon cemeteries and place-names, discrepancy between, 165 f
Anglo-Saxon settlement, 25, 148, 152 f
animals, domestic, 18, 43, 53, 84, 98, 180; wild, 18, 26, 30, 32, 33, 34, 36, 53, 73, 180
animal-head place-names, 163, 223-4
Antonine Itinerary, 112
Appledore, Kent, 180, 183
Appleshaw, Hants, 143, 220
Appleton, Berks, 116
arable land, 22, 83, 120, 170, 172
Arborfield, Berks, 222, Map J
Arcadius, Emperor, 148, 149
Ardington, Berks, 192
Ardleigh, Essex, 221
Arenigs, Merion, 56
Arlesey, Beds, 111
Arlington, Sussex, 184, 186, Map L
Armada defences, 198
Arminghall, Norfolk, 62
Armsley, Hants, 103, 113
Arretine ware, imitation, 117, 124
arrow-heads, Mes, 37; N, 48, 51, 52, 53; EBA, 61
art, Palaeolithic, 31, 33
Artington, Surrey, 91
Arun, river, Sussex, 102, 105
Arundel, Sussex, 22, 186
Asham, Sussex, 105, 186
Ashbury, Berks, 49, 116, 136, 220, 225
Ashdon, Essex, 140, 148
Ashford, Kent, 105, 170; A., Middx, 76, 190
Ashley Green, Bucks, 94
Ashtead, Surrey, 115, 128, 140, 146, Map G
Ashurst, Hants, 220
Ashwell, Herts, 94, 116, 171, 184, 222
Aspenden, Herts, 222

Asthall, Oxon, 159
Aston Rowant, Oxon, 217, 221
Aston Upthorpe, Berks, 135-6, 148
Atlantic phase of climate, 27, 37, 41, 58
Atrebates, 112, 116
Aurignacian Culture, 21, 34
autumn slaughter of cattle, N, 46; IA, 96; S, 162-3
Avebury, Wilts, 47, 56, 57, 67
Avon, river, Hants, 60, 161, Map H
axes, stone, 56, 72; flint, P, 23, 31; Mes, 37 f; N, 44 f, 52, 55-6; bronze, 67, 72, 74, 76 f
Aylesbury, Bucks, 170, 171, 199, Map K
Aylesford, Kent, 49, 67, 111, 125, 129, 161, Map A, Plate 2

BADSHOT, Surrey, 49, 51, 210
Bagshot, Surrey, 20
baileys, castle, 186, Fig 18
Balcombe, Sussex, 39
Baldock, Herts, 111, 153
Baldon, Oxon, 217
Baldslow, Sussex, 188
Balksbury, Hants, 102
Balmer, Sussex, 196, 197, Map L
Balsdean, Sussex, 197, Map L
Banstead, Surrey, 175, 184-5, 199, 217, Map G
Barham, Kent, 174
Barkhale, Sussex, 44, Map D
Barkway, Herts, 143, 149
barley, 48, 65, 72, 78, 97
Barley, Herts, 219
Barming, Kent, 170, Map A
barrows (see long b., bell barrows etc.), 20, 56, 61, 63, 65, 66, 67 f, 76, 98, Figs 5 and 6, Map 4; Belgic 125-6, 128, Map 7; R 139, 140, Maps E, F and 8, Plate 20; S 136, 174, 188-9, 190, 217, 224, Fig 14 and Map 9
Bartlow, Essex, 140-2, Plate 20

Basildon, Berks, 155, Map I
Basing, Hants, 171, 198, Map J
Battersea, London, 37, 167
Battle-axe Culture, 61
Baughurst, Hants, 190, Map J
beaches, ancient, 22, 23
Beaker Cultures, 47, 48, 49, 52, 56, 57, 60 f, 63, Fig 5, 65, 73
Beane, river, Herts, 176, Map F
Beaulieu, Hants, 40, 65, 66, 67, 69, 98
Bede, The Venerable, 159, 164, 173
Beddingham, Sussex, 78 f, 94, 97, 103, 105, 186, Map L
Bedford, 161, 170, 171
beech, 27, 58
Beech Bottom Dyke, Herts, 111, 116, 122
Beedon, Berks, 70
Bekesbourne, Kent, 163
Belgae, 103, 105, 106, 109 f, 128
bell barrows, Figs. 5 and 6, 67 f, 72, Map 3, Plates 5 and 6
bell-disc barrows, 67 f, Fig 6E, Map 3, Map I
Benfleet, Essex, 180, 183
Bengeo, Herts, 223, Map F
Benson, Oxon, 55, 170, 222, Map I
Berechurch, Essex, 120,
Beresford, M. W., 196, 200
Berkhamsted, Herts, 157, 186, 222, Plate 25
Berkshire Downs, 18, 87, 88, 123, 136, 151, Maps B and I; B. Ridgeway, 54, 83, 132, 154, 155, Maps B and I, Plate 12
Bermondsey, London, 154
Bermondspit Hundred, Hants, 189, Map C
Berrylands, Surrey, 14, 227
Bersted, Sussex, 190
Betchworth, Surrey, 171, Map G
Bewsborough Hundred, Kent, 188
Bexley, Kent, 157, 222
bibliographies, Natural Background, 30; P, 35; Mes, 42; N, 59; E-MBA, 73; LBA, 84; IA, 'A', 99–100; IA, 'B', 108; IA 'C', 128–129; R, 149 f; S, 176–7; Med, 199–200; field studies, 215–6; PN, 227; General, 228 f
Bierton, Bucks, 219
Bigbury, Kent, 116, 122, 123, 127
Bighton, Hants, 226
Bignor, Sussex, 44, 140
Binderton, Sussex, 197

Bindon, Dorset, 87
Binsted, Hants, 145
birch, 26, 27, 36 f
Birchanger, Essex, 218, 221
Birchington, Kent, 78
Bishopsbourne, Kent, 139, 142, 174
Bishopstone, Bucks, 171
Bishop's Waltham, Hants, 69, 189
Bitterne, Hants, 126, 134, 148
Black Patch, Alciston, Sussex, 206, Map L
Blackpatch, Patching, Sussex, 48, 56, 58, 63, 206
Blackwater, river, Essex, 77, 131
blade tools, 21, 34
Bledlow, Bucks, 56, 90, 174
Bletchingley, Surrey, 186, 220 223, Map G
Blewbury, Berks, 49, 87, 88, 91, 102, 174, 191, 192, 219, Map I
Blōtmōnath, 162
Boarhunt, Hants, 218
Bodiam, Sussex, 194, 199
Bokerly Dyke, Martin, Hants, Fig 16; Plate 19; Map H; 155, 191, 214
Boldre, Hants, 211
Borden, Kent, 142
Boreal climate, 27, 36
Boscombe Down, Wilts, 83
Bosham, Sussex, 148, Map D
Botley, Hants, 61
Bottisham, Cambs, 62
Bouddican revolt, 132, 152
Boughton under Blean, Kent, 215
Boulder Clay, 20, 22, 205
boundaries, parish, 188, 190–1; shire, 9, 191
Bournemouth, Hants, 56, 62, 73, 76, 230
Bourton, Berks, 219
Bovington, Herts, 148
bowl barrows, Fig 6, a and b; Plate 6
Boxford, Berks, 96, 218, 219
Boxgrove, Sussex, 221
bracteates, Jutish, 164
Bradwell-next-Coggeshall, Essex, 197
Bradwell-on-Sea, Essex, 25, 144, 153, 175, 221
Braintree, Essex, 77
Bramber, Sussex, 186
Bramley, Hants, 94, Map J
Braughing, Herts, Map F; 122, 127, 131, 132, 167, 226
Breckland, Norfolk, 20, 58

Brede, river, Sussex, 132
Brendon Hill, Worcs, 127
Brentford, Middx, 76, 84, 88, 140
bretasche, 186, Plate 26
brick, S, 178; R, 194–5, 212; Belgic, 195; place-names, 218, 227
Brickearth, 9, 19, 43, 140, 167, 178, 196
Bricket Wood, Herts, 218
Bridge, Kent, 174
Brighton, Sussex, 19, 22, 23, 49, 91, 95, 132, 145, 151, 197, 230
Britwell, Oxon, 220, 222
Brixton, London, 188
Broadstairs, Kent, 88, 127, 153, 174
Brockley Hill, Middx, 122, 127, 131, 145, 150
Bromley, its derivations, 202
bronze, 60, 72, 74, 86, 98, 211
brooches, IA, 99, 101, 106, 123, 126; S, 154, 159, 163–4
Broomfield, Essex, 169,
Brown Candover, Hants, 76
Broxbourne, Herts, 37
Broxhead, Hants, 163
Brundall, Norfolk, 153
buckets, 74, 98, 125, 126
Bucklebury, Berks, 218
Bulmer, Essex, 188, 218
Bulphan, Essex, 220
Bulstrode, Bucks, 94, 116
Burbeach Hundred, Sussex, 189
Burgh, Suffolk, 153
Burgh Heath, Surrey, 184, 217
Burghal Hidage, 183, 219
Burghclere, Hants, 184, 192, Fig 19
Burgundians, 152
burhs, Saxon forts, 176–83; in place-names, 218, 222; and see Map 9 and Plate 22
burial customs, N, 48 f, 51; Beaker, 61; Food Vessel, 66; Wessex Culture, 66–70; Urn Folk, 70–72; LBA, 76–7; IA 'A', 98; IA 'C', 109, 125; R, 142; S, 159, 174; and see barrows, cremation, inhumation
Buriton, Hants, 219
Burley, Hants, 146, Map H
Burnham, Bucks, 88, 221
Burnham, Essex, 124
Burpham, Sussex, 65, 94, 183
Burton, Hants, 183, 219
Burwell, Cambs, 157
Bury Hill, Hants, 91, 98, 102, 103, 115
Bury Hundred, Sussex, 189

Busbridge, Surrey, 197
Buscot, Berks, 218
Butser Hill, Hants, 92, 100, 219
Bygrave, Herts, 192

CABURN, see Mount Caburn
Caddington, Beds, 32, 192, 215, 220
calcite, 67
Calleva Atrebatum, 112, Map J; 132, 191; and see Silchester
Callington, Cornwall, 56
camps, Roman, 131, 133, Plate 15
Cams, Hants, 40, 41
Camulodunum, Map E; Fig 12A; 119 f, 128, 130, 131, 150, 157; and see Colchester
Cana Moor, Yorks, 65
canals, 214
Canewdon, Essex, 105, 195
cannibalism, N, 46, 48
Canterbury, 51, 56, 131, 133, 134, 142, 148, 150, 173, 174, 175, 183, 218, Fig 15
Caratacus, 130
Carausius, 144
carpentry, 66, 74
Carshalton, Surrey, 115, 217
carstone, 86, 206
Cassington, Oxon, 62
Cassivellaunus, 111
Castle Hedingham, Essex, 189, 195
Castle Hill, Newhaven, Sussex, 73, 105, Map L
castle mounds, 183-4, 185-7, 199, 220, 226, Fig 18, Map 10, Plate 26
Caterham, Surrey, 137, 199, Map G
cattle, 44 f, 51, 53, 63, 66, 71, 72, 74, 78 f, 96, 98, 123, 135 f, 162, 173, 180, 184
cauldrons, 74
causeway camps, 44 f; description 46; 54, 55, 57, 59; Fig 4, Map 2, Plate 11
cave dwellings, P, 34
Caversham, Oxon, 32
Celtic fields, 59, 78 f; description and formation, 80, Fig 8; 84, 97, 106, 123, 135 f, 150-1, 210 213, Figs 7, 13, 14, Plate 8; and see Regional Maps
Celtic speech, 77, 109, 127, 128; C. place-names, 109, 176
cemeteries, N-EBA, 57; Beaker, 62; LBA, 76 f, Map 4; Belgic,

111, 125, Map 7; R, 142, 153, 222; S, 153 f, 164 f, 198, Map 9; reuse of R cemeteries by Saxons, 175
Cerdic of Wessex, 168, 169
cereals, 51, 72, 96, 123; origin, 43
Chalgrove, Oxon, 56
Chalk, 9, 18 f, 40, 42, 43 f, 55, 84, 190, 196, 201, 205, 206
Challow, Berks, 224, Map B
Chanctonbury, Sussex, 103, 143, 176, 215, 225
charcoal, 58, 63
Charford-on-Avon, Hants, 161, Map H
chariots, 101, 120, 125, 126
Charlton, London, 131
Charney Bassett, Berks, 94, 102
charters, Old English, 190
Chatham, Kent, 139
Checkdendon, Oxon, 220, 224, Map I
Chelsham, Surrrey, 107, Map G
Cherbury, Berks, 94, 102, Map B
chert, 42, 212
Chertsey, Surrey, 221
Cherwell, river, Oxon, 115, 116
Chesham, Bucks, 220
Cheshunt Dyke, Essex, 120; Cheshunt Field, 120
Cheshunt, Herts, 131, 220, 222
Chessington, Surrey, 220
Chi-Rho symbol, 143-4
Chichester, Sussex, 113, 115; Map D; 120, 132, 133, 124, 146, 148, 173, 174, 183; Chichester Dykes, Map D; 113, 157
Chiddingfold, Surrey, 40
Chieveley, Berks, 191
Chignall, Essex, 194
Childe, V. G, 35, 59, 70, 228
Chilham, Kent, 49, 59, 142
Chilling, Hants, 165
Chiltern Hills, 18 f, 32, 44, 49, 55, 83, 90, 155, 161, 167, 168, 170, 176, 186, 192, Map I, Map K
Chilton Candover, Hants, 220, 225
Chinnor, Oxon, 90, 217, 222
Chislehurst, Kent, 34
Chobham, Surrey, 76, 149, 220
Cholderton, Wilts, 83
Cholesbury, Bucks, 94, 116, 194, Map K
Cholsey, Berks, 60, 218, Map I
Choseley, Hants, 113, 123, 128
Christchurch, Hants, 56, 60, 77, 92, 183, 219, Fig. 10

Christianization of Roman Britain, 142, 143-4
churches, siting of, 194 f
Cissbury, Sussex, 48, 56, 58, 88, 95, 102, 103, 113, 116, 154, 213, Fig 11; Cissbury Culture, 102
cists, 66
Clacton, Essex, 32, 41, 47, 52
Clactonian Culture, 21, 23, 32, 33
Clanville, Hants, 140
Clapham, Sussex, 47
Claudius, Emperor, 130
Clausentum, Hants, 134
Clavering, Essex, 186, Map F
clays, 9, 18 f, 140, 191, 205, 206
Clayton, Sussex, 67
Clay-with-Flints, 18 f, 32, 40, 44, 83, 139, 201
Clifton, Beds, 57, 62
Clifton Hampden, Oxon, 218
climatic phases, Charts p. 21 and pp. 28-9; 22, 26, 30, 36 f, 58, 66, 76, 95, 122
cloth manufacture, R, 140, 146; S or Med, 217
Clothall, Herts, 192
coast-line, 20 f, Fig 2, 112, 144, Fig 15
Cobham, Kent, 112, Map A
Cobham, Surrey, 115
coffins, wicker, 65; tree-trunk, 69; oak, 142; stone, 142; lead, 142; 220
coins, IA 'B', 106; Belgic, 112, 113, 115-16, 123, 126, 128; R, 143 f; coin-moulds, 113, 120
Colbury, Hants, 76
Colchester, Essex, 62, 91, 105, 113; Map E; 116, 119 f., 123, 128, 129, 132, 133, 134, 142, 143, 145, 148, 150, 153, 169, 175, 183, 229; and see *Camulodunum*
Cold Ash, Berks, 56
Coldred, Kent, 139, 194
Coleshill, Berks, 218
Colne Engaine, Essex, 224
Colne, river, Essex, 19, 37, 77, 119, Map E
Combe Gibbet, Berks, 49
Combe Hill, Sussex, Fig 4; 47, 51; Map L
Combe Rock, 22, 31
Commius, 112 f, 119
communications, 19, 43, 54, 67, 131-2, 186; and see Regional Maps
Compton, Berks, 135, 142, 150, 197, Map I

Compton, Hants, 98, 174
Compton Beauchamp, Berks, 94, 225, Map B
Constantius, Emperor, 135
Consumpta per Mare, Essex, 25
Conversion of the Anglo-Saxons, 159, 162, 178, 198
cooking, 39, 106, 117, 173
Coombes, Sussex, 190
Copford, Essex, 195, Map E
copper, 60, 61, 63, 65–6, 72, 86
Copthorne Hundred, Surrey, 188
Copythorne, Hants, 224
cores, Mes, 36, 41; c. cultures, 21, 33
corndrying—see kilns
Coulsdon, Surrey, 137, 151, 171, 174, Fig 14, Map G
coulters, plough, 122, 125
Cowfold, Sussex, 226
Cowley, Oxon, 153
Cranbourne Chase, 25, 54, 135, Map H
Cranleigh, Surrey, 146, 171
Crawford, O. G. S., 11, 84, 100, 192, 199, 207, 215, 225, 227, 229
Crawley, Hants, 213
Crayford, Kent, 32, 88, 161
cremation burials, N, 48 f, 54; EBA, 62, 63, Fig. 5, 66, 67; E/MBA, 69 f; LBA, 74, 76; IA, 98, 109, 125–6; R, 142; S, 159 f, 164, 174, 198
Creswellian Culture, 35
Cripplegate Roman fort, London, 133, 150
Crockenhill, Kent, 217
Crofton, Hants, 219
Crondall, Hants, 225
Crookham, Berks, 157
crop-marks, 80–1, 197, 207–9, 216, Fig. 20
cross-ridge dykes, 83–4, 191, 213, Map D
Crowhurst, Sussex, 106, 125
Crowmarsh, Oxon, 155, 184, Map I
Croydon, Surrey, 88, 166, 169, 184, 230
cruciform brooches, S, 163 f, 165, 168, 169
Cublington, Bucks, 195
Cuckhamsley, Bucks, 188, Map B
Cuckmere, river, Sussex, 105, 186, Map L
Cuddesdon, Oxon, 171, 224
Cudlow, Sussex, 25
Cumnor, Oxon, 218

Cunobelin, 116, 119, 126, 130
currency, 101, 106, 113, 123, 148, 159
cursus monuments, 54–5, Fig 5, Map I, Plate 3
Cuthwulf, West Saxon prince, 170, 176
Cuxham, Oxon, 197

DAGENHAM, Essex, 74
daggers, flint, EBA, 41, 60 f; bronze, 60, 65, 67, 72; iron, 102
Dallington, Sussex, 106
Damerham, Hants, 135; Fig 13; 213, 218, Map H
Danbury, Essex, 90, 94, 195
Danebury, Hants, 103, 115
Danish wars, 180 f
Darenth, Kent, 140, 146
Deal, Kent, 111, 153, 230
Debden, Essex, 222
Deddington, Oxon, 223
deforestation, 19 f, 44 f, 53, 58–9, 70–1, 84
Desborough Castle, Bucks, 186, 189
deserted villages, Fig 19; 195 f; Map 10; 225; Plate 28
Deverel-Rimbury Culture, 76 f, 84
Devil's Dyke, Sussex, 95, 106; D. D., Herts, 111, 116, Fig 12B
Dinton, Bucks, 171
Dippenhall, Surrey, 65
disc-barrows, 67 f, Fig 6f, 72, 211; 213, 215; Map 3, Map C, Plate 6
distribution maps, note on, 9
Ditchingham, Norfolk, 49
Ditchley, Oxon, 136
Ditchling, Sussex, 191
docks, Danish?, 183; Med, 194
documentary evidence, 159 f, 183, 190, 194, 197, 198
Dogmersfield, Hants, 197, Map J
dolerite axes, 56
Domesday Book, 26, 124, 162
Donnington, Berks, 221
Dorchester, Dorset, 103
Dorchester, Oxon, 54, 57, 59, 88, 94, 102, 132, 148, 149, 167 f, 174, 175, 222, Map I
Dorchester Culture, N, 52, 54, 66
Dorking, Surrey, 34, 131, 137, 221
Dover, Kent, 144, 174, 183, Fig. 15

Dover, Strait of, formation, 23, 25; Fig 2
drainage ditches, Belgic, 117, 122
Drayton, Berks, 65
Droxford, Hants, 164, 171
Drury Lane, London, 175
Dry Hill, Surrey, 116
Dubnovellaunus, 119
Dummer, Hants, 40, Map C
Dumpton, Kent, 122
Dungeness, Sussex, 20
Dunsfold, Surrey, 226
Dunstable, Beds, 49, 51, 54, 131, 154, Plate 24
Durobrivae, Kent, 131; see Rochester
Durocobrivae, Beds, 131; see Dunstable
Durovernum Cantiacorum, Kent, 131; see Canterbury
Durrington, Sussex, 221
Durrington, Wilts, 53, 210
Dyke Hills, Oxon, 94, 174, Map I

EALING, Middx, 167, 220
Earls Colne, Essex, 221
earth movements, 22 f, 25, 30, 41, 140, Fig. 2
Eartham, Sussex, 137, Map D
Easewrithe Hundred, Sussex, 188, 189
Easington, Oxon, 197
East Barming, Kent, 142
East Dean, Sussex, 221
East Garston, Berks, 218
East Hendred, Berks, 188
East Hoathly, Sussex, 165
East Horsley, Surrey, 55
East Malling, Kent, 53, 170
East Shefford, Berks, 168, 169
Eastbourne, Sussex, 49, 76, 88, 125, 165, 189, 230, Map L
Easton Down, Wilts, 55, 63
Eastry, Kent, 139
Eastwell, Kent, 197
Eastwick, Herts, 223
Ebbsfleet Culture, 47 f, 51, 54, 57
Edlesborough, Bucks, 194
Edmonton, Mddx, 190
Edward the Confessor, King of England, 186
Edward the Elder, King of the English, 176
Effingham, Surrey, 162
Ehenside Tarn, Westmorland, 58
Ekwall, E, 202
Ellesborough, Bucks, 90
Ellisfield, Hants, 189

elm, 27, 97
Elsfield, Oxon, 148
Elstead, Surrey, 67
Elstree, Middx, 145
Elthorne Hundred, Middx, 188
emergence of land surfaces, 22 f
Enborne, Berks, 198
enclosures, earthwork, MBA, 72, 73; LBA, 83; IA, 162; Belgic, 113, 117; R, 135 f; Med, 185, 225; undated, 211, Plate 3, 226, 227
Enfield, Essex, 51
English Channel, formation of, 23; Fig 2; 37, 41, 58
English Place-Name Survey, 180, 202, 217 f, 227
Eppillus, 112, 113, 116
Epping, Essex, 90, 94
Epsom, Surrey, 115, Map G
equal-armed brooches, S, 168, 173
erosion of coast, 22 f, 25
Esher, Surrey, 88
Essex, 18 f
Eversheds, Surrey, 163
Eversholt, Beds, 189
Eversley, Hants, 222
Ewell, Surrey, 53, 115, 171, 173, 217, Map G
Ewelme, Oxon, 171, 217, 222
excavations, 12, 13; Mes, 36, 39; N, 54, 55 and passim; 212
extensive system of farming, 43 f
Exton, Hants, 164
Eynsford, Kent, 221
Eynsham, Oxon, 55, 62, 170
Eythorpe, Bucks, 197

FAÏENCE, 67, 70, 73
Falmer, Sussex, 196, 197
Fambridge, Essex, 196
Fareham, Hants, 42, 221
Faringdon, Berks, 56, 107, 186, Map B
Farley Chamberlayne, Hants, 96, 194, 197
Farley Heath, Surrey, 143, 149, 176, 212
farms, LBA, 78 f, Fig 7, 84; IA, 94, 96 f, 102, 106, 128; R, 132, 135 f, 140, 145, 148, 209, Plates 10 and 21
Farnborough, Berks, 191, 226
Farnham, Surrey, 34, 39, 41, 42, 53, 55, 65, 76, 88, 90, 107, 115, 145, 162, 171, 173, 210, 229
Farningham, Kent, 139, Map A

Farthingdown, Surrey, 139; Fig 14; 174; Map G
Faversham, Kent, 111, 131, 153, 163, 174
Fawler, Oxon, 222
Fawley, Bucks, 221
Fawley, Hants, 219
Feering, Essex, 217
Felixstowe, Suffolk, 153
fences, 46, 73, 78, Fig. 9
Fenland, 23, 25, 58
Ferring, Sussex, 78, 88, 91, 92, 165, 174
fertility beliefs, N, 48; LBA, 78
Fetcham, Surrey, 115, 167, 171, Map G
field-work, 13–15, 201 f, 217 f
fields, N, 45–6; MBA, 72; LBA, 78 f, Fig 7, Fig 8; Med, 191 f, Fig 19; and see Celtic fields and lynchets
Fifield, derivation, 202
figurines, N, 48
Finchampstead, Berks, 194, Map J
Finchingfield, Essex, 218, 226
Findon, Sussex, 56, 62, 63, 88, 96, 97, 101, 102, 113
Fingest, Bucks, 190
Fingringhoe, Essex, 131, Map E
fire-dogs, 125
fishing, P, 34; N, 52
fish-ponds, 184, 197
fish-spears, Mes, 23, 36, 37
Flake Cultures, 21, 32, 33, 34
flake tools, 32
flat cemeteries, LBA, 76
Flaunden, Herts, 222
flax, 72
Fletching, Sussex, 165
Flexborough Hundred, Sussex, 188
flint, 35, 55, 71, 72, 207, 211–12
flint-mines, 48, 55 f (description); 57–8, 63, 71, 213; Map 2, Map D
Floore, Northants, and similar names, 223
Fobbing, Essex, 217
fodder, 46, 162
Folkestone, Kent, 25, 111, 140, 186
Food Vessel Culture, 65 f, 69, 70, 72
foot-ring vessels, Map 6; 106
Fordingbridge, Hants, 103, 113, 161, Map H
Forest Gate, Essex, 169
Forest of Bere, 20, 112

Forest of Dean, 86
forest distribution, 19 f, 26 f, 37, 40, 44, 58, 63, 127, 131, 167, 172, 177, 180, 196, 202, Fig 17A and 17B
Forest Folk, 36 f, 62
forest place-names, 180, 201–2, 223, Figs. 17A and 17B
forest succession, 26 f
forts—see hill-forts, promontory forts and camps
forts of the Saxon Shore, Roman, Map 8, Fig 15, Plates 15 and 16; 22, 144 f, 149, 152, 186, 198
Fosse Way, 149
Foulness, Essex, 142
Fox, C., 15, 30, 177, 205, 229
Foxbury, Hants and Essex, 219
Framfield, Sussex, 221, 226
Franks, 154, 164
Frant, Sussex, 130
Frensham, Surrey, 39
Frilford, Berks, 87, 88, 99, 100, 102, 126, 143, 150, 153, 165, 168, 175, Map B
Frindsbury, Kent, 32, 139
Frisians, 154, 163, 173, 174, 175
Friston, Sussex, 219, Map L
Fritham, Hants, 135, 146, 221, Map H
Froxfield, Hants, 157, 180
Fulham, London, 189
Fulscot, Berks, 197, Map I
funeral furniture, N, 48; Beaker Folk, 61; Wessex Culture, 67; Belgic, 125–6; R, 140; S, 153 f, 159 f, 174, 178, 198
Fyfield, its derivations, 202

GADERBROOK, Middx, 190
Garsington, Oxon, 217, 224
Gault Clay, 20, 86
geological maps, 201, 205
Germanic strain in Belgae, 109, 122, 125, 127
Gerrard's Cross, Bucks, 94, 116
Gilton, Kent, 153
Ginge, Berks, 171
glacial drift, 22, 31, 201
glaciations, chart p. 21, 22 f, Fig 2; 31, 33, 34
glass, beakers, 178; windows, 178
Glastonbury, Som, 103–4, 106
Glatting Down, Sussex, 84, 213
Godmersham, Kent, 139
Godshill, Hants, 113, Map H
Godstone, Surrey, 186, 197, 223, 224, 225, Map G

gold, 63, 67, 123, 164
Goldhanger, Essex, 124
Goodwood, Sussex, 22
Gore Hundred, Middx, 190
Goring, Oxon, 71, 92, 116, 155, 162, 167, Map I
Goring, Sussex, 162
Gorsey Bigbury, Som, 62
Gosbecks site, Stanway, Essex, Map E; 120 f, 126, 143, 150
Graig Lwyd, Caern, 56, 59
grain-rubbers, N, 48; and see querns
granaries, 96, 97
Grand Pressigny flint axes, 57
grassland, 58, 84, 97, 180
gravel-digging, 32-3, 91, 166, 210, 215
gravels, 9, 19 f, 40, 43, 55, 88, 112, 120, 140, 166-7, 201, 205, 206, 212
Graveney, Kent, 224
Gravettian Culture, 34, 35
Great Amwell, Herts, 199
Great Baddow, Essex, 56
Great Bromley, Essex, 90, 202
Great Chesterford, Essex, 62, 65, 122, 134, 142, 148, 153, 169, 175, 219
Great Coggeshall, Essex, 222
Great Dunmow, Essex, 131
Great Hampden, Bucks, 156
Great Henny, Essex, 218
Great Horkesley, Essex, 120, 220
Great Langdale, Westmorland, 56, 59
Great Leighs, Essex, 220
Great Milton, Oxon, 221
Great Missenden, Bucks, 157, 220, Map K
Great Munden, Herts, 224, Map F
Great Oakley, Essex, 65
Great Waltham, Essex, 218, 220
Greenham, Berks, 157, 219
Greensands, 18 f, 37, 40, 41, 71, 86, 107, 116, 190, 206, 212
Greensted-next-Ongar, Essex, 221
greenstone axes, 56, 63; g. wrist-guard, 65
Greenwich, London, 149, 174, 198, 230
Grime's Graves, Norfolk, flint-mines, 48, 55, 59, 62
Grim's Ditches, Berks, 155, Map I; Chilterns, 155-7, 180, 222, Maps I and K, Plate 25; Cran-

bourne Chase, 83, 191, Plate 7; Hants, 157, 180, 213, Map J
Grinsell, L. V., 73, 207, 215, 217
grooved ware, 47
Grovehurst, Kent, 52
Guildford, Surrey, 34, 88, 167, 171, 175, 186

HADDEN HILL, Hants, 76
Hadstock, Essex, 220
haematite slip on pottery, 87, 98, 123
Halling, Kent, 35, Map A
Hallstatt Culture, 85, 86, 88, 90, 98, 101, 106, 107, 127
Hambledon, Bucks, 148
Hampstead Norris, Berks, 191, 222, Map I
Hamwih, Southampton, 178-80, 195
hanging bowls, 136, 153
Hanwell, Middx, 167
Harbledown, Kent, 116, 122, 123, 127
Hardham, Sussex, 131
Harlington, Middx, 88, 98-9, 105, 143, 223
Harlow, Essex, 150, 188, 189, 225
Harpenden, Herts, 142, 219
Harpsden, Oxon, 223
Harrietsham, Kent, 170
Harrow, Middx, 162, 167
Harrow Hill, Sussex, 83, 91, 162
Harrowdown, Berks, 162; H., Oxon, 162, 176, 188
Hartfield, Sussex, 220
Harting, Sussex, 95, 113, 137, 213
Hartlip, Kent, 148, 153, 175
Harty, Kent, 74
harvesting, 27, 97
Haslemere, Surrey, 222
Haslingfield, Cambs, 168
Hassocks, Sussex, 39, 132, 165
Hastings, Sussex, 94, 161, 162, 183, 214
Hatfield, Herts, 188, 222
Hatfield Broad Oak, Essex, 218
Hatfield Peverel, Essex, 218
Hatford, Berks, 102
Hawkes, C. F. C., 16, 99, 100, 128, 205, 228
hay, 46, 96, 97
hazel, 26, 46, 122
Hazeleigh, Essex, 195
Headbourne Worthy, Hants, 128, 213
Headley, Hants, 163

hearths, P 31; Mes 39, 41; IA, 96; S 172; hearth-flints, 207
Hedsor, Bucks, 140
Hellingly, Sussex, 219
Hendon, Middx, 227
Henfield, Sussex, 189, 221
henge monuments, 53; description, 54; 55, 57, 59, 62, 63 f, Fig 5; 70, 99, Map 2, Map I
Hengist and Horsa, 161
Hengistbury Head, Hants, Fig 10; 87, 88, 92, 100, 103-4, 106, 112, 117, 219, Plate 14
Henley, Oxon, 32
Hertford, 176, 183
Hertfordshire, 18 f
Hertingfordbury, Herts, 183, 219
Hexton, Herts, 184
Heybridge, Essex 131, 169
Heyshott, Sussex, 191, Map D
High Down, Sussex, 78, 83, 88, 91, 92, Fig, 11, 154, 165, 174
High Wycombe, Bucks, 157, 186, 189
Highclere, Hants, Fig 19; Map C
Higham Gobion, Beds, 197
hill-forts, Map 5, 88, 91 f, 100, 101, 116-17, 130, 191, 210, 213, Fig 11, Plates, 9, 11, 12, 13
Hitcham, Bucks, 63
Hitchin, Herts, 62, 90, 111, 142; H. Hundred, 189
hoards of axes, flint, 55-6; bronze, 72-3, 74 f, Map 4
hoards of coins, R, 149; probable fifth-century, 154; S, 178; various, 224
hoes, 44, 51, 72, 79
Hoggeston, Bucks, 195
Holdenhurst, Hants, 47, 49, 51, 53, 59, 62
Hollingbourne, Kent, 170, 174
Hollingbury, Sussex, 91, 95
Holwell, Herts, 90, 191
homo sapiens, 33, 78
Honorius, Emperor, 148, 149
Hope All Saints, Kent, Plate 28
Hordle, Hants, 224
Horley, Surrey, 171
Hormead, Herts, 189, Map F
horse, 14, 26, 34, 53, 98
Horsham, Sussex, 39, 42, 220, 221
Horsted Keynes, Sussex, 105, 123
Horton, Oxon, 148
Houghton Regis, Beds, 44 f, 94, 107, 154
Hounslow, Middx, 125

houses, P, 31; Mes, 39; N, 46, 47, 52; Beaker Folk, 62 f; Wessex Culture, 66–7, 70; Urn Folk, 71, 73; LBA, 78 f and Fig 7; IA 'A', 96–7; IA 'B', 106; IA 'C', 117, 120, 122; R, 134, 140 and see villas; S, 172–3, 178–80
Hove, Sussex, 61, 67, 69
Hulberry, Kent, 139, 218, Map A
human sacrifice, 190
hundred, origin of, 188; h.-moots, 184, 188 f, 224, Maps C, D, L
Hundredsteddle, Sussex, 189
Hunsbury, Northants, 102
hunting, 18; P, 33, 34; Mes, 40; N, 48, 52; MBA, 71, 73; LBA, 78; IA, 98, 106
Hunton, Kent, 139
Hurn, Hants, 53
Hurstbourne Tarrant, Hants, 126
Hurstpierpoint, Sussex, 217
huts—see houses
Hutton Moor, Yorks, 65
hypocausts, 135, 140

IBSLEY, Hants, 69, Map H
ice-sheets, 21, 22 f, Fig 2, 26
Iceni, 128, 130, 133
Ickham, Kent, 220
Icknield Way, 20, 54, 61, 90, 92, 132, 154, 155–7, 168, 169, 176, 184; Map I; 190; Map K
Idsworth, Hants, 113
Ightham, Kent, 34, 108, 116, 127, 130, 222, Map A
industry, flint, 42, 55–6; bronze, 60, 72, 74; iron, 86, 116, 124, 132; various, 140, 145–6; Med, 194, 200
Ingatestone, Essex, 222, 225
inhumation, 62, Fig 5, 66, 69; LBA, 76; IA 'A', 98; Belgic, 125; R, 142; S, 136, 159 f, 170, 174, 214; in place-names, 219
Inkpen, Berks, 62, 76, 155, 220, 225
inter-glacial periods, Chart p. 21; 22
Iping, Sussex, 131
Ippollitts, Herts, 189, 224
Ipsden, Oxon, 219, Map I
iron, 86, 124, 172, 200, 211; cinder or slag, 124, 132, 172, 221; ore, 86, 102, 105, 124, 221
iron bloomeries, 106, 116, 124–5, 132, 194
Isle of Wight, 161, 164

Islington, London, 13, 199
Itford, Sussex, 78, 97, 103, Map L

JADEITE axes, 56
Jaywick, Essex, 32, 47, 52
jet, 63, 67
Jevington, Sussex, 74, 51, 219; Fig 4; Map L
Julius Caesar, 85, 102–3, 109, 111, 112, 116, 130
Jutish Culture, 159, 164, 169, 171, 172, 174, 175, 192

KELSHALL, Herts, 222, 224–5
Kelvedon, Essex, 169
Kempston, Beds, 168
Kenardington, Kent, 183, 194
Kendrick, T. D., 205, 228
Keston, Kent, 142,
Kilmington, Wilts, 55
Kilns, corn-drying, LBA?, 78; IA, 96, 97, 122; R, 135, 137
Kilns, potters', 145–6, 194, 221, 225; brick and tile kiln, 146, 218, 221, 226–7
Kimble, Bucks, 186, Map K
Kingsbury, Middx, 190, 194
Kingsclere, Hants, 56, Map C
Kingsey, Bucks, 171, 197–8
Kingsley, Hants, 145
Kingston, Kent, 174
Kingston Buci, Sussex, 63, 88
Kingston Lisle, Berks, 142, 222
Kingston-on-Thames, Surrey, 76, 88, 91, 217
King's Walden, Herts, 171
King's Worthy, Hants, 96, 98, 122, 171
Kintbury, Berks, 218
Kirdford, Sussex, 106, 124
Knapping sites, P, 31, 32; EBA, 63
knives, flint, 65, 73

LACEY GREEN, Bucks, 155, 226
Ladle Hill, Hants, 91, 215, Map C
Lambeth, London, 192–4
Lambourn, Berks, 49, 61, 66, 67, 83, 192, 218, Map B, Plate 6
Langenhoe, Essex, 105, Map E
Langley, Kent, 142
Langrish, Hants, 92
La Tène Culture, 85, 102, 106
Layer de la Haye, Essex, 221, Map E

Lea, river, 19 f, 32, 37, 61, 90 111, 140, 166–7, 176, 180, 183 Map F
Leadenhall, London, 180
Leakey, L. S. B., quoted, 39; 42
leather, 46, 47, 62, 72, 123
Leatherhead, Surrey, 88, 137, 151, 184, 230, Map G
Lee, Bucks, 157, 195, Map K
legions, Roman, 128, 130 f
Leman Bank, North Sea, 23; Fig 2; 37
Letchworth, Herts, 90, 91, 111, 116
Letcombe Bassett, Berks, 218; Map B
Letcombe Regis, Berks, 184, 219
Levalloisian Culture, 21, 23, 32, 33, 34
Lewes, Sussex, 67, 132, 183, 186, 210, 211, Map L
Lexden, Essex, 126, 191, Map E
lignite, 67
Lilley, Herts, 191
Limbury, Beds, 170
lime trees (Tilia), 41, 58, 97
Limlow, Cambs, 92
Limpsfield, Surrey, 153, 175
Lindsell, Essex, 218
linear earthworks, 191; and see ranch boundaries, Grim's Ditches, boundaries and park boundaries
Lingfield, Surrey, 116, 191
Litchfield, Hants, 91, 190, Map C
Little Baddow, Essex, 90
Littlebury, Essex, 189
Little Coggeshall, Essex, 195
Little Hallingbury, Essex, 189
Little Missenden, Bucks, 186
Littleton, Middx, 76
Little Waltham, Essex, 168, 226
Little Woodbury, Wilts, 96–7, 100
Lockinge, Berks, 171
Lockleys, Herts, 128, 151
loess, 19, 43
London, 105, 106, 131, 132, 133, 134, 143, 145, 150, 152, 153, 161, 166, 167, 175, 177, 180, 183, 199, 230
London Clay, 20, 22, 119, 140, 167, 201
long barrows; Map 2, 44, 47, 48 f, 54, 57, 59, 174, 210, 213, Plate 1
Longparish, Hants, 225, Map C
Longstock, Hants, 183
Long Wittenham, Berks, 87, 97, 102, 136, 168, 219, Map I, Plate 21

Longworth, Berks, 162, 218
look-out points, 144, 183-4, 226, Map 10
looms, 78, 173, 178-80; loom-weights, 78, 90, 98, 173, 180
Loughton, Essex, 90
Lowbury, Berks, 116, 135, 148, 150, Map I
Lower Beeding, Sussex, 189
Lower Halstow Culture, 41, 52-3
Lullingstone, Kent, 128, 139, 143, 151, 153, 218; Map A
Lullington, Sussex, 91, Map L; Plate 8
Lurgashall, Sussex, 220
Luton, Beds, 32, 168, 170
Lydd, Kent, 22, Fig 15
Lymington, Hants, 63, 94, 183
Lympne, Kent, 144, 174, 226; Fig 15
lynchets, formation, 80 and Fig 8; and see Celtic fields
lynchets, strip, Belgic, 123; S or Med, 192-4, 210, 213, Plates 23 and 24; modern, 214, Plate 23
Lyndhurst, Hants, 220

MACE-HEADS, Mes, 39, 42; Secondary N, 66
Magdalenian Culture, 21, 35, 66
Maglemosian Culture, 23, 36 f, 41
Maiden Bower, Beds, 44, 47, 48, 94, 107
Maiden Castle, Dorset, 47, 57, 94, 100, 103, 106, 111, 127, 128
Maidenhead, Berks, 140, 223
Maidstone, Kent, 132, 139, 170, 186, 188, 205
Malden, Surrey, 115
Maldon, Essex, 180, 183
Mangravet, Kent, 139
Manningtree, Essex, 76
manorial sites, 173, 184, 195, 197, 129, Plate 27
Manshead Hundred, Beds, 190
Manston, Kent, 101
Manuden, Essex, 194
maps, 14, 151, 176, 177, 190, 201 f, 205, 214
Margary, I. D., 151, 207
Margate, Kent, 87, 88, 101, 127
Mark Beech, Kent, 139
Marks Tey, Essex, 169, Map E
Marlow, Bucks, 43, 47
Marlborough, Wilts, 206
Marnian Culture, 85, 99, 101 f, 109

marshlands, 20 f, 37, 41, 94, 144, 146, 166, 194
Martin, Hants, 83, 155, 191, 214; Map H; Fig 16; Plate 7
mazes, 194
medieval earthworks, various, 194
Medway, river, Kent, 35, 111, 112, Map A, Map 2
Medway Culture, N, 49-51; Map A; 56; Map 2; Plate 2
Meesden, Herts, 190, Map F
megalithic monuments, 49, Plate 2
Mellitus, Saxon Abbot, 162
Meon Hill, Hants, 53, 87, 94, 102, 115, 222
Meon, river, Hants, 164
Michelmarsh, Hants, 47, 218
Micoquian Culture, 21
microliths, 37 f, 40-41
Middlesex, 18 f
migration of village sites, 166
Milston Down, Wilts, 213
Milton Regis, Kent, 163, 169, 174, 180, 183
mints, Belgic, 116, 120
Mitcham, Surrey, 166
moats, 173, 184, 188, 195, 219, 225, Plate 27
Mole, river, Surrey, 186, Map G
moles, 209, 211
Mongewell, Oxon, 155
Monks Risborough, Bucks, 47, 49, Map I, Map K
Moordown, Hants, 62
moots—see hundred
Morden, Surrey, 131
Mortimer West End, Hants, 157, 191
Mortlake, Surrey, 192, 210
mortuary houses, N, 51; Fig 5 (Site VIII); 69-70
Motcombe, Sussex, 189
Motley, Kent, 189
mottes (see castle mounds), 188
Moulsford, Berks, 83, 218
Mount Bures, Essex, 125
Mount Caburn, Sussex, 94, Fig 11, 98, 103, 105, 106, 108, 115, 116, 130, 154, 186, Map L
Mountfield, Sussex, 226, 227
Mountnessing, Essex, 196
Mousterian Culture, 21, 23, 32, 33, 34
Mulberry Green, Essex, 189
Mundon, Essex, 195
Muntham, Sussex, 97
museums, 203, 205, 211, 212, 228; and see Gazetteer
Mustow, Essex, 189; London, 189

Mutlow, Essex, 189, 224
Mutton Lane and Gate, Middx, 190
Mutton Wood, Kent, 189

NATIONAL grid of Ordnance Survey, 9, 203
Nazeing, Essex, 167, 224
Neanderthal man, 33, 34
Nether Wallop, Hants, 103
Netley Marsh, Hants, 161
Nettlebed, Oxon, 221
Nettleden, Herts, 225
Nettlestead, Kent, 139
New Barn Down, Patching, Sussex, 78
Newbury, Berks, 198, 219, 230
New Forest, 20, 40, 67, 71, 107, 112, 113, 135, 161, 165, 171, 180, 196, 199, 211, Map H; N.F. potteries, 145; Map H; 150, 153, 221
Newhaven, Sussex, 73, 88, 91, 220, Map L
Newington-on-the-Street, Kent, 221
Newmarket, Suffolk, 168
New River, Herts, Middx and London, 199
Newtimber, Sussex, 165
North Downs, 18, 44, 49, 83, 88, 170, 171, 186
North Downs trackway, 132, 139, Map A, Map G
Northfleet, Kent, 32, 131, 153, 163, 165, 174, 175
North Hayling, Hants, 226
North Hinksey, Oxon, 218
North Mundham, Sussex, 222
North Stoke, Oxon, 55, Map I
Noviomagus, 115; see Chichester
Nuneham Courtenay, Oxon, 196, 197
Nursling, Hants, 165
Nutley, Hants, 189

OAK, 20, 27, 37, 58, 122
Oareborough, Berks, 191
oats, 97
Ock, river, Berks, 94, Map B
Ockley, Surrey, 163
Odiham, Hants, 113, 123, 128, 171
Odsey Hundred, Herts, 224
Offa's Dyke, 180
Oldbury, Kent, 34, 108, 116, 127, 130, 222, Map A

Old Sarum, Wilts, 161
Old Street, Berks, 191
Old Winchester Hill, Hants, 95
Old Windsor, Berks, 227
Oliver's Battery, Hants, 174
Ongar, Essex, 195; O. Hundred, 184
open-field system, 172
oppida, Belgic, Map 7, 111, 116, 134, Fig 12
Ordnance Survey, 151, 176, 177, 201 f, 215
Orgarswick, Kent, 197
Orpington, Kent, 51
Orsett, Essex, 220, 221
Orwell, Herts, 224–5
Osney, Oxon, 167
Ospringe, Kent, 139, 150
Ossulstone Hundred, Middx. (now London), 188
Otford, Kent, 128, Map A
Otham, Kent, 197
Ouse, river, Sussex, 132, 137, 165, 186, Map L
Overton, Hants, 224, Map C
Over Wallop, Hants, 55
Ower Bank, North Sea, 23; Fig 2; 37
Owzlebury, Hants, 218
oxen, 26, 36, 55, 78, 162
Oxford, 32, 60, 62, 116, 177, 229
Oxted, Surrey, 186

PADWORTH, Berks, 157
palisades, 46, 70, 83, 91, 96, 197, Plate 26
palstaves, 72, 74
Pamber, Hants, 146, 157, Maps C and J
Pangbourne, Berks, 48, 155, 223, Map I
parish, origin of, 190; see boundaries
park boundary ditches, 194, 199, 225, Fig 19
Park Brow, Sussex, 78, 88, 96, 98, 101, 102, 106, 113, 145
Park Street, Herts, 65, 123, 127, 128, 133, 146, 151, 153, 218
pastoralism replaces arable farming, R, 135, 146, Fig 13; Med, 196
pasture, 58, 71, 73, 74, 83, 120, 172, 180
Patcham, Sussex, 165
Patch Grove ware, Map 6; 105 f, 115

Patching, Sussex, 48, 56, 58, 78, 206
Peacehaven, Sussex, 40, 53
Peaslake, Surrey, 56
peat, 17, 25, 41
Pebmarsh, Essex, 218
Pendley, Herts, 197
Penmaenmawr, Caern, 56, 59
Pen Pits, Wilts, 107
Penton Grafton, Hants, 140
Peper Harow, Surrey, 171
Peterborough Culture, 42, 43, 47 f, 52, 53, 54, 56, 57, 63, Fig 5, 66, 70
Petersfield, Hants, 67, 96, 71
petit tranchet arrowheads, Mes, 37, 41; N, 51, 52, 53, 54
Pevensey, Sussex, 20, 22, 25, 144, 149, 161, 186, 198, Fig 15, Plate 16; P. Levels, 20, Fig 15
phallic carving, N, 48; LBA, 78
Picts, 154, 161
Piggott, S., 49, 59, 73, 228
pigs—see swine
Pike o' Stickle, Westmorland, 56, 59
Pimlico, London, 56
pine, 26, 27
Pirton, Herts, 90, 98, 184, 195, Plate 27
Pitchbury, Essex, 120, Map E
pits, as dwellings, 39, 62–3, 65, 96, 97; as hundred meeting-places, 189; ritual, 54, 126, Fig 5; for storage, 78, 96 f, 106, 137, 208, Plates 10 and 21
Pitstone, Bucks, 184, Map K
place-names—forest, 180, 202, 223, Figs 17A and B; pagan, 162, 168; *ingas* etc., 162, 165 f; look-out points, 183 f; hundred-moots, 188 f; R roads, 226; animal heads, 163, 223–4; brick, 218, 227; *burh*, 218, 222; *thing*, 189–90. And see pp. 217 ff
Plaitford, Hants, 76
plant communities, tundra, 26; chalk land, 59, 201; 30; marsh, 201
plateau forts, 90, 94, 120, 219, 222
Plaxtol, Kent, 142, 146, Map A
Playden, Sussex, 73, 79
Pleshey, Essex, Fig. 18; 186, 194, 195
ploughs, 122, 125, 199; ploughing methods, 122, 123, 199
Plumpton, Sussex, 76 f, 86, 91, Fig. 7, Map L
Poling, Sussex, 171

polished flint axes, 42, 44, 48, 54
pollen grains, 58
pond barrows, 67 f, Fig 6h
Porchester, Hants, 144, 161, 183, 186, 220
Portsmouth, Hants, 67, 161
posting stations (*mansiones*), R, 131, 132
pot-boilers, 172–3, 207
potsherds, 207, 211, 212, 221, 225
potter's kilns—see kilns
potter's wheel, 123, 126
pottery, N, 46 f, 52, 53, 59; EBA, 61 f, 65; E-MBA, 67; MBA, 73; LBA, 77; IA 'A', 85, 87, 98, 99; IA 'B', 101 f, 106; IA 'C', 109 f, 117, 122 f, 127, 128; R, 131 f, 148; Romano-Saxon, 152 f.; S, 153 f, 163 f, 178, Med, 194
pottery manufacture, 18, 20, 105, 123, 132, 145–6, 152–3, 194, 217, 221, 225, Map H
Poynings, Sussex, 95, 106
Prae Wood, St. Albans, Herts, 111, 116, 117, 119, 120, 124, 127, 128, 133
Preston, Sussex, 145
Preston Candover, Hants, 174, 189, 220, Map C
Preston-next-Wingham, Kent, 153
Prittlewell, Essex, 88, 90, 169
Procopius, 163
promontory forts, N, 46; IA, 44, 92–4, 120, 213, Fig 10; R, 131; S?, 183
Pulborough, Sussex, 41, 131, 132
Purleigh, Essex, 219
pyres, R, 142
Pyrton, Oxon, 197, 217, 219

QUARLEY HILL, Hants, 53, 83, 87, 91, 92, 213; Plate 9
Quarrendon, Bucks, 197, 198–9, Map K
querns, quarries for, 107, Map B and Map G; rotary, 107, 178; saddle, 78, 97

RABBITS, 194, 197, 209, 211
Radlett, Herts, 145
Radley, Berks, 60, 65, 67, 72, 73, 116, 173
rainfall—see climatic phases
Rainham, Kent, 189

ramparts of hill-forts, 91 f, Fig 11, 94–5, 103
Ramsgate, Kent, 76
Ram's Hill, Berks, 72, 87, 88, 92, 100, 102, 116; 223, Map B
ranch boundary-ditches, Fig 9, 81 f, 84, 211, 213, 214, 222, Map B, Map I; Plates 7 and 9
Rankine, W. F., 41, 42
Ranscombe, Sussex, 92, 94
rapiers, 72
Reading, Bucks, 148, 157, 167, 219, 222
Reculver, Kent, 22, 25, 144, 174, Fig 15
Redbourn, Herts, 94, 222, 223
Red Hills, 124, Map E
Reed, Herts, 184
Regional Maps, note on, 9
register of finds and sites, 203
Regni, 151, 128, 130, 131
Reigate, Surrey, 71, 186, Map G
relative chronology of earthworks, 213–14
Repell Ditches, Essex, 117
Richborough, Kent, 22, 25, 88, 130, 131, 143, 144, 149, 150, 153, 154, 174, 218; Plate 15, Fig 15
Richmond, Surrey, 192, 210
ridgeways, 102, 148, Plate 12
Ridgewell, Essex, 148
ring ditches, Fig 5A, 67, 71–2, 73, 174, Plate 3 and Plate 21
Ringmer, Sussex, 225, Map L
Ringslow Hundred, Kent, 188
Ringwood, Hants, 218, Map H
Ringwould, Kent, 67
Rinyo-Clacton Culture, N, 47 f, 52 f, 56, 57
Ripe, Sussex, 221, 224, Map L
rise in sea level, 22 f, 41
roads, Belgic, 122; R, 131 f, 142, 148, 151, 157, 186, 190, 191, 207, 209, 213, 214, 226; and see regional maps
Rochester, Kent, 131, 132, 133, 148, 174, 183, 189, Fig. 15
Rochford, Essex, 224
Rockbourne, Hants, 135, 150, 194, Map H
Roman Conquest, 115, 117, 127–128, 130 f
Romanization of Britain, 130, 133, 134 f, 143
Romano-Celtic temples, 120, 126, 143, 188; continued veneration of sites by Saxons, 175–6
Romano-Saxon pottery, 152

Romney Marsh, Kent, 20, 196, 197, Plate 28
Romsey, Hants, 218
Rother, river, W. Sussex, 132, 165
Rotherfield, Sussex, 106, 116
Rotherfield Pepard, Oxon, 55
round barrows, N, 51; and see barrows
Rowland's Castle, Hants, 113, 218
Royal Commission on Historical Monuments, 150, 204, 229
Roydon, Essex, 224,
Royston, Herts, 37, 49, 51, 90
Ruislip, Middx, 195
rusticated ware, EBA, 47, 62; S, 153–4

SAFFRON WALDEN, Essex, 117, 174, 194, 195
St. Albans, Herts, 111, 131, 230; see Verulamium
St. Catherine's Hill, Christchurch, 194
St. Catherine's Hill, Winchester, 88, 92, 94, 95, 99, 113, 194, Plate 13
St. Cuthbert, 173
St. George's Hill, Surrey, 115
St. Germanus, 148
St. Margaret-at-Cliffe, Kent, 174
St. Martha's, Surrey, 194
St. Mary Bourne, Hants, 131, 219, Map C
St. Michael's, Herts, 111, 225
St. Osyth, Essex, 221
St. Stephen's, Herts, 65, 123, 127, 128, 218, 222
Salcott, Saltcote, 124
Salisbury Plain, 19
salt-making, 124, 194, 217 (ærn)
Samian ware, 125
'Sanctuary', Overton, Wilts, 57
Sandford, Oxon, 148
sandstones, 9, 19 f, 205 f; and see Greensands
Sandwich, Kent, 126
Sarratt, Herts, 220, 222
Sarre, Kent, 163, 175
saucer barrows, 69, Fig 6g; 76, Plate 6
saucer brooches, S, 165, 168, 169
Saunderton, Bucks, 53, 90, 186
Savoy, London, 175
Sawbridgeworth, Herts, 153
saws, flint, 37, 41, 53, 211
Saxonbury, Sussex, 116, 124

Saxons, 144, 149, 154; of Essex, 169; of Thames valley, 166–8; of Surrey, 171; of Sussex, 165; of Wessex, 161, 168 f; S burial places, 154 (see Anglo-Saxons); re-use of R dwelling-sites, 175
scrapers, flint, Mes, 36; N, 46, 47, 53
Seaford, Sussex, 40, 96, Map L
Seale, Surrey, 65
Seasalter, Kent, 217
secondary neolithic cultures, 51 f, 57, 66, 70, 72
Seddlescombe, Sussex, 105
Selborne, Hants, 218
Selmeston, Sussex, 39, 53, Map L
Selsey, Sussex, 22, 25, 47, 113, 161, 165, 173; S. Bill, 112
Send, Surrey, 221
separation of Britain from Continent, 23, Fig. 2
Setley, Hants, 211
Severn-Costwold Culture, 49, 51
Sewards End, Essex, 195
sheep, 53, 63, 78, 84, 97, 180, 192
Sheepen Farm site, Colchester, Map E; 120 f, 127, 133, 143; Sheepen Dyke, 120, Fig 12A
Shefford, Beds, 62
Shepperton, Middx, 167, 175
Sherborne St. John, Hants, 131, Map J
Shere, Surrey, 56, 224
Sherfield upon Loddon, Hants, 226, Map J
shields, 74
Shillington, Beds, 194
Shinfield, Berks, 218, 225, Map J
shire-moots, 186, 190
Shoebury, Essex, 88, 105, 111, 169, 180, 183
Shoreham, Sussex, 91, 137, 148
Shorthampton, Oxon, 223
Shotover, Oxon, 148
shrines—see temples
shrunken villages, 196–7
Sible Hedingham, Essex, 62, 221, 225
Silchester, Hants, 105, 112; Map J; 116, 120, 132, 133, 134, 135, 143, 146, 148, 150, 153, 157, 175, 191, 209, 213; S. earthworks, 116, 120
siltstone pebbles, 39
Singleton, Sussex, 88, 92, 103, 194
Sittingbourne, Kent, 56, 153
Skara Brae, Orkney, 53
Skirmett, Bucks, 190

skulls, P, 23, 33; N, 57; Beaker
   Folk, 57–8; R and S, 152, 175
slaughter of cattle in autumn, N,
   46, IA, 96; S, 162–3
slaves, 123
sledge, 65
Slindon, Sussex, 31, Map D
slings, 103; sling-stones, 78, 103
Sloden, Hants, 135, Map H
snail-shells, 58, 84, 97
Snodland, Kent, 142, 225, Map A
soils, 9, 19, 22, 30, 43, 71, 112,
   122, 127, 139, 140, 170, 176,
   191–2, 201, 205
soil-marks, 207, 216, 218, Plates
   10 and 21
Soldiers Ring, Hants, 135; Fig
   13; 213; Map H
Solutrian Culture, 21, 34
Sompting, Sussex, 78, 86, 88, 96
Sonning, Berks, 167
Southampton, 178–80, 183, 190,
   195
Southbourne, Hants, 47, 87, 92,
   103, Fig. 10
Southchurch, Essex, 77, 84, 88
South Downs, 18, 40, 48, 55, 60,
   78, 83, 87, 88, 123, 137, 165
   186; S.D. Ridgeway, 84, 131
   132, 190
South-Eastern 'B' Culture, Map
   6; 105 f, 107, 112, 115, 123,
   124, 125, 128, 133, 139
Southend, Essex, 56, 111, 229
South Hayling, Hants, 219
South Malling, Sussex, 92, 94
Southminster, Essex, 111
Southwark, London, 223
spearheads, P, 32; MBA, 72; LBA
   74
Speen, Berks, 131
Spellbrook, Essex, 189
spelt, 72, 97
Spelthorne Hundred, Middx,
   188, 190
Sperberry, Herts, 189, 224
Spitalfields, London, 152
Staines, Middx, 131
Standlake, Oxon, Plate 10
Standon, Herts, 142
Stane Street, Surrey and Sussex,
   131, 132, 213, 225, 226, Map D
   and Map G
Stanford-in-the-Vale, Berks, 148
Stanfordbury, Beds, 125, 129, 142
Stanford Rivers, Essex, 184
Stanmore, Hants, 113
Stanmore, Middx, 122, 127, 131,
   145, 194

Stanstead St. Margaret, Herts,
   162
Stansted Mountfitchet, Essex,
   219, 225
Stanton Harcourt, Oxon, 54, 55
Stanway, Essex, 225, Map E
Staple Hundred, Sussex, 188
Star Carr, Yorks, mesolithic habi-
   tation site, 36
Stebbing, Essex, 218
Stephen, King of England, 184,
   186
Stevenage, Herts, 142
Steyning, Sussex, 219
stockade, 136, 180, 184
Stockbridge, Hants, 67, 71, 73,
   87, 94, 102, 115, 222
stock-raising, 52, 83, 98, 106, 135
Stoke Mandeville, Bucks, 197
Stoke Newington, London, 32
Stone, Bucks, 219
Stonehenge, Wilts, 54, 56, 62, 67
Stonesfield, Oxon, 221
storage pits—see pits
Stotfold, Beds, 111, 226
Stoughton, Sussex, 69, 92, 143,
   165 n., 225, Map D, Plate 5
Stratfield, Hants, 226, Map J
Stratfield Mortimer, Berks, 157
Stratford, Essex, 226
Stratton, Hants, 226
Streat, Sussex, 132, 226
Streatham, London, 226
Streatley, Beds, 54
Streatley, Berks, 136, 155
Strethall, Essex, 226
strip-fields—see lynchets
Sturry, Kent, 163
submerged land surface, 22 f, 30,
   41, 140, Fig 2
subsidence of land surface, 22, 25,
   30, 140
Sulloniacae, Middx, 122, 127, 131;
   see Brockley Hill
Sumner, Heywood, 199, 205–6
Sutton, W. Sussex, 84, 213
Sutton Courtenay, Berks, 55, 56,
   57, 71, 72, 73, 153, 165, 168,
   172–3, 177, 210, Map B
Sutton Hoo, Suffolk, 169
Sutton Valence, Kent, 142
Sutton Walls, Herefordshire, 127
Swanborough Hundred, Sussex,
   188
Swanscombe, Kent, 19, 23, 33
Swanwick, Hants, 218
Swaythling, Hants, 165
swine, 44, 53, 63, 98, 180, 196;
   swine pastures, 170–1, 223

swords, 74, 76 f, 84, 102, 125
Sydmonton, Hants, 192, Map C

TAKELEY, Essex, 224
Taplow, Bucks, 77, 174, 224
Tardenoisian Culture, 21, 37 f
Tasciovanus, 116, 119
Tatsfield, Surrey, 197
Teddington, Middx, 217
temenos, 120, 143
Temple Ewell, Kent, 217
temples, IA, 98–9, 120, 126; R,
   143; S, 162 f, 175–6, 224, Map E;
   and see Romano-Celtic temples
Tenterden, Kent, 170
terraces, gravel, 20 f, 32
Test, river, Hants, 37, 49, 60, 103,
   115, Map C
Tewin, Herts, 167
Thakeham, Sussex, 42, 173, 189
Thames, river, 19 f, 25, 32, 43,
   54, 60, 61, 72, 76, 88, 90, 115;
   T. pick, 41
Thanet, Isle of, 20, 161, 170, Fig
   15
Thatcham, Berks, 37, 148
Thaxted, Essex, 219
theatres, R, 120, 135, 143, Maps
   D, E, J
Theodosian coin-hoards, 149
Therfield, Herts, 192, 195, 224
Thetford, Norfolk, 178
thing in place-names, 189–90
Thomley, Oxon, 196
Thorley, Herts, 191, 197, 220,
   Map F
Thornborough Moor, Yorks, 65
Thorrington, Essex, 195
three-field system of agriculture,
   172, 191–2
Throcking, Herts, 197, Map F
Thundersbarrow, Sussex, 91,
   137, 148
Thundersley, Essex, 162
Thundridge, Herts, 188, 197, 198,
   218, Map F
Thursley, Surrey, 162, 171
Thurstable Hundred, Essex, 162,
   188–9
Ticehurst, Sussex, 106, 162, 165
Tievebulliagh, N. Ireland, 56
Tilbury, Essex, 117, 140, 146,
   198, 227
Tilehurst, Berks, 226–7
tile-kilns—see kilns
tile production, 140, 195
time scale, Charts p. 21 and pp.
   28–9

tin, 72, 86, 102, 123
Tincommius, 113, 116
Tingrith, Beds, 189
Tinhale, Sussex, 190
Titchfield Haven, Hants, 41
Titsey, Surrey, 140, 146, 224
Togodumnus, 130
Tolleshunt Major, Essex 189
tombs, R, 142, 227; tombstones, R, 142
tools, 14; P, 34; Mes, 36 f; N, 48 f, 58; EBA, 63; MBA, 72; LBA, 74; IA, 86, 125; S, 173
Tooting, London, 167
Toppesfield, Essex, 142, 223
Torberry, Sussex, 95, 113
Totternhoe, Beds, 175, 183, 226
towns, R, 131-5, 148-9; occupation by Anglo-Saxons, 174-5
trackways, 22, 78, Fig 7, 80, 131-132, 137, 188, 190
trade, Mes?, 40; N, 51, 55 f; E/MBA, 61, 66, 72; LBA, 74; EIA, 106, 113, 123; R, 131; Sub-Roman, 149; S 178
tranchet axe, Mes, 37, 38, 40, 41, 54
traps for the unwary, 214-5
tree-rings, 215, Plate 6
Tring, Herts, 197
Trinovantes, 111, 119, 120, 127
Trottiscliffe, Kent, 49, Map A
Trundle, Sussex, 53, 88, 92, 95, 100, 103, 113, 194, Map D, Plate 11
Tuesley, Surrey, 162
tumuli—see barrows
Turville, Bucks, 19
Twickenham, Middx, 13-14
two-field system of agriculture, 97, 172, 191-2
Twyford, Hants, 96 f, 113, 122, 123, 128, 140, 199
Tythrop, Oxon, 197-8

UFFINGTON, Berks, 72, 87, 88, 92, 100, 102, 116, 125, 148, 154, 220, 223, Map B, Plate 12, Plate 23
Ufton Nervet, Berks, 157, 213
Upchurch, Kent, 132, 146, 150
Upham, Hants, 220
Upper Beeding, Sussex, 142, 189, 192
Upper Clatford, Hants, 92, 98, 102, 103, 115
Urn Folk, 69, 70 f

Uttlesford Hundred, Essex, 189, 224

Vagniacae, 131; see Northfleet
Vandals, 152
vaults for Belgic burials, 125-6, 129
Veneti, 102-3, 106
Venta Belgarum, 113, 132; see Winchester
Verica, 113
Verulamium, 128, 131, 133, 135, 143, 148, 150, 153, 154, 175, 195, Plates 17 and 18
Victoria County Histories, 150, 203, 204
villages, S, 134, 153, 165-6, 170 f; earthwork defences of villages, 195; Fig. 18; and see deserted villages and migration of sites
villas, 9, 17, 128, 132, 134, 136, 139, 140, 143, 146-8, 151, 209; occupation by Saxons, 175; churches on site of, 175, 194; field-names as a clue to site of, 220-1, 222
Vortigern, 152, 161

WADDON, Surrey, 115
Wadhurst Clay, 86
Walkern, Herts, 217, 218
walled cemeteries, R, 142
walls of R. towns, 133, 134, 135, 142, 148, Plate 17
Wallingford, Berks, 148, 183, 186, Map I; Plate 22
Wallington, Herts, 192, 224
Walmer, Kent, 111, 127
Waltham St. Lawrence, Berks, 149, 219, 220
Walthamstow, Essex, 88, 230
Walton-on-Thames, Surrey, 76, 115
Walton-on-the-Hill, Surrey, 186, Map G
Walton-on-the-Naze, Essex, 41, 52
Wandle, river, Surrey and London, 167
Wandsworth, London, 37
Wansdyke, Berks, 155
Wantage, Berks, 83, 171, 218, Map B
Wantsum, river, Kent, 20
Warborough, Oxon, 184, 217, Map I
Wargrave, Berks, 221

Warnford, Hants, 69, 95
Warnham, Sussex, 226
Wash, The, 61, 90, 144, 154, 168
Washington, Sussex, 103, 132, 143, 176, 191, 225
Water Eaton, Oxon, 222
water supply, 9, 25, 40, 53, 135, 217 (æwiell); water table, fall in, 25-6, 67
Watford, Herts, 91
Watling Street, 131, 133, 145, 227, Map A
wattle and daub, 18, 52, 122, 137, 139, 173, 178; wattlework, 73, 212
Weald, 18, 30, 37, 40, 42, 71, 86, 107, 112, 124, 127, 131, 132, 134, 151, 161, 165, 170 f, 192, 194, 200; W. Clay, 20, 40, 201
Wealden Culture, IA, 14, 105 f, 108, 112, 115, 116, 130
weaving, 72, 78, 98, 173, 178-80
Weedon, Bucks, 162
Welwyn, Herts, 111, 125, 127, 128, 151, 225
Wendens Ambo, Essex, 198, 224
Wendover, Bucks, 157, 176, Map K
Wessex, 168 f
Wessex Culture, E/MBA, 66 f, 70, 71, Map 3, Fig. 6
Westbere, Kent, 163-4, 175, 177
West Clandon, Surrey, 115
West Dean, Wilts, 223
Western Neolithic Culture, 41, 43 f
West Harling, Norfolk, 90
West Harting, Sussex, 213; and see Harting above
West Hendred, Berks, 218
West Hoathly, Sussex, 106
West Kennet, Wilts, 57
West Langdon, Kent, 220
West Meon, Hants, 164
West Mersea, Essex, 142
Westmill, Herts, 226, Map F
Weston Turville, Bucks, 186
West Runton, Norfolk, 57
West Saxons, 161, 168-9, 170
West Tarring, Sussex, 88
West Wycombe, Bucks, 194, Map K
Wey, river, Surrey, 56, 61, 88, 105, 186
wheat, 48, 72, 97
Wheathampstead, Herts, 111; Fig. 12B; 116, 117, 120, 127, 128

Wheatley, Oxon, 171, 220
Wheeler, R. E. M., 100, 128, 150, 177
wheels, 122-3
Wherwell, Hants, 218
whetstones, 86
Whiligh, Sussex, 162, 165
White Colne, Essex, 76
Whitehawk, Sussex, 46, 47, 48, 53, 62
White Horse, Berks, 125
Whiteleaf, Bucks, 49, 51, Map K
White Notley, Essex, 218
Whitsbury, Hants, 213, Map H
Whitstable, Kent, 188
Whyly, Sussex, 165
Wickham, Hants, 218
Widdington, Essex, 162, 202, 221
Widford, Essex, 217, Map F
Wigginton, Bucks, 157, Map K
Wilbury, Herts, 90, 91, 92, 96, 111, 116
Willey, Surrey, 162, 171
Williams-Freeman, J. P., 205
Willian, Herts, 90

willow, 26
Wimbish, Essex, 197, 198
Wimbledon, Surrey, 71, 91, 94, 99, 115, 210
Winchester, Hants, 88, 92, 94, 99, 113, 125, 126, 132, 133, 134, 146, 148, 171, 175, 183, 194, 223; and see Venta Belgarum
Windmill Hill Culture, 41, 42, 43 f, 51 f, 56, 57, 63
windmill mounds, 215
window urns, S, 163
Windsor, Berks, 186
winged axes, 76 f
Wingham, Kent, 153, 175, 221
Winkfield, Berks, 218
Wisley, Surrey, 115
Wiston, Sussex, 191
Witham, Essex, 90, 180, 183
Wittering, Sussex, 25
Woking, Surrey, 224
Wokingham, Berks, 162
Wonersh, Surrey, 76
Woodbury, Wilts—see Little Woodbury
Woodeaton, Oxon, 143, 149, 162, 176, 188

Woodham Ferrers, Essex, 222
Woodhenge, Wilts, 62
Woodnesborough, Kent, 162
Woolmer, Hants, 218
Wootton, New Forest, 40
Wootton St. Lawrence, Hants, 220, Map J
Worplesdon, Surrey, 67, 71, 76
Worth, Kent, 87, 101, 126, 143, 153, 220
Worthy Down, Hants, 113
Worting, Hants, 171, Map J
Wotton, Surrey, 67, 171, 194
Wrecclesham, Surrey, 90
Writtle, Essex, 222
Wrotham, Kent, 32, Map A
Wye, Kent, 139, 162, 188
Wyfold, Berks, 224, 226
Wymondley, Herts, 148, 175, 221

YALDING, Kent, 170
Yeading, Middx, 167
Yiewsley, Middx, 76

ZEUNER, F. E., 21, 27, 30, 35